Henry Ford
and the Jews

Also by Neil Baldwin

Legends of the Plumed Serpent: Biography of a Mexican God
Edison: Inventing the Century
Man Ray: American Artist
To All Gentleness: William Carlos Williams, the Doctor Poet
The Writing Life (Co-Editor)

Henry Ford and the Jews

THE

MASS PRODUCTION

OF HATE

Neil Baldwin

PublicAffairs · *New York*

Book design and composition by Mark McGarry
Text set in Monotype Bell with Clarendon display.

Library of Congress Cataloging-in-Publication Data
Baldwin, Neil, 1947–
Henry Ford and the Jews: the mass production of hate/
Neil Baldwin. −1st ed.
p. cm.
Includes bibliographical references and index.
ISBN 1–891620–52–5
1. Ford, Henry, 1863–1947.
2. Industrialists—United States—Biography.
3. Antisemitism—United States.
4. Jews—United States.
5. Automobile industry and trade—United States—History.
I. Title.
CT275.F68 B28 2001
2001041679

ঞ

FIRST EDITION

2 4 6 8 10 9 7 5 3 1

FOR THE LIBRARIANS

If we want to examine the development of actual belief as contrasted with social norms, we have to examine individual lives, for belief is an activity of individuals; ideas or prescriptions are not beliefs until individuals assent to them.

GAVIN LANGMUIR,
History, Religion, and Antisemitism

✧

I want to live a life. Money means nothing to me—neither the making of it nor the use of it so far as I am personally concerned. I am in a peculiar position. No one can give me anything. There is nothing I cannot have. But I do not want the things money can buy. I want to live a life.

The trouble with people is they do not think. I want to do things and say things which will make them think.

HENRY FORD,
December, 1915, to Rev. Samuel S. Marquis

✧

Ideas and circumstances are the two ends of a stick. There is no question of holding the stick by the wrong end; whichever way we seize it, we are in possession of the two ends and of the element that joins them.

G. J. RENIER
History: Its Purpose and Method

CONTENTS

1	McGuffeyland	1
2	The Great Questions	8
3	Tin Lizzie	20
4	The Christian Century	27
5	Working Man's Friend	36
6	"I Know Who Caused the War"	48
7	The Bolshevik Menace	67
8	Exit Mr. Pipp	92
9	The Jewish Question	108
10	Retaliation	134
11	The Talmud-Jew	152
12	Heinrich Ford	172
13	*Sapiro v. Ford*	192
14	Apology	218

Contents

15 Apostle of Amity   241

16 The Chosen People   255

17 "I Am Not a Jew Hater"   268

18 Hitler's Medal   281

19 The Radio Priest   293

20 Transitions   309

Afterword   321

Acknowledgments   331

Bibliography   335

Notes   353

Permissions   395

Index   401

Henry Ford
and the Jews

CHAPTER ONE

McGuffeyland

A BRIGHT and chilly fall morning, 1879. Henry Ford and his teenaged pals have gathered early before another day of lessons at the Miller School in rural Springwells Township, northeast of Dearbornville, Michigan. Henry, wiry and slight of build, is crouched down at the muddy slope of a ditch draining behind the schoolhouse, busily assembling a miniature waterwheel to run in the dammed stream. Just as the stream begins to rise—the wheel hooked up to an old coffee mill with a rake handle serving as a connecting rod—the bell rings, summoning the reluctant boys to abandon their work and enter the one-room cabin crammed with ten rows of wooden double-desks and stuffy from the heat of an old wood stove. That night, the waterwheel would jam and the ditch would overflow, flooding the neighboring farmer's potato patch.

For the moment, it was time to continue reading in Lesson LIX of *McGuffey's New Fifth Eclectic Reader*: "Shylock, or The Pound of Flesh." The boys are instructed by their burly, moustachioed teacher, a former barrel cooper named John Brainard Chapman, to "stand and read so loud and distinctly, that [I] may hear each syllable."[1]

"I am sorry for thee," the judge, Doctor Balthasar (Portia disguised as a "learned man"), says to Antonio, the seafaring businessman who has lost his ships. "Thou art come to answer a stony adversary, an inhuman wretch, incapable of pity." Enter the "unfeeling" moneylender Shylock, to plead his case. "By our holy Sabbath," here is a man who will "give no reason" outwardly for his deep-seated misanthropy and "lodged hate" of Antonio. This Jew is stubborn, principled, adhering to the letter of the law. "There is no power in the tongue of man" can sway him. Shylock will exact his collateral, a pound of Antonio's flesh. He will not take even twice or thrice or six times three thousand ducats in exchange. The knife is at the ready. Antonio's apologies are futile.

But before the spot nearest Antonio's heart can be cut, Doctor Balthasar warns Shylock that he must not "shed one drop of Christian blood...nor cut less nor more, than just one pound" even to the weight of a hair, otherwise his lands and life will be forfeited to the State of Venice. Shylock, realizing he is trapped by the very law he craves, attempts to withdraw—but there is a further penalty. As an "alien" who has attempted to take the life of a citizen, half his goods are subject to confiscation by Antonio, as the aggrieved party; half must go to the state; and the Jew's life is at the mercy of the court.

Shylock pleads for death, because his funds and possessions, "the means" through which he truly values life, are worth more to him than anything in the world. In a twist of irony, the judge takes the compassionate path, showing the state's "mercy" on the Jew, allowing him to survive among the very people he so despises.

"Why did Shylock choose the pound of flesh rather than the payment of his debt?" the McGuffey exercises inquire of the stu-

dent at the conclusion of the selection. "What does he mean by saying 'my deeds upon my head'? In whose favor does the judge
decide? How does he eventually relieve Antonio from his danger?"

And finally, Henry Ford and his classmates are asked to discuss,
"How is Shylock punished? Was his punishment just? Why?"

Elsewhere in the *Fifth Reader*, the students read of "Paul's
Defense before King Agrippa," in which the apostle laments the
fact that despite his wide-ranging efforts to spread the gospel of
repentance at Damascus, Jerusalem, and along the coasts of Judea,
"the Jews caught me in the temple,
and went about to kill me."[2]

In his *Fourth Reader*, young Henry
had already been forewarned that
"Jewish authors were incapable of
the diction and strangers to the
morality contained in the gospel."
Rather, although the Jews had their
"own sacred volume" known as the
Old Testament, they misguidedly
failed to heed within it "the most
extraordinary predictions concerning the infidelity of their nation,
Jesus' coming, and the rise, progress,

Shylock in 1860

and extensive prevalence of the gospel truth of Christianity." In his
Third Reader, Henry had learned that the unfortunate Jews never
accepted that "the Bible is a Christian book... the Scriptures are
especially designed to make us wise unto salvation through faith in
Christ Jesus."[3]

Henry had also read McGuffey's instructive tale of "The Good
Son," in which a jeweler's child will not sell his diamonds to a
group of Jewish elders because in order to obtain the key to the
merchandise chest the lad would have to awaken his sleeping father.
"At my father's age," the boy explains solemnly, "a short hour of
sleep does him a great deal of good; and for all the *gold* in the

world, I would not be wanting in respect to my father, or take from him a single comfort."[4]

For nearly a century, William Holmes McGuffey's anthologies were the dominant textbook in American schools. More than 122 million copies were sold between 1836, when the first two volumes of primers were published by the venerable firm of Truman and Smith of Cincinnati, and 1921, when the American Book Company brought out the *New Sixth Eclectic Reader.*

"The Old Guff" was born in western Pennsylvania in 1800, second in a family of eleven children. He taught in the country schools of the Ohio Territory, then attended Greersburg Academy and Washington College, both in Pennsylvania, graduating in 1826. He went on to positions at Miami University in Oxford, Ohio, was appointed president of Ohio University, and distinguished himself further as one of the founders of the common-school system in Ohio.

Under a gargantuan ash tree on the West Lawn near Colonnade Alley at the University of Virginia, where he served as professor of mental and moral philosophy from 1845 until his death in 1873, McGuffey would assemble parties of children and teenagers and read to them from selections he was planning to include in revised editions of his *Readers.* Those passages generating interest and excitement were published, while others that failed to ignite the young people's imaginations were rejected. Thus did this "modest, self-effacing teacher bear the torch of education to light the wilderness," setting out singlehandedly to establish the moral (more than intellectual) agenda for American youth at mid-century.[5]

First and foremost, according to this "messiah of education,"[6] Protestant Christianity was the only true religion in America, "closer to Puritanism than Unitarianism.... God was omnipresent. He had His eye on every child every moment of the day and night, watched its every action, knew its every thought."[7] The deeply ingrained "sublime chorus of truths" of the Bible could not be questioned. Equally, the quotidian world was built simply upon a

Calvinist structure of reward and punishment. Hard work, thrift, and rugged conformity were the ideals. Success was desired. Failure was shunned.

In the later *Readers*, excerpts from literary works took the place of many homiletic, homespun parables: John Dryden, Charles Dickens, Samuel Johnson, Walter Scott, Washington Irving, and William Shakespeare.

Throughout his life, Henry Ford expressed indebtedness to McGuffey's teachings. He was proud of his early exposure to this unadorned brand of book-learning, which reinforced an ordered, rigid, and straightforward view of a world where white was white and black was black. Known familiarly as "McGuffeyland," this was

**Henry Ford perusing the works of his favorite author
at the McGuffey Homestead, Greenfield Village, 1940**

a pure and pastoral domain, where a boy worked with his own two hands and benefited directly from the products of hard labor, far removed from urban dens of cosmopolitan iniquity.[8]

As an adult, Ford could quote spontaneously line-for-line from McGuffey. He was an obsessive collector of McGuffey first editions and reprinted all six *Readers* from 1857, distributing complete sets of them, at his own considerable expense, to schools across the United States. In 1934, Ford had McGuffey's whitewashed log cabin birthplace, complete with all its furnishings, disassembled from the Pennsylvania hill country and moved to Greenfield Village, Ford's exhaustive museum of Americana at Dearborn, Michigan. In 1936, Ford served as an associate editor—along with colleagues Hamlin Garland, John W. Studebaker, William F. Wiley, and several others—of a collection of *Old Favorites from McGuffey Readers*. The 482-page volume was dedicated to Ford, "lifelong devotee of his boyhood Alma Mater, the *McGuffey Readers.*"

Although myriad excerpts appeared in *Readers* over the decades—*Othello, Henry IV Part I, Henry V, Henry VIII,* and *Richard III,* among others—only three selections from Shakespeare were chosen for inclusion by the editors: Marc Antony's speech over Caesar's body in *Julius Caesar*; Hamlet's report to his friends on sighting his father's ghost; and Shylock's ignominious defeat from *The Merchant of Venice.*

In May 1914, the local Detroit advisory committee of the fledgling B'nai B'rith Anti-Defamation League, under the chairmanship of Temple Beth El Reform Rabbi Leo Franklin, undertook as its first order of business a vigilance campaign to eliminate the required study and teaching of *The Merchant of Venice* in local public schools. Indeed, the charter of the ADL made a commitment to urge "proper authorities... to remove books which maliciously and scurrilously traduce the character of the Jew."[9] In a vehement letter to ADL founder Sigmund Livingston in Chicago, Rabbi Franklin insisted that the image of "the avaricious, revengeful and bloodthirsty Jew" must be banished from classroom discourse. The following fall, the ADL sent a circular to school superintendents in all cities with a population of 10,000 or more itemizing why *The Merchant of Venice* was not fit for the classroom. Among the complaints listed, "It serves to increase misunderstanding of Jews by non-Jews ... because Shylock is erroneously pictured as typical of all Jews ... [and] Shylock has become an unhappy symbol of Jewish vindictiveness, malice and hatred."[10]

To Henry Ford, Rabbi Franklin's friend and neighbor in Detroit, this national lobbying action was nothing less than a personal affront to his revered mentor, William Holmes McGuffey.[11]

CHAPTER TWO

The Great Questions

———— ✺ ————

An image manifestly comes from somewhere. Stereotypes are
not in themselves a full explanation for rejection.

GORDON ALLPORT,
The Nature of Prejudice, 1979.

HENRY FORD was born on July 30, 1863, twenty-seven days
after the Battle of Gettysburg, on a prosperous farm near Dearbornville, in Wayne County, southeastern Michigan, "the rural
backwoods of fundamentalist America."[1] He was the second of
eight children, and the grandson of John Ford, a Protestant English tenant farmer who had come to America from Ireland during
the great potato famine of 1847. Henry's father, William, worked
eighty acres of wheat and hay, tended sheep, cows, and pigs, and
worked now and then as a part-time carpenter.

Henry's beloved mother, Mary Litogot, was of either Dutch or
Flemish parentage. Orphaned very young, she grew up in Wyan-
dotte, Michigan, as the adopted daughter of Patrick O'Hern (or
Ahern) and his wife, a childless immigrant couple. Mary, an
upstanding Christian woman, died when Henry was thirteen years

old, which caused him great pain, and he spoke reverently and with aching nostalgia for her throughout his life. Before her favorite son entered the country school at age seven, Mary had already led him firmly by the hand across the border into the welcoming terrain of McGuffeyland, where she read every single evening to him of a wonderful country dominated by only the best kinds of boys: "honest boys" against "thieves"; "contented boys" who worked hard, as opposed to "lazy boys" who were "compelled to stand and gaze while shivering in their places"; boys "who knew no such word as fail," never touched liquor, and kept a place for everything and everything in its place; boys who had lost their fathers in shipwrecks at sea and assumed the leadership of their homes.

It was a righteous land where rich men's sons with soft hands had to depend upon the whims of the banks, while poor men's sons were blessed with the desire to work hard and build within themselves "souls shined with labor"; where "barefoot boys with cheek of tan," denizens of the natural world, knew more of real life than any school-bound contemporary ever could and grew up to become independent souls like Nathaniel Hawthorne's "Mr. Toil," who

William Ford, circa 1895   Mary Litogot Ford, circa 1860

lorded over unfortunate and foolish fellows like "Hugh Idle, who only loved to do what was agreeable."[2]

From an early age, like others of his generation, young Henry helped with chores, albeit resentfully. He preferred to forage for what he called "trinkets"—nuts, washers, odds and ends of machin-

Henry Ford at age eighteen,
Dry Dock Engine Works

ery. He spent spare and stolen time at his bedside workbench taking apart watches and putting them back together again, and he thought nothing of walking into Detroit—which could take an entire day—to frequent hardware stores.[3]

Henry was biding his time for the right moment to escape from the farm. On the first of December 1879, in his seventeenth year, he walked into Detroit to sign up for work as a $1.10 per day apprentice at the Michigan Car Company Works. That ill-fated job lasted six days, after which he joined the James Flower & Brothers Machine Shop at the corner of Woodbridge and Brush streets. Henry was assigned to mill hexagons onto brass valves. Within the year, he had moved on to the Detroit Dry Dock Engine Works, the largest shipbuilding firm in the city. Even at this early stage, Henry soon became known as the curious "wanderer" around the shop, happier peering over the shoulders of his fellow workers and commenting upon what they were doing rather than staying put at his own table. To pick up a little extra cash, he worked nights for the jeweler Robert Magill. Lunchtime was the only part of the day he found time to read; Henry favored perusing machine parts catalogs and the pioneering works of James Faraday on the steam engine.[4] There were plenty of such small-business opportunities in Detroit for a young man who liked to roll up his sleeves and even sweat a little bit now and then.

Detroit had grown to become a city of more than 116,000 people, covering an area of seventeen square miles—an industrial, shipping, and railroad hub with nearly 1,000 manufacturing and mechanical establishments, twenty miles of street railways, a telegraph network, and a waterworks.[5]

Henry returned to the family farm after his grandfather died and worked there for three years in the early 1880s. He applied his developing interest in steam traction to building a car-locomotive with a kerosene-heated boiler, enrolled in shorthand and accountancy classes at Goldsmith Bryant and Stratton Business College, worked part-time for the Westinghouse Engine Company and the Buckeye Harvester Company, and took dancing lessons. Henry was becoming a fanatic for self-improvement. During a harvest moon ball at Martindale's Four Mile House, outside Detroit, he met Clara Jane

Henry Ford at age twenty-three

Bryant, the twenty-year-old daughter of a local farmer in Greenfield Township; he told his sister Margaret that in thirty seconds after their first quadrille he knew this was the girl of his dreams. In the spring of 1888, after a two-year engagement, they were married in an Episcopalian ceremony, and Henry set up a circular sawmill on forty acres adjacent to his family's property. Within three years of cutting at the frenetic rate of more than 200,000 feet per year, the timber was gone and Henry was able to load all his household goods into a haywagon and move back into Detroit, snapping up a $40 per month engineering job that luckily came available at the Edison Iluminating Company, leading producers of electrical power for the region's homes.

Clara—or "Callie," as her loving husband called her through

their sixty years together—and Henry moved into a two-story house a few blocks from the Edison substation, where he started on the night shift from 6 P.M. to 6 A.M. Ambitious and driven, he rose to the position of chief engineer at Detroit Edison soon after the birth on November 9, 1893, of his son and only child, Edsel (named after Henry's school seatmate). The brownstone home at 58 Bagley Avenue was half of a two-family house owned by one William B. Wreford. The tiny front lawn by the five-step front stoop was usually scrubby and unmowed. Facing the house, one could discern just to the left a narrow alleyway leading to a workshop shed at the rear. Automotive history would be made there when Henry Ford began intensive experimentation elaborating upon his earlier work with a four-cycle gasoline engine—one-inch bore, three-inch stroke—moving on to a double-cylinder model he had originally conceived as attaching to the rear wheel of a bicycle.

Henry Ford with son, Edsel, 1899

These rudimentary prototypes would become the basis for the horseless carriage that revolutionized American culture and commerce. Henry Ford's gasoline quadricycle, a buggy frame mounted on four twenty-eight-inch bicycle wheels, with a four-horsepower, air-cooled motor handmade from the exhaust pipe of a steam engine by "Crazy Henry" (as he was now known), came trundling out onto the shining cobblestones of Bagley Avenue in the warm and drizzly predawn hours of June 4, 1896. It weighed 500 pounds, had a horn made from a doorbell, boasted a three-gallon gas tank, had no brakes or reverse gear, and ran at two speeds, ten and twenty miles per hour, emitting an other-worldly "chuck-chuck-chuck" sound, "civilization's newest voice."[6]

Two months passed. At the concluding banquet of the seventeenth annual convention of members of the National Association of Edison Illuminating Companies in the grand ballroom of the Oriental Hotel in Manhattan Beach, Brooklyn, the wiry, shy, nervous young tinkerer-engineer met the legendary Thomas Alva Edison. They were introduced with a bemused smile by Henry's boss, superintendent Alexander Dow: "Young fellow here has made a gas car." Edison was curious and began to pepper Ford with detailed questions. Ford was advised by those men seated nearby that he

**"Crazy Henry" driving down Bagley Avenue,
as interpreted by Norman Rockwell**

would have to pull his chair up close to the deaf Great Man and speak loudly into his right ear. He did so, sketching the contours of his machine busily on a scrap of paper. Edison grinned, pounded his fist onto the table, rattling the silverware, and in his peculiarly nasal tenor heartily encouraged the starstruck Ford to "Keep at it!" From that moment onward, Ford's admiration ripened into hero worship "like a planet that had adopted Edison for its sun."[7]

Reminiscing about this incident twenty-five years later, Dow recalled his protégé's behavior in somewhat more critical terms: "Henry used to get *set* when he was a young man, just as he does now. I mean, he would get his mind running on something and think of it to the exclusion of everything else for a while... When Ford gets 'set,' he is set and that is all there is to it. He may be right or he may be wrong—but he is 'set.'"[8]

With no personal finances, Henry Ford resigned from Detroit Edison after eight productive years and leaped into an industry "strewn with the wreckage of failures." As his Detroit Automobile Company was organized over the cusp of the turn of the century—and Henry Ford was forced of corporate necessity to attract investors, raise working capital, find a big enough building on Cass Avenue, and hire a staff of his own—colleagues and employees alike began to detect significant down-shifts in his disposition, from sunny to cloudy to gloomy to authoritarian. "If you didn't agree with Mr. Ford, you would no longer be useful to him," said one old-timer, looking back from retirement. "The fellows that yessed him were the fellows in his favor.... There were too many people who *did* what Mr. Ford thought, and there were not enough people who could *influence* what Mr. Ford thought."[9] Using large carriage tires purchased exclusively from Harvey S. Firestone, twenty-five vehicles were manufactured before the Detroit Automobile Company collapsed, after one year of life, in January 1901.

Henry Ford was in his thirty-eighth year. His first business venture had ended ignominiously and he was considered by many Detroiters to be an eccentric, and with the exception of Clara, his family thought he had been foolish to leave a good position with the Edison Company. Despite his pull-yourself-up-by-your-own-boot-straps philosophy, a narrow but discernible thread of surliness and severity had become woven into the fabric of Ford's personality. "In order to get along with Mr. Ford," another company pioneer recalled, "you had to have a little mean streak in your system. You had to be tough and mean. Mr. Ford enjoyed that."[10]

Dejected and trying to remain undaunted, Ford decided to shift the emphasis of his automobile development from outright consumer manufacturing to the more glamorous (and also headline-grabbing) realm of racing cars. He began to put together a scaled-down, specialized team, working out of a smaller shop. This group became the nucleus for Ford's second short-lived corporate enterprise, the Henry Ford Company, "Builders of High-Grade Automobiles and Tourist Cars." One of the first people he turned to was a younger mechanic, engineer, and draftsman named Oliver E. Barthel, who had been his student eight years back when Ford taught a $2.50-per-session night-time metalworking class at the Detroit YMCA.

Oliver Barthel (left), with two shop colleagues,
October 17, 1902

Barthel prided himself as a spiritual man. He knew that something was troubling Ford deep inside: Was it the forced paring-
down to more modest circumstances (Henry, Clara, and Edsel had
recently moved back in with Father William and spinster sister

**"At Full Speed," Henry Ford (left), at the wheel of his "Old 999"
racing car, versus John Harkness, May 1903**

Jane to save on rent), or was it perhaps having to string together
miscellaneous jobs once more while approaching middle-age? Or
might there even be some kind of religious deficiency? Ford was
nominally an Episcopalian,[11] but sometimes when the two men fell
to chatting as they worked shoulder to shoulder in close quarters,
Ford sounded to Barthel as if he were seeking some higher truth: "I
talked with Mr. Ford to arouse his interest along metaphysical
lines. He listened to me by the hour as I talked with him."

Barthel likewise was disturbed by what he considered Ford's
dual nature, as others in similarly close contact had been. "One side
of his nature I liked very much and I felt that I wanted to be a
friend of his," Barthel remembered, after half a century had passed.
"The other side of his nature I just couldn't stand. It bothered me

greatly. I came to the conclusion that he had a particular streak in his nature that you wouldn't find in a serious-minded person."[12]

On September 6, 1901, President William McKinley was shot while attending the Pan-American Exposition in Buffalo, New York. Eight days later, he died, and the nation went into shock. Mayor William C. Maybury of Detroit—himself a Ford Company investor—declared a day of mourning on the day McKinley was laid to rest, and the men at the Ford shop observed the occasion to put down their tools and engage in some thoughtful discussion of the state of the Union. Everyone liked McKinley. What kind of president would the vigorous, strenuous Theodore Roosevelt make? People felt a stir of excitement, but also of uncertainty.

As they whiled away that sad afternoon in quiet and speculative conversation, Oliver Barthel took a paperbound pamphlet out of his back pocket and handed it to Ford, telling him to read and take solace from it. The book was *A Short View of Great Questions*, by Orlando J. Smith. Henry Ford insisted time and again, well into the late 1930s, that this slim volume "changed his outlook on life."[13] At one point in 1924, Ford misplaced his precious, dog-eared copy, and desperately asked Barthel to borrow his so he could "have a photostatic copy made of each page, after which he returned it." Twelve years later, Barthel loaned his old friend a copy of Smith's subsequent book, *Eternalism*, the 1902 sequel to *A Short View*. Ford never returned that leather-bound tome; it remained in his personal library.

A Short View of Great Questions is a mysterious, multilayered tract. On first reading, it seems as a popular polemic endorsing the theory of reincarnation and metempsychosis (transmigration of souls), which, Oliver Barthel believed, "being in tune with the infinite...came to be as near a religion as Ford ever had."[14] However, to understand the powerful and lasting impact of the booklet upon Ford's thinking (by his own repeated testimony), a slow examination to uncover other pertinent agendas is required.

Beyond his initial mysticism, Smith emerges as a Social Darwin-

ist, superceding "the theory of Creation."[15] Man is at the center of
his own universe, and therefore "he need not grovel or abase himself": "We reap as we have sown. Each man is—mentally and
morally exactly, and to a large degree physically—what he has
made himself.... The strong have made themselves strong, the
weak are responsible for their own weakness."[16]

The author further comes across about midway through the
pamphlet as most resolutely *not* an "Orientalist," which is to say
that he "does not have patience with the Eastern cults of mysticism," nor with "the mythology of the Jews.... In these days of
light and doubt, men's minds are turning somewhat to the philosophy of the Orient. Yet it is not well to discard one authority, and set
up in its place another; for the last may be no better than the first.
The sacred mysteries of the East probably have no merits over the
sacred superstitions of the West."[17]

In Part XXV, "Theology is Artificial, A Revelation," which the
author addresses exclusively "to a Small Number of Men," Smith
hones in on this theme, specifically identifying the insidious source
for skepticism against metempsychosis as "the ancient Hebrew
scripture... a collection of the dreams, legends, poetry, proverbial
philosophy and sacred and historical fables which were current in
the twilight of the Hebrew race.... Early Judaism discredited the
immortality of the soul."[18]

By so doing, insisting upon the exclusive credibility of *their*
"One Book," the Jews set in motion a damaging succession of
"conflicting creeds" and centuries of "fierce and bloody wars" that
determined the dire modern fate of Europe.[19] Smith turns to none
other than "the acute mind of Arthur Schopenhauer [1788–1860]"
to bolster this accusation—in particular *Die Welt als Wille und
Vorstellung* (The World as Will and Idea): "What resists the belief of
metempsychosis is Judaism.... They certainly have succeeded,"
observed Schopenhauer in 1859, approvingly quoted by Smith, "in
driving out of Europe and part of Asia that consoling, primitive
belief of mankind."[20] Smith's explicit link with Schopenhauer is

noteworthy because both writers share a philosophical brand of antisemitism in their conviction that the Jewish race obstructed the integration of purer, ideal values of classical antiquity into the modern-day world.[21]

Smith extends the argument one final step, concluding *A Short View* by drawing upon an even earlier exponent of German race-thinking, Gotthold Lessing [1729–1781], whom he laudatorily invokes as "the Luther of German literature, German drama, German art." In his seminal work, *Die Erziehung des Menschengeslechts* (The Upbringing of Mankind), Lessing had written, "The very same way by which the race reaches its perfection must every individual man—one sooner, another later—have travelled over. Have travelled over in one and the same life?"

"Can he have been in one and the same life," Lessing wonders, "a sensual Jew and a spiritual Christian?"[22]

CHAPTER THREE

Tin Lizzie

EARLY in January 1902, Henry Ford—the development of his racing car perceptibly slower—stopped by to meet and chat with the young engineer and manufacturer Alfred P. Sloan Jr. at the Hyatt Roller Bearing Company booth at the annual Madison Square Garden Automobile Show in New York City. Ford had spent the better part of the afternoon "tromping around" the various exhibits, and he was looking for a place to take a break. He doffed his derby hat, mopped his brow, leaned back in a chair, hooked his heels onto the top rung of the railing in the gallery so that "his knees were at the level of his chin," watched the newest model cars parade by down below, and chatted with abandon for several hours.[1]

At this juncture in his career, restless Ford expressed conviction about a different kind of vehicle; "he was always talking about [wanting to manufacture] a light, trustworthy, powerful, *cheap* car for the common people...and [he said] making them come through the factory just alike."² A compelling paradox coalesced in Ford's mind. How often had he spoken of his aversion to farming chores; try as he might to idealize his childhood, he would always recall rising in darkness to perform an interminable succession of domestic tasks and numbingly repetitive physical labors. These distasteful memories burst into a resolutely commercial notion: Henry Ford would remake himself as the friend of the farmer, consciously channeling his manufacturing energies into a blatantly grassroots campaign to "make the farmer's lot easier"—literally, to emancipate him through technology. He believed this rural outreach held the key to the future of American progress.³

Such rhetoric—be it the farmer's "plight" or his "troubles"— became a mantra during the hectic run-up to formal incorporation of the Ford Motor Company, with all of twelve shareholders, on June 16, 1903. What raised the profile of this endeavor above the 150 other automobile manufacturers then active throughout the United States? The first widespread and successful car, the two-cylinder Model A, was, as promised, lighter, less expensive, and less mechanically daunting than the competition. "*Anybody* can drive a Ford," vowed Henry. The car was dedicated to utility, rather than luxury, "designed for every day wear and tear....Built to save you time and consequent money," bragged the first advertisements, "providing service—*never* a 'sporting car.'"⁴

There was something else about speaking directly to the farming market that appealed to Ford, an affinity of disposition he felt keenly. "From boyhood, I was a farmer...And a farmer is a stubborn rascal," revisionist Henry noted approvingly to a factory visitor. "He doesn't take up with a new idea very fast." Stubborn Henry was the persona everyone on the factory floor came to know so well. In strict control, "he expected obedience on the jump" and was the self-styled final arbiter in all disputes and matters of policy. "I'm the fellow who does that," he would say with pride during his formative years as boss.⁵

"I am trying to democratize the automobile," Ford defiantly asserted in defense of patent-infringement suits brought against the corporate upstart by the Association of Licensed Automobile Manufacturers, a consortium refusing to admit him to membership.

The first Ford

"Progress happens when all the factors that make for it are ready," Ford sermonized.

The Ford car was embraced by the rank and file. Despite a nationwide economic panic in 1906–1907, Ford lowered prices to $500 for a four-cylinder runabout, increased as well as varied production, and racked up gross sales of more than $5.7 million. He pushed onward with his consumer vision of the world, "a car for the great multitude, the Model T. It will be large enough for the family but small enough for the individual to run and care for. It will be constructed of the best materials, by the best men to be hired, after the simplest designs that modern engineering can devise. But it will be so low in price that no man making a good salary will be unable to own one—and enjoy with his family the blessing of hours of pleasure in God's great open spaces."[6]

Ford consolidated his gains and on March 9, 1908, brought down his focus to a single, simple, egalitarian, and uniform car, each one manufactured as much like the next as pins or matches. Just like its five-foot-eight inch, 145-pound creator, the $825 car was "slight yet strong...a machine of lithe toughness with an ability to reach difficult goals." The mass-produced, assembly-line Tin Lizzie rode high off the road on thirty-inch wheels, forged from vanadium steel, and came most commonly in black. On the site of a sixty-acre former race track in the Highland Park suburb of Detroit, inspired by the guiding design genius of architect Albert

Kahn, Henry Ford put up a sprawling four-story glass and steel factory where a Model T would be churned out on the moving assembly line every two hours and thirty-five minutes. Each man was assigned one task and stood in one place, while conveyor belts took the parts to him.[7]

"I KNOW what kind of help I want and I look around until I find the man I am sure will give it," said Henry Ford. However, one kind of help was needed on the assembly line and quite another required to keep up with Ford. He was a hyperkinetic manager with a seemingly inexhaustible reserve of energy. Colleagues quickly learned that the last place to look for him was in his office, because to Ford, thought equaled action. He was constantly in motion—in the machine shop, the power plant, or the drafting room—turning up stealthily one moment at the shoulder of a man deep in his manufacturing chore, handing him a required tool; at another moment, he might be seen disdainfully wiping a thin film of dust off the surface of a lathe, in his fanatic quest to maintain

The classic Ford logo designed by C. Harold Wills in 1903 and used continuously until 1947

perfect cleanliness at Highland Park—and woe to the unfortunate foreman who had neglected this basic responsibility.[8]

There were also the sorts of men Ford turned to for engineering solutions and business partnerships, such as Oliver Barthel, Alex Malcomson, Joseph Galamb, C. Harold Wills, and the brainy strategist, second in command James Couzens. These early and loyal soldiers in the Ford Motor Company ranks were forced to subscribe to Ford's nonhierarchical style of governance. No one man was ahead of or ranked above any other in Ford's way of thinking. This perverse egalitarianism from the original days of Ford's business gave rise to a climate of uncertainty and kept the men off balance, never quite knowing who was "in" or who was "out," which Ford quite enjoyed.

However, when Ford hired Ernest Gustav Liebold as his personal secretary in 1910, he departed from his ostensibly non-structured management philosophy, recognizing in the stocky, soft-

spoken, bespectacled bookkeeper a complete alter ego. Over the ensuing thirty-four years, Liebold grew to achieve an intimate position of un-equaled (and, it would soon tran-spire, pernicious) power within the great industrial empire and partici-pated in all of Henry Ford's whims, enthusiasms—and prejudices. With the taking of Ernest Liebold into his confidence, Henry Ford gave birth to the phenomenon we can only con-ceptualize as "Henry Ford," much the same as Walter Lippmann was

E. G. Liebold, April 26, 1925

writing in 1914 when he speculated about how many hundreds of times a day "The President" may do something he may never even hear of.[9]

Born in Detroit on March 16, 1884, of German Lutheran immi-grant stock, Liebold attended public schools, through Eastern High School, before graduating from Detroit's Gutchess College, where he established a reputation as a voracious reader and majored in business studies, including shorthand. After marrying Clara Reich, also of Detroit, he began work at Peninsula Savings Bank in Highland Park as a messenger, and then advanced to ste-nographer and assistant teller. While at the Peninsula Bank, Liebold met James Couzens, general sales manager of the Ford Motor Company. It turned out that Ford was looking to establish its own bank nearer the factory, to administer payroll and other cash functions for employees (and also to give Mr. Ford more direct, hands-on control of his money, since he was well-known to possess a deep distrust of bankers—especially those on Wall Street—and a fear of personal and corporate borrowing that bordered upon the phobic). Couzens took an immediate liking to the twenty-six-year-old fellow "with the mind like a balance sheet" and made him president of the newly established Highland Park State Bank.

The next year, Henry Ford acquired the failing D. P. Lapham Bank in his hometown of Dearborn (formerly known as Dearbornville) and assigned Liebold to take over its management. Eventually, Liebold was given power of attorney, including signatory responsibility for Mr. and Mrs. Ford's personal correspondence and all their financial transactions. Liebold maintained an office at the Highland Park factory, but his salary was always paid from Ford's separate account at Dearborn, never through the Ford Motor Company.[10]

The socially awkward Henry Ford always had a problem with the so-called rougher chores of management. Thus, when a man needed to be fired, the reluctant Ford sent Liebold to do it. His tough-minded factotum did not associate with many other men inside the corporation.[11] He did not need a set of cronies and preferred to head straight home after work to his growing family. (He would eventually have eight children.)

After the release and success of the Model T, Ford almost immediately began to chafe against the burdens of routine. By the end of 1913, he had presided over the manufacture of 500,000 motor cars, and he was a millionaire many times over. He seriously considering selling the company three times between 1908 and 1916. More and more, Ford displayed listless and dejected moods. Clara worried constantly about his lack of sleep and feared her fidgety husband was heading for a breakdown, although she knew better than to share this apprehension with him.[12] He strayed often from the stresses of factory life. He appeared at the auto plant once or twice a week, then liked to go out for long, solitary walks in the wheat fields of Dearborn, or grab his binoculars and take a solo spin into the countryside to spy upon the inhabitants of the hundreds of birdhouses he had built. Ford even began drafting notes for a book about birds.

At times like these, Ford was grateful for his devoted "watchdog" who stayed behind: "I didn't hire him to like everybody that comes to the gate."[13] Stolid, cold, and austere in manner, Liebold, "the Prussian martinet," turned visitors away from the factory door, insisting to curious journalists he had no idea where Mr. Ford was at the moment.

"I had to protect Mr. Ford from everyone," Liebold explained in a lengthy interview in 1951—and to him, The Boss was always "Mr. Ford," even posthumously. "Everyone who came to see him was carefully screened. You had to be on your guard, every minute of the time." Those few newspapermen who *were* fortunate enough in the first decade of the Ford Motor Company to corner the man himself for a few words of wisdom invariably found Liebold right there by his side: "If Mr. Ford made a statement about doing so-and-so or having something in mind," Liebold said, "you had to sit down and analyze it, figure out what the meaning was. Perhaps after you knew what you were talking about, you could go back and discuss it with him."

Even after seven years in retirement, Liebold maintained lucid convictions about his mission: "All of Mr. Ford's statements, while there was a good deal of logic behind them, unless they were properly interpreted and worded wouldn't mean much to the public."

"Somebody"—Ernest Liebold told his interlocutor with unshakable resolve, as if it were only yesterday, and he was back where he felt most at home, comfortably within Henry Ford's brain—"*Somebody* had to know and understand Mr. Ford who knew what he meant when he was talking about things, or you wouldn't know what Mr. Ford was driving at. He sometimes used different phraseology than other people do, so you had to know what he meant."[14]

CHAPTER FOUR

The Christian Century

AND WHAT *did* Mr. Ford mean when he began to talk publicly about "the Jews"? How did he manage to extrapolate from *A Short View of Great Questions* in general, to the particulars of "the Jewish Question"?

Henry Ford was touched by the Zeitgeist—the civilization and spirit of the times—of nineteenth-century America. By January 1914, when he stepped out of the shadows and imposed himself on the public consciousness, Ford was more than fifty years old and well-formed. He had lived through a maelstrom of changes in the American economic and social structure.[1]

As early as the 1840s, while Grandfather John Ford was working the land in Dearbornville, a firm conviction was already in place among small-town Americans that they were an elect and favored people, doing God's work. As Anglo-Saxons, most thought, they had come into a new territory that was their birthright to be cultivated "according to the intentions of the Creator." It has never been determined conclusively that Grandfather Ford knew he was trying to get close to Nature via a kind of Jeffersonian nostalgia. However, he did share in the belief that savage Indians could not rightfully maintain a claim to his land, because they were not capable of "improvement." Neither were the "oriental" German Jews who had just begun to appear on these shores in modest but visible numbers. These people could perhaps be tolerated; nevertheless they were outsiders, confusing to the vision of America as a place where the industrious many worked by hand, and the Priests of the Soil would always stand superior to the idle few.[2]

The gospel of progress was synonymous with the *Christian* (generally Protestant) way during that "Great Century of Christian Expansion." Henry Ford recalled that he and his younger siblings were raised on a daily dosage of the American Tract Society's *The Illustrated Family Christian Almanac for the United States* topping off the nightly fireside McGuffey readings. The almanac's "Historical Tales for Young Protestants" were classic representations in a widespread and popular genre of evangelical publications predicting, either implicitly or explicitly, that sooner or later, the obsolete Jewish religion would give way entirely to "the new Israel" of America.[3] Who, the little boys and girls learned catechistically, was the ultimate symbol of persecuted goodness? Christ. And who persecuted Christ and crucified our Lord—as the grand old hymn had it? The Jews: "Let our motto ever be, 'None *but* Christ,' and our ever-increasing aspiration, 'More *of* Christ.'" The children were further chastened by the many comforting homilies in their *Almanac* never to forget the "Three Whats:" "What from? Believers are redeemed from hell and destruction. What by? By the precious blood of Christ. What to? To an inheritance incorruptible, undefiled, and that fadeth not away."[4]

John Lanse McCloud served, among other capacities, as head of the Chemical and Metallurgical Laboratory and manager of the

Manufacturing Research Department at the Ford Motor Company, and he knew Henry Ford well from 1914 until 1947. He was one of the old-timers who speculated (after Ford's death, of course) on the earliest root of his friend's anti-Jewish bias, attributing it at first vaguely to "the social atmosphere of the time ... [and] boyhood influences." When pressed by his interviewer, McCloud more precisely pointed out "an anti-Semitic thread observable in the garment of Populism."[5] It is the case that in 1878, when young Henry was a lad of fifteen, the Central Greenback Club of Detroit came forth with a manifesto attributing the American railroad scandals and the economic depressions that followed the Civil War to the "Rothschilds across the water."[6] Other sources aver that "during the agrarian ferment of the years 1870–1896, when he was growing up, the young fellow doubtless heard Populistic speeches."[7] Populists and other opponents of international capitalism did bandy about the name "Rothschild" as a convenient euphemism for "international banker." A typical pulp periodical of the period ranted, "Wherever on the globe commerce exists, there hovers the hook-nosed Jew with his bag of gold, carrying the curse of usury, like the money-changers of old."[8]

These were commonly held attitudes toward Jews contemporaneous with Henry Ford's development at an impressionable age. However, nowhere in the vast biographical literature does Ford make any direct attribution to a Populist rally he attended or to an overt screed he read in the local newspaper. During the late-Reconstruction period, leading into the cusp of the 1880s—as historian C. Vann Woodward pointed out in his classic 1938 study, *Tom Watson, Agrarian Rebel*—the "bitter chorus of shibboleths" around the country became more divisive along predictable economic lines. The domineering capitalists were defined as class-conscious and ruthless Northeasterners, while angry farmers looked to like-minded constituents in the expanses of the West for additional economic clout. Town and country fissured and became clichéd adversaries. Jews were commonly believed to abhor agricultural life and to reside

comfortably among the "detested middlemen" and "Yankee businessmen, tradesmen and corporations" on the one side; desperate, militant farmers and "agrarian masses" stood on the other.[9]

ACCORDING to the Federal Census Schedule, the entire Jewish population in Detroit when Ford was a boy was about 1,000, concentrated into a ten-square block quarter on the eastern side of
downtown known as "Little Jerusalem."[10] Over the next half-
century, Jewish emigration to the United States increased exponen-
tially. Yet by 1920, Dearborn, the site of Ford's sprawling tractor
manufacturing plant, was still a resolutely Anglo-Saxon scene, with
only four Poles and one Russian Jew in residence in the entire suburb.[11] There is no anecdotal evidence that Henry Ford might even
have *met* a Jew before he was twenty years old. Prejudice does not
depend upon actual experience for its power.[12] Antisemitism does
not require the presence of Jews, only their images—as in the powerful image of the profit-motivated Jew, the "economic creature . . .
whose God was money."[13]

In addition to being nurtured upon deeply ingrained Christian
teachings about mythical, ancient, unseen Jews with a broad reper-
toire of fabled (and lethal) qualities, Henry Ford grew up during an
era of economic stress; there has always been a correlation between
economic frustration and "actual or symbolic pogroms," which tend
to remain latent in more ordinary times.[14] Jews are historically disliked most actively in periods of economic depression, when a sense
of disenfranchisement and frustration (as among prairie farmers)
can give rise to illusions of unfair persecution. This, in turn, can
lead to an exaggerated self-image of "goodness" that has been
abused—causing the unsophisticated, "naïve Christian" to turn with
expedient antipathy toward the Jews as the reason for his hardship.

There is furthermore a tendency to focus dislike upon Jews during periods of extreme social change and turmoil. Religious bias
becomes conflated with nationalism. During the Civil War, among

the Union and Confederacy alike, there was rampant distrust of Jews—again, out of proportion to their actual numbers—that increased as Jews moved toward greater involvement in the affairs of commerce. Jews' loyalty and patriotism naturally came under question at a time when the very definition and shape of American nationhood was already so splintered.[15]

Amerika, du hast es besser
Als unser Kontinent, das alte.

America, you are better off
Than our continent, the old one.

The problematic conditions in the so-called Promised Land at the advent of the Great Migration in 1881 no longer resembled the glowing promise embodied in *Amerika*, Johann Wolfgang von Goethe's poem of 1827, a seeming eternity in the past.[16] Quite the opposite: The onslaught of many thousands of unfamiliar Eastern European Jews, with their frenzied, quasi-German speech and ragged, "Oriental" clothing and extreme mannerisms, converted stereotypes into specifics. Lo and behold, these "debased and mongrel" people were "degrading our Commonwealth from a Nation into something half pawn-shop, half broker's office.... You will not find many Poles or Huns or Russian Jews in the clean cattle country!" declared the eternal glorifier of the American West, Owen Wister.[17] It is important to note that the coming of the Eastern European Jews also threw off balance the fragile illusion of acclimation of the German Jews, even as they understood all too well that American Christians were always covertly inclined to conceptualize all Jews as one race. The "debilitated and pauperized" new arrivals and their anxious predecessors might have seen and felt the extreme cultural divide with the Germans, but the confused American public made no such distinction.[18]

The image persisted of displaced Jews in motion, triggered by a wave of pogroms in the years following the assassination of Czar Alexander II by terrorist revolutionaries and the subsequent acces-

sions of Alexander III and Nicholas II. Abandoning the ideal of emancipation in Russia and elsewhere in Eastern Europe, one-third of an entire population moved away, en masse and with uncertainty, leaving their *shtelekhs* and cities behind. The remaining two-thirds would be baptized or starve to death. Like "an advancing shadow," the Wanderers from the Russian Pale of Settlement (themselves comprising more than one-half the Jewish population of the world), from Rumania, and from Galicia came through the cities of

Immigrants arriving in "the golden land"

di goldene medine (the golden land), compromising tightly held urban illusions of American stability.[19] Jewish immigrants, because they were itinerant, were not perceived as new settlers; rather, they were looked upon disdainfully as "bearers of a foreign culture."[20] Unlike those who had staked their claim to America—who were already here—Jews were thought of as having no singular, specifically identifiable national origin. They were "ghost people" with no homeland or sense of nationhood; rather, they had been pathetically dispersed, wraith-like, throughout the world ever since the time of Babylonian captivity. As living symbols of homelessness, the beleaguered *Ostjuden* came into direct contact with an intensely nativist society made doubly uneasy by their presence, an uneasiness compounded with the sheer momentum of their invasion.[21]

The xenophobia and restrictionism characterizing the American response to the Jews was not limited to any one sector of society:

"Brahmins and rednecks, bourgeois and proletarians, reactionaries and populists" all joined in the outcry against this dilution of American identity.[22] The coming of the Jews actually served to galvanize American nationalism; here was a common, Oriental enemy thought to pose a generalized threat to mainstream values.

There was no more popular textual exemplar of the panicked pulse of the period than *Our Country: Its Possible Future and Its Present Crisis,* by the Reverend Josiah Strong, D.D., published in March 1886 and going on to bestsellerdom—an astonishing 175,000 copies sold over the next three decades. Strong understood the mood of Protestant America at this signal point in its struggle to preserve and protect its abiding mission and put a stop to the reckless corruption of our great metropolises by "tainted spots in the body politic."[23] By 1888, there were already over 270 major Jewish congregations in America, 130 of them in New York City. To Strong's way of thinking, the solution to this epidemic was simple: "Christianize the immigrant and he will be easily Americanized. Christianity is the solvent of all race antipathies."[24]

Setting the alarmist tone for a theme that would appear with disturbing frequency over the bridge of the new century and well into the 1920s, Strong wrote vigorously of the superiority of the Anglo-Saxon race, God's truly chosen people, unlike whatever other, shadowy newcomers might believe of themselves.

By the close of the twentieth century, Strong believed, "It is possible that the Anglo-Saxons will outnumber all the other civilized races of the world. Does it not look as if God were not only preparing in our Anglo-Saxon civilizations the die with which to stamp the peoples of the earth, but as if He were also massing behind that die the mighty power with which to press it?"[25]

For this God-given triumph to materialize in the 1880s, it was necessary that "this great focal-point of history toward which the lines of past progress have converged," for the many great identities and "allied varieties of the *Aryan* race," these veritable instruments in the hands of God, to bravely close ranks. They must gird their loins and make ready for the impending Armageddon, "the final competition, for which the Anglo-Saxon is being schooled."[26]

In Strong's dramatic assessment of a lesson to be learned from ancient history, this enterprise of preparation would be no small matter, because the invading army of foreigners that had touched American shores during the past five years was, by his estimation, "more than four times as vast as the number of Goths and Vandals that swept over Southern Europe and overwhelmed Rome," another noble civilization toppled because it did not heed the alarm bells of nativism.[27] The modern American Aryan man of the late nineteenth century had his work cut out for him, but on the other side of his inevitable victory, Strong predicted—with explicit acknowledgement of Herbert Spencer—there would spring forth from the ashes of spiritual carnage "a new and more powerful type of Man than has hitherto ever existed."[28]

HOSTILITY toward Jews in Detroit increased markedly through the 1890s. In March 1893, the Detroit Athletic Club membership committee, dominated by a homogeneous elite of industrialists, blackballed the application of Herman Freund, a prominent Jewish businessman.[29] There were attacks by Irish and Polish working-class youths on Jewish peddlers, to which the police conveniently turned their backs, as well as ethnic slurs in the daily newspapers and strong-arm efforts to prevent Jews from rising too high in city politics, which gave cause to an "all-Jewish political meeting" in 1894. In 1897, inspired by Theodore Herzl's tract, *The Jewish State*, the United Zionists of Detroit Association was founded. But whenever Jews decided to band together in these ways, it only served to inspire further negative opinion and fears of ill-defined conspiracy and also drove Baptist clergy to mount increasingly zealous evangelical outreach efforts into the Jewish community.[30]

These acts in Detroit and elsewhere in fin-de-siècle America were the results of the compulsion to find a "stereotyped other" against whom endangered Christians could measure themselves. In the strange, nervous netherworld blurring the end of one century and the beginning of the next, with the American economy continuing to suffer bewildering fluctuations and booms followed by depressions, there was a vague sense that unseen, hidden, and irrational "market forces" were determining the course of personal destiny.

Christian identity was under siege in this rapidly changing, modern Promised Land. "The Jew was conveniently at hand," enabling the character of early-modern racism in America to be formed on the notion that people who were "different" could be actual instruments of change and therefore could be held accountable for otherwise inexplicable trends in the culture of modernity.[31] Once that blame was affixed, antisemites had latched upon a real reason to criticize, contain, or even control the Jews.[32]

CHAPTER FIVE

Working Man's Friend

ON JANUARY 5, 1914, at the instigation of James Couzens and Horace Rackham, the Ford Motor Company announced that the following week, the work day would be reduced to eight hours, the immense Highland Park factory converted to three daily shifts instead of two—and the basic wage increased from three dollars a day to an astonishing five dollars a day. Male workers over the age of twenty-two, no matter what their color or nationality, would receive profit-sharing sufficient to achieve this level. Unfortunately, the women at the plant, who were paid at a rate of $2.07 a day, had been overlooked. But their turn would gradually come, once the men had been taken care of.[1]

Couzens's inspiration was the bold stroke that brought Henry Ford into the public eye. The Boss took full advantage of the new-found spotlight and full credit for the idea as "the greatest revolution in the matter of rewards for workers ever known to the industrial world."[2] Ford took great pains to deny that it was the lure of the spotlight that had motivated him: "Many employees thought we were just making the announcement because we were prosperous and wanted advertising."

On the contrary, Ford insisted, also denying that his plan was just another method of welfare, "To our way of thinking, this was an act of social justice, and in the last analysis, we did it for our own satisfaction of mind. There is a pleasure in feeling that you have made others happy—that you have lessened in some degree the burdens of your fellow-men—that you have provided a margin out of which may be had pleasure and saving. Good-will is one of the few really important assets of life. A determined man can win almost anything that he goes after, but unless, in his getting, he gains good-will, he has not profited much."[3] Ford was actually shaping a not-so-veiled reply to the editors of the *Wall Street Journal*, who criticized him for injecting "Biblical or spiritual principles into a field where they do not belong," which would result in "material, financial, and factory disorganization."[4] The *Journal* was not far off the mark in suspecting that a moralistic plan lay in waiting just below the surface of Ford's largesse. The wage increase came contingent upon Ford's strict stipulation that "a man who is living aright will do his work aright."[5] This was not going to be "easy money" that flowed directly into the following week's pay envelope without a host of conditions.

Livelihood was to be linked with behavior. Industrial betterment was linked to the straight and narrow path. Henry Ford was often (intentionally) overheard on the shop floor encouraging a foreman to "Go ahead and *make* a man for the job" that needed doing; he said, "You make the man and you needn't worry about your business."[6] As one of several corporate press releases issued over the ensuing weeks blared, "The idea Mr. Ford has in mind is to help the men to a LIFE—not a mere LIVING."[7]

Hence the contingent and immediate establishment of the Ford

Sociological Department, headed by John R. Lee, "a man of ideas and ideals [with] a keen sense of justice and a sympathy with the 'down and outs,' the men in trouble, that leads to an understanding of their problems. . . . Under his guidance, the department [will] put a soul into the company."[8]

To assist Lee as an unpaid volunteer in this new enterprise (and succeeding him in November 1915), Ford persuaded his friend—and Clara Ford's faithful spiritual adviser—the Reverend Samuel Simpson Marquis (1866–1948), to relinquish his post as dean of St. Paul's Episcopal Cathedral in Detroit and come into the welcoming fold of the Ford Motor Company. "I want you, Mark, to put Jesus Christ in my factory!" Ford proclaimed. Marquis was chosen to oversee all personnel issues at Ford because he wholeheartedly encouraged The Boss's view, the watchword of Social Gospelism, that the teachings of Jesus Christ were "the basis upon which a new society must be built." What could be closer to God's work than the improvement of man's condition? In 1912, Marquis had preached a sermon called "The Man: On the Scientific Self-Management of a One-Man Power Three-Cylinder Engine," in which he stressed that all three components of "the human engine—the physical, the mental, and the moral"—be kept "tuned up." Ford was so taken with Marquis's analogy that he had the sermon printed as a little booklet and distributed to all the workers in the plant.[9] Marquis labored for Ford Motor Company for more than five years.

The Sociological Department of the Ford Motor Company was set in motion with a staff of more than fifty "investigators" (Marquis changed their titles to the less-threatening "advisers"), growing to a force of 160 men within two years. The investigators, chosen because of their "peculiar fitness as judges of human nature," were an odd hybrid of social worker and detective, venturing into the crowded back streets of the city with a driver, an interpreter, and a sheaf of printed questionnaires. Their job was to establish standards of proper behavior throughout the company. "If you double a man's wages, and lift him up from living below par, he might go haywire," a Ford adviser theorized. "Hence the Sociological Department was necessary, in order to teach the men how to live a clean and wholesome life."[10]

To qualify for the five-dollar day, an employee had to put up with an exhaustive domestic inspection, show that he was sober, clean of person, saving money through regular bank deposits, "of good habits," and not living "riotously" or taking in too many boarders. Lee and his colleagues believed that roomers were detrimental to the home life of the family: "Next to liquor, dissension in the home is due to people other than the family being there." Cramped living quarters were similarly frowned upon. Married couples were preferred. If an investigator discovered a situation in which a man and a woman were living together who were not married, application was made in short order to Probate Court, so that their union could be legitimized. Ford himself, "highly moral and upright," did not drink intoxicants or use tobacco in any form (he vilified cigarettes as "the little white slavers").[11] If a Ford worker was determined by Sociological Department investigators to be diverting from the path of righteousness in ways either explicit or implicit, he was offered the opportunity for rehabilitation so that he could be "lifted up" to the requirements of the company and "his fellow-men." Then and only then would he certified to receive Ford's "bonus-on-conduct."[12]

Since just after the turn of the century, there had been a concerted effort on the part of the Detroit Industrial Removal Office to bring in Eastern European Jews from the overflow conditions rampant in New York City. The burgeoning local automobile industry was wholeheartedly behind this initiative, because the companies' personnel demands were insatiable. By 1914, more than twelve thousand "Jewish newcomers" had moved to Detroit, thanks to IRO efforts.

At the nonunionized Ford plant, most of the unskilled laborers were of Russian, Polish, Croatian, Hungarian, or Italian descent.[13] "Like all great manufacturing establishments in this country," wrote James Martin Miller, a reporter for the *New York World* and author of one of the first sanctioned, official Ford biographies, "it has been found impossible to get enough workmen from among the American born. Being above all, an American, Mr. Ford is spending money without stint to give the foreign born of his employees a practical knowledge of the English language, and to teach them about the United States Government; in short, to Americanize them."

"Mr. Ford is doing more to industrialize the Jew and make producers, rather than consumers, of them, than any other force in the world."[14]

And, by the way, though it hardly seemed to warrant reiterating, "Those foreign-born employees soon found out that Mr. Ford did not want employees very long who refused to become Ameri-

The Ford Americanization School at Highland Park

canized." A benighted alien, and there were some, who chose at first not to attend compulsory Sociology Department School classes, would be laid off "and given a chance for uninterrupted meditation." Afterward, Lee and his colleagues confidently reported, he "seldom failed to change his mind... He saw that attending the school was the best thing for him to do."[15]

The primary rehabilitation step for immigrant workers, teaching them a practical method for speaking English in classes intentionally mixed by race and country, promoted the overall goal of Ford's uniformity campaign, "to impress upon these men that they are, or should be, Americans, and *that former racial, national, and linguistic differences are to be forgotten.*"[16]

Henry Ford's melange of evangelism and patriotism was in place more than a year before the Detroit Americanization Com-

The Melting Pot ceremony, July 4, 1917

mittee was formed as a consortium of the major corporate players in town, and also before National Americanization Day was officially established on July 4, 1915.[17] The first graduation ceremony from the Ford School was held in a municipal building at the center of Detroit, but after a couple of years it was moved to a baseball field near the Highland Park plant. A huge wood, canvas, and papier-mâché "Melting Pot" was built at second base. There were flights of steps up to the rim on both sides. The audience of families and co-workers settled themselves in the grandstands after a huge picnic had been served. A brass band commenced to play, and a procession moved forth from a gate at one side of the field—men from the foreign nationalities employed at the plant. They were wearing their various native costumes, singing their national songs, and dancing folk dances. The master of ceremonies was the principal of Mr. Ford's School, Clinton C. DeWitt, dressed up as Uncle Sam. He led the group to the ladder on one side of the big pot. Then he directed them up the stairs to the rim, and down inside. One by one, he called the men out again on the other side. Now they were dressed in derby hats, coats, pants, vests, stiff collars, polka-dot ties, "undoubtedly each with an Eversharp pencil in his pocket," singing the *Star-Spangled Banner*—and wearing the distinctive Ford Motor Company badge on their lapels.[18]

Henry Ford's Sociological Department and school flourished at a time when the ideal "national type" was fixed as if in amber. America's self-image in those tense days on the brink of World War I made full use of a *"transmuting* pot" rather than a "melting pot," because all the ingredients of other national identities were compelled to become assimilated into an idealized "Anglo-Saxon model," more familiarly known as the American way of life. The messianic purpose of America in 1914, in Henry Ford's mind, was best expressed as a special kind of civic religion, and he was its chief minister.[19]

Symptomatic of his hermetic identity, Henry Ford as captain of industry grew in power and public stature on a parallel track with

Henry Ford as the most isolated man in America. "Whizzing through the streets in his car in passing from one to another of his plants," Ford was virtually unknown in downtown Detroit.[20] He insisted upon using his 100-ton, customized Pullman railroad coach when he traveled for business, and private cruises aboard his 223-foot-long, two-masted yacht, *Sialia*, when he sailed in the summers for pleasure on Lake Michigan. With the exception of a fourteen-room home, *The Mangoes*, on three and one-half acres of land fronting the Caloosahatchie Bay at Fort Myers, Florida—which Thomas Edison persuaded the Fords to purchase for $20,000 next door to his winter cottage in the spring of 1916—and a plantation at Ways, Georgia, the couple never owned a residence outside Detroit or Wayne County. "He has lived all his life practically in the same spot," Sarah Bushnell, another early biographer and a close friend of Clara Ford, observed approvingly, "and even today he seldom leaves the vicinity of Dearborn for any length of time." Mrs. Ford told Bushnell, "We have lived here always, and here we love to stay."[21]

Since 1909, Ford had slowly acquired many parcels of land in his beloved Dearborn Township, eventually exceeding 1,300 acres along the curving banks of the north branch of the Rouge River. Originally he intended to develop an exclusive wildlife preserve for unfettered ramblings. Clara convinced her husband that "Fair Lane," a great estate of gray, rough-hewn Marblehead-Buff Ohio limestone, should be built on the land, upon a bluff overlooking the Rouge. "Hereafter," came the intention of Ford the recluse, "I am going to see to it that no man comes to know me so intimately."[22]

In the spring of 1913, while the construction of the hybrid Late English-Gothic style mansion and its landscaping took shape under the direction of architects Von Holst and Fyfe of Chicago, Ford built a bird fountain at the base of a hillside near the house, in homage to John Burroughs (1837–1921), the wise and soft-spoken naturalist whose works Ford greatly admired. Burroughs, a white-bearded rustic, had been affectionately nicknamed "the child of the

**Henry Ford and John Burroughs
at their first meeting in Dearborn**

woods" by Henry James and was also a particular favorite of the English critic Matthew Arnold. Burroughs's essays were models of the romantic, pastoral tradition, and Ford fell in love with their self-styled "home instinct," exalting local sights and sounds at the author's doorstep near his stone cottage in the heart of the southern Catskill Mountains, along the Hudson River at West Park, ninety miles above New York City.

Burroughs's writing was infused with a fervent Christian strain that spoke to Ford directly. The godhead was not some remote, abstract concept; it was as near to hand as the sturdy oak just out in back of his house. Thus, "the tenet of sin followed by redemption" was exemplified in Burroughs's descriptions of citizens of the cities who finally saw the light and "returned to seek the pleasure and solitude of the wooded countryside." To Burroughs, cities were places where the "rude and barbarous" gravitated. He believed with all his heart and soul that Modern Man had to learn the hard way of the dire consequences of denying the pristine forest. If the pastoral was fated to suffer defeat at the hands of the greedy "hell of the urban," then the sinner must come around to embrace the ultimate heaven of sylvan glades.[23]

When Ford's ornate bird fountain was ready for unveiling in a little grotto at the center of an array of rose beds, he brought the reticent but flattered Burroughs to Fair Lane for the occasion. The talk at their first face-to-face meeting was of—what else?—birds; to Ford they were "the best of companions." They then turned to the inspirational works of Ralph Waldo Emerson. Through Burroughs's books, Ford had recently become enamored of the Transcendentalists, and now the industrialist was determined to take his naturalist mentor with him on a pilgrimage to visit the homes of Emerson and Henry David Thoreau in and around Concord, Massachusetts, that coming fall.[24]

During the Civil War years, when Henry Ford was but a toddler, Burroughs had met and talked with Emerson at West Point, remembering him as resembling "an alert, inquisitive farmer." Burroughs was impressed by Emerson's "serene, unflinching look. Just the way his upper lip shut into his lower...showed to me the metal of which he is made." Working at the Treasury Department in Washington during the war, Burroughs had hiked through Rock Creek Park with the Good Grey Poet himself, Walt Whitman, describing him in similar terms: "Walt is as great as Emerson, though after a different type....it is as if Nature herself has spoken."[25]

Ford looked to Emerson as a mainstream, popular Christian teacher—as, in the words of Matthew Arnold, who knew Emerson, "the friend and aider of those who would live in the spirit."[26] From the time of Emerson's death in 1882 until well into the 1930s, this was his enduring message for middlebrow American culture. His aphoristic, sermonizing best-selling *Essays: First Series* (which Emerson "toyed briefly" with entitling *Forest Essays*) were reprinted every two years from initial publication in 1841 through the next four decades and were the springboard for his international reputation.[27] Emerson advocated a "new, more natural theology" that found religious ecstasy in the manners of everyday life, honored the "green solitude" of the broad outdoors, and revered the great ideals of Progress with a decidedly capital *P*. Self-reliance diametrically opposed to dependence upon property and government; the exercise of power in motion, never repose; education through experience, not book-learning; focused thought as the key to all other human qualities; trusting your own instincts; beauty found in utilitarianism—such were the fundamental Emersonian principles so attractive to Ford. As he had done previously with Orlando Smith, Ford dug into Emerson's work for "solace and spiritual renewal."[28]

This habit was witnessed by visitors to Ford's home. Aside from carefully examining the morning, noon, and evening newspapers put by his favorite chair and reading light—with particular attention to cartoons and clippings referring to him—Ford made the occasional foray into Tolstoy, Maeterlinck, Darwin, and "several plays" of Shakespeare. "He *actually reads* only two books, as far as I have observed," wrote Allan Benson, "Emerson's *Essays* and the Bible. Mr. Ford knows the *Essays* in his own way, down to the core. He has Bibles all over his house. He does not regard the Bible as a book to be put up on the shelf and never read. He dips into it a great deal." Certain books in Ford's library were noticeably "soiled by frequent use," and "odd copies of Emerson" were always to be found on a side table next to Ford's spot on the couch, where Clara, the bibliophile of the family, read to him of an evening by the hearth. Above the fireplace was carved Emerson's inspirational adage, "Chop your own wood and it will warm you two times."

Ford also carried around a small, light-blue paperbound two-inch-square pamphlet of Emerson excerpts, titled *Gems*, to be pulled from his pocket for inspirational reference as needed. Perhaps he marked the bottom of page nine, where it said that "The soul is no traveller; the wise man stays at home."[29]

In the absence of any spare copies of the *Short View of Great Questions*, Ford favored one work by Emerson above all as a special-occasion gift to be handed out to others, an essay that "came nearer to stating his creed than anything else," called "Compensation."[30]

"All successful men have agreed in one thing,—they were causationists. They believed that things were not by luck, but by law," Emerson wrote. "Belief in *compensation*, or, that nothing is got for nothing,—characterizes all valuable minds." The sagacious man interprets the law of balance or polarity in nature, every action causing an equal and opposite reaction, and applies it to human behavior, "the condition of man . . . in which all things are double, one against the other . . . and every thing has its price." This balancing rule must also be accepted by the wise man to hold true in times of "calamity," when a society's "prosperity" must necessarily be disturbed.[31]

In the essay "Race," written in 1850 and published six years later as a chapter in his book, *English Traits*, also a perennial best-seller, Emerson applied the same metaphorical design, this time adapting a ruling principle in one representative family to the vast arena of humankind. Just as a son inherits the outward and inward character of his parents, so too does "the power of blood or race" take on permanent aspects shared by all its members: "Race avails much, if that be true, which is alleged." For example, he wrote, "Race is a controlling influence in the Jew, who, for two millenniums, under every climate, has preserved the same character and employments."[32]

CHAPTER SIX

"I Know Who Caused the War"

ON APRIL 10, 1915, eight months after the guns of August began to thunder, Henry Ford gave an interview for the *New York Times Magazine*, his first public pronouncement on the "problem" of war. This initial interview, followed by a linked series of bombastic outbursts extending through the anxious summer, is the closest we have come to identifying the beginning of Ford's volatile tendency to blur and often ignore the boundaries between warmongering and international banking (soon enough, both terms were conflated seamlessly with "the Jew"). "Moneylenders and munitions makers cause wars; if Europe had spent money on peace machinery—such as tractors—instead of armaments there would have been no war... The warmongerers urging military preparedness in America are Wall Street bankers... I am opposed to war in every sense of the word."[1]

Less than one month later, the unarmed Cunard passenger ship *Lusitania* was torpedoed in Irish waters, and German U-boats fractured the façade of American neutrality. Over the next two years, before the threat of rampant submarine warfare finally drew the United States into the conflict, this singular trauma at sea precipitated divergent and telling responses from Henry Ford and his minions.[2]

"No animosity for anyone," Ford jotted down laboriously with a pencil stub in one of the little black pocket "jotbooks"—the kind with the hinge on the top that flipped up like reporters' pads for ready access—he kept with him for moments of inspiration, "But people who *profitt* [*sic*] from war must *go*... War is created by people who have no country or home except Hadies [sic] Hell and live in every country."[3]

On June 17, Ford called a press conference to announce with rhetorical flourishes his conviction that "If we keep our people working, America will never be dragged into the war... The parasite known as the absentee owner fosters war. New York wants war, but the United States doesn't. The peoples west of New York are too sensible for war."[4]

On August 15, in New York City, Ford reiterated that he would not be lured into the convenient economic trap of becoming a war-dependent manufacturer: "I would never let a single automobile get out of the Ford plant anywhere in the world if I thought it was going to be used in warfare." War was "a wasteful sacrifice," pushed forward by avaricious, amoral arms makers.[5]

Meanwhile, across the continent, the Second National Conference on Race Betterment, in full swing since the preceding spring, culminated its five-day eugenics-themed sojourn at the Oakland Auditorium, sponsored by the San Francisco Panama-Pacific International Exposition to celebrate the opening of the Panama Canal. One of the most compelling keynote conference speakers had condemned the warring European powers for "committing race-suicide." The renowned orator's name was David Starr Jordan, and he would soon be identified by Louis Marshall, chairman of the American Jewish Committee, as a major influence inflaming Henry Ford's "insane prejudice."[6]

Jordan, a native of Gainesville, New York, and a Cornell graduate, was appointed as the first president of Stanford University in Palo Alto, California, in 1891. He became chancellor of Stanford in 1913 and retired in 1916. He was as obsessed with fish as Henry Ford was with birds. A disciple of the legendary Swiss-born American naturalist Louis Agassiz, and a world-renowned ichthyologist, Jordan founded the Hopkins Marine Station at Stanford and named 1,085 genera and more than 2,500 species of fish in his lifetime of research and field work around the world. His classic *Manual of the Vertebrates of the Northern United States* went through thirteen editions between its publication in 1876 and 1929. Jordan was a tireless exponent of Darwin's work and served as an expert witness on the validity of the theory of evolution at the Scopes trial in Tennessee.

David Starr Jordan is of special interest because of his roles as past president of the World Peace Foundation, past vice president of the American Peace Society, and then president of the World Peace Conference—and because of a series of books reflecting his major nonacademic preoccupation since the turn of the century, among them, *Imperial Democracy* (1899), *The Blood of the Nation*, *War and Waste*, *War and the Breed*, and Henry Ford's inspiration, *Unseen Empire: A study of the plight of nations that do not pay their debts* (1912).

Jordan, also a published poet, was fond of referring to himself self-effacingly in his memoirs, *Days of a Man*, as a "minor prophet of democracy." He used "prophet" because he could be quite outspoken, even inflammatory, when serving up his lethal philosophical brew; its primary ingredient was a synthesis of racism and pacifism. He liked to "approach the subject of peace from a biological angle," arguing that war was detrimental to the health of the blond and muscular Aryan species "because it removed the strongest individuals from the gene pool."[7] Jordan lamented the unwillingness of modern societies to practice selective breeding so that these crucial "best" could be perpetuated: "A race of men or a herd of cattle are governed by the same laws of selection."[8]

It was the new rationale of Social Darwinism to appropriate this deterministic view of the "grim physical laws of the animal kingdom"—seeing biological struggle as the underpinning to all of life—and transpose it to the ways of mankind. By so doing, Jordan admitted into his race-thinking vast and impersonal processes, nameless and secret forces at work threatening to reduce favored, "civilized... yeoman" peoples to mere "pawns." In the end, "natural history became confused with national history."[9]

Despite his lifetime of rigorous training as a taxonomic scientist, Jordan did not possess a concrete definition when he wrote of the Jewish race—it was, rather, an impressionistic idea, a *conviction* of a classification, lacking precise, enumerated characteristics—but which he knew was *there*, discordantly interrupting his ideal hierarchy of the human family.[10] This manufactured fear of the Jews as a united, homogeneous force had accumulated to pressure-cooker proportions by the time Jordan came to write *Unseen Empire*.

In private correspondence with like-minded friends Edwin Ginn and Elbert Hubbard, he had already rehearsed familiar themes, stigmatizing the "Jewish bankers" who had been "mortgaging the continent of Europe" ever since the Napoleonic Wars and whose "allied fortunes... hold the operations of nations in absolute check." He had begun to assemble scrapbooks of clippings in which he kept track of the "stealthy advance" of the Rothschild family along its "sinuous trail" of greed: "That the House of Rothschild had an open sesame upon the purse-strings of all Europe for half a century is a fact."[11]

The *Unseen Empire* that Jordan fantasized about was populated with many more "pawnbrokers of the world," men named "Isaac Goldschmid [and] Maurice de Hirsch [and] Mendelssohn, patron of Humboldt, and Montefiore, owner of Australian debt... and Wertheimer of Austria, scholar and *Judenkaiser*... The financial affairs of Europe, and these include all questions of war and peace, have passed into the control of the moneylenders." Closer to home, and thus even more dangerous, "In the same class belongs the house of J. P. Morgan & Co., in America." This was the kind of scatter-shot terminology Margaret Ford Ruddiman alluded to when she denied that her brother was antisemitic, because Henry "called *all* the moneylenders of the world 'Jews,' regardless of their religion."[12]

Jordan prophesied in 1912 that unless these irresponsible Jewish powers behind the thrones of the world were halted by "the machinery of Conciliation," the result would be nothing short of Armageddon.[13]

THE DETROIT *Free Press* headlines on August 22, 1915, proclaimed that Henry Ford *"Will Devote Life and Fortune to Combat Spirit of Militarism Now Rampant."* In an interview with one favored local journalist, Theodore Delavigne, Ford improvised upon recently coined pacifist sentiments: "I have prospered much and am ready to give much to end this constant, wasteful 'preparation'... I hate war, because war is murder, desolation and destruction... I will devote my life to fight this spirit of militarism."

Two weeks later, Ford announced that he had set aside $1 million "to begin a peace educational campaign in the United States and the world." Much of this funding would be used in a swords-into-ploughshares enterprise, except in these modern times, the ploughshares would become Ford tractors, implements of agriculture, to help turn the workers' thoughts away from munitions and toward feeding their families.

Again, lest they forget, Ford issued an acerbic warning to the "parasites, these sloths and lunatics... apostles of murder" who he felt instigated war. They would suffer greatly in the unlikely event that America were ever attacked as a result of their avarice—but Ford the flag waver could be trusted in adversity to give all of his resources to help the common weal: "Anything that I have is at the disposal of this country for defense. And I would not take one cent of profit."[14]

These erratic ravings proved too embarrassing for James Couzens, whose relations with Henry Ford had been under strain since the new year. On the morning of October 12, Couzens resigned from the Ford Motor Company, telling a friend, Louis B. Block, that "A man sometimes gets to the point where his freedom of thought and independence is greater than all else."[15]

The next day, Henry and Clara Ford, Thomas and Mina Edison, and Harvey and Idabelle Firestone took separate private railroad trips to meet for a leisurely busman's holiday at the San Francisco Panama-Pacific Exposition. The celebrity couples were given a tour of the vast grounds by W. D'Arcy Ryan, chief of illuminations, capped off with a magnificent fireworks display in celebration of "Edison Day" at the fair. Ford took advantage of the adoring crowds following the entourage to declare that he had just opened a "Peace Bureau" in Detroit to "distribute educative materials in the States and conduct a press campaign abroad" for an end to war.[16]

From San Francisco, the party headed up the coast to Santa Rosa for a visit to the nursery, greenhouses, and botanical gardens of renowned naturalist and plant breeder Luther Burbank. Ford expressed particular interest in Burbank's current hybridization experiments with small garden peas; he was working to develop a larger size that could be harvested automatically, by machine. It turned out that Burbank had participated in a symposium at the Race-Betterment Conference in San Francisco in August, sharing the platform with John Harvey Kellogg, of cereal fame; Charles Eliot, president of Harvard; and David Starr Jordan. Following remarks by Kellogg about the urgent necessity of "establishing a eugenics registry to assure obedience to biologic law," Burbank read a new paper in which he suggested that by the use of eugenics, and control of the environment, it would be a "biological possibility ... to create a new race of man ... only the best individuals for continuing the race."[17]

Joined by Ford's secretary, Ernest Liebold, out from Detroit, the group visited San Quentin Prison for an inspection tour, then journeyed down to San Diego for another round of "Edison Day" festivities. There they reviewed a huge display of "Fordson" tractors ready to be shipped to England in aid of the pressing agricultural needs of the war effort. The Firestones hosted a farewell dinner at the Fairmont Hotel in San Diego, and the group split up. Mr. and Mrs. Edison went by railroad back across the country to their home in West Orange, New Jersey, via the Grand Canyon. Mr. and Mrs. Ford took a whistle-stop journey, pausing first in Denver, where Ford theorized that "the war could be over in two months if the newspapers told the people that the money bags of the world's rich men are being added to at the price of countless lives."

In Chicago, interviewed standing on the steps of his private car, Ford once again endorsed a "peace-propaganda plan," alluding vaguely to his desire to oppose the advocates for "preparedness" amassing in Congress.[18]

On November 15, Henry Ford arrived triumphantly back in Detroit, in time to see the one-millionth Model T come rolling off the assembly line—but unaware that his relentless, shrill antiwar media campaign had caught the ear of an ardent and charismatic Hungarian pacifist who had sailed over from London and was on that very day waiting eagerly in her room at the Hotel Tuller on Bagley Avenue for an audience with the great man.

Her name was Rosika Schwimmer.

SHE DESCRIBED herself from the outset of her career as a "very, very radical feminist." Schwimmer grew up in Budapest and in 1913, at the age of thirty-six, was elected corresponding secretary of the Seventh Congress of the International Woman Suffrage Alliance. She moved to London to serve there as press secretary for the alliance. In the early summer of 1914, just before war broke out, she set up a meeting with Prime Minister David Lloyd George. She warned him that the world was not taking the assassination of Archduke Franz Ferdinand seriously enough. At the time, Lloyd George remembered in his *War Memoirs*, he believed Schwimmer was tending toward the "alarmist." But when her premonitions proved correct within a few weeks, he credited her with being "the only person at the time who was aware of the imminence of world conflict."[19]

That fall, she came to America for her first lecture tour, heralded as "Hungary's great Jewess, the darling of women's rights advocates in Europe and America . . . a rarely-endowed woman of a most engaging personality and fine intellectuality."[20] Schwimmer's visit to the United States was sponsored by two leading suffragists and feminist peace advocates—Carrie Chapman Catt and Jane Addams—who were at first unequivocally "thrilled by her presence." "Well aware that she was Jewish," they encouraged Schwimmer to speak to immigrant groups and other diverse audiences about her deepest concerns, which she did, skillfully melding support of suffrage with the cause of continuous mediation as the only certain way to achieve peace. Although it was at times an uneasy alliance, the militant Schwimmer knew that she needed the clout and power of the more moderate Catt and Addams to get her message across. And she did insinuate her way into the White House and state her case to Secretary of State William Jennings Bryan and President Woodrow Wilson, who were noncommittal.[21]

By December, Schwimmer had inspired the formation of the Emergency Peace Federation in Chicago, and in January 1915, Catt, Addams, and Schwimmer joined forces to found the Woman's Peace Party. Their conference in Washington, D.C., brought together women from all over the country to call for a limitation of arms, mediation of the conflict in Europe, and removal of the economic causes of war. There was unification of the peace and suffrage movements when a plank calling for the vote of women was added to the party platform.

The momentum created by the American Woman's Peace Party

carried forward to the first International Congress of Women for Peace at the Hague in late April 1915. More than 2,000 women from both warring and neutral nations assembled, with Jane Addams as chairman. Schwimmer's controversial proposal, delivered with alacrity in an emotional three-minute speech, was to send delegations from the Congress of Women to the capitals of Europe to lobby world leaders and try with personal diplomacy to end the war. Schwimmer—"sure that millions of women in each country feel alike"—and her colleagues traveled to Copenhagen, Christiania, Stockholm, Petrograd, Amsterdam, then back to the Hague. "I want to most indiscreetly report to you of a talk Mme. Schwimmer had with the German ambassador in Copenhagen [at the beginning of June]," Emily Greene Balch, a Wellesley sociology professor and fellow-delegate, wrote to Louis Lochner of the Carnegie Peace Endowment. "The ambassador talked very frankly and was quite international-minded. He thought that President Wilson of the U.S.A. had behaved very badly... It was something unheard of that a great neutral country like the U.S. had not come forward in such a world war." Wilson had recently addressed a meeting of the Associated Press in New York City, in which he emphasized the glory to be gained by standing still in a chaotic world, "the distinction of absolute self-control and mastery, a distinction waiting for this Nation that no nation has ever yet got. I covet for America this splendid courage of reserve moral force."[22]

Undeterred by unwavering presidential sentiments, Schwimmer headed back to New York in September 1915 on board the SS *Ryndam*. Her whirlwind tour of Europe had elicited the repeated urging of five neutral governments that she and her colleagues on the board of officers of the International Committee of Women for Permanent Peace try again to urge Wilson to sponsor a conference of neutral nations—or at least to guarantee the participation of the United States in such a conference if he would not call it himself.

"Have you seen Henry Ford?" the clamoring newspaper reporters on board doggedly questioned the portly, bespectacled

Schwimmer as she paced the deck on her morning constitutional with her traveling companion, the English attorney Chrystal Macmillan. "Do you know of Henry Ford's peace effort?" "Are you going to see Ford?" She heard at first hand from these journalists of Ford's sensational million-dollar peace fund, and she observed that "they seemed to think it was our duty to see him."[23]

From Rosika Schwimmer's dear friend, fellow-suffragist, and lifelong patron Lola Maverick Lloyd came a short note of encouragement: "Detroit for many reasons is the best place for you," she wrote. "I hear that Ford is returning there now. Good luck to you. If he really wants his money to work for peace, he could not do better than to give it to you."[24]

E. G. Pipp

Well aware how difficult access to Henry Ford could be, Schwimmer turned for help to Rebecca Shelly, a Detroit schoolteacher recently converted to community peace activism, in the hope that the young woman could connect her to the inner sanctum. Shelly first approached the Reverend Mr. Marquis, but to no avail. However, Marquis's wife recommended Edwin G. Pipp, at the time managing editor of the *Detroit News* and another crony of Ford's. Perhaps because of the flurry of activity surrounding Ford's tumultuous return to Dearborn, Pipp was also not able to gain his attention. Finally, however, the editor of the *Detroit Journal* put one of his aggressive general assignment reporters, Ralph Yonker, on the case. A phone call was made, and a date set for the following morning, November 17, at the Highland Park factory.[25]

Schwimmer arrived promptly at eleven o'clock and was greeted by Ford. As he took her hand in his—dry, yet warm—she was struck by a strange, contradictory quality in his expression. "His strong, ascetic face reminded me of the portrait of a Greek philosopher I remembered from a rare old book in my parents' library," she wrote, "and when a humorous twinkle lighted his face, he looked like a wistful but healthy boy. This combination of sage and boy seemed to me always apparent in Mr. Ford."[26] Allan Benson later made eerily similar note of his friend's "two personalities. One is diffident, almost to the point of bashfulness, yet very friendly. In ten seconds, for no apparent reason, the smile may flit from his face and you behold a man who, from the eyes up, seems as old as the pyramids. Back of the boyish Ford is the Ford who seems to have lived for ages, to have suffered much, and to have survived from the sheer exercise of the will to live."[27]

Anticipating an intimate personal audience, Schwimmer was startled when Ford ushered her into his private dining room and directed her to take the chair to his immediate right as he assumed his usual place at the head of the long table. There were five men already seated and ready: the Reverend Samuel Marquis, who had by now taken leadership of the Sociological Department; Alfred Lucking, the Ford Motor Company in-house corporate counsel; Charles A. Brownell, Ford's advertising director and the editor of the company's in-house monthly, the *Ford Times*; journalist Ralph Yonker, there to cover the event, or so he thought; and Frederick C. Howe, New York City's commissioner of immigration at Ellis Island.[28]

Overcoming her surprise, Schwimmer broached her number-one agenda item: If President Wilson was going to continue to equivocate on the matter of sponsoring an official peace conference, then an "unofficial" gathering with the sole purpose of adhering to "continuous mediation" would have to come from the private sector. It was at this point that she put forth the idea of a "Peace Ship" that would sail from America to Europe, drawing in its wake the kind of public attention to galvanize world opinion once and for all.[29]

"In the midst of the animated conversation" that ensued,

Schwimmer was quite pleased to realize that "Mr. Ford showed himself an absolutely clear and radical pacifist with deep-going views expressed briskly, logically, in a vigorous tone and in colorful language."[30]

Her relief was short-lived. Suddenly, Ford paused, and then burst out, "I know who caused the war—the German-Jewish bankers!" He slapped his breast-pocket, "I have the evidence here. Facts! The German-Jewish bankers caused the war. I can't give out the facts now, because I haven't got them all yet, but I'll have them soon."

Ford's tone shifted and became "flat as a pancake as he came forth with this cheap and vulgar statement." He placed no emphasis on any word in particular. He spoke with "that lack of conviction with which a schoolboy would recite something about the supreme happiness of being good and virtuous." The remark fell upon the assembled group "like a new poison bomb from a mysteriously invisible airplane."[31]

Ford appeared as if "he had stopped thinking, as if [his] heart made a strange pause while beating. A strange shadow crept across his face as he uttered the disconnected phrase. The expression of the sage and the boy was gone." He gazed slowly around the table. Schwimmer sensed that Marquis, seated just to her right, "exchanged a triumphant glance" with Lucking and Brownell to his right. Marquis then turned slightly in his chair and "challenged [her] openly on who caused the war."

"Oh, how well I knew that trick!" Schwimmer thought. "But, tired as I was, I stuck to my refusal to discuss that question in spite of the Dean's pressing challenge."

"You are right, Madam," interjected Ford, seeming to come out of his trance and speak with his old vigor. "It is useless to discuss the causes of the war at a time when to a real pacifist the only problem is how to end this terrible slaughter."

Then, just as quickly, Ford returned to his prior statement, "I know who caused the war. The German-Jewish bankers. I have the evidence here. Facts. The German-Jewish bankers caused the war."

Again he looked down the table at Marquis, Lucking, and Brownell—and again the same look of satisfaction seemed to flit across their faces.

"That one parrot-like reiteration," Schwimmer thought, "that one phrase—never a word more or less... It was the age-old trick of pulling The Jewish Question into the problem. Repressed tears were burning behind my lids and I was suffering with such pain, as if the martyred victims of war were my own sons."

She was desperate not to show "feminine weakness," and finally managed to break up the party. As the men stood up from the table, Yonker darted across the room, buttonholed the mercurial Ford, and tried to elicit a summarizing statement from him, but at the insistence of Schwimmer, Ford demurred: There would be "no statement to make to you, my boy." Walking Schwimmer to the elevator, to her even greater surprise, Ford asked her to come see him and Mrs. Ford for supper the following day at home.[32]

Rosika Schwimmer awoke in her hotel room the next morning feeling defensive and confused enough to wire Pipp at the *Detroit News* and complain bitterly about the "hostile, skeptical and doubtful" reception she had received. Seeking to head off possibly negative publicity (and how prescient she was in this respect, as unfolding events over the coming months and years would attest), Schwimmer asked Pipp (whom she knew to be sympathetic) to communicate with Jane Addams at Hull House in Chicago for a character reference as to her industrious work at the Hague Conference the preceding spring, and the sincerity of her ambassadorial energies. Pipp also took it upon himself to set in motion arrangements through the *Detroit News* Washington Bureau for Schwimmer to meet with President Wilson later that month. "In the meantime," Pipp told Addams, "we are anxious to have the press of the country take a more friendly attitude toward the peace movement."[33]

There was no love lost between the *News* editor and Ford's private secretary. Ernest Liebold was jealous that his boss had taken a liking to Edwin Pipp ever since the fellow first arrived at the *News* more than a decade before. At unpredictable moments, the auto magnate slipped away for impromptu "jawing" over at Pipp's office—man-to-man, feet-up-on-the-desk types of conversation—off the record, of course. Schwimmer would not have made it in to see Ford as quickly—if at all—if Liebold were not still on vacation with his family in California. Liebold was out of the loop during those crucial late-November days. He admitted that he did not like being out of town when Ford was in the office at the factory. Liebold "had a premonition" while he was on the West Coast that he really should be heading back to his guardianship responsibilities when he first got wind of Schwimmer's inevitable course toward Detroit. "Of course, she was a Hungarian Jewess," the secretary recalled, exasperation still evident even after thirty-five years had gone by. "She got to Pipp, who was then managing editor of the paper."[34]

As for Ford's "German-Jewish bankers" mantra, Liebold had a matter-of-fact explanation: "The international Jewish interests play behind the scenes and carry on different activities, [men] such as Mr. Ford referred to as warmongers...who were interested in carrying on the war for profit. Mr. Ford's definition of Wall Street was the Jewish interests who operated on that type of proposition."[35]

Schwimmer and Liebold never met, predominantly through Liebold's stubborn designs. However, in the days following the luncheon with Ford, Schwimmer did intuit that—as she expressed in multiple metaphors—"someone had tried to harness Ford's pacifism into [sic] the wagon of Anti-semitism...He linked the institution of war and the Jewish race together. This is the grossest exhibition of his mental dependance [sic] on others in questions where his intuition fails to serve as a flashlight...Like managers of a puppet show, they have succeeded in connecting war and Jews in Ford's mind...administering the anti-semite poison."[36]

While there is no way that Schwimmer could have known definitively "who handled the hypodermic needle" at that earliest time in her relationship with Ford,[37] she had witnessed the man in action, "scuttling back to the facts like a rabbit to its hole," manifesting the rigid, assertive manner in which people who profess chimerical beliefs typically behave. Some scholars speculate that Ford did not realize Schwimmer was Jewish; this seems unlikely when one considers the degree of national and international press she had already received. Perhaps with his inimitable ability to compart-

Rosika Schwimmer, Henry Ford, and Louis Lochner,
December 3, 1915, New York City

mentalize, Ford simply did not associate her, just yet, with the subversive financial plot he envisioned.[38]

Schwimmer was a savvy enough diplomat to avoid confronting Ford directly on his views, especially while her major solicitation was still in play. The Ford company car and driver arrived at her hotel. Schwimmer enlisted the willing company of Louis Paul Lochner, a fellow peace activist and writer, and together they were driven to the Ten Eyck Farm House on the grounds of the Fair Lane estate, because the sprawling, $3 million, fifty-six-room main residence was still under construction. Lochner had recently met President Wilson for the first time, accompanying David Starr Jordan, representing the American Peace Society, on an unsuccessful visit to the White House. Lochner, too, felt that perhaps a less formal, more "populist" approach to the president was needed, and that Ford might be the man to bring it off.[39]

During this late-afternoon suburban visit in more relaxed circumstances, Ford took Lochner aside for a ramble through the woods, leaving his wife and Schwimmer to talk together in the front parlor, looking out over the geranium-studded window boxes. "What do you think of the Hungarian's ideas?" Ford asked the young man, who endorsed his colleague's purposes, while Schwimmer spoke passionately to Clara Ford about the horrors of the current conflict. It was a successful get-together. A motivational spark had been touched off in Henry Ford. He proposed relocating temporarily to New York City and commissioned Lochner to assemble a crusading brain trust to meet at the McAlpin Hotel during the week before Thanksgiving, including Jane Addams, Oswald Garrison Villard of *The Nation*, and George Kirchwey, dean of Columbia College—passionate pacifists all. Schwimmer's "Peace Ship" concept took hold. It was something tactile that Ford's empirical, restless mind could appreciate.[40]

Ford's forthright offer to pay for an official neutral commission to discuss ending the war if the president would appoint one was rebuffed at the White House when he finally did meet with Wilson. Ford dismissed him as "a small man"[41] and seized the moment to take responsibility for shutting down the warmongers himself. "Out of the trenches by Christmas, and never go back!" he declared impulsively. He moved to more commodious headquarters in Suite 717 at the Biltmore Hotel, where a telephone, telegraph, and letter-writing blitz was mounted to convince other patriots to join the crusade against the kaiser and book passage aboard Henry Ford's chartered steamship, to stop the carnage of "twenty thousand men killed every twenty-four hours."

To his unsuspecting dismay, Ford was greeted with a torrent of ridicule in the daily press and quickly vilified as "God's Fool," "a jackass and a clown." His massive invitation campaign to "respond to the call of humanity . . . to establish an international conference dedicated to negotiations leading to a just settlement of the war" was an utter flop. William Howard Taft, Charles Steinmetz, John Dewey, Robert LaFollette, Walter Lippmann, William Dean Howells, Ida Tarbell, Lincoln Steffens, Julius Rosenwald, and John Wanamaker, along with every college president and forty-seven out of forty-eight state governors—and yes, even his friends Thomas Edison and John Burroughs—conveyed regrets. David Starr Jordan, while asserting that "the Germans are extremely anxious for peace," declined to join the ranks of "the peace pilgrims," warning Ford that "Schwimmer [was] too emotional" and advising him several times that his great wealth would be better applied to establishing a *College* of Internationalism, rather than a simple conference.[42] Clara Ford, who always believed in women's suffrage, pledged $10,000 to the Woman's Peace Party. But she pleaded with her husband not to embark.[43] Wasn't it enough that Henry had already laid out more than $500,000 to rent the ship and stock up with provisions—was it really necessary that he leave home and hearth for the high seas? Ford stubbornly refused to back down, and so, at Clara's tearful behest, Dean Marquis agreed to go along for the voyage and keep a vigilant eye on her foolhardy husband. Weighted down with a chaotic melange of college students, eccentric "peace-nut pilgrims," and journalists, the *Oskar II* pulled out of the pier at Hoboken, New Jersey, on the frigid Saturday afternoon of December 4, 1915, bound for Christiania, Norway. "Tell the people to cry peace and fight 'preparedness,'" Ford promised. "If this expedition fails, I'll start another!"[44]

In the early morning hours of the ninth day out at sea, in the midst of a raging storm, Henry Ford emerged from his stateroom onto the upper deck of the *Oskar II* to take the air, as was his routine, rain or shine. The ship hit a wave and pitched sharply upward. Ford slipped on a water-slick and tumbled, dropping his gold-headed cane. The drenching left him with a terrible cold, which quickly became the grippe, and he was confined to his cabin, hors de combat for the remainder of the voyage. It was the beginning of the end of the tragicomedy for the "international harlequin."[45]

Ford was absent from subsequent public events after the ship docked, remaining in seclusion in his room at the Grand Hotel in Christiania. On December 23, Ford whispered hoarsely to Lochner from his sick bed that he "had better go home to Mother... I told [Mrs. Ford] I'll be back soon. You've got this thing started now and can get along without me." In the pre-dawn hours of Christmas Eve, accompanied by the ever-faithful Marquis, Henry Ford departed.

Ford's seeming defection caused a degeneration in Rosika Schwimmer's status from which she never recovered. She had publicly allied her fortunes with his, preemptively, it would seem, boasting openly to her comrades ten days before the ship sailed about Ford's pledge of "two hundred thousand dollars for the work of the International Committee of Women." Schwimmer told Lola Maverick Lloyd that she had "succeeded in gaining Henry Ford's full support for our movement." She assured Ethel Snowden, another Women's Committee delegate, that "Henry Ford has fallen in line and stands with his personality and his money for what we are standing."[46]

The promised funds were never received, and Schwimmer fell prey to accusations of embezzlement from Aletta Jacobs and Carrie Chapman Catt, who had been among her staunch supporters.[47] Schwimmer, in turn, remained suspicious of "foul whisperings" from the Ford inner circle. She was appalled but not surprised to read Dean Marquis quoted in an article by William C. Bullitt in the *New York Times* of January 31, 1916, accusing her of "toying with Mr. Ford" and of "desiring... to control the stream of money which Mr. Ford is anxious to pour out for peace." Marquis suspected Schwimmer of subverting his special relationship with his chief.

Schwimmer was then informed by members of the Neutral Con-

ference in late January that Liebold had cabled Gaston Plantiff, the
Ford Motor Company representative in charge of its New York
City office, with the demand that she be eliminated from further
authority under the banner of Ford's mission at the mediation conference in Stockholm. She offered to resign on the spot. Despite the
fact that Ford wrote back the next day that he had "not lost faith in

you or the expedition," Schwimmer
gave up her position in disgust. Upon
his return to Detroit, Ford had
stopped by friend Pipp's office at the
Detroit News to discuss the vicissi-
tudes of his idealistic trip. Pipp asked
Ford point-blank to talk about
Schwimmer, and Ford declared, "She
has more brains than all the others on
the peace ship put together."

"What about reports of her having
received money from you?" Pipp continued. "She never asked for any,"
Ford responded. "Did she get any?"
"Not a cent," declared Ford. Yet when

**Rosika Schwimmer
on board the Peace Ship**

Schwimmer finally appeared at Ford headquarters in the summer of
1916 with the intention to clear the air of these persistent ambigui-
ties, she was told by Theodore Delavigne—who had by now graduated from working journalist to full-time member of Ford's
personal staff—that Henry Ford did not want to see her. By the
time the United States declared war on Germany, Schwimmer was
back home in her native Hungary, and then moved to Vienna,
where she would remain until 1921.[48]

CHAPTER SEVEN

The Bolshevik Menace

EARLY in the new year of 1916, Ford decided that he wanted to expand the Highland Park factory to twice its size and also build a blast furnace and a foundry at a separate site on the River Rouge. During the time of construction, he suspended all stock dividend disbursements; he took $58 million of accumulated profits and put it back into the business while simultaneously, as a marketing ploy, reducing the price of the Model T by $66 per car.

These bold strokes caused great consternation to two major Ford shareholders in particular, John and Horace Dodge, rival manufacturers who since 1913 had been taking advantage of Ford's cash flow to finance their own modestly priced sedan. The Dodge Brothers filed suit against Ford to restore distribution of dividends and also obtained a restraining order "to prohibit the use of company funds for plant expansion." Judge Henry Butzel of the state circuit court ordered the Ford Motor Company to halt the River Rouge expansion and to initiate a special dividend payment of almost $20 million. On appeal, Ford was able to obtain clearance to proceed with his necessary construction but the cash outlay stipulation held.[1]

In the spring of 1916, despite Ford's insistence that he would never stand as a candidate for president, the Republican Party of Michigan put him on the presidential-preference ballot. He went on to win the Michigan primary, and then, in absentia, almost won the Nebraska primary as well. In the summer of 1916, his name was placed in nomination at the Republican National Convention, where he received thirty-two votes on the first ballot but did not survive a second vote. Two years later, running (again, he said, reluctantly) as Michigan's Democratic candidate for the U.S. Senate against GOP candidate Truman H. Newberry, Henry Ford lost by a hair's breadth.[2]

Both forays—industrial and electoral—demonstrated to Ford that even in defeat he could come out ahead if he took his case directly to "the common man." In the Dodge suit, Ford exploited the daily deposition transcripts in the national press to harp upon his determinedly altruistic desire "to do as much as possible for

Highland Park assembly line, two views

everybody concerned... to send out the car where people can use it
... and incidentally to make money." On the campaign trail, Ford
made an explicit point of not spending any money; rather, he struck
the pose of the little guy at the mercy of the people's will: "If they
want to elect me, let them do so."[3]

An idea had been percolating in Ford's imagination ever since
his return from abroad: Why expend so much energy to seize headlines? Why not cobble together his personal soapbox in the press?
Why not set up a weekly forum for his own ideas, "a private appara-
tus for molding public opinion," unmediated by any intervening
editorial sensibility—except his?

By deciding to take this step into the media world, Henry Ford
joined a genre with a well-established tradition. *Tom Watson's Magazine* was probably the most outspoken exponent; founded in 1905
by the firebrand Southern Populist on the abiding principle that
"The day of the Common People is at hand," its editorials had
proudly attacked Wall Street, "the professional boodler and grafter
in both the old [political] parties," and "that brace of rascals in
New York." In its first week of publication, *Watson's Magazine* broke
the 100,000 circulation mark.[4] Up until 1915, "a score of less successful imitators appeared," rustic Protestant journals in Mankato,
Minnesota; Anderson, Indiana; Magnolia, Arkansas; and Moravian
Falls, North Carolina.[5]

Thus, the informing seeds were sown for the *Dearborn* (Michigan) *Independent*, "The Ford International Weekly," with its
highflown motto as "Chronicler of the Neglected Truth." There
was only one man seasoned—and idealistic—enough to edit it:
Ford's trusted sounding-board and kindred spirit, Edwin G. Pipp
(1868–1935). Born in the town of Brighton, Michigan, Pipp began
his career as a reporter in Kansas City; by 1903, the "gangling
young man" had moved to Detroit and become the Wayne County
Building and City Hall correspondent for the *News*. Insinuating
himself into the corridors of power, Pipp "waged a merciless war
against privilege and monopoly." His investigative, muckraking

acuity and "flair for going behind the scenes" resulted in major exposés of wrongdoing at the City Public Works Department and the Detroit United Railway. Pipp was rewarded by a steady rise through the newspaper hierarchy to become city editor, managing editor, and then editor in chief. In addition to this early reputation as a "persistent fact-finder ... with a feeling for the human side of the news," Pipp also possessed a deeply cultivated social conscience and empathy for the downtrodden, spending many off hours raising funds for new sanitarium facilities and treatments for tuberculosis patients and sufferers. Henry Ford was the most generous (and anonymous) donor to Pipp's causes, sending him money "many a time, and it ran into the thousands, to care for the sick."[6]

But life was not all laboring and charity for Pipp. He was the proud father of two sons, Gaylord, a printer who worked closely with him during the glory days of the *Independent* and afterward, and Frank, who became a radio operator for the Police Department. Pipp was a big man, well over six feet, and a devoted baseball fan; his nephew, Wally, played first base for the New York Yankees. Each spring, Pipp organized the company ball game, through his civic connections simply "borrowing" Navin Field for an afternoon when the Tigers were away, and cheerfully choosing up sides. It was always a delightful outing for *News* staffers and their families. Addicted to a popular card game of the era called "pedro," jovial "E. G." would ask colleagues over to his home after work for a few rounds, which he invariably won.[7]

More than two years before Henry Ford finally acquired a countryside broadsheet that had marginally been in business since the turn of the century, and before the first issue of the *Dearborn Independent* appeared revitalized and expanded under his auspices, the auto manufacturer broached the idea to Pipp to come on board as inaugural editor. It was the fall of 1916. Ford struck his favorite pose when behind closed doors in Pipp's office, leaning back in an armchair with hands clasped together behind his head, and his well-polished, black cap-toed shoes planted firmly on the edge of the editor's oak desk. This was of necessity a confidential chat, Ford cautioned Pipp, who seemed sorely tempted to seize the opportunity for greater autonomy despite his exalted status at the *News*. Ford "rather doubted the real interest of the press in promulgating his ideas... The press was owned body and soul by bankers," he said, "When they tell it to bark, it barks.... The Peace Ship," continued Ford, "confirmed his opinion that if his ideas were to be properly expressed, he had to do it himself."[8]

Quiet, exploratory talks soon extended beyond Ford's by-now familiar (to friend Pipp) compulsion to fight back against the oft-invoked entrenched economic and social trends that had become the bane of his existence. Their newspaper was going to be more than a force to right wrongs in American society. Pipp's recollection of their planning parleys tended toward the benign and philosophical: "There was strife, bitter strife in the world. There was a great need for kindliness, and [Ford and I] were going to try to make the world more kindly, to spread the gospel of tolerance.... Dearborn was your home town," Pipp wrote in retrospect, directly addressing his old comrade, "and you wanted Dearborn to become known the world over as the place where kindliness is preached.... You asked me to help establish a publication that was to be an instrument of good will throughout the world."[9]

However, other weighty matters intervened. On November 1, Edsel Ford, now twenty-three, married the lovely Eleanor Lowthian Clay, niece of J. L. Hudson, founder of the upscale Detroit department store. Edsel had become intimately involved with the family business since his teen years. After graduating from Detroit University School, Edsel was dissuaded by his anti-intellectual father from entering college. Under the aegis of a new corporate entity, Henry Ford & Son, Edsel took a higher corporate profile. He was named to the board of directors of the Ford Motor Company, and then became secretary of the executive committee.

By the middle of 1917, Ford the pacifist became expeditiously transformed into Ford the war-worker when America was drawn

into the conflict. Edsel was supervising the manufacture of ambu-
lances, Liberty aircraft engines, Eagle boats, and tanks with Model
T innards. When it came to the welfare of his only son, however,
Henry Ford kept his pacifist leanings. Edsel was browbeaten by his
father into requesting a military deferment. Henry said that the
young fellow "was more valuable to his country in Detroit than in a
mudhole in France." Tortured by widespread criticism of her son,
Clara was helpless to intervene.[10]

Pipp was sent overseas to cover the European scene for the
News. He resigned from the paper upon his return in the fall of
1918, then joined Ford's payroll as an adviser for his abortive presidential run. On Armistice Day, the two men shook hands in final
agreement that the *Dearborn Independent* must hoist its banner as
soon after the new year as possible. It was time to staff up.

IT WAS incumbent upon Ernest Liebold that he assume a personal
role in every project of Henry Ford's outside the corporate purview
of the Ford Motor Company. The nascent *Dearborn Independent* certainly fit this definition, promising from the day of its public conception to become one of Ford's most prominent (and costly)
undertakings. To serve as administrative umbrella for the *Independent,* an entity was established called the Dearborn Publishing
Company. Henry Ford put himself in place as president. Clara
Ford was named vice president. Edsel Ford was named secretary-
treasurer. Liebold was appointed general manager. The office space,
including production facility, was set up on the premises of the
Ford tractor plant in Dearborn.

Liebold required a chief assistant with direct reporting responsibilities to him. The paper could use some younger blood to keep it
moving along. Fred Lee Black was at that time a "very genial"
twenty-seven-year-old salesman and advertising representative in
Detroit for the Whitaker Paper Company in Cincinnati. Working
for Whitaker, Black had sold goods to Gaylord Pipp, E. G.'s son,

who owned a printing plant on Grand River Avenue. Gaylord put
Black in touch with his father at just the right moment, and "E. G."
introduced the fellow to Henry Ford, who with characteristic
impulsiveness added the title of business manager to Black's portfolio, since he had solid experience in budgeting for the printing

Dearborn Publishing Company typsetters and printers,
April 23 and 27, 1923

trade. The first thing Black did was go out and find a fine old 1890
printing press for $5,000 and have it installed in the *Independent*'s
new premises. Henry Ford rolled up his sleeves and took some
elbow grease to the dusty, gear-laden machine until its brass trim-
mings shone like new.[11]

For his part, E. G. Pipp knew as soon as he had decided to join
up with Ford that he was going to need a strong, consistent writer
to crank out copy on a weekly basis. That man would have to be
William John ("Billy") Cameron (1878–1955). Canadian-born,
Cameron moved to Detroit with his family when he was a boy. Billy
went back to Hamilton, Ontario, for his high school education and
also took some courses at the University of Toronto. Blessed with a
sonorous voice from youth, he had a desire to become a preacher,
although he was never ordained. He spoke at the People's Church in
Brooklyn, Michigan, on Sunday mornings, and then after his mar-

riage, became a familiar guest-sermonizer at community churches throughout Detroit.

Cameron's skills as a moralistic wordsmith landed him at the *Detroit News* as a reporter and staff writer in 1904. There he met and became fast friends with Edwin Pipp, moving up with Pipp's endorsement to become chief editorial writer. "And on that morning when we drove out to Dearborn to buy the Independent," Pipp

Fred Black

remembered, "I felt that I would be lost in newspaper work without Billy Cameron. He was one of the few star reporters I had. Billy wrote his own feelings, poured out his own soul, and there never was an unkind thought in them. I wanted that kindly soul in our work. I wanted his splendid writing in our pages." And Henry Ford said—instantly, of course—hire Cameron and offered to pay him a lot more money than he was making at the *News*, just as Pipp was being remunerated at a salary higher than he had ever received in his career as a working journalist.[12]

The division of functions at the newspaper was clearly laid out from the first meeting of these men: Although it was indeed the case, as Henry Ford had declared, that Pipp was editor and Liebold was business manager, there was one bridge over that barrier. In each issue, Henry Ford would have a prominent feature, called his "Own Page," written or "translated" by William Cameron and then essentially signed off on by Liebold wearing his other hat as Ford's private secretary. Pipp said that was "more than agreeable to [him] from the start, and as time went on [Pipp] seldom read [Mr. Ford's

Own Page] before or after it got into the paper." Although Liebold tacitly agreed with Ford's stipulation that Pipp had been hired to govern the newspaper's editorial content, privately he believed that "as far as editorial policy was concerned, I think perhaps I might say that I may have been the deciding factor." Liebold also understood in the beginning that "Mr. Ford's Own Page" would be crafted by Cameron—"but I talked a great deal to Mr. Ford about what his policy was going to be. [Ford] said [to Liebold], 'We are going to educate people and we are going to show blue-prints.'"[13]

Eager Fred Black tried to sit in on as many of the *Dearborn Independent* editorial get-togethers as he could while the much-anticipated inaugural issue was in the works toward the end of the year 1918. Ford came across to young Black in these settings as a "fundamentalist. He expressed a great many truths that people didn't understand at the time he said them." An interesting choice of words, giving added weight to an impression shared by both Liebold and Cameron, but for different purposes. Liebold had been with Ford for eight years by now and had presumed from the start that his boss needed a lot of help getting his message across to the outside world. Cameron—as did colleague Pipp—began working closely with Ford in a more conciliatory fashion, separating the rhetorical wheat from the chaff when The Boss came out with one of his (as he called them) "*intuitions.*"[14]

Just the way Ford liked to take advantage of the element of surprise around the automobile plant, he would frequently appear in the *Independent* office unannounced, and so a "committee meeting," in the conventional sense, could hardly ever be formally scheduled. One morning, Ford might shake hands all around, sit down, and blurt out in a general way, "I have an idea!" Then the men would discuss it and "flesh it out" while he leaned back and listened. But Ford would not tolerate lengthy discourse about any matter, large or small. He would attend to a presentation or a plan for an article for a few minutes—fifteen minutes was considered the outside limit—and then "on the basis of a *hunch*, come to a decision." He was impatient to get on with things. This often led to Henry Ford's well-known inclination to jump to conclusions on the basis of too little information. "We used to say around Dearborn," Fred Black remembered, "that if Henry Ford saw three blackbirds in the morning, all birds were black that day."[15]

Ford preferred that letters, article ideas, and pertinent documents be digested ahead of time and then read to him rather than having to spend the effort reading them himself. He might stop the reader at some point to ask for a brief clarification. Ford did not like to be told too far along in a discussion that someone did not agree with him. If you were going to go out on a limb in a conversation, and take the chance to differ with his point of view, common knowledge held that you should do it soon. You always ran the danger that he would arbitrarily cut off the flow of talk, or just get up out of his chair and leave the room before you had finished a sentence. Ford had the last word, and he thought of his conclusions as salutary, no matter what the eventual consequences were: "He wanted men [around him] who worked out not their ideas, but his" and felt that "you could only harden people by opposition." One of Ford's favorite mottoes, which he had typed up and placed under glass on the top of his desk, was "He is your friend who makes you do what you don't want to do, rather than what you want to do."[16]

At the end of December 1918, Henry Ford resigned from the presidency of his company "to devote my time to building up other organizations with which I am connected," a way of saying that it was time to focus upon the burgeoning tractor business, representing his undying persona as "friend of the farmer," and his imminent "International Weekly" newspaper. At a salary of $150,000 a year, Edsel succeeded his father as president, while Ford remained on the board. Edsel's appointment turned out to be an empty honor. Within a matter of months, Henry had crept back into his old position. He just did not know how to let go. By the following summer, the Ford family had bought out all other stockholders, at a cost in excess of $105 million, taking sole possession of the firm.[17]

Henry Ford sat down with William J. Cameron to expostulate on the first appearance of "Mr. Ford's Own Page" in the *Dearborn Independent* of January 11, 1919. He wanted to strike his most comfortable pose, as just folks: "I have never pretended to be a writer or an editor, but I can talk with plain Americans in a way that we can understand each other." He wanted to sound an optimistic note: "This paper exists to spread ideas, the best that can be found. It desires to stir ambition and encourage independent thinking." He wanted to come across as the stern pedagogical advisor: "One of the chief objects of this paper will be to point out to its readers the opportunities that lie everywhere about them, and advise how they may be used to their best advantage." He wanted to lay the blame for public venality on the doorstep of "the speculative capitalists [who] are always trying to get hold of what another has built up. Too many businesses have been morally ruined by this method. It is not human. It does not produce anything." And he wanted to make it crystal clear that his newspaper would avoid entangling

**Henry Ford and W. J. Cameron
in Cameron's office**

commercial alliances and not carry advertisements: "The Dearborn *Independent* [is] an organ of unbiased opinion. We are first making our own character."[18]

Billy Cameron then took over to do what he did so well. Henry Ford's spontaneous and heartfelt dicta were shaped, given rhythm and cadence and authority. And the sixteen-page, large-format journal sailed forth, at a bargain-basement price of five cents a copy,

The inaugural "Mr. Ford's Own Page," in the
Dearborn Independent, January 11, 1919

one dollar a year. At the helm of the new enterprise, steering into the choppy waters of postwar America, was E. G. Pipp, his vocabulary filled with the spirit of entrepreneurialism, emboldened by this golden opportunity to be captain of his own publication. "Into the new time with all its prophetic forces, the Dearborn *Independent* comes to put its shoulder to the car of social justice and human progress," Pipp enthused. "The new society is forming under the crust of the old, and to live only on the crust is to be shallowly rooted."

Pipp was true to his mission. His personal causes were evident from the outset. He ran a variety of features of interest to the "modern" woman—articles on child-rearing advice, the virtues of maintaining a well-run, spotless home, as well as the new challenges of the workplace, pictorial spreads on the latest fashion styles, and a regular column called "In the Realm of Women." As a result of his wartime stint reporting from abroad, Pipp demonstrated an ongoing commitment to following world news. There were frequent two-page photo displays of noteworthy events from the capitals of Europe, especially, of course, "the gathering in France ... [where] the real purpose of the Conference," Pipp opined on February 1 in a bylined, front-page article, "Not a One-Man Affair," "is to arrange the differences among all the nations that were directly interested in the war, to insure the peace of the world." He weighed in frequently and high-handedly on how the world powers should "serve the interests of all humanity."

The editor of the *Dearborn Independent* had strong faith in what one of his special correspondents, Cyril Arthur Player, called the ultimate "sanity of nations." Pipp believed that eventually the great powers would work out their differences and come together to shape a glorious future.

Another big theme in this new "organ of unbiased opinion" was the glorification of the working man in his never-ending struggle to make a better life for himself and his family. Several major articles in the first weeks of the *Independent* were conspicuously

devoted to chastising big business, calling upon the major corporations to look within their souls and "commit as all human minds
must be to the welfare of man.... This is possible in any industry."

Running in tandem with Pipp's known concern for the security
of the common man, "the plain people of this country,"[19] was serious advocacy of proper and respectful treatment for our "boys"
returning from overseas. "They ought to fit back into business life
as readily as they fit into the army.... Or leave the big, unsettled
tracts of the West for wholesale reclamation and power projects....
Enlist an army of men to make our deserts bloom! *That* would be
an Army of the United States indeed!"[20]

It was not long, however, before Mr. Ford's irrepressible pet
peeves insinuated themselves into the pages of the *Independent*. His
"Own Page" took on a strident tone as Ford lashed out once more
against unnamed, hidden influences that continued to trouble him,
"The Dark Forces—whether political, military or capitalistic... The
power that would gamble with men's lives on the battlefield is the
power that always gambles with their lives in industry."[21] And in
another piece, "What of the Melting Pot?" the (unbylined) writer
answered his own question with a disturbing euphemism, "The
problem is not ... with the pot so much as it is with the base metal.
Some metals cannot be assimilated, refuse to mix with the molten
mass of the citizenship, but remain ugly, indissoluble lumps. How
did this base metal get in? ... What *about* those aliens who have
given us so much trouble, these Bolsheviki messing up our industries and disturbing our civil life?"[22]

To understand how—and why—fissures appeared so quickly
admitting the pernicious "Red Scare" and its "spectre of Bolshevism" through the supposedly smooth façade of Henry Ford's
weekly, it is necessary to examine the tenuous relationship between
Pipp and Liebold. From the start, Pipp took his editorial outreach
mission with the utmost seriousness. He set about to make the
Independent truly international, as the masthead defiantly proclaimed. He lined up correspondents in Paris, Brussels, Tokyo, Lon-

don, Dublin, Toronto, and Sydney, as well as in many points throughout the United States, and went about the business of collecting as much good material as he could.

In so doing, Pipp tried conscientiously to avoid—as expressed in his inimitable manner—"any earnest chewing matches" with Liebold. The arrangement was such that if Liebold wanted to get something into the paper (outside of "Mr. Ford's Own Page," of course) he was supposed to come to Pipp and talk about it first. "He didn't like it," Pipp said, "but he came just the same." One day early in the life of the newspaper, Liebold appeared in Pipp's office to show him a letter from an émigré named Boris Brasol, with whom Liebold was already acquainted, suggesting that he could give the paper "a very interesting article on Russia, then in chaos and puzzling the world considerably." It appeared to Pipp that Liebold "took an unusual interest" in endorsing Brasol who was, at that time, vice chairman of and major spokesman for the General Committee on Russian National Defense and—by dint of his decorated service in the Imperial Russian Guard infantry during World War I—vice chairman of the Russian Officers' Union in America. In line with the worldwide purview of the *Independent*, Pipp followed up dutifully on Liebold's tip and wrote to Lieutenant Brasol, commissioning the "rather well-written" essay, "The Bolshevik Menace to Russia," subsequently published in the April 12, 1919, issue of the *Independent*.[23]

Boris Brasol

By the time this article was published, Boris Brasol had been residing in the United States for nearly three years. He served as Imperial Russia's representative to the Inter-Allied Conference until 1917, when—as an outspoken, loyal monarchist and frustrated supporter of the ousted czar—he summarily resigned rather than serve the new post-Revolution Bolshevik regime. Brasol went to work for the United States War Trade Board after the Armistice was signed in 1919. Smooth-talking and adept, as a confidential adviser Brasol moved easily into high circles of the Military Intelligence Division. The American Constitutional League hired Brasol to make a speaking tour of the Midwest. He soon became well-known as a darling of conservative patriots concerned about the widening stain of revolution overseas, touching a nerve especially when he warned that "this country, too, will have to decide whether it would be prepared to see American homes looted ... the American flag trodden down, and America given up for the benefit of a gang of criminals who have no other aim than the Great Divide."[24]

One of the members of the military intelligence community with whom Brasol struck up a key connection in early 1918 was Harris Ayres Houghton, a physician stationed at the War Department's Eastern Department on Governor's Island in New York City. Houghton, a hard-core nativist, was a "zealous counter-subversive, obsessed by the Jewish threat to America's war effort." Well-aware of her employer's ideological affinities, his administrative assistant, Natalie de Bogory, a young woman of Russian parentage, acquired from Boris Brasol a copy of a rare edition of an arcane book by Sergei Nilus (1862–1930) published in Kiev in 1917 called *The Protocols of the Learned Elders of Zion*. Brasol worked closely with de Bogory—paid out of Houghton's personal funds—on a translation of the *Protocols* from Russian into English, the first such version in existence on American soil. Their twenty-four section typescript was completed by early June.[25]

The *Protocols* is a "spurious document" purporting to be the minutes and proceedings of a Jewish conclave led by the Grand Rabbi and held during the first Zionist Congress in Basel, Switzerland, in 1897. The purpose of this secret meeting of "the innermost circle" of worldwide Jewish leadership was to structure a "blueprint" for world domination reducing all non-Jews to slavery and then to set the schedule for subsequent gatherings every 100 years by an endless succession of "autocrats of the House of David."

"Our power in the present tottering conditions of all forms of power," ominously begins *Protocol I*, "will be more invincible than any other, because it will remain invisible until the moment when it has gained such strength that no cunning can any longer undermine it."[26]

The book in Brasol's possession began its most recent iteration as a forgery created by the Okhrana (Secret Police) of Imperial Russia under the supervision of their chief, Pyotr Ivanovich Rachkovsky, some time between 1894 and 1899. It first appeared in 1903 and served to point an accusing finger at the Jews and their Satanic cohorts, the Freemasons, for inciting the 1905 Revolution. The 1917 edition that Brasol provided Houghton was the fourth version, "edited" and improvisationally expanded by Nilus, a Nietzsche-admirer and mystic. Subtitled *It Is Near at Our Doors!* Nilus's version extended the "Judaeo-Bolshevist" threat further into the racial realm, drawing a graphic analogy between the pair of crossed triangles composing the Jewish star and the seal of the Antichrist. When the Jews take over human society, "The mark of the serpent's evil will be stamped on every man's brow, and none will be able to make the sign of the cross."

Antichrist and his emblems. The six-pointed Jewish star was considered one of his "trademarks"

There could no longer be any doubt among Judaeophobes by the time Boris Brasol showed his hand that the *Protocols* were warning of the inevitable death struggle between Aryans and Jews. How else explain the religious symbolism displayed by the Bolshevik assassination of the czar and his family on July 17, 1918?[27]

As soon as the English translation was done, Brasol and Houghton moved into high gear to disseminate their valuable findings. The trail is erratic, but traceable. As early as September 1918, Brasol's name turned up in an article in a Brooklyn newspaper called *The Anti-Bolshevist,* blatantly claiming that the Jews—unleashing their favorite "stock weapons," Liberalist revolution and class war—were responsible for pushing the United States into World War I, and furthermore that they were operating behind the scenes to prolong it. As the *Protocols* made clear, the Zionist Jewish state in Palestine established by the Balfour Declaration of November 1917 and destined to become the "headquarters of the Jewish world masters" never could have come to pass without the systematic destruction of gentile Russia and Germany.

Houghton managed meanwhile to show the *Protocols* to Chief Justice of the United States Charles Evans Hughes, who in turn sent it to Louis Marshall, president of the American Jewish Committee. Other typescript copies made the rounds of the Smithsonian Institution, the Justice Department, and Military Intelligence Division Headquarters in Washington.[28]

In the new year, Houghton approached Frederick Ohl, managing editor of the *New York Herald,* with a "very important document concerning the Jewish people and their role in world affairs." Ohl turned to Herman Bernstein, the paper's highly respected staff correspondent recently returned from overseas, for his opinion. When Bernstein conducted a private interview with Houghton, the good doctor went so far as to reveal to the reporter that the *Protocols* had been "prepared by Theodore Herzl, the father of modern Zionism" and that the document had been formally adopted as the cornerstone for the Zionist movement. Houghton also told Bernstein that various members of President Wilson's cabinet had seen the secret manifesto and were "deeply impressed with its astounding revelations." Houghton "pointed to Bolshevism in Russia as the fulfillment of the plan" set forth in the *Protocols.*[29]

Houghton offered to leave this "treasured document" in Bernstein's possession on the strict condition that he sign a receipt guaranteeing to read the *Protocols* in secrecy and return it in three days. This Bernstein did, certifying to editor Ohl that they were "a clumsy falsification" and not to be published in the *New York Herald*. Despite additional skepticism expressed at the level of a Senate subcommittee investigating it in February 1919, the *Protocols* continued to wend a stealthy way by *samizdat* among delegates to the Versailles Peace Conference and began to appear on the desks of cabinet members and civil servants in London, Paris, and Rome.[30]

It was at about this time that Boris Brasol and Ernest Liebold crossed paths, their meeting of the minds leading to Brasol's article scheduled for later in the spring. It is difficult to determine who approached whom, even though Pipp asserted two years later that Henry Ford "had the files of the [*Dearborn Independent*] correspondence" between the Russian expatriate and the private secretary, wherein was described "what was back of all of it, just how [Liebold] worked to give the man with Brasol's Russian record a standing in the newspaper." These corporate files were destroyed in the 1960s.[31]

Brasol's polemic warning of "the Bolshevik menace" provides substantial insight (from his embittered perspective) into sensitive issues of nationalism, worker sovereignty, Russian unity, and the imbalance of power in Western Europe at a hair-trigger and uncertain moment in its modern history.

The essay is marred by the author's apocalyptic broad-strokes depicting a ruined motherland "bow[ing] to the tyrannic, inhuman, and illiterate rule of international mobs..." Brasol concludes with a flourish, "Why should humanity submit its will to a tyranny which is worse than Oriental autocracies which ruled over mankind at the dawn of its history?"[32]

The agenda of the *Dearborn Independent* mutated with greater speed in the ensuing months. Liebold's first signed article, published four weeks later—"Speculation vs. Production: Which Creates Wealth?"—read as if it were drafted in dialogue with Brasol's.

"Financial interests played a deep and sinister part in creating the conditions which finally exploded in a state of war," Liebold stated, well-convinced for his part that "No one needs to be warned today about the danger to international peace which comes from the insistence of the owners of gold that will be out everywhere earning interest."[33]

The newspaper was taking on an uncomfortably schizophrenic quality. Pipp's sermons on the importance of, say, maintaining a social conscience through the act of being an informed consumer ran just a few pages away from Mr. Ford's/Cameron's gloomy sentiment that "something is wrong with the body politic. . . . there is a great deal of shiftlessness in the world." Every time Pipp came out with his cheerleading voice to encourage Woodrow Wilson and the League of Nations, running front-page cartoons that chastised the dilatory Senate and portrayed a worried Uncle Sam always on the verge of joining in but not quite, Cameron found a way to "curse" the practice of "diplomacy-in-the-dark."

Pipp praised the Southern Race Congress convened in New Orleans in the early summer of 1919, an event to be welcomed, he wrote, by "all lovers of our universal humanity." He scorned faithless commentators who looked with wariness upon the recent migration of southern Negroes northward, and found it encouraging that minority races would gravitate to the larger urban areas of America. Meanwhile, on his "Own Page," Ford was outspoken in his conviction that "the modern City concentrates within its limits the essence of all that is wrong, artificial, wayward and unjust in our social life."[34]

AND Henry Ford was battling another set of demons. In May 1919, his million-dollar libel suit against the *Chicago Tribune* finally came to trial in the town of Mount Clemens, Michigan, the Macomb County seat twenty miles northeast of Dearborn known for its supposedly therapeutic, noxious sulphur springs. Three years earlier the newspaper had labeled the automobile manufacturer an "ignorant anarchist" for saying that he was unequivocally opposed to "cowardly and unjust" American military involvement in border disputes with Mexico: "Better to put the Mexican peon to work," Ford said, "then there would be no more talk of a revolution. Villa would become a foreman, if he had brains. Carranza might be trained to be a good time-keeper."[35]

Weeks of detailed questioning by the *Tribune*'s adept attorney, Elliott G. Stevenson, sought to "expose Ford's mind bare" and establish him as pitiably naïve, ill-educated, and unpatriotic. It became painfully clear that the Flivver King was ignorant of most basic textbook facts: the fundamental principles of government, the dates of the Revolutionary War ("1812?" he asked tentatively), and the identity of Benedict Arnold (Ford thought Arnold was "a writer," confusing the traitor with Arnold Bennett, apologists insisted, because at the moment the question was posed, Ford was preoccupied on the witness stand, scraping mud off the sole of his cordovan shoe with a penknife).

But what did these so-called facts matter in the end, an exasperated Ford blurted out late one afternoon, since "History is more or less the bunk." Twenty years on, he was still trying to clarify what he meant by that infamous statement. He was really talking about—had *always* been referring to—the authors of history *books* that "weren't true. They wrote what they wanted us to believe, glorifying some conqueror or leader or something like that."[36]

When the jury finally heard enough verbiage from both sides and withdrew to deliberate in "the weary summer of 1919," Ford, feeling dispirited and vindictive, sought to distance himself. He was overdue for another restorative excursion with sympathetic friends. Accompanied by Edward G. Kingsford, manager of the Ford Motor Company for Michigan's Upper Peninsula, Ford sailed on Lake Erie from Detroit to Buffalo aboard the night boat of August 3. There he was met by Harvey Firestones Senior and Junior, coming in from Cleveland via Akron. A six-car entourage of Cadillacs, Lincolns, and Pierce-Arrows was assembled for the ramble eastward to Syracuse, New York. After a night's rest, the group set forth for Albany, where Thomas Edison and John Burroughs completed the happy band. They pitched a compound of tents at Green Island,

"Roughing it" around the lazy Susan. Mina Edison seated to the left of the tent-pole, Thomas Edison, Clara Ford, Warren B. Harding, Idabelle Firestone, Henry Ford, and others

north of Troy, where Ford had just purchased a large plot of land upon which he was planning to build a Fordson Tractor factory.[37]

After an afternoon of woodchopping and riflery, and dinner served around a big table with a bountiful lazy Susan in the middle, the campfire talk on the night of August 5 was dutifully recorded by John Burroughs in his private pocket notebook. Ford was in an especially dour mood. He strayed off the safe, jingoistic path, and attacked the Jews, Burroughs jotted down, "saying the Jews caused the War, the Jews caused the outbreak of thieving and robbery all across the country, the Jews caused the inefficiency of the Navy."

Then Ford lashed out at railroad magnate Jay Gould as "a Shylock" and the prime example of the kind of avarice he abhorred. Burroughs was forced to join the argument; Gould had been his childhood wrestling playmate and was a tried-and-true Presbyterian.

Such satisfaction was momentary, for Jew hatred was now an entrenched, persistent stain on Ford's psyche. Stunned and embarrassed by the depth of his friend's aggressive language, Burroughs did not transcribe this aspect of the fireside debate into the published version of his camping story, "A Strenuous Holiday," an otherwise affectionate reminiscence that appeared in his 1921 book, *Under the Maples*. Nor did Burroughs ever mention Ford's bias in any other related essay about their customary outings together, save to say that "not much of the talk that night around the camp fire can be repeated."

Burroughs sensed correctly that Thomas Edison was empathetic with Ford's prejudices, although in a less strident, more stereotypical manner. The Jewish businessmen in Germany, Edison chimed in, according to Burroughs's notes from that same August night, were "keen and alert...efficient," in contrast to the lowbrow German industrial and military leadership, wrongfully taking possessive credit for the past prosperity of their nation. Five years earlier, indignant at a similar manifestation of Edison's typecasting published in an interview in the *Detroit Free Press*, the banker Jacob H. Schiff, chairman of Kuhn, Loeb & Company, dashed off an angry letter asking Edison to deny his "flighty...assertion[s]." Edison drafted a conciliatory response insisting he was only trying to give credit where credit was due. If Schiff wanted to discover the secret of the "enormous industry of modern Germany," he had merely to "dig up [*sic*] a Jew who furnished the ability and that made them a success."

Edison elaborated upon his theory about where Jews did and did not belong in society in a subsequent letter to Isaac Markens, author of *The Hebrews in America* (1888) and *Abraham Lincoln and the Jews* (1909). "The Jews are certainly a remarkable people," Edison conceded, "as strange to me in their isolation from all the rest of mankind as those mysterious people called Gypsies. While there are some 'terrible examples' in mercantile pursuits, the moment they get into art, music and science, and literature, the Jew is fine." To Edison, it was a troubling "racial" characteristic, a "natural talent" for becoming rich, that had caused the meddling Jew to be "disliked." Hopefully, through continued exposure to modern American democracy, the Jew "in time will cease to be so clannish." Edison excised the next sentence of his letter with black pencil before having it typed up for sending to Markens: "I wish they would all stop making money."[38]

The recent ideological conflicts over the signing of the Treaty of Versailles in late June were on everyone's mind and also tainted the Ford-Edison dialogues that summer. Infuriated with the "Carthaginian" solution to the war concocted by the Council of Four and excessive reparations reducing Germany to servitude for a generation—and especially disillusioned with the behavior of President Wilson—the young economist John Maynard Keynes had summarily quit as an adviser to the British Peace Conference delegation. Keynes notified Lloyd George that he was "slipping away from this scene of nightmare...in the dead season of our fortunes. The battle is lost." Keynes was horrified by the way in which the governments of Europe, in their "racial or political hatred" euphemistically condemned the "international financiers...profiteers and traders" for the postwar chaos of their economies. The insinuating and bitter shadow of Versailles thus fell most ominously over the Jews, triggering a "fourth wave" of American anti-alienism to break in 1919.[39]

In considering the nuances in their different attitudes toward Jews at this volatile juncture in the Ford-Edison relationship, the observations of Leon Poliakov, investigator of Nazi war crimes for the Nuremberg trials and author of one of the definitive histories of antisemitism, prove useful. He makes the important distinction between those who "merely hold negative stereotyped value-judgements about the Jews to be true; and those who openly express a desire to have Jews restricted in any way." In both cases, Poliakov says —and there is no question of Ford's susceptibility here—the degree of intolerance expressed is "often a function of the hostile individual's anxiety."[40]

Aside from a run of public-relations blunders and hypersensitivity to postwar consequences in Europe, Henry Ford suffered from other anxious matters. The nation had been crippled by a series of big labor strikes since the new year—harbor workers, sedan- and open-car body manufacturers, and railroad shopmen, with further disturbances brewing from coal miners and steel workers—not to mention an impending raise in the discount rate by the Federal Reserve Board. Ford was looking at unprecedented consumer demand for his cars, but he was frustrated by disruptions in the interlocking chain of industries that inhibited his ability to meet consumer demand.

When Ford returned from the summer travels and refocused attention with hopes of solace upon his beloved *Dearborn Independent,* he discovered stagnant circulation and a hemorrhaging budget as the first year of the paper's life moved toward conclusion. Something had to be done to improve matters. "Find an evil to attack, go after it, and stay after it," advised Joseph Jefferson O'Neill, a veteran *New York World* reporter lured away from his job to try to help Ford manage his faltering public persona during the *Chicago Tribune* trial. "PUSSY FOOTING and being afraid to hurt people will keep us just where we are if not send us further down the ladder.... If we get and print the right sort of stuff, ONE SINGLE SERIES may make us known to millions.... LET'S HAVE SOME SENSATIONALISM."[41]

CHAPTER EIGHT

Exit Mr. Pipp

THE 1920s may have been "roaring" to some American flappers and champagne-swillers; to others the period touched off an unprecedented blossoming in literature and the arts, a great coming-to-maturity for the modernist ethos. But it was not a good time to be a Jew in America at the onset of the "peculiar force and magnitude" of the Anglo-Saxon decade, the decade of anxiety, an historical threshold "sad for those of us who have hitherto been proud of our fine traditions," wrote Louis Marshall in characteristic solemnity, "noting what a change has occurred since the Armistice."[1]

More than 120,000 European Jews passed through the somber brick portals of Ellis Island in 1920, and their arrival provided a convenient and familiar scapegoat for the country's swelling unemployment. Detroit was vulnerable to the twin postwar tensions of immigration and economic depression. By the end of the year,

Henry Ford had cash-flow problems so extreme that he shut down the Highland Park plant as a protest against the extortionate "war prices" he believed were still being charged by his raw material suppliers. But he was adamant about not succumbing to the speculative Wall Street vultures circling above, waiting for Ford to ask for a loan of tainted "eastern cash": "I would tear down my plants, brick by brick, with my own hands, before I would let Wall Street get ahold of them."[2]

In 1920, also, the U.S. Bureau of the Census declared that for the first time the majority of Americans lived in cities and their adjacent burgeoning suburbs. Detroit at this time boasted a population of 993,678, making it the fourth-largest city in the United States and the country's fastest-growing industrial center. The automobile industry employed 45.4 percent of the manufacturing labor force in Detroit. The city had evolved steadily into a dramatic portmanteau symbol of the new industrial society, crowded as it was with all of the pluses and minuses that such a condition implied. Surges of new arrivals meant an increasing stratification of class-consciousness. "Native white industrialists"—Republican, Protestant, and socially prominent—called the shots from above, determined to control their workforces, giving Detroit the depressing reputation among trade unions as "graveyard of the organizers."[3]

At the same time, from below, immense numbers of workers flocked to the embracing ranks of the newly revived Ku Klux Klan, finding a strong sense of community in "traditional nativism's last stand," fighting for prohibition and 100 percent Americanism. "Against us are all the forces of the mixed alliance composed of alienism, Romanism, hyphenism, Bolshevism, and un-Americanism," proclaimed a contemporary Klan spokesman. The working men looked around at the recurring alien tides, peered far upward at the captains of industry, and turned with self-righteous vengeance against the blacks, the Catholics, and (last, but not least) the "cross-breeding hordes" and "Christ-killing monsters of moral corruption"

—in what the American historian John Higham identifies as the "central apotheosis of the tribal spirit." Soon after his outspoken entry into the Zionist movement, Justice Louis Brandeis observed during a visit to Detroit that "anti-Semitism seems to have reached its American pinnacle here."[4]

By 1921, Michigan's 875,000 Klan members represented the largest group in the United States. The Klan's special "Black Guard," founded as an elite force and soon spun off as a related cadre, claimed more than 24,000 hard-core "Night Riders" in Michigan alone. Among the guard's most active members were the mayor of Highland Park—stationed near the Ford factory complex—and the police chief of Royal Oak, both Detroit suburbs.[5]

In Washington, Woodrow Wilson's appointee as attorney general, A. Mitchell Palmer, often referred to as "Uncle Sam's Policeman," was exercising his own brand of venomous rhetoric against "the aliens on the steerage steamers who were not of our sort ... and were hostile to American institutions." In Palmer's mind, there was no doubt that the leadership of this radical and anti-Christian creed, "eating its way into the churches, schools and homes of the American workmen," could be found banded together as "a small clique of autocrats from the East Side of New York," disciples and allies of "Leon Bronstein, the man who now calls himself Trotzky." In the attorney general's mind, there resided a clear correlation between the influx of such libertine aliens and the increase in crime rampant throughout the land since the end of the Great War. Bolshevism had already "looted Russia not only of its material strength but of its moral force," and it was Palmer's mission to warn the United States against a similarly lawless overthrow of its own government.[6]

Encouraged by Congress, and legitimized by the Espionage and Alien Acts of 1918, Palmer's high-profile deportation raids against thousands of members of the Industrial Workers of the World (the "Wobblies"), radicals, factory strikers, and indiscriminate leftists of all kinds earned him accolades as "The Fighting Quaker of the

Cabinet." In August 1919, Palmer created an "intelligence depart-ment" to delve more deeply into the purported machinations of anarchists, and he appointed J. Edgar Hoover to lead this enter-prise, resulting in the names of many more "subversives" coming to public attention. Twenty state governments picked up the federal baton and passed their own legislation against "criminal anarchy."

On Friday, January 2, 1920, Palmer launched his most ambitious and widespread series of raids "to tear out the radical seeds that have entangled American ideas in their poisonous theories." Dozens of meeting halls and homes in cities across the land were hit hard, without regard for due process, warnings, or warrants. In Detroit, the House of the Masses, headquarters for the city's Com-munist party, was ransacked. Eight hundred men were arrested and imprisoned without food or water in the dark, unventilated hall-ways of the old Federal Building downtown.[7]

E. G. Liebold was talking.

He was talking to Henry Ford.

Mr. Liebold tilted back his chair, unbuttoned his coat, put his thumbs into the armholes of his vest, expanded his chest, and said:

"Mr. Ford, *YOU* don't have to think as other men think; *YOUR* thoughts come to you like a flash, from a sub-conscious mind, and you have your problems solved."

Mr. Ford, who usually sits well settled down in his chair, straightened up a bit, his shoulders went back a bit, his chin raised a bit, and his eyes sparkled.

A look of satisfaction spread itself over Mr. Liebold's counte-nance.

It was the look of satisfaction which comes to a man's face when he feels that he has put something over.

... The door to the Ford mind was always open to anything Liebold wanted to shove in it, and during that time Mr. Ford developed a dislike for the Jews, a dislike which [grew] stronger and more bitter as time went on.... In one way and another the feeling oozed into his system until it [became] a part of his living self.[8]

ALL WAS NOT WELL around the offices of the *Dearborn Independent* as the paper struggled toward its first anniversary. Liebold's drive for power took on renewed vigor, with Ford willing to cede more and more territory to his secretary. The attack dog was still firmly tethered to his leash, but the leash was played out farther and farther. Commensurately, Liebold began to go out of his way *not* to pay attention to E. G. Pipp, disparagingly remarking that he "didn't find Mr. Pipp of any value [and] ignored anything and everything that he said." Their arguments became more frequent and public, the heretofore-mild-mannered Pipp getting red in the face and pounding his fist upon Liebold's desk in full view of co-workers. Fueled by Liebold, the power behind the throne, "substantial rumors about the rift between Pipp and Mr. Ford" began to swirl.[9] The secretary's behavior was also noticeable to outsiders. Another Michigan newspaper publisher complained privately to Edsel Ford that Liebold's grip on the *Independent* and "his great greed for power and more power have driven him to action akin to Kaiserism."[10]

Henry Ford tallied up his losses at year-end and found to his dismay that the newspaper was $284,000 in the red. Circulation was languishing, even though Ford had sent a memo out to all of his agents and dealers across the country that he was establishing a quota system whereby every purchaser of a Model T was going to have to buy an automatic subscription. It was about this time, in the emotionally fraught and divisive editorial atmosphere of late 1919 and early 1920, that Ford's obsession with the health of his newspaper came into direct convergence with the inspiration for the Jewish campaign—or, as it was more casually described in hindsight by surviving members of the younger staff, "the old Jewish thing." They had gathered for a meeting, significantly, in Liebold's office,

not Pipp's, and Ford looked around the table at his men and asked
what kind of readership the newspaper was reaching; they quietly
told him the dismal figures, and The Boss sprung out of his chair
and said, "We want a million by next week! You run a campaign
next week!"[11]

Pipp's writing took a defensive turn. "Facing 1920," he confided
to his readers, "there never was in America's history a beginning of
a twelvemonth which more seriously, more solemnly, called for
thought, for ambition, for resolution... Problems beset us, conditions beset us... What is the price we must pay to live?" Was he
talking to the readers of the *Dearborn Independent*, or was E. G.
Pipp preparing himself for the inevitable denouement of his own
career? "It is your Paper," he wrote in February, again turning his
emotional editorial voice into a confessional of sorts. Pipp decided
to "pause," and "discuss our aims, that we may go along the road
together with mutual good understanding... All we ask of our writers is to write what they know to be true."

The liberal, Catholic Pipp's influence receded rapidly as Ford and
Liebold "commenced to talk persistently about a series of articles
attacking the Jewish people," an ongoing "educational" series that
would, as Ford envisioned it, "tell all—just open up and let some air
in" on the Jewish Question—once and for all, with the eventual goal
that the Jews would then "clean up their own house." Toward that
goal, Ford, devotee of the assembly line, ordered up one article written each week, "as he gives orders for so many cars or tractors to be
built." In contrast to Pipp's bitterness, the response of the junior
staff was benign, as befitting their relative distance from the depth
of Ford's venom. They sympathized with Mr. Ford about the pain he
still harbored from the attacks he had received in the press after the
Peace Ship debacle. After all, their boss was a man who came from
simple, "sturdy," traditional midwestern stock. He feared "encroach-
ments... along the lines of Jewish influence" upon his cherished,
Victorian model of life; and so, if Mr. Ford wanted to use the soapbox of his newspaper to "preserve American tradition," that was

acceptable to these men. As for Ford's cranky attitude against Wall Street, why, "that old idea likewise went back to the period when he was raised . . . that was the whipping boy of the country." In summary, Ford's attitude "wasn't unusual," concluded Fred Black, and colleagues Ben Donaldson and Walter Blanchard. His was the kind of thinking "shared by many people in the country, and in small towns" during "the F. Scott Fitzgerald era when the younger generation was seen as going to hell. That was all there was to it in the minds of people like Mr. Ford."[12]

To breathe the life of language into Ford's melange of antisemitic notions, Liebold turned to "the walking dictionary," Billy Cameron. His writing talents were especially suited to the task proscribed, because Cameron, as a dedicated British-Israelite, believed that contemporary Anglo-Saxons were descended from the Ten Lost Tribes of Israel and that Great Britain and the United States were the true Holy Land. Thus, the Anglo-Saxons were the true "chosen people"—and not the "Modern Hebrews," who were actually usurpers worshiping the subversive doctrines of the Talmud. According to British-Israelite lore, Jesus was not a Jew, but rather the forefather of modern Germans, Scandinavians, and British. The Anglo-Saxon, Celtic race was the "Ruling People," destined to master the world. Despite this religious conviction, Cameron confided in his friend Pipp on several occasions that he was sickened by the prospect of such an ugly assignment, and he began taking to the liquor bottle with greater frequency. Cameron, perceived as a congenial sort, comes across as docilely following orders, perhaps out of deep-seated fear of Liebold, not to mention the omnipresent threat of the wrath of Ford. When Pipp—disenfranchised and frustrated—resigned in mid-April, 1920, Cameron was devastated, immediately turning sour against the man who had originally brought him to the paper: "You could see that [Pipp] was disappointed. He had been head of the *Detroit News* and he wasn't head of anything [anymore] out at Ford."

Pipp's name was removed from the masthead of the *Independent* as of the April 17 issue.[13]

Pipp made a point of going on record that although he had been on the staff at the *Independent* as the anti-Jewish articles were in planning and preparation, he left before any of Ford's "gospel of bitterness and poison gas of race-hatred" was published. While it is the case that the first explicit "International Jew" article with its blazing, italicized headline came forth on May 22, there actually had been several thinly veiled implications in the half-year running up to it. The paper had speculated on "Who Will Be the King of Palestine?" the previous fall, going into detail about "the drama of the Jewish people" in their unrelenting quest for a homeland, and theorizing that the ambitious brothers Nathan and Oscar Straus were interested in ascending to the "throne" of this monarchical state once it was established. Another candidate for ruler of the new nation was speculated to be the writer Israel Zangwill. But the most likely to take power, according to the *Independent*'s analysis of the situation, would surely be someone from the omnipotent House of Rothschild. "In any event," the newspaper complained, "it seems that the Zionists will have their way."

Through the month of April, Mr. Ford hoisted once again his flag of warning against "the dark forces of war," invoking on his "Page"—the "Own" of the title having been dropped, perhaps as an admission that it was not written by him?—the ability of mysterious and anonymous individuals to "manipulate certain instincts and passions with a skill which could only emanate from Satan himself." He went on to cast a critical eye on the persistent "immigrant problem" interfering with his campaign of Americanization of aliens. There must be some more forceful way, Ford believed, to "stem the tide of undesirables."[14]

Pipp's Weekly—the plain-spoken and bluntly written periodical through which E. G. struck back at his old boss, commenced publication on June 19, advising readers that "We do not claim to be a

Jewish paper, nor devoted entirely to the cause of the Jew. We look on the Ford attacks on the Jew as an attack on Americanism and as such believe it the duty of non-Jews to answer the attacks."[15]

It was a dark and miserable spring for Pipp, who had come on board at the *Independent* with high hopes such a short time before. To the alienated Pipp, "it was as though an idol had fallen." To add insult to injury, Ford and Liebold had spared not an instant to find someone "willing to help gather the stones and throw them at the men, women and children of a whole race of people," and—ironies of ironies—they alighted upon Billy Cameron.[16]

Pipp's sleepless anguish—he made a regular point in his news-paper columns of telling *Pipp's Weekly* readers that he stayed up many nights until dawn worrying and writing about the tragic turn of events—was derived in large measure from the distasteful idea of Cameron's wasted talents as a writer. Pipp persisted for years afterward in pitying Cameron as a victim coerced to redirect his inherently positive energies into "tearing down people."

Pipp felt sorry for his former employer and confidant. He feared that once the "International Jew" articles hit the newsstands, this great man's legacy would be indelibly corrupted—Henry Ford, larger-than-mere-mortal, pioneer of American industry, already "past the middle hour of life . . . would let the memory of him be the memory of a nation set against a race that is part of that nation."

ACROSS the seas, like a restless serpent, the *Protocols of the Learned Elders of Zion* continued its slithering progress. Funded by the Pan-German League, the Berlin edition was first to succeed the Russian Nilus version. It was grandiosely dedicated "to the princes of Europe" and brought to public attention in the middle of January 1920 by Gottfried zur Beek, pseudonym for Ludwig Muller von Hausen, a retired army captain and editor of the antisemitic monthly, *Auf Vorposten* (On Outpost Duty). The German version was noteworthy for a new embellishment explaining in breathless detail how the *Protocols* had been stolen by a Russian spy from a Jewish messenger on his way from the secret Zionist meeting in Basel to a "Jewish Masonic lodge" in Frankfurt. The evil "Judeo-Mongols" had instigated a war to "stab Germany in the back" and were now embarked upon a "golden international" racial and "Mammonistic" rampage that had to be halted soon.

An abridged version of the *Protocols* appeared the following month in Alfred Rosenberg's newspaper, *Völkischer Beobachter*, (The Racial Observer), published just one day after the February 24 meeting at the Munich *Burgerbraukeller* where thirty-one-year-old Adolf Hitler spelled out the inaugural "Twenty-Five Point" program for the emerging National Socialist German Workers' Party before a crowd of more than 2,000 people: "Only a racial comrade can be a citizen. Only a person of German blood can be a racial comrade, without regard to religion. Consequently no Jew can be a racial comrade." Zur Beek's book was "a great sensation" and sold 120,000 copies, soon earning the subtitle *The Bible of the Antisemites*. It was reprinted in Germany thirty-two more times over the next thirteen years.[17]

Almost simultaneously, the *Protocols* were published by the venerable London firm of Eyre and Spottiswood under the title *The Jewish Peril*. The translation was by George Shanks, a Russian émigré. The book was received with alarmist declarations in the press. On May 8, 1920, under the headline "A Disturbing Pamphlet: A Call for Inquiry," the *Times of London* wondered, "What are these '*Protocols*'? Are they authentic? If so, what malevolent assembly concocted these plans, and gloated over their exposition?" One week following, the *London Spectator* joined the chorus, stridently evaluating the *Jewish Peril* as nothing less than a tract of "moral perversity and intellectual depravity."

In Paris, the French antisemitic daily newspaper *La Libre Parole* serialized the complete *Protocols*; in Warsaw, the Polish edition appeared; and a Russian-language edition sprung up as far afield as Tokyo.[18]

Into the epicenter of this multinational cyclone stepped the *Dearborn Independent* of May 22, 1920, bearing "The Jew in Character and Business" on page one, as the first of ninety-one successive articles devoted to examining "The International Jew: The World's Problem" in exhaustive detail. How proud Liebold was of this project, now that he had clambered decisively to the top of the heap. Even though it was common knowledge by now around the *Inde-*

"The International Jew,"
May 22, 1920

pendent that Liebold was the "spark plug in the Jewish series, and that he was antisemitic in terms of wanting to eradicate the Jews," Mr. Ford's secretary was always careful to maintain respect for the source of authority, conceding that "Everything that was being done was being done because of Mr. Ford's wishes in carrying out the idea of revealing to the public the facts pertaining to Jewish activities." Liebold was also careful to give all due credit for the excellent analytical writing to "the man most active in collecting and compiling the information, Mr. Cameron." "Mr. Ford intimated to me that he was going to show up this group of international Jews," Liebold recalled. "He said, 'We are going to print their names. We are going to show who they are.'"[19]

There was only one innovation Liebold was convinced he had the right to take credit for: "I suggested the name 'The International Jew,' as segregated from others. I believed that the trend of the campaign would be along that line. Mr. Ford's answer to that was,

Pipp's Weekly strikes back

'Well, you can't single them out. You have to go after them all. They are all part of the same system.'"[20]

Liebold's claim needs some perspective. By mid-1920, Henry Ford had long since built up considerable momentum as an ambitious and determined international business imperialist. As early as 1904, barely one year after Ford Motor Company had opened its doors, he had capitalized the Ford Motor Company of Canada. In its first three years, Ford-Canada sold 540 cars—but it was a start. That same year, Fords were sent to appear in the showrooms of London. The Model A was exported to France, Belgium, Mexico, and subsequently—via the first automotive assembly plant ever built in Argentina—throughout Latin America. Ford Motor Company (England) was soon to follow and flourish as the largest branch of Ford in the world outside Detroit—nonunion, to be sure—under the faithful and watchful eye of Percival Perry. Before World War I, there was a major Ford factory constructed in Hamburg. Faraway outposts were also found in Odessa, St. Petersburg, Estonia—and Vladivostok, Russia, where an impressive 90 percent of all the cars were Fords. Assembly plants in Japan and Turkey soon followed. Ford understood from the outset that it was cheaper to ship "knocked down" rather than "built up" cars. By 1919, with the Model T riding high, Ford's foreign and domestic sales exceeded 1 million units, "a feat never before achieved by any motorcar manufacturer." Thus, Henry Ford had more than enough reason to fear all manner of threats—real or perceived—to his farflung corporate empire.[21]

So much for the "International" dimension of the title. As for usage of "the Jew" in the singular mode, found frequently in the particular language of antisemites, this is traceable to the propensity for abstraction syntactically carrying more effective weight as fraught with menace. Making the assumption that "one Jew is identical with all others" means that the "race" can justifiably be impugned as a whole—hence the aptness of Henry Ford's imagination of a "system."[22]

In tone and language, the article on "The Jew in Character and Business" served to set all the salient themes in motion for the ensuing *Independent* series. For several years following publication, everyone who came to Dearborn to meet with Henry Ford would first be asked to take a seat in a quiet waiting room, and spend fifteen minutes reading an offprint of this inaugural article before the business at hand could be addressed.[23]

Even the opening sentence, "The Jew is again being singled out for critical attention throughout the world," is replete with implications—the singular reference to "the Jew," the idea that the global problem he has instigated is persistent, the sense that the Jew stands unique, that his ubiquity is common. Within four paragraphs, the word "control" recurs five times, most often in connection with the Jew's annoying propensity for business. From this platform, the writer reflects upon the beginnings of the Jew's history, his earliest formation into a "money aristocracy," his "dispersion" to wander among the nations for the past twenty-five centuries, causing him to be always *in but not of* the countries he inhabits. He is the perpetual alien, "a corporation with agents everywhere"—a reference that brings to mind the structure of the Ford Motor Company itself.

Coupled with his alien personality, according to the article, is the Jew's urge to create a nation that will master the rest. This nation—his "headquarters," known as Zion—will bring together all Jews, congenitally "linked in a fellowship of blood" with each other. The fear of Jewish unity is traced back to the Middle Ages. Even then, it was thought that the Jews knew more of what was going on in Europe than any individual governments. Their secret knowledge has always had at its fundament financial sophistication; thereby do the Jew "great masters," the bank directors and the rabbis, exercise a collective, invisible hand over the enterprises of modern society as they have done for all time. The latest example of this influence was vividly seen in "stricken Germany," and America would likewise soon fall prey unless "the proud Gentile race" woke up quickly and armed itself against these "few super-men of a long despised race." All the more reason to endorse "a candid examination" of the Jewish problem now, in the pages of the *Dearborn Independent.* It was to be noted, however, that this was conceived at first as a racial problem, *not* a religious one.[24]

ITS NOBLE posture struck, proposing to shine a cleansing, visionary searchlight to probe into the dark, musty corners of the "Jewish Question," the *Dearborn Independent* began erecting the walls of its paper pogrom. A country newspaper in 1920s America, the *Independent* fit squarely into a thousand-year-old continuum of Jew hatred, thick taproots sunk deep into the archetypal, richly poisoned soil of medievalism. Early church fathers had feared the "magical sorcerers' language" of Hebrew, believing it tampered perversely with the text of the true Bible. They sounded warnings of deviant, blasphemous rabbis assembling "to conspire with secrecy in Cairo." They portrayed Jews as "enemies of the people," ready at any moment to betray the countries that harbored them—a message which would become so elaborately presented in the Russian *Protocols*. By the fourteenth century, pathological fantasies about plots hatched by deicidal "Jewish monsters" came to full flower. The final goal of the Jews—this camouflaged body of dispersed, "wandering" (and therefore even more dangerous) people in concert with lepers and Saracens—was to murder a large part of Christendom and enslave the survivors.

Likewise out of the fourteenth century emerged a character prefiguring Shylock, the usurer demanding his pound of flesh. The moneylending Jew was another familiar medieval figure with no legal rights, a chimerical "black beast" populating fabulous stories drawn from the exotic Orient and told throughout Europe. There was no one more despised than the usurer demanding payment from unwilling citizens. The stereotypical Jew in business disdained by Ford and Edison possessed a mirror image in the minds of feudal lords. Ford labeled Jay Gould and J. P. Morgan "Jews"; a medieval cliché allied Christian moneylenders with the Devil as their shadowy partner and vilified them for "Judaizing." The reason the Jews were essentially cornered into moneylending ten centuries ago was because so many other professions had been denied to them: "They were not hated because they lent money; they lent money because they were hated."[25]

Many of these and other antique, regressive, prejudicial social attitudes survived intact into and through the late-eighteenth century phase of Jewish "emancipation" and enfranchisement in

France, and from thence for another 150 years into the third decade of twentieth century ("modern") America. *Emancipation* is in quotes because it ironically had the opposite effect. The Jew had been confined for hundreds of years to the margins of society, to follow legally delimited paths of livelihood. Although he was "allowed to intermingle" with surrounding bourgeois culture, the fear of his presence and always-exaggerated power was still not dissolved. Rather, with the coming of emancipation, demonological fear had to be transformed into something political, even scientific—call it racism.

Medieval, religious Jew-hatred evolved into modern anti-semitism, a term and a movement invented by the radical pamphleteer and politician Wilhelm Marr in Germany in 1879. They should be recognized as different factors within the same tradition. Both passions are infused with a pathological requisite to find someone to *resent*.[26]

CHAPTER NINE

The Jewish Question

—⚬—

To answer feeds the vehemence of the attacks. Not to answer seems unmanly, and gives the enemies a chance to say our silence acknowledges our guilt.

RABBI HENRY PEREIRA MENDES,
Sephardic spiritual leader of Congregation Shearith Israel
in New York City, to Louis Marshall, president of the
American Jewish Committee[1]

BY THE summer of 1920 the Jewish community in America was faced with a complicated dilemma: how to counter Henry Ford's considerable efforts to spread his antisemitic views without adding fuel to his fire—and how to coax both "uptown" and "downtown" Jewish leaders into making a concerted stand. Three men, Jacob Schiff, Cyrus Adler, and Louis Marshall, joined forces in a triumvirate of *yahudim* elite and challenged the Flivver King's efforts.[2]

The leading representative light was Jacob Schiff (1847–1920), head of the banking firm of Kuhn, Loeb and Company.[3] Ironically, it was Schiff and his bank that, alongside the Warburgs (subsequently related by marriage), became the "symbol par excellence" of malevolent Jewish financiers in the pages of the *Dearborn Independent.*[4] The son of a dealer in shawls who became a stockbroker, Schiff was born in Frankfurt-am-Main. From childhood, he knew

Hebrew well and was a constant reader of the Bible, "calling it the book that had the greatest influence on him." By the age of fourteen, Jacob had already left school. After a few years in the Frankfurt mercantile milieu, the young man was itching to leave for America. In August 1865, he arrived in New York. Over the ensuing decade, during a time when the number of Jews in New York City catapulted to well over 100,000, Schiff became a naturalized citizen, securely integrated within the tight company of "uptown" German Jews. He married into the prosperous Solomon Loeb family, rose to partner in the powerful and venerable Kuhn, Loeb investment house, built a new mansion on Fifth Avenue, joined the Reform Temple Emanu-El, and sent his children, Mortimer and Frieda, to private schools.

From his early association with Kuhn, Loeb—he took charge in 1885, upon Loeb's death—Jacob Schiff worked to develop favorable reciprocal connections in other countries, as far away as Japan and China, and helped to make the com-

pany into a powerful contender not only in Europe but around the world. By the turn of the century, Kuhn, Loeb was second in size only to the House of Morgan. Not long after, Schiff made overt forays beyond pure business dealings into the more delicate world of international Jewish affairs, personally intervening with President Theodore Roosevelt on behalf of persecuted Jews in Romania and Russia; in fact, from the 1890s until czarist Russia's fall in 1917, Schiff was engaged in a

Jacob Schiff

virtual "private war" against that country. He was alert for discrimination, exclusionary practices, and slurs against Jews, socially and in the newspapers; with respect to Thomas Edison, the banker's acerbic pen was quick to act in the spirit of righteousness.

In the decade before World War I, Schiff "reached the pinnacle of his career." More and more in the public eye, he persisted in trying to distinguish business life from Jewish life. This schism became increasingly difficult to maintain as Schiff's natural inclination to seek power among the Jewish "stewards" who were his contemporaries—Louis Marshall, Cyrus Adler, Oscar Straus, Judah Magnes, Mayer Sulzberger, and others—grew stronger and stronger, at the same time that amicable ties with Christian capitalists were likewise required of him.

Schiff's philanthropic generosity toward "the deserving poor" was seemingly inexhaustible. Intense biblical immersion had created in him an abiding belief in the sacredness of *tzedakah*—the performance of good deeds as a good Jew's obligation to God.[5] Within a few years of his arrival in the United States, he had already made a modest gift to Mount Sinai Hospital. By mid-life, Schiff was supporting institutions as diverse as the American Jewish Farmers, Montefiore Hospital, the Industrial Removal Office, the Jewish Publication Society, the Stephen Wise Free Synagogue, the Lillian Wald Settlement House, and many other such havens for European newcomers on the Lower East Side, including the Educational Alliance.

Schiff struggled for his entire life with the problem of Zionism, linked in his philosophy to the "extreme" of nationalism—both ideologies posing as incentives to antisemitism. The dilemma was exacerbated by the influx of immigrants before World War I. Schiff and his well-to-do, quasi-assimilated colleagues were patronizing in their approach to the matter of what to do about and with their "co-religionist" *yidden* from Eastern Europe. On the one hand, Schiff (who never learned to read Yiddish) fought for the right of unrestricted immigration to America; on the other, once the "downtown" hordes had arrived, Schiff believed that he should have a say in where they lived, going so far as to sponsor resettlement efforts in the South and Midwest, anywhere outside the ghettos within which, he believed, Jews should not be constrained.

Zionism had its sources in the pluralism of Theodore Herzl, and so, if most of the masses adhered to that way of thinking, then the Jews could face trouble maintaining their solidarity. "Speaking as an American," Schiff declared, "I cannot for a moment concede that one can be at the same time a true American and an honest adherent of the Zionist Movement." He feared the establishment of "a nation within a nation." What could possibly appear more threatening to the antisemites than that image of the Jews?

During the first years of World War I, Schiff expressed pacifist views and was vilified as partisan and pro-German. For a brief period in 1915, his activities dovetailed with Henry Ford's peace mission to preserve American neutrality. It was not long before Kuhn, Loeb became the subject of deep suspicion. Schiff was caught on an untenable middle ground, as the convenient nativist phrase "German-Jewish bankers" entered the public discourse, sullying Jacob Schiff's impeccable reputation and wobbling the tightrope upon which he and others of his milieu had balanced so deftly for half a century. The popular equivalence of "Jew=Bolshevik" followed soon thereafter with the overthrow of the czar in the spring of 1917.

In the final year of Schiff's life—when he acknowledged for the first time the "chaotic" situation among American Jewish leadership—he cautiously endorsed the *principle* of a Jewish homeland, but one that would be free of ideological imperatives and would not cause Jews in America to forget that they still had to tend to their situation at home. "There is a great difference," he told the members of the Zionist Organization of America at their annual dinner on February 1, 1920, in New York City, "between a national homeland and a self-governing nation. We are not prepared to build a nation in a land where today there are practically no Jews."[6]

In the winter and spring leading up to the first inflammatory outbursts of the *Dearborn Independent*, Schiff's global preoccupations spread into the realm of Jewish war relief efforts and the progress of the Joint Distribution Committee, "the fate of our brethren . . . and the plight of terribly suffering Jewry in the Near East."[7] There was also continuous distraction caused by the recently established American Jewish Congress, scheduled to convene in Philadelphia in early June. Schiff had neither hope for nor patience with yet another demonstration that Jews were organizing themselves. He worried, on the contrary, (and prophetically) that publicity about the A.J.C. would exacerbate "that terrible prejudice that has been oppressing us for so long."

"There has been a woeful lack of the spirit of amity and compromise," Schiff wrote in weary despair to his friend Louis Marshall on April 24, one month before Ford's inaugural "International Jew" article hit the newsstands. "Obstinacy and willfulness have done their share to produce the present hopeless condition of the world. I find that my habitual optimism has been strained almost to the breaking point. The Jews, too, seem to have eaten of the insane root. They seem to think that . . . all that is necessary to do is to hold a convention or congress, national or international, and that by means of rhetoric and denunciatory resolutions our age-long sorrows can be ended."[8]

On June 9, Schiff, his health failing, strongly cautioned Cyrus Adler and Marshall against taking any concerted effort to discredit the *Dearborn Independent:* "If we get into a controversy we shall light a fire, which no one can foretell how it will become extinguished, and I would strongly advise therefore that no notice be taken of [the articles] and the attack will soon be forgotten."[9] The elder statesman's moderating warning came too late. The fires raged even more wildly through the summer and beyond.

Jacob Schiff died on September 25, 1920, three days after fasting for Yom Kippur, the Jewish Day of Atonement.

THE SECOND member of the trio, Cyrus Adler (1863–1940), was born in Van Buren, Arkansas, the son of German immigrants from the first wave who arrived in America before the middle of the nineteenth century. Adler remained proud of his Americanness throughout his life. His mother, Sarah, was a member of the Sulzberger family; when her husband, Samuel, died, the family moved to Philadelphia, where four-year-old Cyrus was raised by his uncle, David Sulzberger. In 1883, Cyrus graduated from the University of Pennsylvania and embarked upon the study of law with his cousin, Mayer Sulzberger. However, the young man discovered that he was at heart a scholar of antiquity, and he shifted careers, enrolling at Johns Hopkins University in Baltimore to pursue a doctorate in semitics.[10]

Cyrus Adler

Adler joined the faculty of Johns Hopkins in 1887, then moved on to become librarian of the Smithsonian Institution in Washington. He was one of the founding fathers of the American Jewish Historical Society in 1892. From this important platform, the erudite Adler advocated the supreme importance of Judaism as a proper *intellectual* discipline in its own way as valid as the observance of traditional synagogue rituals. Thus he served with enthusiasm as editor of the "Jews in America" section in the omnibus *Jewish Encyclopedia* published by Funk and Wagnalls, and he crusaded tirelessly through his work in the Jewish Publication Society to promote the responsibility of American Jews to learn more about their heritage.

During the late 1890s, in the wake of the First Zionist Congress in Switzerland, Adler weighed in with his views on this agitating movement. He struck a chord similar to Jacob Schiff's in his belief that, as espoused by political Zionism, a Jewish state might well be an appropriate goal for the refugees in Eastern Europe; however, *American* Jews must preserve and protect their internal identity,

and in their own country. In succeeding years, even with the advent
of the harsh Russian pogroms (and the bloody, antisemitic oppres-
sion of the Balkan Wars of 1912–1913), Adler flatly rejected elabo-
rations on the separatist-Zionist ideal expressed in subsequent
congresses, preferring to oppose restrictionist legislation and push
for free and open immigration to America. Adler persisted in his
dismissive view of Zionism as "an expression of mere material
nationalism." It was one thing to be devoted to rebuilding a homeland; it was quite another to be dedicated to the essential tenets of
the Jewish *religion.* "I have never felt any fear of the disappearance
of the Jewish people," he said, "as long as Judaism survived."[11]

Toward that end, at the turn of the century Adler—in concert
with Schiff and Marshall—recruited the distinguished English
rabbinic scholar Solomon Schechter to leave Cambridge University
and come to New York City to head the Jewish Theological
Seminary, an institution Adler believed would "unite the various fac-
tions of American Jewry ... and develop worthy leaders of *Israel in
America.*"[12]

Under Schechter's leadership over the ensuing decade, the Jewish Theological Seminary became the wellspring for the United
Synagogue of America and the nucleus for the Conservative movement of American Judaism. Adler was elected president of the
board of trustees of the seminary, and thereafter extended his passionate commitment to identity-formation of Jews in the United
States "as a religious and social body" by helping to found the
American Jewish Committee in 1906.

When Adler announced that he envisioned the A.J.C. as an
organization "which may act for all of [us] with authority ... and
with a sane and conservative tone ... on behalf of the oldest settled
Jews" and when he insisted upon "quiet diplomacy on behalf of Jewish causes," he set a theme that would come to characterize his public persona when he was forced to deal with the *Dearborn
Independent.* Adler never warmed to the idea of Jews drawing attention to themselves as Jews "when the facts have no relation to being

a Jew or to Jewishness." He told Adolph S. Ochs, publisher of the *New York Times*, in February of 1912, "If we want to remove the use of the word in scandalous connections because it has nothing to do with the scandal, we must also remove it from the honorable connection if it has nothing to do with the honor."[13]

With the advent of World War I, divisions were heightened within the already short-tempered leadership of the American Jewish Committee. Accusatory barbs were flung against the so-called elitists from the offices of the newly founded Yiddish newspaper, *Der Tog* (The Day), edited by Herman Bernstein, emblematic of the widening gap between "downtown" and "uptown." This irrepressible behavior pained Adler greatly. In this respect he sided with Jacob Schiff in feeling entitled to call the shots for the behavior of all American Jews, no matter what end of the socioeconomic spectrum they inhabited—including those Lower East Side "Socialists" who had the nerve to publish a newspaper on Saturday in Yiddish, which Adler (like Schiff) could not understand.

The war also inspired Zionists to bring back to the fore their idea of an American Jewish Congress with democratically elected (and therefore more representative) members, an attempt to rebalance power among the leadership of American Jewry. Adler and Marshall were adamantly against this initiative, which they viewed as "too public...just so much noise," "politically intrusive," and therefore dangerous to the welfare of already-endangered Jewish communities.

In the aftermath of the Armistice, a postwar "America for Americans" nativistic fervor swept the land, and Adler and his colleagues were again forced to divide their energies between rumblings of discrimination at home, and—via the work of the Joint Distribution Committee—the welfare of their brethren abroad. Adler was chosen by the American Jewish Committee to represent it at the Paris Peace Conference. He was a vocal supporter of the League of Nations. At the end of the summer of 1919, he returned to a hothouse climate of "Jewish factionalism" in the United States.

Within four months, Adler received a copy of the "much-discussed" *Protocols of the Elders of Zion* from Louis Marshall, who told his friend that although the work might appear to be "exceedingly silly" at first glance, the documents had already been circulated within government circles and so "must be reckoned with." Adler "set them down as the work of a disordered mind...My advice," he told Marshall, "is that you initiate an investigation both as to the origin and circulation of this document through the people from whose hands you secured it... [We must] denounce it for the fraud that it is." Still, Adler took his accustomed high road at this crucial moment, for he honestly believed that the most civilized defense of all against antisemitism would be for American Jews to "enlighten" Gentiles by "becoming even more exemplary in their conduct."[14]

WITH ninety-five cents in his pocket, nineteen-year-old Jacob Marshall arrived in New York City from Germany. The year was 1849. He went to work for the railroads and wended his way upstate, settling in Syracuse. Six years later, established in the hide and leather business, Jacob married Zilli Strauss. On December 14, 1856, Louis, the first of their six children was born. From childhood, Louis Marshall was a scholar and linguist. All the way through high school—even as he helped in the family business, buying skins from trappers and salting hides—Louis applied himself to learning French, German, Latin, Greek, and, of course, Hebrew. He also wrote an indignant eleventh-grade essay in defense of Shylock as "the only real human and consistent character" in *The Merchant of Venice*.[15]

Taking the opposite path of his eventual colleague and "intimate collaborator" Cyrus Adler, Marshall—the third member of the triumvirate—turned from bookish pursuits to the profession of law. He apprenticed in the Syracuse offices of Nathaniel B. Smith and then, harnessing a prodigious memory for facts and citations, did double time at Columbia Law School, taking the first-year set of classes in the afternoon simultaneous with second-year courses in the morning. In 1878, Marshall was admitted to the bar. Over the ensuing sixteen years, he made his mark in Syracuse as an energetic and devoted citizen across a spectrum of legal and religious activities ranging from the New York State constitutional convention to nature conservation and voting rights to the daily community affairs of his neighborhood Temple Concord.

In 1894, having outgrown the hospitable, comfortable boundaries of his hometown, Marshall accepted the invitation of Samuel Untermyer to join as a partner in his law firm in New York City, thus gaining entrée to the established German Jewish Reform community there. Through the Untermyer family, Marshall met their cousin, Florence Lowenstein; the couple were married in 1895 and

Louis Marshall

took up residence in a brownstone on East Seventy-Second Street where they raised four children. Possessed of an enduring fondness for nature, Marshall purchased several acres near Lower Saranac Lake and built a house there for weekend retreats. But he was never one to relax. Even in the country, he was plagued by insomnia and worked around the clock.

Setting down roots in New York City marked the beginning of Marshall's inevitable, ever-deeper involvement over the next quarter-century with Jewish affairs on a broader scale. He joined Temple Emanu-El and eventually became its president. He joined the board of the Jewish Theological Seminary and in 1905 became chairman. He served on Mayor Seth Low's committee to help remedy conditions on the Lower East Side. At the same time, together with Jacob Schiff and others, Marshall set up the *Yidishe Velt*, a newspaper that was meant to be "everything that existing Yiddish newspapers [*Forvert* and *Tageblatt*] are not, namely, clean, wholesome, religious in tone." With its patronizing attitude toward "Oriental" Jews, propagandizing for "Americanism," and advocating gratitude for all that the *yahudim* were doing for those less fortunate, the *Yidishe Velt* was doomed to failure. As Irving Howe trenchantly observed, "Uptown was uptown, downtown downtown, and it would take another half-century in the warmth of affluence before the twain could meet."[16]

Joining forces with Adler and Schiff as they feared growing discord and decentralization in Jewish communal life, Louis Marshall began in 1906 to advocate the formation of an American Jewish Committee, to, as he put it, "make order out of chaos." In so doing, Marshall struck a self-contradictory theme that would come back to haunt him fifteen years later when he was drawn—passionately, despite himself—into the Ford debacle. "I am trying to avoid, more than anything else," he wrote to Rabbi Joseph Stolz, "the creation of a *political* organization." Both Adler and Schiff cautioned that the only way this committee could be made to work was if it would "unite all elements that might possibly seek to father a national movement . . . to bring into this organization men of every shade of opinion . . . everybody who, if outside of it, would be a freelance, and a power for evil." This underlying, presumptive desire to round up (or co-opt) other segments of American Jewry cast the well-intentioned but hermetic committee in an "oligarchic" light until the 1940s. Marshall was president of the A.J.C. from 1912 until his death seventeen years later.[17]

In 1915, Louis Marshall passionately argued the landmark miscarriage-of-justice case of *Leo Frank v. the Sheriff of Fulton County, Georgia*. The young Jew was convicted of murder in Atlanta, and lynched. From that pivotal moment, Marshall dedicated even greater energy to fighting all manner of civil liberty discrimination against Jews, in schools, the professions, the corporate workplace, the armed forces, YMCAs, private and university clubs, summer hotels—as well as in the complicated arena of immigration restric-

tion. In wartime, relief for Eastern European Jews preoccupied
Marshall just as it did Schiff and Adler; he joined these two men in
their opposition to the Zionist image of Palestine as the only viable
place for modern Jews to gather permanently in an ideal and final
return from exile. With the fall of the czar, Marshall came to accept
the more moderate tenets of the Balfour Declaration and also went
on record as supporting the League of Nations. But he was never
taken into the complete confidence of the Zionist leadership.

After the war and the Paris Peace Conference, Marshall's attentions reverted to overt domestic antisemitism. He argued against
the contention that the United States was a Christian government.
Marshall was the first of his circle to point out the racial biases in
Stanford President David Starr Jordan's writing and to prove the
popular influence of Jordan's tract, *The Unseen Empire*. During the
years of the Red Scare, Marshall was astute in his observation that
"Bolshevism is the creation of non-Jews," asserting that "the Jew is
not by disposition a radical. He is essentially conservative, wedded
to the ideals of his forefathers."

Then Louis Marshall read the May 22 and 29, 1920, issues of
the "insidious and pernicious" *Dearborn Independent*. The incendiary
spectre of "the mob spirit," in Jacob Schiff's metaphor "enkindled by
mere suggestion," flared into public view, and the respected Jewish
attorney who had up until now consecrated his life to scrupulous
behind-the-scenes diplomacy in defense of his people had no choice
but to change tactics and confront Henry Ford.[18]

The second openly antisemitic issue of the *Dearborn Independent*
exploited an analogy that would become frightening in its implications over the decades to come: the Jew reviled as an unhealthy irri-
tant "encysted in the flesh" of the body politic. With special emphasis
upon the situation in Germany, the writer noted the parlous state of
"national hygiene" overseas, fearing that the economic collapse that
descended upon Germany after the Armistice would only become
worse as the Jewish virus spread wider and wider. As bracing tonic
against this disease in America, the *Dearborn Independent*, unlike the

German press, was not dominated by Jews. Rather, Henry Ford's newspaper, distinguished from those in Berlin, Munich, Frankfurt, and "their spiritual dependents," stood proudly as an Anglo-Saxon bulwark against "the most closely organized power on earth, even more than the British Empire . . . the journalistic performance of *All-Judaan* . . . controlling the world's sources of news."[19]

These assertions drove Louis Marshall to take direct action. He dispatched a telegram to Henry Ford accusing him of making "palpable fabrications." He went on to say, "They constitute a libel upon an entire people who had hoped that at least in America they might be spared the insult, the humiliation and the obloquy which these articles are scattering throughout the land and which are echoes from the dark middle ages." Marshall asked Ford point-blank "whether these offensive articles have [his] sanction . . . and whether you shall remain silent when your failure to disavow them will be regarded as an endorsement of them by the general public. . . Three million of deeply wounded Americans are awaiting your answer."[20]

Marshall received an immediate, harsh response from the Dearborn Publishing Company: "Your rhetoric is that of a Bolshevik orator. You mistake our intention. You misrepresent the tone of our articles. . . These articles shall continue and we hope you will continue to read them and when you have attained a more tolerable state of mind we shall be glad to discuss them with you." A.J.C. board member Louis L. Berlin, president of Prest Sentinel Publishing Company in Chicago, was among many others who sent letters and telegrams of protest to Ford by the end of May. Berlin received an even more acerbic reply: "Here is a world fact," declared the unnamed spokesman for the Dearborn Publishing Company. "The astounding facility with which a numerically inferior race maintains a degree of control which makes them the virtual ruler of many countries. How is this to be accounted for? The fact is here and it calls for explanation. . . The Dearborn Independent believe[s] that openness of statement is sanitary."[21]

On June 5, Marshall fired back to the anonymous editorial correspondent: "Your telegram in answer to my personal message to Henry Ford has just been received from which I infer that your answer is authorized by him and betokens his sanction of the articles in the *Dearborn Independent* to which I have taken exception in words that I shall be able to justify." Against his better judgment, Marshall henceforth could not remain silent. Surprised by the depth of his own vehemence, nevertheless, from the outset Marshall pushed for "the matter [to] be brought out in the open... [we must] hit it as hard as possible," and he set out upon a nonstop, day-by-day effort to rally the A.J.C. troops.[22]

This was far easier said than done. Four days later Jacob Schiff sent a cautionary message expressing fear of the result if Ford's wrath were further provoked. The august Schiff's dignified and temporizing disposition continued to cast a powerful shadow over his disciples: Cyrus Adler was not as certain of which way to go as his friend Marshall seemed to be, answering Schiff that "while I hate to 'lay down' under the [Ford] attack," he did concur with the elder statesman that "such a controversy in the American press would exaggerate what is already too much exaggerated there about Jewish affairs."[23]

Further complicating matters was the local-level intervention already underway—at this moment unknown to Adler, Marshall, and the New York mandarins—by Rabbi Leo Franklin, since 1899 leader of Detroit's most important Reform Temple, Beth El. On the evening of May 22, the Wednesday Night Club had assembled as usual at the Phoenix Social Club in downtown Detroit for their weekly convocation. The atmosphere in this group of twenty prominent Jewish professionals and businessmen, usually a hubbub of talk and vigor, was unusually somber that night as they silently read the inaugural issue of the *Dearborn Independent.* "Such venom could only come from a Jew-hater of the lowest type," wrote Rabbi Franklin in his diary, "and here it was appearing in a newspaper owned and controlled by one whom the Jews had counted among their friends. It was veritably a bolt out of the blue."

The consensus among the Wednesday Night Club was that surely Mr. Ford did not know anything of this matter. As soon as it came to his attention, the men hoped, "he would vigorously deny it and make those who were responsible for it pay the penalty of their cruel defamations of a whole people." They decided to let the matter rest and to "wait patiently" for the following week's issue—only to discover with horror that "the second article was more full of

Rabbi Leo Franklin in his study

rancor than the first had been, and that if the writer of this first article had dipped his pen in vitriol, he had used a more malignant poison when he wrote a second time."

As Henry Ford's former neighbor and longtime friend, Leo Franklin was in the unique position of being one of the only Jews whom Ford actually knew personally, and he had always been able to gain access to him with little difficulty through the years of Ford Motor Company expansion. With the astonishing publication of the second "International Jew" article, Franklin was delegated by his club colleagues—a task he accepted with great reluctance—to visit Ford in his office at Dearborn and discuss the newspaper campaign first hand. Franklin was greeted by E. G. Liebold and William J. Cameron, in Ford's company. They rambled on for "many hours." Franklin was in the middle of this "long conference" with Ford and the others when Louis Marshall's incensed June 3 telegram arrived. Franklin subsequently told Marshall that at that very juncture, "Ford [had] called in a stenographer" and was on the verge of being convinced that perhaps he should "dictate...and sign a letter" and "issue a partial retraction...which would appear in his paper or under his name ... when he changed his mind...It was the receipt of your message," Franklin wrote Marshall, "that changed [Ford's] decision on the matter."

Ford read the telegram, "his face flushed, he literally jumped out of his chair and he said, 'Let's go to lunch.'" The four men went over to another building across the way and dined with other executives of the company, during which time Ford did not make a single reference to their previous conversation. When the meal was over, Franklin suggested to Ford that they all adjourn to his office and finish drafting the letter. To the rabbi's amazement, Ford said flatly, "I am not going to sign it."[24]

The ensuing dispute between A.J.C. leader Marshall and the rabbi simmered on through the end of the year and was never resolved to either man's satisfaction. Marshall complained to anyone who would listen that the "puerile and amateurish" Rabbi Franklin naïvely assumed Ford was "the victim of evil advisers." Franklin insisted, both at the time of the immediate conflict and as long as seven years later, that "a little more patience and a little more tact exercised at the beginning of [Henry Ford's] crusade of vituperation might have brought about a recantation" and that "personal conferences" would have accomplished more than orchestrated letter-writing.[25]

Others were quick to weigh in. David Brown, a "pugnacious, charming, and charismatic" lay leader in Detroit, had served as head of the Joint Distribution Committee Fundraising Drive there, and was the first director of Detroit's Community Fund in 1918. "Do-It-Up" Brown, as the flamboyant, white-haired, blue-eyed philanthropist and businessman was affectionately known, was the preeminent donor to Temple Beth El, an intimate friend of Rabbi Franklin, and the first to defend him against Marshall's disdain. "*Every* person here is in the dark," Brown confided to fellow-midwesterner Jacob Billikopf, who had moved east via a succession of Jewish community-welfare positions in Chicago, Cincinnati, and Kansas City to become executive director of the Federation of Jewish Charities in Philadelphia. "What is on [Ford's] mind, and what does he hope to accomplish?" Brown stood on Franklin's side, reassuring Billikopf that the good rabbi had "been on the job since the very first article and informed me some few days ago [June 7 or 8] that he had hoped to accomplish something with [the Dearborn Publishing Company]." Brown had heard from Franklin of Marshall's untimely, threatening intervention and agreed that Marshall could "not make much progress" from New York City.[26]

Michigan Supreme Court Justice Henry Butzel was another prominent member of the Detroit Jewish lay leadership and also a Temple Beth El congregant. Justice Butzel had ruled against Henry Ford in the Dodge Brothers lawsuit four years earlier. He took a different perspective from Brown, implying to Marshall that Rabbi Franklin was "flattering himself as to what he might accomplish." Butzel confirmed that Ford's prejudices were longstanding, reporting to Marshall that the automaker and his cohorts "had for a long time past been gathering a complete library of antisemitic literature," and also filling Marshall in on the history of the E. G. Pipp fiasco, culminating in the journalist's high-minded resignation that past spring.[27]

COULD it be that only one year earlier, Rabbi Franklin had been feted as "one of the creators of the city's soul," on the occasion of his twentieth anniversary in the pulpit of Temple Beth El? How did he end up in this untenable bind, as the touchstone for the Detroit Jewish community's quandary about Henry Ford and simultaneously the object of Louis Marshall's scorn?[28]

Born March 5, 1870, in Cambridge City, Indiana, Leo Morris Franklin was the only son (he had four sisters) of Prussian-born tailor Michael Franklin and Rachel Levy. Franklin received his B.A. from the University of Cincinnati and was ordained as a rabbi from Hebrew Union College in 1892. He served as rabbi of Congregation Temple Israel in Omaha, Nebraska, from 1892–1899, marrying Omaha-born Hattie M. Oberfelder. While still in his twenties, Franklin was already known as a searching, eloquent—and idealistic—preacher. One of his prominent admirers was William Jennings Bryan, who often went to hear Franklin speak. Franklin's dreaminess, limited not only to his youth, may have evolved into a defect of character that Marshall perceived as naïveté.[29]

One of Franklin's Omaha sermons, dated November 13, 1896, provides some hint of that naïveté. In it, he approaches the question, *"Can Antisemitism Find a Foothold in America?"* He takes listening congregants swiftly through the entire historic span of "a whole people, scourged with the scourge of malice...the scape goat of the nations." The Jewish people persisted "patiently" through one suffering era after another—in Egypt, Babylon, Rome and the destruction of the Temple, Spain, the Crusades, France, serfdom in Germany, expulsion from England, all the way up to Russia and modern Germany—always "with Cain's mark set upon them, but without Cain's sin."

Surely then, when the Jewish people finally traversed "the vast expanse of ocean...to find freedom of speech and of thought... how shocking it was to find that there are men in this fair land who are as deeply steeped in bigotry as the most ignorant fanatics of Europe."

"Oh! Friends, what a blow it is unto idealism...to see harrowing prejudices before our very eyes in free America!" And where had

Rabbi Franklin come across this shocking example of bigotry? In the pages of the popular *Frank Leslie's Illustrated Weekly* issue of October 29, 1896, under the headline, "Down With the Jew." "It is the poison of German Anti Semitism transplanted to American soil," the Rabbi declares. The article was by Hermann Ahlwardt, an Austrian agitator who had come to the United States one year earlier to stir up anti-Jewish antagonism. Despite the fact that upon his arrival in New York City he was greeted by rotten eggs thrown by young Jews, Ahlwardt did gain outlets for his work in some of the more hostile periodicals. Rabbi Franklin warns that "Ahlwardt will find that America is not the place for him... [his] weed will not flourish in liberty's garden where the air is laden with the invigorating oxygen of freedom."

In a haunting phrase foreshadowing his encounter with Henry Ford's prejudices a quarter of a century later, young Rabbi Franklin concludes by expressing "pity for the few fanatics whose souls are yet in bondage."[30]

As the eleventh rabbi of Temple Beth El, Leo Franklin succeeded Louis Grossmann, who left to assist Isaac Mayer Wise at Congregation B'nai Jeshurun in Cincinnati in January 1899. The evangelical new Reform rabbi set forth as his goal "to revitalize Judaism" in his congregation. He reintroduced Friday evening services and inaugurated Sunday morning services as well; organized a children's choir and Bible classes for young people and adults. He revived Jewish festival days such as Purim and placed emphasis upon them as Jewish holidays with religious themes. He organized the Temple's Sisterhood and Brotherhood. He revitalized the Temple *Bulletin.* Four years later, the congregation moved from its outmoded quarters on Washington Avenue to the Albert Kahn-designed Temple on Woodward Avenue and Eliot Street, where it remained until 1922. Franklin wanted this new building to be what he called an "open temple," and he desired to bring more of an American democratic ethos into the congregation: "Judaism is my religion; America my country!" Thus, despite opposition from some of the older families in the community, he pushed for doing away with the wealthier congregants' tradition of purchasing pews, so that all members would be on "an absolute plane of equality."[31]

By 1912, Leo and Hattie Franklin had three children: Ruth, Margaret, and Leo. They built a house for their growing family at 26 Edison Avenue, two doors from Woodward Avenue on the north side of the street. Except for the home of attorney Horace Rackham (one of Ford's first investor-partners), there was only one other neighboring family on Edison at that time—Henry, Clara, and Edsel Ford had lived for four years at number 66, a big, red brick Italian Renaissance Revival–style house with landscaped grounds on four adjoining lots at the northeast corner of Second Avenue. It was to be the Ford's last residence in town before moving out to the Fair Lane Estate. Henry Ford used to drive by the Franklin home on his way over to Woodward and thence to the company's Piquette Street and Highland Park plants. Occasionally, he would stop his car for a cordial, perfunctory chat. One day about a year after the Franklins had settled in, mutual friend Albert Kahn, chief architect for the Ford Motor Company, approached Rabbi Franklin on Ford's behalf and asked if he "would be insulted if Mr. Ford presented [him] with a car." Why was this offer made through an intermediary? "Because," Kahn replied, "Mr. Ford was fearful lest [the rabbi] would misunderstand his motive." It was the first of seven customized Model T's that followed and which Franklin gratefully accepted—until the fateful summer of 1920.[32]

Even as he kept up a steady pace of innovation and "democratization" at Temple Beth El during his first two decades at the helm, Rabbi Franklin also assumed wider leadership roles within and beyond Jewish communal life. He founded and served as editor from 1901 to 1911 of the *Jewish American*, Detroit's first Anglo-Jewish weekly, published by the Chamber of Commerce. He was one of the co-founders of the United Jewish Charities, and in 1914 he established the Jewish Student Congregation at the University of Michigan in Ann Arbor, forerunner of the Hillel Society in colleges and universities across America. He reached out to the Conservative and Orthodox congregations of Detroit and its environs. He founded the Detroit Interdenominational Thanksgiving in 1906 and spoke often at church groups throughout the area in attempts "to bridge the gap between Jews and non-Jews."

However, Franklin's extensive journalistic, diplomatic, and philanthropic enterprises always took a back seat to his tireless efforts against discrimination. He was a member of the first executive committee of the Anti-Defamation League in 1913. In his role as chairman of the local Advisory Committee of the ADL—and in alliance with Henry Butzel's brother, Fred, an attorney—Franklin set up a Citizens' Vigilance Committee over the school curricula. Their first public endeavor was to lobby to eliminate the teaching of *The Merchant of Venice*. Franklin was outspoken in letters to W. N. Moffatt, superintendent of schools in Detroit, on the matter of employment of more Jews as teachers in the school system. After James Couzens resigned from the Ford Motor Company and took up the offices of police commissioner and then mayor of Detroit, he found himself head-to-head with Rabbi Franklin on the issue of restricting performances of *Merchant* in the city's theaters. When the Detroit Athletic Club refused to admit Jews, Franklin declined to attend any further community meetings there, stating that he could not "directly or indirectly accept the hospitality of that

"The Jew in the United States"
in the Dearborn Independent,
June 5, 1920

institution and retain my self-respect." For half a century, from
1900–1950, there were no Jews on the club's roster. The rabbi also
kept attuned to employment practices in the auto industry. He
heard that the Liberty Motor Car company had turned down a
"Jewess" who had applied for a clerical job and immediately wrote
to Percy Owen, president of the company, to complain.[33]

When the June 12 issue of the *Dearborn Independent* provocatively broached "The Jewish Question—Fact or Fancy?" the editors
said they were operating at a
disadvantage, because of "the
supersensitiveness of Jews and
non-Jews concerning the whole
matter ... [who] would prefer
to keep it in the hazy border-
lands of their thought, shrouded in silence." The desire to
sweep "the Question" under the
proverbial rug only leads to
further aggravation. Once
again, the editors wrote, the
issue is one of "control," far out
of proportion to the meager
number of Jews, at most recent
count making up only 3 percent of the American pop-
ulation. The commercially
successful "modern Jew" in
America prides himself as hav-

"The Jewish Question"
in the Dearborn Independent,
June 12, 1920

ing a monopoly on the values of "humanitarianism" in the host
society, making it even more difficult to criticize him, and to try to
"solve The Question... This series of articles is already being met
by an organized barrage of mail and wire and voice," the editors
complain indignantly, "every single item of which carries the wail
of persecution." The magnitude of protests against the articles after

a mere three weeks validates the editors' tautological contention that time-tested, historic antagonism hardens and strengthens "a race whose persistence has defeated the utmost efforts made for its extermination." the *Dearborn Independent* believes, in other words, that the lamentable behavior of the Jews has brought about the necessity to raise "the Question" among fair-minded non-Jews.

All of this despite the fact that not once is there any reference to a single, well-defined question. By invoking "the Jewish Question" in this reactive manner, without defining it—or, for that matter, asking it—the *Dearborn Independent* took another giant step into the antisemitic rhetorical tradition. This was a slogan with a long pedigree, traceable to the middle of eighteenth century England. At that time, the "Question" was whether a Jew born within the British dominions could be allowed to become a naturalized subject and own land. Similar questions were posed at this time in France and Germany: Could Jews "be permitted full commerce and traffick in the country?" The answer invariably fell back upon the universally held presumption that the Jews themselves, an isolated people by nature, had "no desire to be incorporated," and so there was no need to alter the status quo. Besides, if the Jews were allowed to own land, the next consequence would be their dominance of real estate.

During the period of emancipation in France, *La question sur les juifs* arose as a legislative matter in the National Assembly, and reappeared in 1834, four decades later, in the context of considering the citizenship status of Polish Jews. Upon his accession to the throne of Prussia, King Friedrich Wilhelm IV took a restrictive view of the degree of personal freedom he would allow Jews in his country. He preferred that they take on the status of a corporation within the larger context of the state as a whole; thus, the Jews could be *in, but not of,* the encompassing state of Prussia.

This political hairsplitting laid the groundwork for the defining essay by German Protestant theologian and philosopher Bruno Bauer, bringing *Die Judenfrage* (The Jewish Question) (1843) squarely into the modern framework—Is the Jew to be considered once and for all just like any other element in society or does he remain as part of an "extraneous community?" Bauer came down on the latter side; he believed that the Jew himself—obsessed with identity-preservation—had encouraged this way of perceiving him as someone ultimately "incompatible with the requirements of general emancipation."

However, "If the Jews want to become real," wrote Bauer, "they cannot achieve it in their *chimerical* nationality, only in the *real* nations of our time living in history... They have to sacrifice their disbelief in the other nations and the exclusive belief in their own nationality."

Thus did the Jewish Question evolve over the centuries into an ideological trap for the Jew, no matter how he may have wanted to respond. As a community issue, apart from a religious one, it was a powerful statement about the devaluation of Jews as full citizens; Bauer believed that "emancipation" (in the eighteenth-century sense) would never survive as a concept in modern society, as long as Jews so tenaciously preserved their collective identity. Bauer further castigated the Jew for "proclaiming that his religion was the highest principle of morality." And he concluded by warning that even though it might be feasible legislatively to circumscribe the political powers of the Jew, it would continue to be in the Jew's nature to find ways to "wield immense economic power," which could (in all seriousness) eventually lead to an all-out war on mankind.

Here is the crux of Bauer's Jewish Question, with its clarion call to the non-Jew. The rhetoric echoes so familiarly through the June 12 *Dearborn Independent* that it is reasonable to imagine Bauer's book as a cornerstone of the accumulating antisemitic texts stored away in the newspaper offices at the Ford tractor plant. Bringing the Question up to date with implications for 1920s Detroit, the *Independent* piece focused on the more-assimilated, socially ambitious, "new" German community, the Franklins and Butzels and Kahns, who had worked to be both Jews *and* Americans. Now they were reminded how easily their hard-won acculturation could be stripped away at any time, through accusations of tribalism emanating from Henry Ford's weekly.[34]

Not only the German Jews of Detroit felt the sting of Ford's threats. The word was spreading rapidly. Cyrus Adler noted with mild apprehension to Jacob Schiff and Louis Marshall that "the Jewish press all over the United States has itself taken up this subject. In both East and West I see editorials, and the chances are that Mr. Ford will get a form of publicity which will not be particularly helpful to him." For example, the Detroit Yiddish-language community weekly, *Der Veg* (The Way) fought back with a passion in its issue of June 14 against "the antisemites with silk shirts...Now 'our' Ford comes and rebukes us [in the *Dearborn Independent* of May 29] for the Germans, by saying that we are the cause of their misfortune."

In a riposte to the recent warnings about Jewish "dominance" voiced by Ford's newspaper, the editorial in *Der Veg* proclaimed, "One hears from Jewish leaders in every movement because they are the most talented; therefore one hears from Jewish activists in every new trend because they are more feeling, idealistic, and—purer. And precisely because of this, they hate us. Only because of this!!!"[35]

As for the patient and hopeful Rabbi Franklin, the most recent *Independent* article pushed him to the breaking point. He conceded to colleagues on the executive committee of the Anti-Defamation League that his recent meeting in Ford's office "showed all too clearly that the ordinary methods of appeals to reason and justice would be of no avail." To the *Detroit News*, Franklin said, "Few thinking men have given any credence to the charges offered against the Jews. But Ford's publication has besmirched the name of the Jews in the eyes of the great majority, and especially in the small towns of the country, where Ford's word is taken as gospel. He has fed the flames of anti-Semitism throughout the world."[36]

On June 14, Franklin returned the customized Model T he had

most recently received from Henry Ford, with a melancholy letter blaming "the last issue of the *Dearborn Independent* [wherein] with the desire of establishing the truth of an unfortunate idea that has taken possession of you, you are determined to continue the series of articles that must inevitably tend to poison the minds of the masses against the Jews. You claim that you do not intend to attack all Jews but ... [I hope] that you may come to realize the enormity of the injury which you are doing to a[n entire] people." The reply to these painful sentiments came back through the correspondence of E. G. Liebold, chastising the rabbi and hoping in return that "conditions will so adjust themselves as to eventually convince you that Mr. Ford's position is correct."[37]

Within days, a genuinely astonished Henry Ford phoned the rabbi to ask, "What's wrong, Dr. Franklin? Has something come between us?"[38]

Ford's apologists sounded the same incredulous refrain. Fred Black recalled how caught off guard Ford was when the rabbi returned the car: "He was very much surprised that the Jews he considered good Jews were opposed to this. I think he expected people like Rabbi Franklin, who had been a very good friend of his, not to be so opposed to this campaign." Authorized corporate biographer James Martin Miller was similarly appalled that Franklin did not understand that the newspaper articles, "in their frank and open discussion of the Question," were addressed as a sanitizing remedy only to "a certain type of Jew, [to] open up the way for those Jews' self-correction."[39]

CHAPTER TEN

Retaliation

—⌀—

It is the anti-Semite who defines the Jew. The Jew then has no alternative but to define himself.

Jean-Paul Sartre,
Reflexions sur la question juive (Anti-Semite and Jew), 1946

AN ENDURING fear of the antisemite is the image—one might even go so far as to call it the specter—of Jewish "unity," and it was upon this dimension of the Jewish problem that the editors of the *Dearborn Independent* next chose to shine their searchlight. This chord was first struck in the issue of June 19. It would be reprised in the issue of August 28 and on at least three more occasions, in February, March, and November of 1921. "To this end we must organize. Organize, in the first place, so that the world may have proof of the extent and the intensity of our desire for liberty," was the above-the-headline citation taken from a speech on Zionism by Justice of the Supreme Court Louis D. Brandeis, "Organize, in the second place, so that our resources may become known and be made available...Organize, organize, organize, until every Jew must stand up and be counted." The provocatively titled essay, *Anti-*

Semitism—Will It Appear in the U.S.? went on to answer its own query by warning against "the united action by which ... [is] attained Jewish commercial success."

The gadfly *Der Veg* was quick to respond, this time with a sardonic essay by Yisrael Rabinovitsh (pen name "Yisraeli"), a prolific Yiddish journalist and writer who lived in Montreal: "A Jew, according to the anti-Semite of the *Dearborn Independent,* is a synonym for superhuman strength and world domination." But on the contrary, "Our kingdom," Yisraeli pointed out, "is not more than a piece of fiction of anti-Semitic minds."[1]

The concept of covenanted community is among the most ancient and revered in Jewish history. It is found in the traditional national and spiritual Hebrew phrases for the Jewish people: *Am Israel,* the *People* of Israel; and *Keneseth Israel,* the *Congregation* of Israel. The ideal that it was incumbent upon Jews to come together in these representative ways can be found as far back as "the process of electing kings in ancient Israel, constituting the Council of the Four Lands in late-medieval Poland, or forming communities in the modern United States." The Hebrew root word for this dynamic of *congregating* as an organized community of equals is *kahal* or *kehillah,* and any ten male Jews can create such a self-governing group.

To the editors of the *Dearborn Independent,* the imagined machinations transpiring within these *kehillot* represented a constant source of potential harm to the surrounding society. Did not the Seventeenth *Protocol* of the Elders of Zion warn of this ever-present possibility, when it spoke of "the obligation to denounce apostates or any person known to be opposed to the *Kahal*"? "When our kingdom comes," the *Protocols* reputedly said in the oracular voice of imagined rabbis, "it will be necessary for all subjects to serve the state in a similar manner..." As defined in the *Independent,* "The Kahal is the traditional Jewish political institution during the dispersal of the race among the nations." As far as the *Independent* was concerned, the kehillah of antiquity had now reached modern iteration in one dangerous organization, the New York Kehillah.[2]

It made sense that the first efforts to found some kind of single, coherent Jewish self-government agency in prewar America—predicated upon the sixteenth and seventeenth century Eastern European model—took place in New York City, home to more Jews than anywhere else in the country. The valiant man who took up the kehillah presidential reins was the San Francisco–born Judah Magnes (1877–1948), the young, magnetic, and talented associate rabbi of Temple Emanu-El and one of the founders and then the secretary of the American Zionist Federation. Magnes believed that "uptown" and "downtown," Eastern European and Western European, cosmopolitan and Yiddishist—all must work together under his banner of Jewish peoplehood. He was determined to find a way to honor Jewish culture *within* American culture: "We must, all of us, accommodate ourselves to our surroundings," Magnes preached from his Emanu-El pulpit in February 1909. "But this does not, however, by any means, imply that therefore a man's traditional national culture must be abandoned... [A] parallelism is desirable."

Judah L. Magnes

More than 350 delegates representing more than 200 Jewish organizations convened at the founding conference of the Kehillah in October 1908. The organization was divided into linked bureaus, each one meant to focus upon a different aspect of Jewish activity, from education, to industry, to controlling the special problems of burgeoning crime and social hygiene in the ghetto. Magnes hoped through his quest for order to teach New York Jews that they were "one people with a common history and common hopes." They would set an example for the establishment of *kehillot* in other cities in America. Sadly, this "ambitious goal" was "doomed from

the start . . . disunity and contentiousness remained a constant" in
the fourteen-year lifespan of the Kehillah until 1922. The organization was boycotted from the outset by radical socialist and labor
groups. The Yiddish *Tageblat* newspaper was ambivalent about the
influence of Schiff and Marshall, saying "we wish them to work
with us and not over us." Despite Schiff's philanthropic generosity,
especially in the area of education, the Kehillah was plagued by
financial problems from the outset.

By 1918, the Jewish Communal Register of New York City, published by the Kehillah, listed an astounding 3,997 organizations in
the metropolitan area, one for every 375 Jews. In the war years, the
competing American Jewish Congress assumed a more prominent
presence on the scene. Despite the connotations of its name, the
congress created a "cacaphony" of conflicting ideologies among
Jews rather than a synthesis of the proliferating "tribes."

Ironically, this was why the Kehillah failed. Its structure could
not keep pace with the accelerating arrival of Jews to these shores.
No single organization could possibly have appealed to all interests.
When war came, the attention of American Jews shifted to the fate
of their brethren overseas. Finally, Rabbi Magnes, who through
sheer force of his personality had provided institutional staying-
power, came reluctantly to understand that the Kehillah could not
exercise compulsory membership authority in the free and volun-
tary environment of America. It could merely hope to exercise
moral and spiritual—*not* ethnic—influence among Jews. In 1922,
Judah Magnes left for Palestine, where he became the first president of the Hebrew University of Jerusalem.[3]

To W. J. Cameron and E. G. Liebold, the continued "meekness" of
American citizens against the "clan solidarity" of the Jew was
tremendously frustrating. The very fact that the majority of the
American public had never even heard of this "center of Jewish
world power" called the New York Kehillah was the most convinc-

ing testimony to its subversive might as the "Judaized Tammany Hall." And yet, since the original Diaspora, the Jews always had to find a way to stick together, using a mode of coherence that defied the acceptable, Aryan definition. In East Coast America, that far-away "whispering gallery" known as the Kehillah was not only the glue that kept Jewish organizations "interlaced and dovetailed," it worked simultaneously as a crafty public-relations machine to produce the widespread illusion that Jews remained divided among themselves. How absurd, that Kehillah leaders sought to counteract the *Independent*'s assertions by protesting that their huge organization was weak. How absurd, that the Kehillah should try to convince God-fearing Americans that the Schiffs and Speyers and Warburgs were *not* in alliance with the "Polish Jews who monopolize the hat, cap, fur, garment and toy trades."[4]

It was therefore no coincidence that Rabbi Magnes was Louis Marshall's brother-in-law. Ever since he had stepped forward to defend Leo Frank, Marshall had been the "most powerful agent" linked to perpetuating the Jewish problem. He was the man who headed the American Jewish Committee, seeing to it that a member of his own family assumed control of the Kehillah; the man who consistently fought against restrictions in immigration from Eastern Europe; the man who insisted that any language pertaining to the identification of the United States as a Christian country be expurgated from public discourse. The *Independent* found this last crusade by the attorney Marshall especially distasteful—that a member of "a race which had no hand in creating the Constitution" possessed the audacity to question such nomenclature.[5]

Responding to these accusations came the knowing voice of E. G. Pipp, ploughing ahead with his *Weekly* as a local counterstress to the *Independent*. Pipp had been on the inside of the Ford machine. He knew better than any other journalist of Liebold's intimate trepidations. When he wrote back to his old boss, Mr. Ford, "You and your associates were never more mistaken in your lives [than in] picturing the Jews as one unified whole," Pipp was on the mark. The so-called Eighth Generation of Jews, those who characterized American Jewish presence from the late 1870s through World War I, lived through what is now understood to have been an organizational free-for-all, an era of great fragmentation in American Jewish life, when the boundaries of self-governance seemed to disappear, despite immense efforts toward unification rising in repeated waves.[6]

We need look no further than the workings of the executive committee of the American Jewish Committee to find evidence of great difficulty reaching common ground, insofar as deciding what, if anything, should be done about Henry Ford's recent behavior. At a meeting on June 23, 1920, in New York City, Cyrus Adler began by reading aloud to his colleagues Jacob Schiff's stern letter of two weeks earlier ("we shall light a fire ..."), cautioning against any premature reaction. Even though the A.J.C. governors readily admitted to being in "an anxious frame of mind" about the *Independent* articles, they felt that the agitated "Jewish press" editorials (such as they had seen from publications like *Der Veg* and *Tageblat*) advocating a consumer boycott against Ford products were impractical and in poor taste. Perhaps Marshall should write confidentially to selected editors of the Jewish (read Yiddish) newspapers and exercise quiet pressure upon them to tone down their separatist and all-too-visible rhetoric for the time being, advocate a posture of wait-and-see, and say that "a counter movement is not wise at the present time..." Now that they thought of it, perhaps the A.J.C. should write to all active members and ask them to clip news stories displaying evidence of antisemitic behavior around the nation as instigated by Ford's newspaper and forward them to the New York office, so that an archival brief could be assembled with an eye to future action. Perhaps it would be sagacious to purchase, say, 10,000 copies of a recently published book by the late Joseph Jacobs, a respected former professor at the Jewish Theological Seminary and editor of *The American Hebrew*, entitled *Jewish Contributions to Civilization* (1919). The volume could be sent, along with a well-constructed covering letter, "as an antidote" to "all sorts of

[Gentile] public men"—to launch an intelligent and educational "enlightenment" campaign dedicated to elevating commonly assumed perceptions of Jews, rather than needlessly antagonizing Ford by going head-to-head with him.[7]

Meanwhile, over the river in downtown Brooklyn, assisted by a part-time secretary, Boris Brasol had been huddled since early spring in a claustrophobic "nasty little office" in the Prince George Hotel, feverishly working to complete the American edition of his magnum opus, *The Protocols and World Revolution,* to be brought out by Small, Maynard & Company in Boston. At the same time, he was painstakingly developing a list of more than 4,000 people to receive the slim volume by direct mail order. "I know my enemy [the Jew] very well," Brasol wrote to a friend as publication neared. "I know his strength, his diabolical cunning, and his systematic treachery and yet I refuse to believe that the final victory will be his." The plain brown envelope version of the *Protocols* enjoyed robust sales. But Brasol craved more. When it soon became evident that his book was not going to be offered in Brentano's or any other respectable trade outlet—nor receive the kind of widespread attention he was anticipating in the mainstream review media—Brasol turned to friends in Dearborn for solace.

First, he offered encouraging commentary on the inaugural issue of the *Independent,* flattering the newspaper for making "numerous and frequent references … to the scheme for Jewish world domination." But then Brasol went on to complain to Cameron that the Judaeophobic message was still not getting across, because the *Independent* was not widely enough available on newsstands in New York City.

In late May or early June of 1920, a stenographer in Washington, D.C., made a copy of the complete Harris Houghton/Boris Brasol text of the *Protocols* for W. G. Eynon, district supervisor for Ford Motor Company operations in Delaware. On June 10, Eynon sent the English version of the *Protocols,* accompanied by the original Russian text, to E. G. Liebold.[8]

On June 26, three days after the American Jewish Committee decided to maintain its low profile, the text of the *Protocols* began to appear in the *Dearborn Independent*, starting with "The Seventh Protocol," a ringing manifesto about the Jews' need to control the press throughout the world. Over the ensuing three months, the *Protocols* was serialized and excerpted richly, freely, and systematically: On July 10, the "super-mind" Zionist Theodore Herzl was again vilified as one of the authors of the modern version of the *Protocols*. The July 24 issue featured a primer-like "Introduction to the 'Jewish Protocols,'" providing a brief history of their origins as rabbinical lectures promulgating the "secret Jewish Sanhedrin," and recommending them to "all those who are interested in the theory of Jewish World power." On August 7, the *Independent* disparaged the "purported statesmanship" of the *Protocols*, urging readers to exercise "alertness" in perusing the documents, because the Jews' obsessive insistence upon their identity as "The Chosen People" inspired cause for "alarm." On August 14, the focus shifted to an examination of the many ways in which the *Protocols* advocated a "breakdown of society [by the Jews] ... to wear out and exhaust the Gentiles by dissensions, animosities, feuds, [and] famine."

On August 21, the editors soberly proceeded to "a more detailed study of the connection between the *written* program of the documents and the *actual* program as it can be traced in real life." On September 11, the theme of Jewish control of the press was traced through all twenty-four sections of the *Protocols*. The September 18 issue published a warning against the Jews' ambition "to become rulers" and laid out the potential threat of continuing to allow the flag of Palestine to "fly without hindrance."

"If the *Protocols* had not been authentic, we never would have published them," said Liebold. "We took the *Protocols* at their face value of what the *Protocols* say is what happened. That's all we tried to do. In the various activities they [the Jews] performed, we could show a definite trend or definite instance of the actual things as set forth in the *Protocols* and where they took place."

Thirty years after the fact, Liebold still insisted, "That's even happening today. You can read the *Protocols* and find out exactly what's going on. I think I have it around [my office], because I never wanted it to get out of my hands." Here resides the crux of the matter as the *Protocols of the Learned Elders of Zion* embarks upon widespread American dissemination through the financial resources of the Dearborn Publishing Company: The antisemite cannot be bothered with empirical reality; neither should the *Protocols* be merely dismissed as a work of "fiction." Rather, the *Protocols* are dangerous because they treat fundamental abstractions and outright fantasies *as* reality. The true believers in the *Protocols* dehumanize people—Jews—about whom they do not possess any experiential knowledge.

Hannah Arendt has cautioned that the mission of the historian in confronting a complicated, multiversioned textual situation such as this is not to resolve to "discover" a forgery. *The fact that a patent forgery is being believed* is more meaningful to acknowledge as an outrage to common sense, as opposed to embarking upon exhaustive attempts to track down the ultimate source for the *Protocols* themselves.

It is useful to reflect upon Henry Ford's earlier dictum that "History is more or less the bunk," with the awareness that, as Arendt describes it, this kind of "backstairs literature" had become the main inspiration for rewriters of history by the 1920s. The goal of the fabricators of the *Protocols* and other such concoctions was "to reveal 'official' history [Ford's reference to the accepted textbooks] as a joke, to demonstrate a sphere of secret influences, of which the visible, traceable, known historical reality was only the outward façade erected to fool the people."[9]

PREOCCUPIED with the relentless flow of essays emanating from Dearborn, Cyrus Adler was blindsided when toward the middle of October he received an advance copy of a new antisemitic tract in a bright-red jacket, to be published by the reputable firm of G. H. Putnam & Son, called *The Cause of World Unrest*. An extended series of essays on the *Protocols*, the text was introduced with a new preface by H. A. Gwynne, editor of the *London Morning Post*, wherein the articles had first appeared. It finally dawned upon Adler that "we have lost a lot of time by following the advice of Mr. Schiff, who I am sure did not realize the extent of the propaganda... At no time, in my opinion, even in the darkest days of the Middle Ages, has the danger been so great or the enemy so powerful or united... There are reactionary forces hitting at the Jew ... endeavoring to bring back the old order as it existed before the War." The formidable Jacob Schiff had passed away three weeks earlier. Adler felt free now to try to break out of his respectful silence: "It is really necessary now for decent Jews to show themselves among men," he told his wife, Racie.

Upon receipt the same day of his personal copy of the book, Louis Marshall noticed that *The Cause of World Unrest* advertised the *Protocols* on its back cover. Marshall was so incensed that he dashed off a letter directly to Major George Haven Putnam, condemning him for disseminating among the American people "these outpourings of malice, intolerance and hatred, this witches' broth of violent poison ... this stupid drivel ... seeking to make the Jew, as he has been in all the centuries, the scapegoat of autocracy... Mr. Putnam, whoever touches pitch is defiled... [You are] sheltering yourself behind the bulwarks of an infamous pasquinade of the guttersnipe variety."[10]

Major Putnam did not try very strenuously to defend himself. He fell back upon the freedom of speech argument that he felt was every American's right. He pointed out that he was not endorsing the authenticity of the *Protocols*, merely putting them on view for the public to judge. He also leaned heavily upon the well-worn anti-Bolshevik rationale, saying that he was acting to expose that pernicious movement and prevent its further invasion of native shores. And finally, he wrote, if the book was good enough for British society, then surely it was worthy of American consumption.

In the end, after a few days (during which time he also received the brunt of Oscar Straus's anger) Putnam agreed *"not* to proceed." However, unbound copies of *World Unrest* suspiciously found publication in New York City by an establishment called "The Peter Beckwith Company" within one month after Putnam's hasty concession to Marshall.[11]

Marshall had barely caught his breath when the Dearborn Publishing Company produced its most damaging literature to date, a twenty-five cent, 250-page paperbound anthology of articles published in the *Independent* from the inaugural issue of May 22 through the issue of October 2, called *The International Jew: The World's Foremost Problem.* A brief preface dated October 1920,

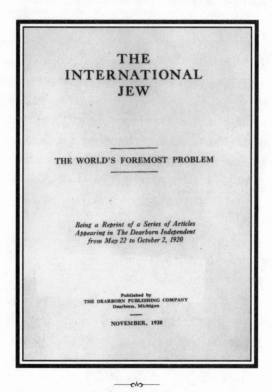

The International Jew,
Volume I, November 1920

introduced "this little book" as "the partial record of an investigation of the Jewish Question," and pointed out that the editors felt
this was the only way to satisfy the huge demand for back issues of
the newspaper. Estimates of the size of this first edition—three
more similar anthologies would follow over the next eighteen
months—ranged from 200,000 to 500,000 copies, many of which
were sent gratis to "locally influential citizens, especially clergymen, bankers, and stockbrokers."

Liebold wisely never copyrighted *The International Jew*, "and
therefore we had no lawful authority to stop anybody [from publishing it themselves]." The book went on to be translated into sixteen different languages—including six editions in Germany alone
between 1920 and 1922. This infamous tract has remained in the
public domain for more than eighty years. "All in all," the historian
Norman Cohn has noted, "*The International Jew* probably did more
than any other work to make the *Protocols* famous."[12]

Despite the anger of Cyrus Adler and Louis Marshall, the
American Jewish Committee still maintained institutional silence.
The Central Conference of American Rabbis, the National Council
of Jewish Women, and B'nai B'rith approached the Anti-Defamation
League in Chicago and beseeched it to counteract Ford's work. The
league published a pamphlet by Sigmund Livingston, *The Poison
Pen*, "Being An Exposure of the hoax which is being foisted upon
the American public by Henry Ford."

"Attempting to reach the sane public," Livingston assessed "the
irresponsible recklessness ... [of] the Hebromaniac" Ford's actions
over the previous five months and drew upon a recent, refreshingly
pertinent critique by Theodore Roosevelt to the effect that "Ford
makes a good car for the money and in his sphere has done very
good work. But he won't stick to his sphere... Many, many persons
hardly as ignorant as Ford think him wise in all things and allow
him to influence their views."

Contrary to inflated statements put forth by the Dearborn Publishing Company about pent-up demand, *The International Jew*

booklet series was disseminated as a way to remedy the fluctuations in the unsteady circulation of the *Independent*. The newspaper was kept afloat during its first years because of Ford's strict subscription quota policy among car dealers in the field. Ford salesmen were informed by the home office that the *Independent* was a Ford product just like any other; every customer should become a regular reader. To avoid the wrath of Liebold, dealers spent their own money on complementary subscriptions for friends and acquaintances, Rotary members, local fraternity brothers, Chambers of Commerce officers, and so on. Many dealers said they never even read the *Independent*, but even if they did, they certainly were not about to complain about its editorial stance. In another attempt to boost the paper's numbers, the Ford Motor Company produced two promotional films about the *Independent*, to be shown at state fairs and in theaters, newsreel-style. Toward the end of 1920, circulation stood just shy of 300,000—however, three and one-half months later, it had dropped to less than half this figure, as commitments from the first wave of the concerted dealer subscription campaign ran out. The readership base was also vulnerable because only a small fraction of published copies were ever found on newsstands due to the intentionally low five-cent cover price.[13]

As *The International Jew* reached the public eye, the flow of mail into the headquarters of the American Jewish Committee grew to an avalanche. While the true nature and extent of Henry Ford's personal involvement in the campaign remained a mystery to the outside world, more comments and rumors about Liebold's shadowy influence emerged. An attorney named Henry Sachs of Colorado Springs, Colorado, wrote, "I have been told that Henry Ford's private secretary, named Leopold [*sic*] was a Jew, but has developed into a renegade." The former A.J.C. executive secretary, Herbert Friedenwald, told Louis Marshall he had heard that "Ford's guide, philosopher and friend in his Dearborn anti-Semitic propaganda is one Meyer or Myer Leibold [*sic*] *a born Prussian* [underlined thus in letter]. So now we have this definite evidence that the Ford brand of anti-Semitism like all the rest is 'made in Germany,' and is a direct importation." Closer to the heart of the matter, Ivan G. English, editor of the *Escanaba* [Michigan] *Daily Mirror*, assured Marshall, "I do not like the stand Mr. Ford has taken and have told him so and also tried to argue it out with his editor who prepared the articles, a fellow-journalist [W. J. Cameron]...Mr. Ford is all right himself," English attested, "but he is dominated by one man: Mr. Ford is being exploited by his private secretary, E. G. Liebold, and much against the wishes of his wife, his son and his friends."[14]

Finally, on November 14, in response to a united petition for action issued by the Zionist Organization of America, the Union of American Hebrew Congregations, the Union of Orthodox Hebrew Congregations, the United Synagogue of America, the Provisional Organization for the American Jewish Congress, the Independent Order of B'nai B'rith, the Central Conference of American Rabbis,

the Rabbinical Assembly of the Jewish Theological Seminary, and the Union of Orthodox Rabbis of the United States and Canada—all agreed to co-sign a manifesto—the American Jewish Committee published its first formal response to Ford. The slim pamphlet

———o\o———

Editorial in The Day/The Warheit (Der Tog),
New York, December 2, 1920, "The Stupid
Slander Against the Jews." "Henry Ford
started a campaign against the Jews...
We can only answer it with a smile of
contempt...We are firm in our belief
that stupidity cannot triumph..."

was called *The "Protocols" Bolshevism and the Jews: An Address to Their Fellow-Citizens by American Jewish Organizations*, and it was written "with honor," characteristic disdain, and unmediated condescension, by Louis Marshall. After conceding that his organization had declined at first to respond to Ford's accusations because that would have been beneath its dignity, Marshall wrote that it was now impossible to keep silent because of the "puerile and venomous drivel" emanating from Dearborn. Henry Ford could not be excused from responsibility. Marshall stated unequivocally that Ford "in the fulness of his knowledge" had given his imprimatur and sanction to "those who have set in motion this new onslaught" of slander.[15]

Thanks in part to a vigorous mailing and telegram initiative out of Chicago headed by Julius Rosenwald, A.J.C. vice president, the statement was reprinted in its entirety in numerous newspapers and magazines across the country. Much to Marshall's delight, editorial response from the *non*-Jewish press was sympathetic to the plight of Jews in America, with tacit understanding of the dilemma the Jews faced in attacking Ford too harshly. A common theme emerged from such heartland quarters as the *Pittsburgh Post*, the *Toledo News-Bee*, the *Chicago Tribune*, the *Springfield Republican*, and the *St. Louis Times*. Ford was depicted as "the tool of a very dangerous organized intrigue, of men cleverer and far more subtle than himself," the "victim of hired writers," a man whose mind was "being diverted from the big problems" of the day, and whose "misfortune" it sadly was "to permit visionaries to adventure with his name."[16]

In response to the publicity around the A.J.C. pamphlet, unexpected support came from another quarter of the Gentile world in the person of noted Fabian social reformer John Webster Spargo (1876–1966). Born in Stithians, Cornwall, England, he was trained as a stonecutter and then became a lay Methodist minister. Spargo moved to New York City at the turn of the century and was fiercely involved in labor rights issues, working to promote laws to regulate child and woman labor. He founded a settlement house in Yonkers, New York. With Samuel Gompers and George Creel, Spargo created the American Alliance for Labor and Democracy. He established his muckraking literary reputation as the author of many books, including *The Bitter Cry of the Children* (1906), *Applied Socialism* (1912), and *The Psychology of Bolshevism* (1919). Spargo had first come into contact with Henry Ford in 1915 when invited to sail on board the Peace Ship, which he declined. Even at that time, Spargo was suspicious of Ford's ideological judgment—"Historical study is not one of Mr. Ford's strong points," he said—although he praised the man's sincerity and idealism. Invoking Theodore Roosevelt, Spargo came around to much the same position as the former president: Henry Ford was treading upon uncertain ground when he became entangled in international questions and issues of racial conflict.

Offended by the "low level" to which Ford had "descended" in proliferating the *Protocols of the Learned Elders of Zion,* Spargo took it upon himself to seek out Harris Houghton and to question his intent in promoting the *Protocols* in the first place. Houghton cast aspersions on the motives of Louis Marshall and the American Jewish Committee and pointed to the Zionist movement as proof that the greatest goal of the Jews was to establish a power base in the community of nations. Spargo took his inquiries directly to Marshall, and as the two strong-minded men engaged in more extensive correspondence, Spargo was inspired to such a degree that within the space of one month he produced a 150-page book, published by Harper & Brothers, *The Jew and American Ideals.* It was the first major defense against Ford written by a well-known social critic, "a plea for Christian civilization."

In Spargo's well-reasoned view, it was a shameful time for America. The *Dearborn Independent* and *The International Jew,* "personal organs of Henry Ford," testified to his inherent hypocrisy—could this be the same man who five years earlier stood for peace in the world? As an acknowledged expert on the inner workings of Social-

ism and Bolshevism, Spargo was also going on record to say
that—contrary to the assertion by the *Dearborn Independent* that "the
bolshevik and the union leader are united under the flag of
Judah"—neither movement by any stretch of the imagination could
be construed as symptomatic of a global Jewish conspiracy.

Toward the conclusion of his study, Spargo made an ominous
point: "There is no reason for believing that here in the United
States we possess a special immunity from the worst forms of anti-
Semitism." Why *couldn't* the pogroms be reenacted here, in an
atmosphere already replete with "hereditary jealousies and
antipathies?" Why *couldn't* our native land become susceptible to
"inflaming passion, as the wind-blown dry autumn leaves are susceptible to the flame of the torch?" If that dreaded time ever did
dawn, Spargo was not shy about saying that Henry Ford and men
like him would have to bear the responsibility and guilt. On behalf
of his "fellow citizens of Gentile birth," John Spargo prayed that
such a day would remain forever locked in the realm of his darkest
fears and never arrive.

Spargo's book was purchased in lots of 10,000 for distribution
by the American Jewish Committee. But the determined author did
not stop there. Spargo composed a statement called *The Perils of
Racial Prejudice* on behalf of more than 100 "undersigned citizens of
Gentile extraction and Christian faith" strongly disapproving of the
current campaign of prejudice and hate "introducing into our
national political life a new and dangerous spirit," and saying that
"it should not be left to men and women of the Jewish faith to fight
this evil, but in a very special sense it is the duty of citizens who are
not Jews by ancestry or faith . . . to strike at this un-American and
un-Christian agitation." Spargo's signatory list was a roll call of
public personalities—two presidents and one president-elect—
William Howard Taft, Woodrow Wilson, and Warren G. Harding
—nine secretaries of state, a cardinal and other ecclesiastical digni-
taries, university presidents, businessmen, and writers: William Jennings Bryan, Paul D. Cravath, George Kennan, Clarence Darrow,

W.E.B. DuBois, Evangeline Booth, David Starr Jordan (in an apparent reversal of former sentiments), Jane Addams, Charles A. Beard, Robert Frost, Franklin K. Lane, and Ida Tarbell, among many others.

The Perils was published in newspapers all across the country on January 16, 1921, under the banner headline, "President Wilson Heads Protest Against Anti-Semitism". "After a few weeks," observed Leon Poliakov, chronicler of antisemitism from antiquity to the modern era, "it was clear that Henry Ford stood alone in the United States."[17]

CHAPTER ELEVEN

The Talmud-Jew

THE AUTOCRAT appears to stand alone, when, in fact, he is intent upon tightening his inner circle so that it is safely composed of men who reinforce and reflect his way of thinking.

On December 31, 1920, E. G. Liebold cabled Warren C. "Fuzzy" Anderson, Ford's representative in Britain and a sixteen-year veteran of the company, and told him to "Secure passage on earliest date possible and report to Detroit immediately upon arrival.... Arrange matters so that you will not be inconvenienced if you do not return to England." Not once during his brief return to Detroit did Anderson ever see Ford face to face. He was simply dismissed, told by sales manager William A. Ryan that "he had not shown stature" of late and that he had left the European dealership structure in disarray.

In this preemptory assessment—which the crestfallen, bitter Anderson never understood—Liebold and Ryan were strongly backed by another tough-minded colleague, Charles Emil Sorensen, who contributed his opinion that Anderson had "fallen short in financial and sales affairs." "Cast-Iron Charlie" had been on the Ford payroll for fifteen years, beginning as a $3-a-day assistant to Fred Seeman, head of the pattern department. As such, he was closely involved in the production of the Model T—including the design for its unique, one-piece, seemingly indestructible engine block. Hence his colorful nickname. Sorensen went on to help plan the first assembly line at Highland Park. During World War I, he was sent overseas to set up the inaugural tractor plant in Britain. He returned to take over tractor manufacture at the expanding River Rouge plant, which was still under construction, gearing up for massive production as Highland Park operations commensurately wound down.

And so it was that Charles Sorensen presided over the departure of several faithful Ford managers in 1921 and after. William S. Knudsen had consulted closely with longtime Ford architect Albert

Henry Ford, P. E. Martin, and Charles "Cast-Iron Charlie" Sorensen, watching Edsel Ford at the wheel of a vintage 1906 "Model N"

Kahn on the design of more than a dozen Ford plants. In 1915, he was given oversight for all thirty branch assembly facilities across the country. But after the war, "Big Bill," as the burly fellow was affectionately known, found himself in conflict with Sorensen, who Knudsen felt was encroaching upon his territory, spending too much time at Highland Park. The two men nearly came to blows on several occasions. After a brief and sadly inconclusive conversation with Ford, Knudsen resigned, was interviewed by Alfred P. Sloan Jr., and went to work as a consultant for arch-rival General Motors, where he soon was elected a vice president and became general manager of the Chevrolet Division, leading it to great success.

Frank L. Klingensmith, as vice president and treasurer of the Ford Motor Company, had developed a warm rapport with Edsel Ford, which his father did not appreciate. Henry Ford likewise frowned upon Klingensmith's stock investments in other companies. Sorensen was well aware of these personal tensions. He seized the opportunity to remind the boss that "Kling" had approached several Wall Street firms about taking out a loan to help the company through its cash-flow problems. Both Liebold and Sorensen claimed to have taken a hand in showing Klingensmith the door soon thereafter—Liebold reminded Ford that the treasurer was "half-Jewish, you know," and Sorensen criticized the treasurer for not understanding that you could just as easily improve the company balance sheet by controlling inventory and requiring agents in the field to take on more spare parts storage.[1]

The most symbolically significant departure from the Ford Motor Company was of the man whose unhappiness represented more than anyone else's "the dissipation of the bright dream of 1914–1918": personnel manager Samuel S. Marquis. As with the others, the rupture could be traced to Sorensen's heavy hand. His territoriality with respect to the innards of Ford manufacturing operations was equaled only by Liebold's vigilance elsewhere. Sorensen told Ford that Marquis's Sociological Department advisers—modified under the reverend's supervision to be called the Education Department—were disrupting production, pulling too many men off the assembly line during the working day to counsel or question them on domestic affairs. There came a verbal confrontation in Ford's office: "Many times in my life I have been called an s.o.b.," Sorensen readily admitted, "but never before or after that [meeting] was I called one by a supposed man of God." Marquis

Rev. Samuel S. Marquis and his wife, Gertrude

discovered to his discomfort that Sorensen was accusing him of "petty tyranny" behind his back. Ford was inclined to support Sorensen openly—in front of both men, which was even more embarrassing—and furthermore, "Mr. Ford and [Sorensen] were set on keeping his [Marquis's] nose out of the plant."

To the melancholy Marquis, Henry Ford had tragically and inexplicably become a different person over the final five years of their long friendship. Marquis would go home at night and confess to his wife, Gertrude Lee Snyder, and their two younger children that he did not know how much longer he could take the stress of working at the factory. He was waking up in the middle of the night and having trouble breathing. "The baffling thing in him," the minister observed of Henry Ford, "is the puzzling mixture of opposing natures. There rages in him an endless conflict between ideals, emotions and impulses as unlike as day and night—a conflict that makes one feel that two personalities are striving within him for mastery....[He] overestimates his judgment on questions outside [his] proper sphere." Marquis finally resigned on January 25, 1921. The *Wall Street Journal* reported breathlessly the following week that Henry Ford had summoned Marquis to his office, "denounced him as the author of sundry leaks, [and] denounced the Christian Church as vigorously as he has denounced the Jews."[2]

Marquis returned to St. Joseph's Church, where he had served upon his arrival in Detroit in 1899, and then, at the request of newspaper magnate George G. Booth, went on to become the first missionary and then rector of Christ Church at Cranbrook, which Booth founded in the countryside of Bloomfield Hills. Marquis presided at Christ Church until 1938.[3]

In the fall of 1922, after considerable soul-searching during a solitary summer writing retreat at a secluded cabin in the woods, Marquis published a series of syndicated newspaper articles through the *Detroit News* tracing the passing of the old "Ford spirit." Before Christmas, he received word from Little, Brown and Company that it was interested in a full-fledged memoir, to be called *The Real Life of Henry Ford*. Marquis's first galleys were so morose, so critical of Ford's "brutal and unnecessary butchery" leading to the "executive scrap heap," that publisher and editor H. F. Jenkins mused on more than one occasion that perhaps the author "had gone too far in reflecting upon the hard-boiled methods of the present executives that surround Ford.... If you will permit us to soften a few expressions here at the office," Jenkins wrote, the book might reach a wider public. Gertrude Marquis emphatically agreed.[4]

Marquis's book was published in March 1923, the title changed to the more benign *Henry Ford, An Interpretation*. It is difficult to determine if Marquis's book was toned down, because the manuscript has not survived. However, his bitterness shines through, especially with respect to "the Jewish Question." At one point, Marquis likens Henry Ford as a "dreamer" to the Biblical figure, Joseph, parenthetically pausing to wonder whether Ford will "pardon [him] for discovering this striking resemblance between himself and a man of a race in which he seems able to see so few virtues and so many faults."[5] Ford instructed his men to buy up as many copies of the book as they could get their hands on, and get it off the market; to this day, it remains practically impossible to find, even in libraries. Marquis family lore had it that Ford bought up the rights to the book and then had the plates tossed into the Charles River (in fact, they were melted down in 1928).

Clara Ford was so offended by the book that she never spoke again to Gertrude Marquis or to Samuel Marquis, who had, not so long before, been her faithful confidant. How could the dean turn upon her beloved husband so viciously—how could he write that Mr. Ford's "tenacity borders at times on obstinacy," that "the isolation of his mind is about as near perfect as possible," that "his Jewish diatribes" demonstrated that "he is not a team man, he must play the game alone and for himself"?[6]

HENRY FORD'S impromptu visits to the familiar domain of his auto plant became more surreptitious. If the men "don't know when to look for me," he would say, "that keeps them on their toes and guessing all the time." Ford would telephone Harry Herbert Bennett, manager of the River Rouge Employment Office (and unofficial director of plant security), and tell him to rendezvous in his office at an odd hour—sometimes two or three in the morning. "Poking around" among the night shift, Ford made it a point not to engage with the foremen. Rather, he approached men working on the line and conspiratorially asked them to fill him in on the latest gossip. When they were finished conferring, Ford would say to the astonished worker, "Now, if you hear anything else, just call me on the phone." Bennett—and Raymond Dahlinger, general manager of the Ford Farms, who often tagged along on these tours, since it was he who picked up Ford at Fair Lane and drove him to the factory—used to enjoy a silent chuckle over that remark. It was common knowledge that Henry Ford "was about as easy to reach on the phone as the President of the United States . . . or the Pope in the Vatican."[7]

Some inflated press reports trumpeted that "Henry Ford believes he is sitting on top of the world." If it got cold and lonely up there from time to time while harsh and critical pamphlets and petitions were published, longtime colleagues and allies were fired and departed—and his son and wife resigned their positions on the board of the Dearborn Publishing Company—Ford gave not one

Ray Dahlinger and Harry Bennett

public indication. However, at some point during this difficult, tumultuous period at the turn of the year between the end of December and the beginning of January, Henry Ford suffered a nervous breakdown, the effects of which kept him predominantly out of the public eye for four weeks and more. After confiding in a handful of close friends that Henry had been "unwell," Clara summoned Dr. Frank Sladen—since 1913 trusted chief of medicine at the Henry Ford Hospital—to attend to her anxious husband.[8]

From the enforced seclusion of the library in his country estate,

Ford tried to manage the spin control counteracting rumors that his corporation had entered dire financial straits. He turned away the "Wall Street bankers" who persisted in calling upon him after the dismissal of Klingensmith.[9]

Still hovering in the corridors of power and instrumental in constructing the Ford image in the press was "hard-drinking, hard-working" Joseph Jefferson O'Neill, now promoted to an editorial position at the *New York World*. His close rapport with Ford went back to their days together on the Peace Ship and subsequently when O'Neill had managed the impromptu Ford News Bureau —issuing daily press releases from Mount Clemens during the protracted *Chicago Tribune* lawsuit.[10]

O'Neill was called to Detroit in February to help Ford issue a reply to the recent proliferation of Jewish publicity against the *Dearborn Independent* articles. Although it seemed to Ford that the "defensive action [of the Jews] was practically a confession," he was determined to speak on the record. The detailed dialogue in the *New York World* of February 16, 1921, was forthright from the beginning: "'Peace' Object, Says Ford, in an Attempt to Justify His Anti-Semitic Attitude." The two old friends made no pretense at journalistic impartiality. "Hundreds have sought him," O'Neill bragged. "Fragmentary talks with him have been printed. But this is the first real interview in which he has been outspoken and unreticent... This was the first time, [Ford] said, he had ever discussed his views freely and frankly with any newspaper writer."

And so, let there be no doubt: "Henry Ford holds the belief that 'international Jewry with its racial programme of domination' is an evil influence in America and the world ... Those who have profited [from the World War] and are profiting now are the international financiers—the Jews." Let there be no ambiguity about the thrust of the *Dearborn Independent* articles in progress. They are "lessons" for the American public to "learn," not "attacks" as has been commonly misconstrued: "We do not hate the Jews," Mr. Ford insisted, assuming the benign, pedagogical tone he occasionally favored. Nevertheless, "no matter what others may think or say, [Henry Ford] holds to his idea ... that there is a Jewish evil, an attempt on foot by the Jews to dominate the world."

Mr. Ford was certain that once the American public understood his "educational campaign" was intended to result in an "investigation ... of the facts of the Jewish question, then every one can cooperate for the general good." O'Neill took pains to stress the authenticity of the conversation, because a tightening of official Ford policy had been instituted, and all interviews had to be thoroughly vetted before they were sent off for publication: "In fact, all the direct quotations from Mr. Ford which appear in this article were read and formally O.K.'d by him."

Speaking of the facts, Mr. Ford cleared the air about the *Protocols of the Elders of Zion*: "They fit with what is going on. They are sixteen years old, and they have fitted the world situation up to this time. They fit it now." Liebold agreed, disparaging "some theory that the *Protocols* were faked by the Russian government. My only answer to this is what Mr. Ford said, 'Here we have the *Protocols*, and this is what happened.'" Moving quickly to fill the management gap at the Dearborn Publishing Company, the serene and unimpressionable Liebold assumed the additional posts of vice president as well as treasurer.

Upon reading the O'Neill piece, E. G. Pipp observed that his former boss had neglected history to master the mechanical world. All the more reason for Henry Ford to refrain from "trying to instruct the world in history" out of a mind polluted to apparent distraction with prejudice and misinformation. As other men had of late also been complaining, Henry Ford got into trouble when he meandered outside his rightful intellectual territory.[11]

UNDER such heated circumstances, Rosika Schwimmer could not have chosen a more inauspicious moment to return to New York with her mother and sister in hopes of re-establishing herself in the womens' movement by writing articles and lecturing. There had been no love lost between J. J. O'Neill and Schwimmer on the Peace Ship. She singled out the reporter to her friend Jane Addams as one of those on board who "hated her." From the earliest hours of the trans-Atlantic trip, O'Neill's dispatches were filled with scornful comments about "The Queen of the Peacers" and her "associates." Although Ford was shown the contents of these cables, he did not censor them. During the continuous mediation conference in Stockholm, complaining to Ford Company officer Gaston Plantiff, O'Neill openly challenged Schwimmer's authority.[12]

Schwimmer suspected an orchestrated smear campaign when the *New York World*—of all newspapers—just happened to publish an article on March 27, 1921, headlined "Jewess Tricked and Fooled Ford," attributing Ford's current desire "to cool his revenge" to her past influence. "It was she who persuaded him to undertake the Peace Expedition. It embittered him. Hence his attacks on the Jewish Race. Perhaps it is not anti-Semitism at all. Perhaps it is Rozika Schwimmer."

The accusation appeared under the name of the Reverend Dr. Charles Aked, pastor of the First Congregational Church in Kansas City, another libertarian fellow-voyager on the Peace Ship who had begun as a sympathetic member of the committee on administration of the expedition. Aked eventually turned against Schwimmer before they reached the Stockholm conference, which he referred to in retrospect as "the greatest mistake in my life."[13]

It was difficult for Rosika Schwimmer to find a forum in which to defend herself against such vilification. After having been away from the United States and therefore out of public view for three years, she now found herself the victim of a postwar, conveniently revised tale wrought by the skillful hands of Ford's apologists—a story in which she played the role of being "accountable" for his antisemitism (even if Ford said that he disliked categorizing it as such).[14]

WHILE Henry Ford resolved to educate fellow self-respecting Americans on the Jewish Problem, W. J. Cameron at the *Dearborn Independent* also kept up a blistering pace. He had no choice. The magnitude of "the Question" required full attention—after all, "it is a very big one, the material is of mountainous proportions. The method therefore," he explained, "has been to lay the observable every day facts alongside the Program, to see if they agree." From the *Independent*'s point of view, the articles thus far published "have been denounced and misrepresented, but not answered." The reason the articles had not been answered was "the essential facts are the same." From the first time Henry Ford had confidently patted his breast pocket at that luncheon meeting with Rosika Schwimmer more than five years previous, until the current tirade, the "facts"—stated and unstated—had been a dire refrain singing against the Jews, whoever and wherever they were.[15]

According to the *Dearborn Independent*, the Jewish Program even invaded the American theater—how else explain the continuous, two-decade popularity of the play *Ben-Hur*, one of the most successful prosemitic shows of all time? (Not to mention the campaign against *The Merchant of Venice*.) The program also encompassed American movies, a "Jewish production" from top to bottom, and American baseball (how dare the Hebrews defile "the cleanest game"), and American jazz and American popular songs—why, the Jewish influence could even be seen in the gradual degeneration of Fifth Avenue in New York between Fourteenth and Thirty-Fourth streets, "the sweatshops in the very heart of Goy respectability."[16]

E. G. Pipp's persistent rebuttals against the *Independent* began to take on a David and Goliath tone. His was the still, small voice crying out in the Detroit wilderness. One night in March, Pipp paid a visit to the Young Men's Hebrew Association meeting downtown. The fellows had huddled around a recent issue of the *Independent* in which Ford had the temerity to attack "the young Jews of the United States... as traitors to this blessed land." The men were aware they were being slandered by one of the world's richest men;

and yet, as testimony to their race, "there was no rancor that night." Pipp was there to bear witness to the integrity of the scene. All he wanted to do was report back to Mr. Ford—"Will he begin to look into things himself and see what great injustices are being done under his order of having 'One article a week' written against the Jews?"[17]

The reply was a redoubling of efforts, and no target was spared Cameron's eclectic pen, whether it was Disraeli, the liquor business, the nomination of judges to the bench, Tammany Hall, William Howard Taft, the Warburg family and the corrupted Federal Reserve system, the New York press held hostage to the Jewish "whispering drive," the Paris Peace Conference, Jews' inordinate demand for civil rights, their pitiful protestations against religious persecution, and the push for "race consciousness and race peculiarity" in Zionism: "Let it go on! Multiply the instances! Each act simply gives a local proof, visible and intelligible to each community where it transpires, that what is written about the Jews is true!"[18]

To this stream of invective, Louis Marshall and his American Jewish Committee colleagues had no further overt reply. They believed their recent publication refuting the *Protocols*, as well as a plethora of intelligent, well-disseminated subsequent books and articles by others, had sufficiently and reasonably made their case, avoiding (Marshall's term) "hysteria." In recent months, Marshall had stubbornly rebuffed appeals for more retaliatory measures such as a libel lawsuit against Ford; a public debating panel composed of seven Jews (nominated by the A.J.C.) and seven Gentiles (nominated by Ford and Cameron); sponsorship of legislation against Ford's newspaper; and a massive, organized boycott of Ford products. Such actions, he said, would "play into Ford's hands." Besides, Marshall wrote—perhaps wishfully?—in April, from his perspective, "the entire Ford movement is dying a lingering death." These premature, optimistic sentiments were echoed overseas by the London *Times*, whose editors asserted that "the legend [of the *Protocols*] may be allowed to pass into oblivion."[19]

In December 1921, Henry Ford took a field trip with Thomas Edison to Muscle Shoals, Alabama, to inspect the massive, unfinished Wilson Dam on the Tennessee River and talk about investing "in the greatest single prospect ever held out to the American farmer and manufacturer." As the two men were walking into a meeting with eager officials from the Tennessee Valley Authority, they were buttonholed by the Florence, Alabama, correspondent for the *New York Times*, who raised a question about the "Jewish articles." Violating the public relations rule against the hazards of his verbal spontaneity, Ford invoked the Peace Ship's mission five years earlier; he recalled that one of the "prominent Jews" on the ship had actually told him "of the power of the Jewish race, of how they controlled the world through their control of gold, and that the Jew and no one but the Jew could end the war." The following month, Ford would identify that Jew by name as journalist Herman Bernstein, author of a recent exposé of the *Protocols of the Elders of Zion*, called *The History of a Lie*; Bernstein later successfully sued Ford for libel. [20]

**Henry Ford and
Herman Bernstein on
the Peace Ship**

RETURNING to Dearborn, Ford burst into Cameron's office and told him, over the protestations of Liebold, that "The Jewish articles must stop." He then spoke with Allan L. Benson, a frequent contributor to the newspaper, in the same terms, saying of the series, "There is too much anti-Semitic feeling. I can feel it around here." Ford biographers Allan Nevins and Frank Ernest Hill, writing in 1956, were at a loss to explain this "impulsive" turn of mind, confessing "we will never know" what drove Ford to such an apparently drastic change of sentiment.[21]

There are two plausible reasons. Ford had had a long year-end meeting with Gaston Plantiff, his business representative in New York City. Although 1921 had been decent for Model T sales, Plantiff reported there were some "spots" around the country where revenues had declined. There had not been an organized Jewish boycott of Ford, yet figures for the New York City area had gone down "in the thousands of cars." Fearing a dangerous trend in the making, Edsel Ford was able to convince his father that the company needed a high-profile acquisition to help its sagging public relations image. In February 1922, the Leland brothers, Henry and Wilfred, sold Ford their moribund Lincoln Motor Company outright for $8 million. Edsel took on the job of redesigning the Lincoln from top to bottom, repositioning it as a luxury sedan: "Father makes the most *popular* car in the world," Edsel said. "I want to make Lincoln the *best* car in the world."[22]

Furthermore, Henry Ford was known at this time to be flirting again with the idea of running for public office. He was well aware that no man had ever been elected president in the past sixty years who had not captured the electoral votes of Ohio and New York —states where Jews held decisive sway.[23]

Economic and political considerations aside, taking a closer look at the "final" words in the ninety-one-issue run, Cameron hardly sounds as if the door is firmly closed. On the contrary, Ford may have decided to diversify the outlets for his opinions "now that a bunch of keys has been provided by which the people may *unlock* doors and make further inquiries. . . . *The Dearborn Independent* will follow other aspects of the Question, discussing them from time to time as circumstances may warrant." Explicit antisemitic references became sporadic rather than regular in Ford's newspaper over the ensuing two years; however, a mere four months later, Volume IV of *The International Jew* anthology was published.

Henry Ford's personal rhetoric did not diminish either. When the English novelist G. K. Chesterton, on a tour of the United States, came to Dearborn to pay homage to Ford, he was treated to an earful. Chesterton, already predisposed against Jews, came away from meeting with this exponent of "the simple rural life" observing with admiration that "There is something of the artist in [Ford], and he is a fighter.... If a man like that has discovered that there is a Jewish problem, then there is a Jewish problem. It is certainly not due to anti-Jewish prejudice." Irrepressibly, on August 27, Ford could not help reminding the *Detroit Free Press* of "the greed and avarice of Wall Street kikes."[24]

He authorized continued acquisition of antisemitic research materials, amassing a cache of literature deposited day by day in tin boxes in a factory vault. Ford also hired a "highly educated" Dutch scholar and translator to set to work exclusively on a text of the Babylonian Talmud. There had appeared a reference in the November 5, 1921, issue of the *Independent* to "the Jewish New Year just past," saying that the sacred Yom Kippur *Kol Nidre* prayer originated "not from the Bible but from Babylon"—it was a "Talmudic rallying-cry," one of "many dark things in that many-volumed and burdensome invention." The essay mentioned the American Jewish Committee by name and caught the suspicious eye of Cyrus Adler: "I know that a policy of silence has been adopted [by the A.J.C.] and it may be right, but I think we are making a big mistake when we assume that this material is not spread in the community."[25]

According to Orthodox Jewish tradition, the Talmud ("study") began as the original commentary, or Oral Law, aligned with the giving of the Torah (Written Law) to Moses on Mount Sinai. The Talmud records the rabbis' legal and ethical discussions about and interpretations of the 613 commandments in the Torah evolving through the ages. The Talmud has been said to offer "How God wants Jews to live." In approximately A.D. 400–450, the accumulated mass of these debates were codified into the first edition of the Talmud, known as "the Palestinian," or "Jerusalem," although actually produced in the Galilee. The first English edition of this Talmud is still in progress. A century or two subsequently, a second Talmud edition, known as "the Babylonian," was compiled; this has become the more frequently studied. The first complete English translation of the Babylonian Talmud was published by the Soncino Press of London in 1935.[26]

"Let me tell you," U.S. Representative Fiorello LaGuardia of New York City joked to a reporter in 1922, "the average Republican leader east of the Mississippi doesn't know anything more about Abraham Lincoln than Henry Ford knows about the Talmud."[27] To LaGuardia, the anti-nativist and new-style urban liberal politician, Ford's latest exegetical witch-hunt was worth a good laugh. But when serious members of the Jewish stewardship read the *Independent* treatise against the *Talmudjude* they heard disturbing echoes.

In thirteenth-century Paris and Rome, by order of Pope Gregory IX in June 1244, twenty-four cartloads of Talmud copies were burned in public after Nicholas Donin, a Jewish apostate, submitted a declaration accusing the Talmud of expressing hatred for Christianity and blaspheming against Jesus and Mary. Twenty years subsequently, King James I of Spain ordered Jews to erase passages from the Talmud that were objectionable to Christians. In the latter half of the sixteenth century, during the infamous *Index Expurgatoria*, there were

Contra hebreos retinentes libros in quibus aliquid contra fidem catholicam no tetur vel scribatur.

Romæ apud Antonium Bladum Impressorem Cameralem.

⸻ ✦ ⸻

Papal bull of Julius III, Contra hebreos retinentes libros, 1550–1555, resulting in a radical program of confiscation and burning of rabbinic literature, with emphasis upon eradication of the Talmud

repeated and continuous Talmud burnings. Christian leaders had come to the conclusion that if the "perversely heretical" Talmud were destroyed, Jews would be more likely to convert.[28]

More than a dozen additional references to Talmud-cremation are cited in the *Encyclopaedia Judaica*. The editors of the *Dearborn Independent*, proposing that "the whole fabric of Talmudic teaching be consumed in the bright light to which general attention would bring to it," allied Henry Ford with this attenuated and fiery course of persecution.[29]

The nineteenth century was a time for resurgence of Talmud-persecution literature, and judging from the tone of the *Independent*, perhaps Henry Ford's hidden library included such popular classics as Jacob Brafman's *Book of the Kahal*, published in Vilna, Russia, in 1865. Purporting to be the minutes of an official Jewish congress held in Minsk fifty years previously, it was meant to expose a widespread Jewish organization [a "kehillah"] armed with despotic power. *The Book of the Kahal*, embellished with fake Talmudic quotations, was issued at public expense and sent to all government officials in the area surrounding Vilna to "help" them understand the Jewish population. It eventually found its way to America.

August Rohling's *The Jew According to the Talmud* was first brought out in Munster in 1871, then Prague in 1874, and saw English publication in the form of a sixty-four-page pamphlet by the Titus Publishing Company in New York City in 1892, called *The Talmud-Jew, A True Exposure of the Doctrines and the Aims of Judaism*. It is generally recognized as the basis for most subsequent anti-Talmudic writings in America and as "the most violent foundation of the pseudo-science of special anti-semitic literature" in this country. *The Talmud-Jew* went through seventeen editions and hundreds of thousands of copies. Rohling's study was followed the next year by *The Talmud Unmasked: The Secret Rabbinical Teachings Concerning Christians*, by Father Justin Bonaventura Pranaitis. Again, we find a concoction of spurious passages from the Talmud condoning ritual murder. Cameron and Liebold might also have come across another widely distributed text of the early 1920s, *Secret Societies and Subversive Movements*, by Nesta Helen Webster. In her analysis, the Jewish dream of world domination, logically culminating in Bolshevism, was expressed in passages in the Talmud and the Kabbalah.[30]

Translations of the Talmud were especially favored by antisemites after the war in order to break loose the book's "evil secrets" and reveal its web of subversive community laws—including the familiar blueprint for Jewish world domination, a critical ideological point of convergence with the *Protocols*. In this regard, the informing slogan of the *Dearborn Independent* as "The Chronicle of Neglected Truth" takes on added resonance, as well as a measure of irony, when revisiting the furor over Kol Nidre. The prayer is recited on the first night of Yom Kippur, to inaugurate the service. It means "All Vows," and the supplicant is asking to be released in advance from any vows made and not kept. Contrary to the facile interpretation found in the *Independent*—assuming this "indefensibly immoral" prayer emancipates untrustworthy Jews from the obligation to fulfill their oaths—Kol Nidre does *not* nullify promises made to other people. The prayer book explicitly says, "I do not ask for release from those vows from which I cannot be released."[31]

To the modern antisemite, the impenetrable Talmud was a threat, viewed "as if it were somehow endowed with life." Written in a combination of Hebrew and Aramaic, a cognate language, the Talmud reinforced the deeply held stereotype of the insular Jew "separate from the rest of mankind." American sociologist Robert E. Park commented in *The Immigrant Press and Its Control* (1922) that "the masses of the Jewish people remain imprisoned within the walls of the Talmud, knowing nothing of modern science or modern thought."[32]

AND those masses persisted in the drive to reach America, resulting in a gradual tightening of federal immigration policy in the early 1920s. The current quota law, extended in mid-1922 for two more years, "still admitted more than 150,000 people from southern and Eastern Europe annually." That figure—including 119,000 Jews—was still far too high for "hold-the-line" nativists, in Cyrus Adler's bitter observation, "drawing back in affright from the great numbers of what it considered undigested human material in [their] midst."[33]

The "gospel of racism" permeated American academia, making such views commonplace and respectable to the culture at large. Professor William MacDougall of Harvard spoke of the superiority of the Nordics in his series of lectures, *Is America Safe for Democracy?* Henry Pratt Fairchild of New York University supported the lawmakers in Washington in their zeal to keep America pure because "Racial discrimination is inherent in biological fact and in human nature. It is unsafe and fallacious to deny in legislation forces which exist in fact."

In the writings of Henry Fairfield Osborn, Theodore Lothrop Stoddard, Clinton Stoddard Burr, Kenneth L. Roberts, and Burton J. Hendrick—remarkable for being tightly clustered in 1921–1922—is a rich lode of antipathy, a consistent vocabulary arrayed against "the increasing tide of Oriental and decadent European influence ... the tide set flowing [from Europe] by Rousseau and his ilk ... the Tartars and other Asiatic nomad elements ... the races impregnated with radicalism, Bolshevism and Semitic anarchy ... Asiatic conceptions, repugnant to the Western mind."[34]

The particular bias against the "Oriental" or "Asiatic" strain was another euphemism for the Jewish Problem. These loosely applied labels expressed generalized uneasiness about "otherness" to which Jews had historically been susceptible as representatives of cultural difference drifting in from a "mysterious, duplicitous and dark" realm of Eastern Europe. Henry Ford was in tune with this rising chorus when Doubleday, Page & Company published the first volume of his three-part memoir-manifesto, *My Life and Work* in 1922. He, too, took note of "a question which deeply affects the country

... a nasty Orientalism which has insidiously affected every channel of expression... [T]hese influences are all traceable to one racial source."[35]

"If an idea seems good or seems even to have possibilities," Ford said in the introduction to the widely selling book, speaking through his collaborator, Samuel Crowther, "I believe in doing whatever is necessary to test out the idea from every angle." Ford was referring to the process of running experimental prototypes for the Model T—at the time of this writing, Ford Motor Company manufactured more than 50 percent of all the cars sold in the United States—but he might just as well have been reflecting upon the ninety-one-issue run of the *Dearborn Independent*.

Picking up where the *Independent* left off, Ford shifted gears in a potpourri section at the end of the book, "Things in General." He defended with pride the recently concluded series, "Studies in the Jewish Question." He had already commented more than a year previously upon "the whole Oriental mind, the Jewish mind, [as] different from the Anglo-Saxon, the American mind." So now, Ford was not the least apologetic. Unlike the prejudiced hypocrites who spoke praisingly to the Jews while condemning them in private, he continued to take the most direct route.

He believed that the "intelligent" members of the Jewish community would understand, and ultimately be grateful.[36]

CHAPTER TWELVE

Heinrich Ford

———◁▷———

It is one of the cruel ironies of history that the savage anti-Semitism which developed in Germany after the First World War should have been stimulated in part by an American industrialist who, in a number of respects, was so typical a product of American culture.

CAREY McWILLIAMS,
A Mask for Privilege: Anti-Semitism in America (1948, 1975), p.34

PROCEEDING up the stairs to Adolf Hitler's modest office at Schelling Strasse 39, headquarters in Munich of the National Socialist German Workers' Party in the winter of 1922, then entering the waiting room, visitors immediately noticed a large table covered with multiple copies of *Der internationale Jude: ein Weltproblem: Das erste amerikanische Buch uber die Judenfrage, herausgegeben von Henry Ford.* The preface to *The International Jew* lauded Henry Ford for the "great service" he had provided to America and to the world by attacking the Jews. "The younger generation looked with envy to the symbols of success and prosperity like Henry Ford," recalled the Reich Leader of the Nazi Students' Federation and eventual Hitler Youth leader, Baldur von Schirach, who had read *Der internationale jude* in 1924 in his home in Weimar at the age of seventeen, a year before he even heard the Fuehrer speak. "And if

Henry Ford said that the Jews were to blame, why, naturally we believed him."[1]

The publisher of the Ford pamphlet—an abridged, two-volume German version translated in 1921 by Paul Lehmann, and by 1922 already in its twenty-first printing—was Hammer Verlag, a Liepzig firm run by Theodor Fritsch (1852–1933). It was appropriate that Fritsch had unleashed this text upon the German public. Known for decades as the tireless *Altmeister* (Grand Master) of antisemites, he was on the verge of issuing a new, eighty-page *Die zionistischen Protokolle* (The Protocols of the Learned Elders of Zion) like *The International Jew* graced by his own preface and afterword. Fritsch's crusade originated with the immensely popular *Antisemiten-Katechismus* (1883), later renamed *Handbuch der Judenfrage* (Handbook of the Jewish Question) in 1887 and published in more than forty editions before 1936. Long revered by the Nazi elite, Fritsch shipped at least half of every propagandist printing of his various texts free of charge to youth groups, influential individuals, and nationalist organizations.[2]

Reprint of "Heinrich Ford" article with admiring comments by Adolf Hitler, in March 8, 1923 issue of the Chicago Tribune

If a person were summoned from the waiting room into Hitler's private office, he would be somewhat taken aback to see hanging on the wall beside the massive desk a large portrait of Henry Ford—Why here? And why now, ten years before Hitler assumed the chancellorship?

Attempting an explanation—determining points of convergence and personal and/or ideological affinities between these two men, as well as *"idees fixes"* they had in common—requires turning back to the moment when Hitler made his earliest extant public statement about "the Jewish Question."[3]

On September 16, 1919, while employed in the Press and Propaganda Office of the Wehrmacht, Hitler issued the oft-quoted declaration that antisemitism should not be based "upon emotional grounds," but, rather, on "realization of the facts," [*Antisemitismus der Vernunft*], the primary fact being that "Jewry was a race, not a religion."

The final iteration of rational antisemitism, Hitler concluded, must be "the removal [*die Entfernung*] of the Jews altogether." This extreme, eliminationist doctrine does not apply to Henry Ford's species of Jew-antipathy. However, the primary, so-called factual principle, the repeated references to "clarity" in referring to the Jews (setting aside the validity of those facts) is familiar.[4]

A crucial component of Hitler's formative period, after age thirty—and, for that matter, of postwar Germany as a whole—was the coming-into-its-own of the conservative *Völkisch* (race-soul) movement, characterized at heart by romanticization of essential German culture found in its heroic, peasant past and by faith in its potential for a vigorous and healthy future. The movement held beliefs similar to the outspokenly anti-liberal Ford, the wiry, competitive man of the people who liked to imagine himself as a "farmer" when he leaped over wooden pasture fences and sprinted across fields without warning or surveyed his tractor manufacturing plants. Belief in a kind of anti-intellectual and strongly anti-modernist education, learning the lore of the land through pragmatic experience rather than dessicated books, was of primary importance if *Völkisch* Germany were to prosper as a nation. This ideal was achieved through building up and glorifying one's physical form in woodland tramps and hikes over mountains, enjoying in solitude the unspoiled, divine purity of the natural world and the intoxication of the air. A widespread, sentimental revival of rustic folk music and indigenous dances was also an integral component; Henry and Clara Ford made pioneering efforts in this area as well.

Camping out, birdwatching, vegetarianism, teetotalling, and avoiding smoking were expected as part of a cult-like reverence for the rural landscape, in contradistinction to the widespread condemnation of the alien, decadent "asphalt men" who polluted the immoral metropolis—these were the Jews, the foreigners, who had no roots in the soil. They espoused an effete and ultimately vulnerable cosmopolitan lifestyle.

Linked with physical perfection, the *Völkisch* people were required to be persistent and rigorous in their exclusion of every unlike strain of intellectual, moral, and economic influence—like 100 percent Americans—if the ideal national community of Germanic racial unity (*germanische Blutseinheit*) were to take shape successfully.[5]

Hitler, like Ford, needed special philosophers, his own populist versions of Liebold and Cameron and Crowther. He also relied upon a *Mannerbund* (union of men) in the innermost circle whom he could trust to articulate for him these and other anti-Marxist, anti-Jewish, "Christian" racial values, be they abstract or generalized. And, like Ford, Hitler required a regular forum in which to disseminate his strong-willed ideas through the medium of print, another key *Völkisch* ideal.[6]

Many of Adolf Hitler's immutable, hypnotic fixations about Jews and other social and economic matters were inspired by the imagination of a man who has been called The Fuehrer's "chief ideologist" and "closest co-thinker"—the reserved, dogmatic, fair-haired and arrogant Alfred Rosenberg (1893–1946). Born into a bourgeois household in the Baltic village of Reval (Tallinn), trained in architecture in Moscow, the young man fled from Russia during the revolution, worked in a Munich soup kitchen, and then joined the National Socialist German Workers' Party as a proud, self-defined "fighter against Jerusalem" in 1920. The following year, Rosenberg was appointed editor of the *Völkischer Beobachter* (The Racial Observer), a weekly Munich gossip sheet rescued from near-bankruptcy and purchased by the Nazis when Hitler—desperate to "have his newspaper"—found out the tabloid was in danger of falling into the hands of Bavarian separatists. Wanting the paper to achieve broader circulation and appear in "larger, American-style format," Hitler authorized the acquisition of two rotary presses; by February 1923, the *Völkischer Beobachter* had become a full-fledged daily. It served from the outset as an ongoing, unexpurgated record of Hitler's public speeches, transcribed as they were uttered before ever-growing crowds in the early years of his ascendancy to leadership in the Nazi Party.

Over the five-year span from 1919 (when his first published pamphlet appeared) to 1924, Alfred Rosenberg amassed an influential body of work dealing with the "facts" of Jewish identity inside the Bolshevik revolution, the "yoke of Jewish Mammonism," the "wirepullers" in the Zionist conspiracy, the biological perils posed by the Jewish race threatening the glorification of the Aryan—and above all else, the validity of the *Protocols*. He took great pains to bring them up to date through extensive commentaries within his book, *The Protocols and Jewish World Policy* (1923), which ran through three editions within the year, and made a particularly strong impression upon Hitler. Rosenberg's staunch advocacy of the *Protocols* from the first moment he arrived in Munich led to Hitler's acceptance of their authenticity as one of Nazism's core texts in the pages of *Mein Kampf.*

Just like the *Dearborn Independent*, Hitler's newspaper, guided by Rosenberg, found distribution outside its provincial boundaries but remained a forum that was never able to turn a profit; instead of regional automobile dealers and distributors being compelled to seek subscribers, the *Völkischer Beobachter* depended upon the persuasive abilities of S.S. troops "to recruit readers and advertisers." Like the *Independent*, the *Völkischer Beobachter* was written almost single-handedly by one man "with the energy of the possessed, gathering anti-Semitic material on all sides." And also like the *Independent*, Hitler's newspaper provided the raw text for political pamphlets as well as an anthology of direct transcriptions of his public statements, a volume of about 150 pages titled *Adolf Hitler, His Life and Speeches*, going on into several editions after its initial publication at the end of 1923.[7]

IF Alfred Rosenberg was Hitler's intellectual younger brother, then Dietrich Eckart (1868–1923) was his spiritual godfather and first mentor. He was born of middle-class parents (his father was a notary) in the town of Neumarkt in Northern Bavaria, twenty miles southeast of Nurnberg. After trying to drink his way through medical school, Eckart fell into journalism, wrote poetry, and achieved a measure of fame with a new translation of Henrik Ibsen's *Peer Gynt* (1912). During a dissolute, itinerant stretch in Berlin, variously attempting to enhance his visionary range, Eckart used peyote and heroin. He was in and out of mental asylums, for a time dabbled in neopagan magic, and considered himself an occultist as the modern reincarnation of the ninth-century mystic, Bernard of Barcelona.

Eckart returned to Munich in 1913, joined the Thule Society—an esoteric club of several hundred wealthy *völkischers*—and founded an antisemitic, nationalist weekly, *Auf Gut Deutsch* (In Plain German), hiring Rosenberg as a staff writer.[8] Eckart and Hitler met at a Nazi Party meeting toward the end of 1919. Through his social connections the older man helped raise money to purchase the *Völkischer Beobachter*, becoming its first publisher. The witty, mercurial Eckart soon grew to look upon "the party's new recruit as his own protégé," reputedly helping Hitler improve his speech and mode of dress and introducing him to society. Eckart—outspoken and demonstrative where Rosenberg was reticent—made a powerful first impression on Hitler, "shining in [his] eyes like the polar star." In those early days, Hitler remembered more than two decades later, he felt himself to be "intellectually a child still on the bottle" until Eckart and Rosenberg entered his life. "What's the meaning of that word, *Beobachter* (observer),"

Eckart once said with fanatical fury in a booming bass voice, raising his horn-rim glasses up onto his forehead to reveal a piercing
gaze. "I could [better] understand something like 'chain-smasher!'"
In such a frenzied state, he looked for all the world like "an irate
Teuton god, grim and formidable."[9]

Where Rosenberg's bias against the Jews was predominantly
racial, Eckart's was complementarily spiritual. To Eckart, the Jews
had no soul. Echoing Arthur Schopenhauer, an ideological hero, he
defined the Jewish God as "nothing but the projection of their
innate essence." Their danger to pure German society resided in
the way the Jews undermined Christian ethics. The Jews, Eckart
wrote with disdain, were "in and around us," and had long been
"the true makers of our misery."

Beyond fear of religious corruption, Eckart defined himself as a
radical, politically. He desired a thorough revision of German society. He wanted new leaders to take the reins—a new generation
must come forward with "a fellow at the head who can stand the
sound of the machine-gun." As the standard-bearer for the old
guard, it was Eckart's responsibility to issue the clarion call for the
new, which he did in several early essays for *Auf Gut Deutsch*.[10]

Dietrich Eckart's collaboration with Hitler provided evidence of
the latter's awareness of the ideas of Henry Ford: *Der Bolschewismus
von Moses bis Lenin: Zweigensprach zwischen Adolf Hitler und mir*
(Bolshevism from Moses to Lenin: Dialogues Between Hitler and
Me). The pamphlet, published in Munich by Hoheneichen Verlag in
March of 1924, had been roughly and incompletely drafted by the
two men in October and early November the preceding fall, just
before they both were arrested as a consequence of the failed
Munich Beer Hall *putsch*. Hitler was released thirteen months later.
Eckart, already seriously ill when he entered prison at Stadelheim,
died of heart failure on December 23, 1923, and was buried at
Berchtesgaden, in the Bavarian Alps near Austria.

As the title indicates, Dietrich Eckart's "last earthly work" was
supposedly composed of extracts from actual conversations

between the master and his disciple. Recent German scholarship has cast aspersions on the authenticity of this claim.[11] However, even the nature of the dispute about the authorship of *Der Bolschewismus* brings parallels with Henry Ford, Cameron, and Liebold to mind. Hitler needed to have an amanuensis. In order to publish propaganda "by" himself he needed to lean heavily upon a variety of articulators.

Hitler might very well have said by this point in the *crystallization* of his developing antisemitic attitudes and his even broader philosophy of history (to borrow historian John Lukacs's metaphor) that "The Jew's aim is to dominate others in order to extort from them at his leisure." This statement sets the tone for the rest of the tract.

With Eckart's prompting, Hitler repeatedly imports the words of Luther and Schopenhauer, defining the Jews as "the dregs of mankind, a beast, the great masters of the lie....It applies without exception to every Jew equally, whether high or low, stock exchange tycoon or rabbi, baptized or circumcized." Orlando J. Smith, Henry Ford's long-ago inspiration, had also referenced Schopenhauer for authority—accusing the Jews of having exorcised spiritual ideals from Europe—in his *Short View of Great Questions*, the pamphlet that so affected the young automaker in 1901.[12]

No province of the Jews remains exempt in a conversation spanning from the Talmud to Old Testament texts ("The Book of Hate") to the present-day Problem. "They are a rank growth over the whole earth.... Zionism is the visible, surface aspect.... Whoever doesn't become sickened and nauseated upon making a closer acquaintance with the Talmud [Hitler said] can put himself on display in a circus side show.... The truth, [Hitler] said, is indeed as you [Eckart] once wrote: One can only understand the Jew when one knows what his ultimate goal is... beyond world domination, the annihilation of the world.... If a halt is not ordered, he will destroy all men."[13]

Midway through the joint diatribe, Hitler turned his attention to America, and the special problems there involving the attitudes of "faithless" German Jews "toward the country where they live, of the fact that they have united themselves with the rest of the world's Jews toward the ruin of Germany"—as "the American, Ford, well knew" and had lately written. "It's clear that they have had America by the throat for quite a while," Eckart agrees. In his eyes—and, we can safely interpolate, therefore Hitler's—Henry Ford was sympathetic to Germany's burden as the scourge of the world's community of nations in the aftermath of the Great War and the Treaty of Versailles.[14]

During the year spent in a comfortable room at Landsberg prison fifty miles west of Munich—"his university paid for by the state"—Hitler had plenty of free time to read, reflect, and apply the many valuable lessons he had acquired during the previous four years from Rosenberg and Eckart. This tutelage resulted in Hitler's writing his blueprint for the future, *Mein Kampf* (My Struggle). "He occupies himself every day [during the summer months of 1924] for many hours with the draft of his book," reported the prison governor, Otto Leybold. "It will contain his autobiography, thoughts on the bourgeoisie, Jewry and Marxism." The originally intended, bitter title of Hitler's memoir/opus was *A Four and One-Half Year Struggle against Lies, Stupidity, and Cowardice: Settling Accounts With the Destroyers of the National Socialist Movement.*[15]

The first volume was dictated by Hitler to two men who were in prison with him: at first his chauffeur, Emil Maurice, and then for the most part one of his closest comrades, Thule Society alumnus and faithful party secretary Rudolf Hess, who acted as a "human tuning-fork" for Hitler's unformed ideas. Editing and publication of the second volume, dedicated in December 1926 with respect and affection to the memory and legacy of Dietrich Eckart, was supervised by Josef Cerny, a staff member of the *Völkischer Beobachter*. Volume Two of *Mein Kampf, The National Socialist Movement,* is also noteworthy for its tribute to "only a single great man, Ford,

[who], to [the Jews'] fury, still maintains full independence ... [from] the controlling masters of the producers in a nation of one hundred and twenty millions."[16]

"The aim of history," Hitler wrote, "can never be to learn historical dates by heart and recite them by rote." Like Henry Ford, he was a consistent matriculator in what both men would have concurred was "the real university of one's existence ... the real world, not the world of the so-called intelligentsia." Therefore, the constant purpose of reading was utilitarian, to work toward retaining the essential nature of facts as they stood, avoiding nuances or interpretations from received texts.[17]

Also like Ford, "it is difficult if not impossible for me to say," Hitler wrote euphemistically, "when the word 'Jew' first gave me ground for special thoughts." However, as for many modern antisemites, there was a vital connection between his antisemitism and Zionism, because that movement was the first codified expression in contemporary times perceived to be the Jews' impulse to unite in world conspiracy. As for the *Protocols of the Learned Elders of Zion*, "so infinitely hated by the Jews," Hitler fell into familiar rhetoric, stating within *Mein Kampf* that "they are based upon a forgery ... the best proof that they are authentic. ... The best criticism applied to them is reality."[18]

Four days following his release from Landsberg, Hitler spent Christmas Eve with the family of another member of the trusted old *Mannerbund*, Ernst "Putzi" Hanfstaengel, his wife, Helena, and their little son, Egon, at their home in the Munich suburbs. "Upper crust in Hitler's pot-pie," the tall, Harvard-educated, half-American Putzi was a financial and social patron who would eventually become Hitler's foreign press chief.

After a rich dinner and sweet pastries, followed by the host's impromptu, virtuosic piano recital of Hitler's favorite Wagner songs, the friends exchanged gifts. Hitler was moved to receive a popular new book bound in gray cloth, *Mein Leben und Werk* (My Life and Work) by Henry Ford, translated by Curt and Marguerite Thesing.

The volume went on to a long life in The Fuehrer's possession. Twenty-one years later, during the American occupation of Munich in May 1945, a small collection of Hitler's books and papers was salvaged from his work room in the spacious Brown House mansion, Nazi Party headquarters on Brienner Strasse. (Hitler was rarely, if ever, to be found in his office; he was always on the move, making decisions impulsively and in transit from place to place.) Among several books and manuscripts brought back to New York City by "a young American bibliophile lieutenant," and put up for sale by Scribner's Book Store—including works by Alfred Rosenberg and Ernst Rohm, captain of the Storm Troopers—only one literary artifact "showed evidence of thumbing," the well-worn copy of *My Life and Work* inscribed by Ernst Hanfstaengel to his beloved colleague those many years ago.[19]

IN the spring of 1921, two and one-half years before he was offered official Nazi credentials as Adolf Hitler's fundraising emissary to the United States—before he had even met Hitler—a well-to-do bon-vivant *weltbummler* from Berlin named Kurt Ludecke arrived for a "hurried visit" to Ford Motor Company headquarters in Dearborn, Michigan, by circuitous way of London, Paris, Vienna, Rome, and New York City. Ludecke had read about the "famous articles" in the *Dearborn Independent*, and he wanted to meet the editor of the paper. William J. Cameron, "the capable journalist who had so successfully phrased Ford's inarticulate racial uneasiness," received the young man with enthusiasm. They talked "at length," and Ludecke came away bearing the first two *International Jew* pamphlets containing a wealth of antisemitic articles spanning the period from May 22, 1920–March 19, 1921.[20]

By the summer of 1922, Ludecke had alighted in Munich, where he heard Hitler speak in public for the first time on August 16—blasting forth his inspirational call, *"Deutschland Erwache!"* (Germany, awake!) After a four-hour private audience in the dingy back room of a café on the Korneliusstrasse, sealed with a hand-shake and a look deep into Hitler's "domineering" blue eyes, the thirty-two-year-old Ludecke became an immediate convert to the cause.[21]

The story of Hitler's early efforts to obtain funds from Henry Ford for his nascent political movement remains to this day episodic and contradictory. It is well-documented that financial support came into the offices of the *Völkischer Beobachter* before 1923 from

Kurt Ludecke, October 1938

Czechoslovakia, Switzerland, and France, among other countries in Europe. In early 1922, according to a claim by Erhard Auer, presi-dent of the Bavarian Diet (and one of Hitler's political adversaries), an agent of the Ford Motor Company had approached Dietrich Eckart "seeking to sell tractors." This overture would have come upon the heels of a year during which only three Model T's and six Fordson tractors had been sold in all of Germany. Shortly there-after, it was alleged, Eckart reciprocally solicited this "agent" for funds to support the "anti-Semitic movement" in Germany, and

"Mr. Ford's money began coming to Munich."[22] Pool and Pool, in their provocative (if erratic) *Who Financed Hitler?* identify this Ford Company "agent" as Warren C. "Fuzzy" Anderson. However, Anderson had been summarily recalled to Dearborn and dismissed at the end of 1920. E. F. Posekel, a subsequent Ford representative in Germany, was able to obtain approval from the Ministry of Agriculture in 1922 to sell a small number of Fordson tractors there.[23]

In the fall of 1922, Henry Ford had been alluding to the idea of making a run for the U.S. presidency, even while continuing to complain to Allan Benson, one of several official biographers, that he knew the Jews' opposition to him would make it difficult: "Ford made statements to me [in September 1922] that made me feel he might be a dangerous President.... I never printed them because I did not wish his Wall Street friends to have another club to hammer him with."

It comes as no surprise that the leadership of the American Jewish Committee viewed the prospect of a Ford presidency as nothing short of a "calamity to the Democratic party and to the Nation." Rabbi Samuel Schulman, spiritual leader of Temple Beth El in New York City, agreed with these foreboding words of his friend Cyrus Adler, observing that Henry Ford "is being taken seriously by men of all parties, and there is quite a large element in the American people who would like to see him as a candidate. If he runs on a third ticket, we may have some very disagreeable surprises."

Ford could not help adding fuel to this fire when Charles W. Wood, a reporter for *Collier's Magazine*, sat down for a lengthy "tell-all" conversation about his political views, during the course of which Ford (heavily edited by Cameron) nevertheless still sounded so extreme that Wood was finally driven to ask if he weren't perhaps advocating a system of government based more upon "autocracy" than democracy. Ford neatly sidestepped the question by donning his C.E.O. hat and asserting, "Efficient service demands that we get rid of things that have outlived their usefulness. If the Government doesn't do this, the Government will go down, that's all."

Failing to avoid the subject of the Jews entirely, Wood conceded that any conversation with Henry Ford these days was "sprinkled quite generously" with choice comments such as "When the Jews take hold of anything, it goes down.... You probably think the labor unions were organized by labor. But they weren't. They were organized by these Jew financiers."[24]

From across the sea, someone was still listening to Henry Ford's rhetorical flourishes. With intensifying rumors of an impending *putsch* adding fuel to his own political ambitions, Adolf Hitler expressed an enthusiastic wish that he "could send some of my shock troops to Chicago and other American cities to help in the elections.... We look to Heinrich Ford as the leader of the growing Fascist movement in America."[25]

But neither man achieved his goal—at least immediately. President Warren G. Harding died in August in San Francisco. Vice President Calvin Coolidge moved into the White House. Ford hinted he would support Coolidge if he promised to enforce Prohibition. As a show of solidarity, Coolidge said he would not oppose Ford's bid to take over the Muscle Shoals dam from the jurisdiction of the Tennessee Valley Authority. On December 20, 1923, Ford took his hat out of the ring, where it had been placed through the enthusiasm of others more than his own, and endorsed Coolidge's candidacy.

Meanwhile, an imprisoned Hitler managed to sign a letter for Kurt Ludecke asking him to "solicit in the interests of the German Liberty Movement in North America, and especially to assemble financial means for it." Embarking from cloudy Cherbourg in early January for the voyage to New York City, Ludecke's ultimate goal was Detroit—there he hoped to gain "a word in Mr. Ford's presence, a hint, a request."[26]

In the intervening years since his initial visit to America, Kurt Ludecke had become a tireless promoter of the Nazi cause, successfully raising funds for the party in Italy and Hungary. He had also invested his own income into the movement at a time when it was sorely needed. Hitler now placed faith in Ludecke to do the same in America.[27]

Arriving in New York, Ludecke met up with Siegfried and Winifred Wagner. The son of the renowned composer was embarking upon an American concert tour, also hoping to raise funds for the rehabilitation of the Bayreuth Opera Festival. Mrs. Wagner, English by birth, had become enamored of Hitler and offered to pave the way for Ludecke to meet Henry Ford by interceding socially with the Fords. And so, the trio headed west together.

In the early evening of January 31, 1924, the Wagners were entertained in splendor by Henry and Clara Ford in the formal main floor dining room at Fair Lane. In the parlor, after dinner, as was his wont, Ford became vociferous about the Jews. Mrs. Wagner observed that "the philosophy and ideas of Ford and Hitler were very similar." More than half a century later, she recalled Ford telling her "that he had helped to finance Hitler with money from the sale of automobiles and trucks that had been sent to Germany." As she promised Ludecke, Mrs. Wagner seized this opening to ask if her friend could visit to talk with Ford about "further cooperation" with Hitler.[28] That night, before the concert at Orchestra Hall downtown, Ludecke met Winifred Wagner in her reserved box. She signaled him with a "charming smile" that the mission had been accomplished. They sat together and watched her husband conduct the Detroit Symphony in a broad Wagnerian repertory, received with a standing ovation.[29]

At nine the following morning, E. G. Liebold picked up Ludecke at his hotel and drove him to Dearborn. Henry Ford—"the modern myth"—greeted the visitor warmly, and the two retired to a private room. By Ludecke's account, Ford was quiet and receptive, smiling gently, fixing his alert, gray eyes upon the visitor and relaxing into his familiar pose, one foot propped upon the edge of his desk, hands clasped over his knee. Ludecke was well aware that "Ford was

—⁂—

The dwarf against giants: Roosevelt,
American patriot; Lincoln, liberator of
slaves; and Washington, the father of
America, gaze down upon Henry Ford,
holding a sack labelled, antisemitism

—⁂—

Ford on Uncle Sam's scale:
"Even with the Klan, he doesn't out-
weigh American freedom"
The Klan's toy: The papers on the table
next to the Klansman read, "Elders of
Zion," "Henry Ford for President," "Accusations Against the Jews," and "Down
with the Jews"

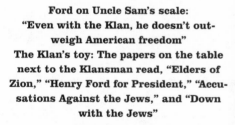

engaged in a campaign tangent to our own"; but this shared ideology was not sufficient reason to assume financial support. Ludecke
knew that any such support would be forthcoming only if he were
able to convince Ford that "the racial theories which Cameron's
work was merely stating in the abstract" would be concretely
enacted by Hitler's emerging Nazi movement. Ludecke further rea-
soned that in launching the attack on the Jews, Ford surely must
have had some ultimate goal (or consequence) in mind. Ludecke

therefore took a logical angle, telling Ford that when Hitler inevitably rose to power he would "inaugurate the social program for which the *Dearborn Independent's* articles provided such suggestive material."

"I know...yes, the Jews, these cunning Jews" nodded Ford with a faint smile, listening attentively but offering little else in the way of what Ludecke hoped would be confirmation that he saw the benefits of working together with the Nazis toward resolution of the commonly reviled "Jewish Problem."

When Ludecke finally developed his courage to make the pitch, Ford, "with consummate Yankee skill," steered the conversation away from money and back to stereotypes. He did not appear to grasp Ludecke's vision of Germany as the staging ground for a "popular movement" to "unseat the Jews from their position." Nor did Ford seem receptive as a businessman to any salutary economic outcome of such a drive; Ludecke speculated that once the Nazi regime had taken hold, there could conceivably ensue a reopening of the Russian market. He surmised that Ford never had given much thought to the ultimate consequences of the grandiose social theories his newspaper promulgated. Perhaps—as with the ill-fated Peace Ship—Ford's entrancement with an idea was sufficient to motivate him.

"Well, that you talk over with Cameron," Ford finally replied, a convenient way of saying that his attentions were waning. He took Ludecke into the editor's office and left the two men together. Ludecke had already met Cameron and was astute enough to notice that without clear marching orders from Ford, Cameron—"strongly imaginative, but not given to action"—was useless. The next day, sure enough, a terse telegram arrived from Cameron on his boss's behalf, "The proposal will probably not be entertained."

"What a resounding syllable is a rich man's *No!*" Ludecke thought as his inaugural but "unprofitable American begging-tour" to Washington, Pittsburgh, Cleveland, Chicago, Milwaukee, and St. Louis, among other cities, came to an ignominious conclusion. He headed home dejected to Germany. Ludecke would be back in Dearborn soon, in dramatically-different circumstances.[30]

Did Winifred Wagner embellish in some fashion upon her longpast memories? Did Henry Ford make a promise of financial support in his one-on-one meeting with Ludecke, the proviso being that the German emissary deny that a funds transfer ever took place? It is impossible to be certain. Over the ensuing decades, Ford Motor Company officials denied that Henry Ford ever supported Hitler financially. There exists no evidence in company records to support the charge.[31]

THE German consumer market, insistent after the war upon the primacy of home-made products and vigilant about protecting its own make of cars, did not open fully to the Ford Motor Company until late in the first quarter of 1924, when a substantial number of Fordson tractors were imported for sale. Edsel Ford was informed in November that a relaxation on the ban of foreign car manufacturers would come soon. It was time to set up a German affiliate. On January 5, 1925, Ford Motor Company A. G. (*Aktien Gesellschaft*) was incorporated. The management and floor superintendents were predominantly Danish (brought in from the successfully run Copenhagen plant) and American; however, the assembly-line laborers were German. By the spring of 1926, Model T's were rolling off the line at suburban West Harbor, Berlin-Plotzensee. General Motors and Chrysler also gained footholds for assembling cars and trucks in the vicinity of Berlin at this same time.[32]

Four years later, Henry Ford laid the cornerstone for the new Ford factory in Cologne, remarking (in what some uncomfortable observers believed was an ill-conceived tip of the hat to Hitler), "What Europe needs is leaders. What is a leader, anyhow? It is a man who visualizes what the people want and goes ahead and produces it." Mrs. Wagner may have had her chronology off, but she was correct in intuiting that Hitler and Ford shared a common industrial affection for the automobile. In 1920, despite his dire financial position, Hitler insisted upon having a car to travel from place to place in Munich. He believed that the car provided a certain dignity and made it a point thereafter never to take a tram or any public transportation. Throughout his life, Hitler often spoke with fervor of how "great roads" defined "the beginnings of every great civilization" above all other manifestations—"beautiful broad, white *Autobahnen*" teeming with the *Volkswagen* would be his most lasting legacy: "It was reading Ford's books that opened my eyes to these matters," he said.[33]

By 1930, the doctrine of *Fordismus* had moved far beyond the boundaries of Nazi appropriation to become a popular byword throughout the intellectual communities of Weimar Germany. The translation of *My Life and Work* sold more than 200,000 copies in 1923–1924. It was followed within a year by two important and widely read critiques of Ford's methods, wedding them to the

The Ford plant in Cologne

prized German work ethic: Professor Friedrich von Gottl-
Ottlilienfeld of the University of Berlin collaborated with influential allies Werner Sombart and Max Weber in an endorsement of
Ford's progressive philosophy. They applauded his insistence upon
production "for the common good" rather than "profit making."
They welcomed Ford's ability to relate to the working man, elevating the worker's conditions of life without dangerously inciting
him to reach too far beyond. And Professor Paul Rieppel went so
far in his study of Ford's methods as to christen him "the greatest
Prussian in America," standard-bearer for the noblest Spenglerian
values.

These opinions were bolstered by the publication in Germany in
1927 of the second volume of Ford's memoirs, *The Great Today and
the Greater Tomorrow* (*Das grosse Heute und das noch grossere Morgen*),
an inflated version of the more modest American title, *Today and
Tomorrow*. This was the beauty of Henry Ford's gospel: Its appeal
covered the spectrum of German social theory from left to right.
At both poles, Ford tapped into attributes of German culture
prophesied for the hoped-for new era ahead. Progressives saw him
as a rational technologist who aimed to perfect the common weal.
Volkischers claimed Ford as a commercial purist whose energies and
exclusionary doctrines fulfilled all that could be desired within the
highest Aryan.[34]

CHAPTER THIRTEEN

Sapiro v. Ford

FOURTEEN years had passed since New Year's Day, 1910, when the Ford Motor Company Highland Park plant opened its doors. The first Model T factory rose up on a 230-acre plot on Woodward Avenue, site of a former race course, at that time several miles beyond the Detroit city limits. The original four-story building was almost 900 feet long and 75 feet wide. It fulfilled Henry Ford's earliest, highly systematized manufacturing plan, to consolidate as many functions as possible involved in the making of the car. Highland Park symbolized the final transition from the industrial-revolution piecework model of labor. Workers no longer focused upon responsibility for bringing their individual specialized item to a stationary car chassis mounted on sawhorses in the middle of the floor. Rather, on a moving and increasingly accelerated assembly line, the Model T was put together through many stages of devel-

opment. Over the ensuing three years, production of the Model T
doubled each year. Highland Park outbuildings were constantly
under construction from the day the place opened—administration
building, power plant, machine shop, and so on.[1]

The criss-crossed conveyors at the River Rouge plant, 1927,
by Charles Sheeler. Aerial conveyors for coke and coal,
and the eight stacks of Power House No. 1

Impatient to perfect his seven interlocking and unchanging fundamental production principles—"power, accuracy, economy, continuity, system, speed, and repetition"—Ford was constrained almost from the outset by Highland Park's multistory design limitations. By 1915, he preferred to imagine a vast factory complex made up entirely of one-story buildings; no more inefficient elevators, no more ramped conveyor belts upon which constant assembly was not feasible. The new complex would be structured around the momentum of the process-line. It would be the largest self-contained manufacturing site in the world, this "River Rouge Plant," reaching out over 2,000 acres southwest of Dearborn, ten miles from Detroit, where the Rouge met the Detroit River near Henry Ford's Fair Lane estate. It would go beyond simply being a place where the car was built. *All* the constituent materials contributing to the creation of the automobile from the ground up would converge there: iron and timber and rubber from Ford-owned mines, forests, and plantations clattering overland on Ford-owned rail lines and sailing in on Ford-owned freighters by sea, via Great Lake ports and the St. Lawrence River, enacting the captain of industry's obsession with self-sufficiency. Glass plant, coke ovens, by-products plant, job foundry, cement plant, and motor assembly building were in place by the year 1924. Eventually, 75,000 men worked at the Rouge, and it encompassed twenty-three main buildings, dozens of subsidiary structures, ninety-three miles of railroad track, and twenty-seven miles of conveyor belts moving raw materials.[2]

At the beginning of 1924, old Highland Park's evening star was fading, while the rising Rouge heralded the dawn of an industrial era beyond belief. There it stood, a mile and a half long and almost a mile wide, a futuristic colossus "like some inflexible, calmly feeding steel monster, already detaching, unit by unit, the proud home of the first moving assembly line."

To the west of the Rouge, south of Michigan Avenue, the Ford Motor Company was beginning to lay out a broad residential area where an expanding workforce and their families would live in close, convenient (and therefore, management believed, more productive) proximity to this vast array of poured-concrete buildings punctuated by looming coal mountains amassed against pale, depthless skies. The power plant's eight towering smoke stacks sent forth white plumes. Covered, squared-off conveyor belts threaded impossibly from building to building in defiance of gravity. Perpetually running blast furnaces surrounded by glowing orange auras fed into a deafening foundry casting engine blocks. Surveying the Rouge nearly

Albert Kahn in his office

half a century after it was largely completed, the *New York Times* summarized it as "one of the most important structures in the history of architecture."[3]

The Highland Park and River Rouge plants were built as a result of the drive and money of Henry Ford. However, it required the consummate abilities of one equally driven man to make Ford's often-inarticulate vision into a reality: his architect, Albert Kahn. Kahn was the oldest of eight children, born in Rhauen, near Mainz, Westphalia, Germany, on March 21, 1869. Albert's father, Joseph, was an itinerant rabbi. His mother, Rosalie, possessed an artistic soul. She played the piano and sketched, and these were valuable legacies to her son.

After several years in Luxemburg, the Kahns emigrated to America in 1880 and made their way to Detroit. Albert's formal schooling was curtailed by this move, and he never went back into a classroom. Rabbi Kahn found work far afield, in Florida and New Jersey, but was not able to provide any sustained income. With Albert's "bent for drawing," at age fifteen he took a job, at first without pay, in the Detroit architectural firm of Mason and Rice. There, under the tutelage of partner George D. Mason (who saw Albert's "enormous capacity for concentration and study"), the astute office boy quickly picked up the requisite drafting skills, bringing home $3.50 a week in wages to assist the growing family.

In 1890, at twenty-one years of age, "A. K." as he later became known, was awarded the $500 Traveling Scholarship given by the *American Architect and Building News*. Borrowing another $500, he spent the next two years abroad, in England and throughout the Continent, visiting cathedrals and monuments and countryside villages, amassing a thick portfolio of plein air sketches. Kahn was deeply influenced by a stint in Florence with the architect Henry Bacon, who was later to design the Lincoln Memorial in Washington, D.C. Upon his return, Kahn was made chief designer for the Mason firm. By the new year of 1896, he felt it was time to move on. The firm of Nettleton, Kahn, and Trowbridge was established.

Small in stature, short-legged, stocky in build, stubborn by disposition, and by nature a self-effacing fellow, Albert Kahn liked to characterize himself as more inclined to listen than to speak forthrightly in social intercourse: "Nine-tenths of my success has come because I listened to what people said they wanted and gave it to them," he once said. More accurately, Kahn was never in doubt of his ideas, never felt the need to prove himself with friends or clients. He was not a theorist: "The 'architecture of tomorrow' had little interest for one so engrossed in creating the architecture of today." Kahn rather considered himself to be a "good craftsman," a hands-on, inveterate empiricist who designed himself—or supervised and approved the final designs—of every building he ever put up.

Kahn preferred long working hours to the placidity of domestic life. He was devoted to his wife, Ernestine, but even after the children arrived, Kahn's idea of an evening at home usually meant late dinner, a brief chat about the events of the day, a restorative fifteen-minute catnap—and then, back to work at the drafting table in his study, poring over plans carried home from the office. He would often stay up through the night and into the early morning hours. Only on Sunday afternoons, frequently spent in his Walnut Lake home twenty miles out of town, would Kahn deign to relax and listen to the Metropolitan Opera on the radio. During these sacred hours, he and Ernestine were not to be interrupted.

After the turn of the century, at last heading his own firm, the entrepreneurial Kahn took on all manner of commissions, including Temple Beth El on Woodward Avenue and the Conservatory in Belle Isle Park. Kahn the pragmatist did not shy away from the industrial jobs most architects of the period felt were beneath their dignity. All his life he reveled in "the common-sense solution of the factory building." In 1901 Kahn designed a small plant for the Boyer Machine Company on Second Avenue in Detroit. His first major corporate client was the Packard Motor Car Company, headed by Henry B. Joy, for whom Kahn eventually designed ten buildings, culminating in Detroit's first large auto plant, the first reinforced concrete auto factory in America, derived from a method the architect had first observed on his European travels. The building was situated in northeastern Detroit, on the north side of East Grand Boulevard, near Mt. Elliott, between Packard and Concord avenues. Free of timbers, it was fireproof, cheap, and characterized by unobstructed vistas of interior space. It is still standing today, sturdy as ever.

The 1905 Packard building was the first representative of the signature "Kahn System." The trussed-concrete George N. Pierce Plant, built on Elmwood Avenue in Buffalo, New York, for the manufacture of the Pierce-Arrow car, followed one year later. Then came the Chalmers Motor Company building back in Detroit. It was only a matter of time before Albert Kahn's unadorned, sensible, consummately utilitarian style caught the competitive eye of Henry Ford, whose antiquated factory at Piquette and Beaubien streets was not suited for further growth.

It was toward the end of 1907 when the telephone rang in the Kahn studio. "Mr. Kahn, I want to talk to you about a new building we are planning," said Henry Ford, "I want the whole thing under one roof." Kahn recalled, "Ford could not explain just what it was he wanted. But when I showed him the first rough drawings," his new client was able to think more clearly. "That's the way he always was," Kahn said, "I would take [Ford's] instinctive hunch and reduce it to a working formula." By mid-1908, the Highland Park plant was in its early design phase, Albert Kahn firmly at the helm. More than 50,000 square feet of glass "let in floods of sunshine on bright days, leading some to call it The Crystal Palace." Highland Park, the largest building of its kind in the state of Michigan, was the first of more than 1,000 commissions over a lifelong collaboration between the two men.[4]

"THOSE around him have hastened to make a difference between the 'Jewish International Bankers' and other Jews not so employed, pointing out that since Mr. Ford has so many Jews working for him, and a Jewish architect, and many Jewish friends, he has no prejudice against Jews as such.

"But in talking to Mr. Ford it is obvious that, being of a simpler construction of mind, divisions of a subject do not come easily to him, and that when he says 'the Jews are the scavengers of the world,' he means what he says, and no more, because that is the full extent of his thought on the matter.

"From a hunch it has grown into an explanation with many applications, and hardened into a cherished obsession."[5]

Albert Kahn led the life of a thoroughly assimilated German Jew. He did not associate with East European Jews. He insisted that the children, Lydia, Rosalie, Edgar, and Ruth, employ proper American English elocution in the home. The Kahn family was not religiously observant. Even though father designed the 1903 domed Temple Beth El building, as well as its prepossessing successor in 1927, he rarely attended services or observed Jewish holidays or Sabbath traditions.

Albert Kahn designed Grosse Pointe Farms and Grosse Pointe

Shores mansions for the Dodge, McMillan, Macauley, and New-berry families. One of his most inspired creations was the family home at Lake St. Clair for Edsel and Eleanor Ford and their children. In the style of a rambling Cotswold manor, it faced a 3,000-foot shoreline. Kahn also designed, and joined, the Franklin Hills Country Club and subsequently he became a member of the Bloomfield Hills Country Club.

However, despite the architect's adroitness at moving fluidly between divergent strata of Detroit society, according to his nephew William Kahn, it was still "very much of a blow to Uncle Albert" when the first antisemitic issue of the *Dearborn Independent* was published and especially painful over the summer of 1920, when excerpts from the *Protocols of the Learned Elders of Zion* began to appear. "Deeply hurt," from that time forward for the next ten years, Albert Kahn did not visit the expanding River Rouge job site. Instead, he sent representatives—his brother Louis (1886–1945), who had joined the company in 1910, his brother Moritz, or other emissaries from the 200-member architectural firm—to meet with Henry Ford and Charlie Sorensen, who had taken a powerful managerial role in the innermost executive circle at the Rouge.[6]

Kahn was on extended sojourns in Europe during the height of the *Dearborn Independent*'s attacks in 1921. Like other prominent Detroit Jewish businessmen in his tightly knit community, many of whom engaged in commerce with the Ford Motor Company, Kahn did not want to confront Henry Ford publicly on his antisemitism. This behavior was not borne out of hypocrisy. It was inspired by economic necessity. Ford was an omnipresent fact of life in Detroit.

On a few occasions, Kahn departed from habitual stoicism to express private misgivings to brother Louis about his powerful yet simple-minded client. In one surviving letter—albeit obliquely phrased—to wife Ernestine, written in the spring of 1923 when she was on holiday with daughter Lydia, Kahn spoke of "continuing to take in new work, largely from Ford.... Whether we can hold them is of course always a question. We'll try our darndest."

"Hold them" he did—as well as Kelvinator, Republic Steel, General Motors, Chrysler, and Burroughs—for another twenty years and more, because although by religion a Reform Jew, by profession Kahn was a businessman with a gift for attracting industrial clients—and a patriot, too, with a principled allegiance to the American society that had allowed him to prosper. Kahn's firm fulfilled more than $200 million in defense contracts from 1939–1942. His last major commission from Henry Ford was the Willow Run bomber plant at Ypsilanti, Michigan, where the B-24 Liberator was mass-produced.

In June 1942, the American Institute of Architects held its seventy-fourth annual meeting in Detroit. The Special Medal of the A.I.A. was presented to Kahn for his "outstanding contribution to the nation's war effort." Just before Albert Kahn's death on December 8, 1942, following a heart attack and a prolonged and debilitating bronchial infection, this prolific and introspective artisan, working even from the sick bed, put forth a final doubt about the paradoxical Henry Ford, who, Kahn at last conceded with a measure of understatement, "once had a prejudice against Jews....He is a strange man. He seems to feel always that he is being guided by someone outside himself. With the simplicity of a farm hand discussing the season's crops, he makes vast moves." The pastoral analogy was appropriate.[7]

"Vast moves," indeed. Henry Ford, hanging on in his twentieth year as the head of the company bearing his name, was determined to maintain a high level of productivity on all fronts, be they ideological or mechanical. His declaration that the *Independent* antisemitic articles "must cease" was for public consumption—or meant to throw adversaries off-guard. As scholar Leo P. Ribuffo points out, past historians have taken Ford's impetuous command for granted and thus "paid slight attention to [the] second wave [of] attacks on Jews" spanning 1922–1925: President A. Lawrence Lowell of Harvard was praised in the *Independent* for his endorsement of admissions quotas for Jews; the Dawes Plan was ridiculed as a "subtle scheme" to aggrandize the Warburgs; and Calvin Coolidge's rivals, Senators Hiram Johnson and Robert LaFollette, were suspected of being backed by the "wire-pullers."[8]

Even the distinguished Julius Rosenwald, chairman of Sears, Roebuck—who had not that long before received an invitation imploring him to come aboard the Peace Ship—was singled out for an ad hominem attack. In the February 10, 1923, issue, the *Independent* disapprovingly accused Rosenwald of direct responsibility for the Negro exodus from the South to Chicago during World War I. According to the *Independent*, thousands of poor migrants, seeking employment and a roof over their heads, and "going to Rosenwald for help," were tempted by him with bargain plots of land along Grand and Prairie avenues and, after a meager down-pay-

Julius Rosenwald

ment of fifty dollars, permitted to move in, corrupting the neighborhood, driving away older owners, and leading to the race riots of 1919.

The *Independent* alleged that this "tide of white dispossession" instigated by Rosenwald's economic incentives set off a disturbing domino effect linking Jewish money with "the Negro problem." Vice resorts and gambling dens "under Negro supervision sprang up" soon thereafter. Blame for this chain of corruption was laid at Rosenwald's doorstep. The *Independent* also said that Rosenwald subsequently rebuffed entreaties by Chicago Police Chief Charles C. Fitzmorris to step forward and undo what he had so expediently and thoughtlessly done to tear the fragile fabric of Chicago's landscape.

This litany was brought to Rosenwald's attention several days following publication by Samuel P. Thrasher and William C. Graves of Chicago, two colleagues with whom he served on the Committee of Fifteen, a group of civic-minded men dedicated to aid public authorities "in the enforcement of laws against pandering and to take measures calculated to prevent traffic in women." The usually reticent Rosenwald preferred to keep a modest profile regarding his countless beneficent urban works and philanthropic enterprises. However, in this case, he was driven at the insistence of his attorneys to issue an extraordinary five-page point-by-point refutation of the *Dearborn Independent*'s "misstatements, false insinuations and innuendos." Addressing Henry Ford personally, Rosenwald went public with the documentation that his committee had, in the year 1922 alone, identified owners and agents of more than 400 "immoral establishments"; since 1913 the Committee had spent more than $300,000 in a vigilant crusade to keep Chicago free of corruption.[9]

Thrilled by opposition, Henry Ford plucked up his bullhorn to broadcast other scattered opinions, not satisfied with castigating a rich Jew audaciously exploiting Negro migrants. Labor unions "make a great deal of trouble," too. Europe "is in a bad way to-day, because Europe doesn't know anything, and therefore isn't working." The U.S. trade tariff "is a joke." The trouble with farming? "It involves too much unnecessary work.... The farmer must turn his attention to the modern industrial methods instead of to the problem of borrowing money." Speaking of which, Ford noted, the best way to deal with Wall Street was to "abolish interest." The downfall of liquor? "Booze had to go out when modern industry and the motor car came in." World peace could only be "assured through world service.... There is going to be another World War anyway," Ford predicted, "and the United States ought to get into it at the beginning and clean them all up." And as for the Women's International League for Peace and Freedom, that left-wing organization— along with many other women's social activist and reform groups no longer exempt from Henry Ford's ire—was the focal point of the *Dearborn Independent*'s "Second Red Scare" crusade heading into the mid-1920s.[10]

Within earshot of these assorted dicta, the Associated Advertising Clubs of the World, meeting at its annual summer convention in Atlantic City, voted Henry Ford the best-advertised individual in America. On August 17, 1923, Ford signed off on an unprecedented infusion of more than $7 million to be budgeted toward promoting the Model T brand in all print media across the land, following five years during which he had managed to coast along without spending anything at all for this purpose. Heretofore, Ford proudly swore that he did not believe in advertising. But his impact upon the culture at large could never be measured simply in relation to dollars and cents spent upon the company's most-visible product. In survey after national survey—the most recent of which drew upon a sample of more than 125,000 people—the king of the Flivvers was named, with affection, "the greatest man in the country." In the eyes of the average (that is, disenchanted) American citizen, Ford loomed as an "enlarged crayon portrait of himself," a man who had succeeded, year after year, surviving caricature and ridicule, in achieving the American dream of self-made wealth without ever losing sight of his pioneer, homespun roots.[11]

Louis Marshall took a divergent point of view with respect to Ford's aggressive advertising drive, especially when Morris Weinberg, president of the Yiddish daily, *The Day*, came to him asking whether or not it was appropriate for that newspaper to carry ads for Ford cars and tractors. "I have no hesitation in answering the question in the negative," Marshall replied in agitation on November 24, 1923. "Ford is not only seeking to sell his wares, but he is trying to keep the name 'Ford' before the public in order to... gain a following in all of his divagations. I cannot see how a self-respecting Jewish newspaper can lend itself to his aggrandizement."

Soon thereafter, Marshall lashed out against the business manager of the *Daily Forward*, Baruch Charney Vladeck, who insisted, despite Marshall's furious protests, upon accepting ads from Ford because, he wrote, "it would be very poor policy on the part of the Jews to boycott a product or refuse channels of publicity to a product because of the views of the manufacturer." The decade between the end of the First World War and the beginning of the Great Depression was the period of greatest prosperity for the Yiddish press. For example, average daily advertising revenues for the conservative *Morning Journal* during the 1920s reached $3,000 per issue. These and other Jewish newspaper and periodical publishers transcended whatever momentary qualms they felt—and took the Ford Motor Company's money.[12]

FARMERS did not require an advertising blitz to encourage them to buy Fords. They had been Henry Ford's best customers since the beginning, for cars, trucks, and the workhorse Fordson tractors. Ford believed he had the farmers' best interests at heart because he was just like them—rural by birth, rugged individualist, woodchopper, traipser through shoulder-high wheat, possessive of his lands. Imagine Ford's chagrin when an audacious, entrepreneurial

Aaron Sapiro

Jewish organizer appeared on the scene to rally American farmers and inspire them with the promise of deliverance from perennial economic hardship through marketplace solidarity.

Aaron Sapiro (1885–1959) was born in Oakland, California, and raised in an orphanage. Graduating from high school, he pursued a course of study at Hebrew Union College in Cincinnati with the goal of becoming a rabbi. After eight years, he left rabbinical school and returned to San Francisco, where he took a degree from Hastings Law School in 1911. He then joined the California State Market Bureau, working for its director, Harris Weinstock. For five years, Sapiro studied the legal history of cooperatives harking back to the colonial period, and also represented California farmers in their efforts to organize more effectively.

The informing goal of the cooperative was to provide the farmer with more clout through control over the sale of products by minimizing the role of middlemen, thereby achieving greater profit margins. The movement touched upon an exposed nerve in the farmer's psyche—that he was being victimized by an oppressive and interfering economic system, the classic "price-cost squeeze," which made him pay out more than he could earn. By the time Sapiro left the State Market Bureau in 1919 to set forth full-time upon his travels, "preaching the virtues" of the cooperative as "the only hope of the man who tills the soil or cares for the orchard," the movement was already catching fire; within two years, American farm cooperatives would handle more than $1 billion worth of business.[13]

Sapiro is recognized as the originator of the California school or model of farming cooperatives because he came out of a region of the country where many different kinds of specialty crops were grown in smaller, separate areas—as opposed to the great Midwestern plains states. Sapiro pushed to correct imbalances in grower treatment by structuring direct-membership organizations, along commodity lines, that would effectively influence terms of trade leading to "just and stable prices for the farmer." He stressed the importance of maintaining longer-term contracts between growers and cooperatives that bound each tightly to the other. He advocated quality control, pooling, and grading different products stringently before they were brought to the consumer, then packaging and selling them in a systematic fashion, protecting the market against so-called dumping, so that harvest-time was less chaotic.

To create more dependable cash flow, farmers would ask to receive part of the payment for their crop at delivery, the remainder coming in stages from the pooled reserves of their "central" cooperative during the year. In short, Sapiro advocated "organizing agriculture just like industry."[14]

Sapiro's West Coast base as representative for the biggest marketing associations in California provided the launching pad for a blazing crusade of speeches throughout the United States and Canada, during which he became revered as "the evangelist of cooperation" and—somewhat more hyperbolically—as the "agricultural Napoleon of the twentieth century... who stirred the entire country." Orations by "this tireless genius," known to last as long as five hours, were acclaimed as "unforgettable, magnetic, and convincing." The rank and file began by being enamored of Sapiro's revivalist fervor, but the inevitable consequence was that they could not help but feel dependent upon him.

By 1922, Sapiro had created the National Council of Farmer's Cooperative Marketing Associations. Aggressive outreach efforts resulted in his coming to represent more than sixty cooperative associations in wheat, cotton, tobacco, fruit, dairy, and vegetables, generating market revenues in excess of $400 million per year. He hired a staff of lawyers working full-time in San Francisco, Dallas, Chicago, New York, and Washington, D. C., and was also instrumental in establishing a division of cooperative marketing in the U.S. Department of Agriculture.

During these intoxicating times, Sapiro gradually traversed the spectrum from idealistic advocate to rigid autocrat. His "iron-clad" contractual stipulations and strictures began to antagonize some of the more traditionally minded farming associations and interest groups, especially the powerful American Farm Bureau Federation, where Sapiro was an increasingly vocal council member and gadfly. Deeply ingrained traditions of autonomous, independent action died hard among those intrepid men and women whose families had worked the land for so many generations. Many cooperative members began to look for loopholes and tried to extricate themselves; spreading defections led to the costly "escape" of tonnage from produce levels guaranteed years in advance. Early in 1924, amidst complaints about his high fees—and broader danger signals in the American economy which Sapiro had nothing to do with and no way to ameliorate—he was forced to step down from the AFBF.

"I don't believe in cooperation," Henry Ford not-surprisingly asserted at this same time, "What can cooperation do for farmers? All it amounts to is an attempt to raise the price of farm products." Ford and his *Dearborn Independent* colleagues had already been casting a wary, suspicious gaze upon Sapiro's trajectory for several years. The perfect opportunity now arrived to speak out against him.[15]

The very notion of Jews interfering with farming was anathema to Henry Ford. The issue had been addressed four years previously, at the height of the first wave of antisemitic articles in the *Dearborn Independent*. "How the 'Jewish Question' Touches the Farm" laid explicit Gentile claim to the birthright of the soil, because "The Jew is not an agriculturalist"; only "land that produces gold from the mine, and land that produces rents" is of relevance to him. As early as 1920, the *Independent* warned of "a new movement" fueled by "Jewish millions," to take control of America's precious farmlands. The target was the independent farmer. The Jew, always the duplicitous trickster, would attempt to subvert the American farmers' tenacious autonomy and seduce him into a show of unity, thereby controlling him.

The invasion had been prophesied long ago, in the arcane pages of *The Protocols of the Learned Elders of Zion*, where it was written in *The Sixth Protocol*, "We shall soon begin to establish huge monopolies, colossal reservoirs of wealth, upon which even the big Gentile properties will be dependent. . . . That the true situation shall not be noticed by the Gentiles prematurely, we will mask it by a pretended effort to serve the working classes." *The Twelfth Protocol* advanced the argument one step further, advocating exploitation of the farmers' mistrust of the cities. "Already the poison is working," intoned the *Independent*, advising that "the farmers look past the 'Gentile fronts' in their villages or principal trading points, to the real controllers who are hidden."[16]

The *Independent* patiently held fire, lying in wait until Aaron Sapiro began to run into problems keeping his momentum going.

Just as the *Protocols* predicted, farmers began to become disen-
chanted with him, especially in Canada, where an open rift developed
early in 1924 over allegations that Sapiro was misappropriating
membership funds and charging excessive fees for his legal services.
Clippings containing correspondence published in Canadian newspapers following the entire controversy—erupting first within the
ranks of the Canadian wheat farmers, and then among apple-growers
in the Pacific Northwest—were carefully accumulated in the *Independent* files as Ford's writers built up a head of steam.

The Dearborn Independent, August 30, 1924

Finally, on April 12, 1924, the first of a series of articles under the byline of Robert Morgan (pseudonym for Harry H. Dunn) appeared in the *Independent*, "Jewish Exploitation of Farmers' Organization—Monopoly Traps Operate Under Guise of 'Marketing Associations.'" Hitting "the self-appointed apostle" Sapiro when he was down, the essays did not let up for an entire year. The level of detail and extensive field research for the series leaves no doubt that it was planned and commissioned long before Morgan's inaugural piece was published.[17]

The agenda set in the first sentences is driven home relentlessly: From the Appalachians to the Rockies and onward to the mighty Pacific, "a band of Jews—bankers, lawyers, money-lenders, advertising agencies, fruit-packers, produce-buyers, experts—is on the back of the American farmer.... This organization [was] born in the fertile, fortune-seeking brain of a young Jew on the Pacific Coast a little more than five years ago."

Raising the spectre of characteristic Jewish behavior—unity as the benign mask for conspiracy—under the banner of "cooperatives," the articles sound much the same warning as did many predecessors in the *Independent* dealing with the New York Kehillah. This time, however, the setting is rural and "horticultural" rather than urban, and the "national associations" which result are in country towns rather than on the Lower East Side. "White, free, American men," according to the *Independent*, are pitted in age-old struggle against the relentless machinery, the interlocking cabal of "Oriental financiers dedicated to the business of establishing control and leadership...Lasker, Baruch, Weinstock, Honig, Levy, Steen, Fleishhacker, Rubinow, Kahn, Meyer...Rosenwald." Formal portrait photographs like elegant mug-shots of these and other Jewish bankers all in a row, buttoned up in stiff white collars and smiling slightly, are juxtaposed against Currier-and-Ives-style, rustic pastoral images: small flocks of innocent sheep grazing peacefully, unaware they have been "bound over to pay the salaries of the officials of the California Plan of Marketing [espousing] principles of Bolshevism and the communistic movement... flitting about in Europe"; cattlemen of the West minding their herds, unaware that "the Sapiro Plan will get 'em if they don't watch out"; strawberry pickers laboring in the beating sun between endless furrows vanishing into the horizon "on their knees to the controllers of American farm products"; "singing Negroes in the cotton fields paying tribute to exploiters... more destructive than the boll weevil"; and Oregon hop-harvesters, straw hats tilted back upon sweaty brows, sleeves rolled up above their elbows, leaning wearily against waist-high straw bushel baskets filled with bounty gathered under the oppressive, alien rule of "the Jewish ring."

About one-third of the way through the course of the series, an *Independent* editor, perhaps W. J. Cameron, felt it incumbent upon the newspaper to insert a sidebar denying a charge by *The Scribe*, a Jewish weekly published in Portland, Oregon, "that these articles insist too much on Aaron Sapiro being a Jew." Rather, there was a far graver threat to examine, beyond Jewish financiers huddling in support of Sapiro. Once the Jewish powers took over the farmers' co-ops, they intended to follow up that effort with a movement to take over the boys' and girls' farm clubs as well. Eleven million children on the more than 7,000,000 farms in America would be endangered, representing "the men and women of America of tomorrow... Trained to communistic ideas, these boys and girls would become as modeler's clay in the hands of the internationalists."

On January 6, 1925, Sapiro sent a formal letter to Henry Ford demanding he retract the entire series on "Jewish Exploitation" to date. With nary a reply, the articles continued blithely on for another three months, concluding with a most serious summation on April 11, alleging "World Cotton Control by Sapiro Plan—Evidence That Many Minds Worked Together to Tie Up Farmer." No less an economic powerhouse than Goldman, Sachs & Co. was now getting into the agriculture business, offering revolving credit lines to finance cotton farm bureau associations in Texas; so that now we are looking at a firm of "New York Jewish bankers" pushing their way into the wide open spaces of the largest state in the union, allying themselves with a fellow-Jew, Sapiro, for mutual advancement.

Making matters more suspicious, the Federal Reserve Bank—according to the *Independent* commonly known to be an institution invented by a Jew—was refusing to advance funds to the Texas cotton farmers and scheming in collusion with the New York moneylenders, clearing the way for their exclusive, private, (and carpetbagging) investments. The boxed-in farmers, with no other recourse for seeking credit available to them, were held hostage by the stringently fixed marketing requirements of Goldman, Sachs attached to a $10 million credit line channeled by the bank through the Sapiro organization. Robert Morgan claimed with a final flourish, "here is the most brilliant example the writer has yet uncovered" of the manner in which farmers across America had become beholden to the "international banking ring" and its ruthless Wall Street representatives.

Ten days after this article was published, Aaron Sapiro filed a libel suit against Henry Ford and the Dearborn Publishing Company in the amount of $1 million, for defamation of character, "to vindicate myself and my race."[18]

To readers of the *Dearborn Independent* during the extended run of Sapiro articles, there would have been nothing new in this most recent of a long line of accusations against German-Jewish bankers. The link with the Federal Reserve System was eminently logical by now. E. G. Liebold's convictions about the central bank found early roots in a conversation he had with Dr. Roy Donaldson McClure (1882–1951), chief surgeon of the Henry Ford Hospital, when the two men began to work together as close colleagues in 1915, creating and then managing the institution. Ford assigned Liebold to the post of general manager with responsibility for staffing the hospital, and Liebold, in turn, reached out to McClure, a distinguished graduate of Johns Hopkins. McClure, along with Dr. Frank Sladen, became one of Henry Ford's personal physicians, gave his boss a daily checkup at home, and enjoyed a standing luncheon appointment with him.

According to Liebold, McClure revealed to him the intriguing story of the Jekyll Island Talks: "The Frankfurters [that is, German Jews from the city of Frankfurt, an obvious example being Jacob Schiff] were down there," Liebold remembered,

Paul Warburg

albeit loosely, "and other prominent Jewish financiers.... That was where they conceived the idea of a Federal Reserve Bank ... where the idea was discussed and talked over.... That would be prior to 1912."[19] In fact, as early as November 12, 1907, in the wake of that fateful year's unsettling speculative economic "panic," Paul M. Warburg (1868–1932) published a seminal essay in the *New York Times'* Annual Financial Review, an overt appeal for a centralized cash reserve fund based upon the concept of the German Reichsbank and other European institutions, ideally to operate "independently of government." At the time "A Plan for a Modified Central Bank" was brought out, Warburg was half-partner in M. M. Warburg & Company, the firm in Hamburg where his family had, since the eighteenth century, made its mark and amassed capital, as well as half-partner in Jacob Schiff's firm, Kuhn, Loeb & Company in New York City (through marriage in 1895 to Nina Loeb, half-sister of Schiff's wife). Warburg's article caught the attention of Senator Nelson W. Aldrich of Rhode Island, influential chairman of the Senate Finance Committee and head of the National Monetary Commission. Aldrich eventually asked Warburg to become an unofficial adviser to this group, and he began to speak out more aggressively in favor of an overhaul of the American banking system. Over the ensuing couple of years, following several sojourns in Europe, Senator Aldrich came around to Warburg's way of thinking.

The time had come for a meeting of the minds. Shrouded in secrecy, one evening early in November, 1910, Paul Warburg and five other men, including Henry Davison, senior partner at J. P. Morgan, and Frank Vanderlip, president of National City Bank, made a train trip at Aldrich's invitation in his private railway car, from Jersey City down to Jekyll Island, off the coast of Georgia, traveling incognito. There, over the course of ten days of free-wheeling debate, they came up with the first draft for a bill proposing a "National Reserve Association" with the authority to issue elastic notes based upon gold and commercial paper, complete with a central hub as well as regional divisions. The bank "would serve as fiscal agent for the U.S. government...and a lender of last resort to the American banking system."

President Theodore Roosevelt's endorsement was obtained a year later; ultimately, Woodrow Wilson signed the Federal Reserve Act at the end of 1913—"a signal achievement," said Warburg, and an idea for which he tried diplomatically to avoid claiming full credit. But Warburg could not turn down the president's request, "despite vehement objection from many populists," that he step up as one of the Fed's seven inaugural governing board members.

As a prosperous, immigrant German Jew, and therefore a visible target subject to nativist vilification, Paul Warburg was labeled "the father of the Federal Reserve," one of the co-conspirators giving birth to a "banking cartel...a legal private monopoly of the money supply, operated for the benefit of the few under the guise of protecting and promoting the public interest."[20]

The *Dearborn Independent* weighed in during the summer of 1921 with its own interpretation of the "Jewish Idea of a Central Bank for America," throwing Warburg's theories scornfully back in his face, attributing the *"private"* nature of the Federal Reserve to the Jewish mentality, which made the system's design all the more insidious. The *Independent* became carried away by its own zeal, however, mistakenly accusing Warburg of advocating only one central bank, when in fact he had pushed from the beginning that the core be tied to diversified branches. The newspaper also took offense at Warburg's (to their eyes) ungrateful snobbery vis-a-vis "the benighted state in which he [said that he] found this country" when he first arrived. The *Independent* may have taken offense at Warburg's oft-quoted, early assessment that "The United States is at about the same point [in managing its currency] that had been reached by Europe at the time of the Medicis." Perhaps that was why he had waited until 1911—ten years after he established permanent residency in the United States—to become a citizen. Overall, Warburg's consistently elitist cast of mind was contributory to his desire to "change and mold our financial affairs more to his liking."[21]

That same year, Max Warburg, Paul's older brother, sued Theodor Fritsch over the popular German translation of *The International Jew*, because it included a fabricated letter encouraging Bolsheviks to deposit their money in the account of M. M. Warburg. In 1923, the *Völkischer Beobachter* attacked Max, Paul, and younger brother Felix. In 1925, Fritsch retaliated with another inflammatory pamphlet published by Hammer Verlag, *My Battle With the House of Warburg*. Once more, for good measure, Fritsch painted an image of the Federal Reserve Bank as "ostensibly a state institution, when in truth it is completely in Jewish hands."[22]

DEPOSITIONS were taken during the year following the filing of Aaron Sapiro's lawsuit. A trial date of March 1926 in Detroit was initially set. Ford sought and was granted a continuance until September 14 by the United States District Court, upon which date Ford filed an affidavit disqualifying Judge Arthur Tuttle from trying the case. Judge Thomas Hough of Columbus, Ohio, was named to hear Ford's motion for a further continuance, which the court granted for another six months. A new trial date of March 15, 1927, was then scheduled.[23]

Meanwhile, the *Independent*'s sporadic observations about "the Jewish Question," continued, attracting the attention of an outspoken member of the New York German Jewish community, Nathan Straus (1848–1931). Born in Otterberg, Rhenish Bavaria, Straus emigrated to America in 1854. He became co-owner of R. H. Macy's Department Store with his brothers, Oscar and Isidor, in 1888. Straus was a passionate supporter of the first American public health efforts to pasteurize milk and distribute it to poor children in thirty-six American cities. During the depressions of the 1890s, he paid for coal, bread, and groceries at community-based lodging houses and relief depots. In 1909, he built the first tuberculosis preventorium for children. In the final two decades of his career, Straus served three terms as president of the American Jewish Congress, and, as a committed Zionist, provided finances for the construction of health and welfare stations in Palestine.[24]

In early December, 1926, Nathan Straus—already singled out by the *Independent* during its early years—decided that he had had enough of the "educational" campaign. In a "combative and pugnacious" speech in Boston, the feisty philanthropist issued a public challenge to Henry Ford, a definitive way to test the "campaign of slander against the Jewish people" once and for all. Straus offered to set up an independent jury of ten distinguished Christian clergymen, and ask them to deliberate upon the credibility—actually, the existence—of the so-called "Jewish Question."

In angry reply on December 11, the *Independent* released advance proofs to the national press of a tartly worded editorial entitled, simply, "Mr. Nathan Straus"—"one of whose department stores operated under the Christian name of R. H. Macy"—in which the cast-down glove was speedily taken up. The *Independent* welcomed the opportunity to recapitulate many charges with reference to the Jew going back seven years and offered to go one step further and provide to the panel of clergymen the documented results of their exhaustive research. Special emphasis was placed upon the reiteration that "the International Jew invented our financial and interest system, and is today in direct control of all financial centers of government, including the United States Federal Reserve

System, which he organized and is now perfecting according to his original plan."[25]

Precipitated by the "zestful, uncalculating enthusiasm" of Nathan Straus's words, the ongoing Federal Reserve debate attained critical mass. On December 18, a member of the House of

Representatives, Sol Bloom of New York, chairman of the House Foreign Affairs Committee, submitted a formal resolution (H.R.335) to Rep. Bertrand H. Snell, chairman of the Rules Committee of the House, calling for a select committee of seven members to investigate the "grave charges" made by Henry Ford (or, as the *New York World* diplomatically phrased it on its editorial page, "the gentleman who does his antisemitism for him") regarding the Federal Reserve System; and "to inquire into the truth or falsity of said statements

Nathan Straus

and recommend such action as it may deem necessary." Bloom urged Snell to invite Ford to testify before the Rules Committee to substantiate "the facts that he claims he has ... [and] to lay them before the Congress, the people."[26]

Bloom took the high road, making it clear that he was proposing such action "not as a Jew, but as an American, in behalf of my constituents, non-Jewish as well as Jewish." He conceded that it was not necessarily the province of Congress to investigate Ford's multiple charges against the Jews, but it was certainly Congress's right to take up any aspersions cast upon the integrity of the U.S. government. "Mr. Ford is a public man," Bloom wrote. "When he speaks, he has a national audience.... If he has proof that any voice but an American voice—the voice of a Jew or of a non-Jew—has a controlling influence in shaping the financial policies of the Gov-

ernment of the country which has favored him so highly, it is trea-
son for him to withhold it."[27]

Attempting to rally respected Jewish leadership, Bloom sent
copies of H.R.335 to Louis Marshall and Cyrus Adler, hoping to
solicit comments and develop momentum in support of his intent
to subpoena Henry Ford. Adler was blunt and patronizing in turning away Bloom's entreaties. "With all due respect to Mr. Nathan
Straus, I think his challenge to Ford was unwise," Adler said. In
Adler's view, "The Ford agitation has died down.... Most people
[now] consider him a fool. That a fool should make money is nothing new.... So my dear Mr. Bloom, now that your first indignation
has worn off, I think it would be wisest to let this matter drop. I
want to say that I have not discussed your letter with anybody and
would not have discussed this subject with you had you not asked
me for my opinion."[28]

H.R. 335 never made it out of the House Rules Committee.
However, on Judge Fred S. Raymond's docket at the United States
District Court in the Post Office Building of downtown Detroit,
Sapiro v. Ford was fast approaching.

CHAPTER FOURTEEN

Apology

AARON SAPIRO was represented by attorney William Henry Gallagher of Detroit and former Judge Robert S. Marx of Chicago. They asserted that the paper was "Ford's mouthpiece" and that "abuse was the general policy of the *Dearborn Independent*." The attacks therein upon Sapiro—a Jewish humanitarian dedicated to the alleviation of American farmers' economic tribulations—were by extension slanderous against all Jews. The articles had succeeded in undermining the faith of the farmers in the cooperative marketing movement. "The Jewish Question? Oh no, we can't discuss *that!*" declared Gallagher sarcastically in his opening statement, asserting to the contrary: "There is no use trying to pull the wool over our eyes and tell ourselves this is only an attack on Aaron Sapiro.... If the first article in the series had not been followed by subsequent articles, Aaron Sapiro never would have had the right to bring action on it."

Henry Ford's chief counsel was the impeccably mannered and mellifluous Senator James M. Reed, Democrat of Missouri, assisted by a team of seven attorneys. Ford's response read in part that "defendant avers that the plaintiff is in fact a member of the Jewish race and that the statement that he is a Jew casts no reflection upon him and is not defamatory.... If Henry Ford authorized an attack on the Jewish *race*, that is something for which no *individual* can recover damages." Ford served as an officer of a corporation legally known as the Dearborn Publishing Company. An instrument of that company, the *Independent*, had printed articles critical of "The Sapiro Plan," and so, whatever might have been in the articles, right or wrong, was the responsibility of the corporation, and Mr. Ford could not be seen as having undertaken any personal liability as president of such corporation unless it were demonstrated that he "instigated and directed" the articles to be written. Furthermore, the term "conspiracy" had never been employed in any of the *Independent* essays.

Judge Raymond ruled that Sapiro was bringing suit as an individual, and therefore Ford's alleged libels toward "the Hebrew race in general" could not be entered into the record. Ford, meanwhile, had already been subpoenaed by Sapiro's attorneys. He came to the Post Office Building on the first day of the trial, remaining secluded in his lawyers' quarters. The prospect of Ford being called to the stand at first appeared advantageous to his side; he was, after all, quite a celebrity. As three days of opening statements came and went, it became clear that the other side had changed tactics, realizing that with Ford as their witness there would be no opportunity to cross-examine him. The Flivver King became more apprehensive; the 1919 Mount Clemens trial debacle remained fresh in his memory.

On March 18, William J. Cameron was called as chief witness for the defendant, and it was announced that following the conclusion of Cameron's testimony, Aaron Sapiro would speak for himself as the plaintiff. "With this postponement," recalled Harry Bennett, responsible for driving Ford downtown and sitting by his side throughout the long hours of waiting, "Mr. Ford's nerve began to fail visibly."[1]

For six and one-half days, Gallagher, hammering away at the steadfast Cameron, tried to establish that Henry Ford was directly responsible for his editor's actions. How frequently did Mr. Ford visit the newspaper offices? "Oh, he dropped in from time to time." Did Henry Ford's philosophical attitudes appear on "Mr. Ford's Page"? "Not in detail; sometimes in a general way." Had Cameron ever discussed with Mr. Ford the editorial policy in the *Independent* with respect to "the international banking ring"? "We discussed the banking ring, but not the attitude of the *Independent* toward it...I've tried to discuss things with Mr. Ford," Cameron conceded, "but I can't discuss policy with him because he won't do it." Had Mr. Ford ever read the *Dearborn Independent* in his presence? "Well, I have tried to get him to, but I don't recall now that I ever succeeded." Did Cameron ever read to Mr. Ford any articles dealing with the so-called international banking ring? "No," Cameron replied flatly. Had he ever discussed with Mr. Ford the articles involved in the current case, specifically about the farmers' organizations? "The only definite recollections I have of a discussion regarding the Sapiro articles," Cameron said, "was at the time the demand for retraction was made. Any discussion I had with Mr. Ford was in the midst of other discussions. Hundreds of people called upon us about the matter."

Sapiro's letter demanding a retraction was received on January 6, 1925. Cameron remembered that he did then have a conversation with Mr. Ford: "I told him that, for the first time in my newspaper career, a statement for which I was responsible had been challenged by a demand for retraction. He [Ford] said, 'On what?' I said, 'On the Sapiro articles.' He said, 'What are they?' I tried to explain to him, but he passed it off with a wave of his hand and said: 'If you're wrong, take it back. If you're right, stand by it.'" That being the case, Cameron was asked, did he ever have any conversations with Mr. Ford about the parameters of his editorship of the *Independent*?

"When there were differences of opinion, he told me that I was the editor," Cameron replied.

Judge Raymond eventually loosened his initial stricture against any testimony pertaining to overall Ford comments about "the Jewish race," allowing Gallagher to present Cameron with back issues of the *Independent* and copies of the four-volume *International Jew* anthology in order to help refresh his memory. The judge also permitted counsel for the plaintiff to question Cameron about "particular Jews," such as Bernard Baruch, Louis Marshall, Paul Warburg, and Otto Kahn. Resistant to Gallagher's prodding, Cameron could not recollect conversations with Ford "about any articles about any individual Jews," adding that he did "recall one or two or three articles relating to Bernard Baruch's testimony on his conduct of the War Industries Board . . . and a discussion in connection with the Federal Reserve System, and not Mr. Warburg particularly." After he was excused from the stand, Cameron took off on an extended, unannounced vacation to the northern wilds of his native Canada.

Twenty-five years later—and following the death of Henry Ford—Cameron, interviewed by an oral history team working for the Ford Archives, still "accepted the scapegoat's burden" and stuck loyally to his guns: Ford had given the seasoned journalist and his staff carte blanche in determining the editorial direction of the newspaper. Ford was "simply an innocent bystander when the staff allegedly used the *Independent* to malign a race or an individual." Cameron met his interviewers with "I don't know," or variants thereof, professing ignorance in response to a series of questions about the Sapiro libel suit having led to banning the *Independent* in certain cities; the fluctuating circulation of the newspaper; Rabbi Franklin's intervention; the day to day editorial decisionmaking process; and so forth. The official historians of the Ford Motor Company, Allan Nevins and Frank Ernest Hill, were driven by common sense to express shock and indignation in their epic, three-volume chronicle in the late 1950s and early 1960s, declaring that "the idea that [Ford] did not know the contents of the anti-

Semitic articles is absurd. E. G. Liebold states that 'they were prompted largely by Mr. Ford"; [and] that 'he kept in touch with every phase.'"[2]

Louis Marshall, like much of the nation, followed Cameron's testimony closely, as extensive transcripts of the sensational trial were published daily in the *New York Times* and many other newspapers. Marshall expressed regret that Sapiro had brought suit against Ford, because, as Cyrus Adler and other American Jewish leaders never tired of pointing out, the trial only "gave Ford more of the publicity which he has craved."

One night at the end of March, that publicity took a strangely opportune twist. Driving alone in his coupe down Michigan Avenue toward his country estate, Ford said that he was sideswiped by a big Studebaker touring car with two men in it. The little Model T lumbered down a fifteen-foot embankment and into a tree. Bruised and disoriented, Ford managed to pick himself up and stagger home. There seemed to be no reliable witnesses to the accident. Ford was spirited off to his eponymous hospital and remained under doctors' supervision for two days before being sent back to Clara's care to recuperate. One of the Ford Hospital physicians later "revealed that Ford may have had a temporary blackout."[3]

A statement was issued by the company strenuously denying foul play. However, Mr. Ford's injuries would prevent him from testifying at the Sapiro trial for the forseeable future. "The papers said you have a broken rib," Harry Bennett remarked to his boss, laid up on the living room couch by the fireplace, "Did they?" Mr. Ford said, "Well, maybe I have." Bennett said, "I'm going to find out who knocked you into the river if it takes me the rest of my life." "Now," Mr. Ford demurred, "you just drop this. Probably it was a bunch of kids."[4]

AARON Sapiro's testimony, under Gallagher's expert guidance, began with a moving reminiscence of the adversities of his child-

hood and youth: father's early death, Aaron out on the street as a
ragged match-seller to help scrape some coins together, poverty-
stricken mother's agonizing decision to send the lad and three of
his six siblings into an orphan asylum "barracks," where the boy
became "a puppet in a cold, unfeeling system," long preparation for
the ministry as a means to bring a higher sense of moral purpose to
the society that had shunned him. Sapiro also read aloud to the jury
one of the many inspirational organizing speeches he had written
to gather the farmers together, telling the six men and six women
who sat in judgment that "there is no worthier thing under the sun
to which you can consecrate yourselves [than serving the farmer]."
Over the ensuing week, Senator Reed, exhaustively cross-
examining, dug fiercely beneath the veneer of Sapiro's altruistic
posture, questioning the religious fervor of his past career, empha-
sizing yet again the high fees Sapiro charged for his services—
"more than any good corporation lawyer would receive."

On April 10, Reed's session with Sapiro began to wind down,
and there was some brief questioning of Fred Black, who by this
time had risen within the ranks of the Ford organization to
become liaison with Albert Kahn's office in planning the engineering department at the River Rouge complex. Following Black's
stint, Gallagher began to make noises about what he openly called
Ford's "faked" accident, asking the judge to summon Henry Ford
into the courtroom for a bona fide physical examination to determine the extent of his injuries and to require him to present testimony. And then, at long last, Sapiro's team served E. G. Liebold
with a subpoena.

Ford's side, sensing the trial was drifting into dangerous waters,
had not been lying idle during this pressurized period. The day
after Liebold was called, Ford's attorneys presented affidavits to
the judge saying that one of the jurors "had lied during the *venire*
and had then been offered a bribe by a Jew." Despite Judge Raymond's warning to the press that there must be no published
account of the alleged transgressions until they were verified,

Harry Bennett, operating behind the scenes, encouraged a reporter for the *Detroit Times* to leak the inflammatory story, complete with the indignant woman juror's vehement words in self-defense. Sapiro offered to stay the course with eleven jurors, but the defense instantly moved for a mistrial, which was granted on April 21. A new trial date was set for September 12.[5]

Soon thereafter, Henry Ford, still in seclusion, phoned Fred Black and summoned him to Fair Lane. "There was a little general conversation about his health, and then Ford suddenly said [in the same impulsive manner he had used with Cameron five years earlier] 'I want to stop this *Dearborn Independent!*' Black asked, 'When do you want to stop it, Mr. Ford?' He said, 'Well, you work out a plan and then let me see it.'" Without pause, Ford segued into the next topic, "'Of course, you know about us bringing out this new car?' Black said, 'Yes, sir, I know about that.'"

How could he not? For the past six months—ever since a one-week December plant closing for inventory, when it was revealed that total employment at Ford had dipped to just over 210,000, 50,000 men *fewer* than the same quarter one year previously—rumors had been flying throughout the company of heated, fractious disputes between Henry Ford and his son over which direction the corporation should take.[6]

Ford said, "Well, you know we're going to have to advertise this new car and tell people about it, because it is going to be something entirely different." Before the summer was out, Black would be working closely with Edsel Ford and the N. W. Ayer & Son Agency on an expensive media campaign for the "Model A."[7]

Fred Black astutely caught the synaptic link in Henry Ford's mind between the problems with the *Dearborn Independent* brought before the public eye through the obsessive coverage of the Sapiro trial; the slow, inexorable decline of the Model T; and the necessity—faced with reluctance—to bring forth a new automobile for a new era in American consumerism.

For eighteen years, the Model T reigned triumphant over the

American automobile market. Fifteen million of them ranged the roads. The Ford gospel was engraved into every salesman's mandate: Stick with a standard model. Make all the cars alike. Produce inexpensively and in mass quantities. Forget about "knick-knacks and frills." Luxury and beauty did not belong in a car that exemplified unfettered production above all other virtues. The rattling Tin Lizzie's "chattering transmission bands ... squeaking little cast-iron brake shoes," sputtering radiator, and knocking connecting rods were sentimental, now vestigial voices in the cacophony of American industrial progress.[8]

But the last big year for the Model T came with 1923, when 7,000 of them a day rolled off the River Rouge assembly line. The competition kicked in, and cumulative numbers tell the story. From 1924–1926, the hand-throttle Ford's total production, including trucks, declined by more than 400,000 vehicles; during the same timespan, the pedal-accelerator Chevrolet went up by 350,000, and Dodge by more than 70,000—and, equally telling, Ford's proportion of motor vehicles sold overseas and in America went down dramatically, from 48 percent to 30 percent. By 1926, five makes of car besides the Ford sold for under $1,000.[9]

With energetic Alfred Sloan succeeding Pierre S. du Pont at the helm in May 1923, General Motors was committed to decentralizing authority for manufacturing operations. Unlike Ford's retrograde practices, G.M. could respond nimbly and flexibly to the demands of customers, adding new body styles and paint finishes each year (for example, there were 500 lacquer colors and upholstery options to choose from in the 1926 Cadillac; Fords were available in red, green, blue—and black). G.M. introduced four-wheel brakes and improved the mechanical operation of the engine with such innovations as six cylinders, increased fan belt durability, and much greater mileage between oil changes.

Chevrolet's banner year, exceeding the combined total production of its entire first decade, was 1926. By this time, G.M. was well along in developing a speedometer, shock absorbers—and some-

thing revolutionary to eliminate "clashing" of gears during shift-
ing, eventually called "synchro-mesh transmission." But Henry
Ford held fast to the planetary transmission of yore and remained
oblivious to these and other telltale signs of progress. He ignored
the reports of his field managers and went ahead with expansion of
the Rouge complex for an unchanging motorcar.

In the succinct words of "Cast-Iron" Charlie Sorensen, "Henry
Ford did not want to be told by anyone how he should build a
car."[10]

Henry Ford grappled simultaneously with "the Jewish Question" and the "Model T Question." Both problems were complicated by over-production and under-consumption—ideological and
material. Both problems could only be resolved by a shift in public
perception of Henry Ford, a corrective that Ford believed he alone
had the power to make. And the resolution of both "Questions"
required that Ford overcome his swirl of angry, resentful feelings,
stop licking his wounds, and make some
kind of clear statement to the world at
large, sooner rather than later. Was he
capable of doing this?

The immensity of Ford's dilemma was
revealed by the popular author Hamlin
Garland (1860–1940). Born on a farm
near West Salem, Wisconsin, Garland
grew up in the rural Midwest. In his
early twenties, beginning to find himself
as a writer, Garland moved to Boston for
three years, where he met and came
under the wing of William Dean Howells. He returned to the wider expanses of
the West and churned out dozens of

**Hamlin Garland, inscribed
"for Mr. and Mrs. Henry
Ford from his friend"**

romance novels between 1895–1916. In the final phase of his
career, Garland came to terms with the enduring literary currency
of the "middle border" territory of his youth and wrote a succession

of bittersweet autobiographical memoirs that achieved great com-mercial success. The best-known were *A Son of the Middle Border* (1917), which led to his election to the American Academy of Arts and Letters, and *A Daughter of the Middle Border* (1921), for which he was awarded the Pulitzer Prize.

Garland, a conservative writer of resolutely middle-brow, home-spun taste, professed an abiding love for American material culture and "old time" native values. He was passionate about what he called *veritism*, the strength of local truths. He wrote emotionally of his fears that "the sons and daughters of Jewish, Russo-Semitic, Polish, and Slavic European peasants who fill our streets . . . the floods from southeastern Europe [would] sweep away all that Whitman and Emerson stood for." To Garland, Ralph Waldo Emerson's prose was the veritable touchstone, "the blessed relief" against which he measured the failures of the "journalistic slang" so prevalent in the disturbing "modern" era.[11]

Garland's social and aesthetic inclinations made him a natural fit for the *Dearborn Independent*. Emerging poet Robert Frost began to have his verse published in the *Independent* in 1926. Frost advised Fred Black to get in touch with his friend Garland. It so happened that some years earlier, John Burroughs had also com-mended Henry Ford to Garland as "a natural philosopher," saying "There's a lot more to him than just automobiles." Garland and younger daughter Constance were given a tour of the *Independent* offices by W. J. Cameron, Black, and advertising manager Benjamin R. Donaldson in late December 1926, after which the author wrote in his diary, "I like these young editors of the *Inde-pendent*"—sadly, it was within a year of the newspaper's demise—"and I shall cooperate with them in their plans for an American magazine."[12]

During the meeting, Henry Ford came quietly into the room and sat down. Garland was handed an open copy of *A Son of the Middle Border* and asked to read the famous passage, particularly beloved by Ford, in which he paid tribute to the McGuffey *Readers*, "almost the only counterchecks to the current of vulgarity and baseness which ran through the talk of the older boys [at school]," Garland read, "and I wish to acknowledge my deep obligation to Professor McGuffey for the dignity and literary grace of his selections.... From the pages of his readers... I got my first taste of Shakespeare... Falstaff and Prince Hal, Henry and his wooing of Kate, Wolsey and his downfall, Shylock and his pound of flesh, all became part of our thinking." Garland's reading "deepened Ford's interest in [him]," and the two men began to trade quotations from the *Readers*. Garland would begin to recite a poem from memory, and Ford completed it. "In the mellow mood of the hour," Ford

Fair Lane, on the banks of the Rouge River

plucked three first edition *Readers* from the shelf and inscribed them to Garland on the spot.[13]

Garland's next encounter with Ford took place on April 22, 1927, one day following the declaration of a mistrial in the Sapiro matter. The author was on a lecture tour of the Midwest, and was invited to bring another daughter, Mary Isabel, and her husband to dinner at Fair Lane. Mrs. Ford met the group and proudly conducted a tour of her vast, newly planted rose garden, several hundred yards north of the river. As they were strolling slowly back from the pergola through the summer house, and then came within sight of the mansion, Ford came out to meet them, "bareheaded and alert, a slender figure, thinner than usual by reason of an accident in which he had been nearly killed.... Ford may be the remorseless businessman ... 'The Dearborn Despot' that some writers report him to be," Garland noted, "but I know nothing of that side of him."[14]

The third time they met, less than two weeks later, Ford was singing a markedly different tune. Garland received a telegram while in Chicago, saying Ford would like to see him again. After a quiet dinner at the Dearborn Country Club—constructed in the Old English style and funded with Henry Ford's money; hence no drinking or smoking allowed on premises—they engaged in an hourlong talk. "He sat opposite me and we had an exchange of opinion," wrote Garland. "He uttered some extreme judgments, the kind of pronouncements which have laid him open to criticism." Even though much of Ford's rhetoric was benign and "kindly, [and] shrewd" Garland could not suppress his dismay: "He is an internationalist in theory but does not commend the bankers who practice it to their personal advantage. His talk was vital and pungent," Garland wrote, striving for the right euphemisms.

The next morning, May 5, Garland awoke with agitation in his bedroom at the Country Club and immediately put pen to paper, his "mind still occupied by the psychological puzzle involved in Ford.... Ford himself is a conjuration, an inexplicable psychical phenomenon. Those who know him best confess that they do not understand him." With these perceptions, Garland stepped into place in a long line of mystified interlocutors. "He speaks at times with an air of great finality, as a man who has received a revelation or has secret sources of information on the great subjects of the day," former colleague Samuel Marquis had written in the memoir so abhorred by his old friend, and sounding as if he, too, (like Rosika Schwimmer or E. G. Pipp, for that matter) had been seated in a nearby armchair in the parlors of the Dearborn Country Club the night before: "He has a way of discoursing on one of his favorite themes—Wall Street, the Jew, international bankers sitting in a secret conclave somewhere and planning another war—in a way that produces among his listeners a profound and embarrassing silence."

And many newspaper reporters assigned to the "Dearborn beat" over the years would have nodded their heads in agreement with a comment by Dudley Nichols in the *New York World* about "Mr. Ford's insistence upon embodying racial animadversions in his statements ... time and again when interviews on other matters were being sought."[15]

Gordon Allport, in his classic work on *The Nature of Prejudice*, positioned the syndrome of "antilocution" at the lower end of a five-point scale spanning the diversity of activities that emanate from prejudicial feelings. Allport wrote that most people who experience prejudices feel the compulsion to talk openly about them with like-minded friends, and even occasionally with strangers.

Henry Ford's antilocution had a way of betraying every initiative he (or surrogates) said he intended to make to the contrary, from the beginning to the end of his career.[16]

The "Model T Question" was the first to be answered publicly, after a protracted struggle. As Ford sales declined and G.M.'s trajectory continued to climb, outside investors sensed an opportunity and came calling. Howard Bonbright of The Old Colony Trust Company of Boston, and then John W. Prentiss of Hornblower &

Weeks, each made an offer of $1 billion to recapitalize the corpora-
tion. Ford laughed them out of his office. Meanwhile, the clamor for
styling and engineering changes among Ford car and truck dealers
grew louder, and not only at home, where Mr. Ford had been turning a deaf ear for nearly three years. The news was equally dire in
foreign markets, especially in Germany, France, and England, from
which Edsel Ford received word that the company had been
"defeated and licked. . . . People cannot understand why we stand
back without combating in a more emphatic way the competition
with which we are faced," complained head of British operations
George D. Jenkins. Widespread layoffs had been rolling on for
more than a year in Manchester, Cork, Berlin, Antwerp, and Tri-
este, and would eventually surpass the 100,000 mark company-
wide, the biggest ever to hit the industry. Many European dealers,
unappeased by sporadic dispatches from the Detroit office that a
new model Ford was just around the corner, responded to the dip
in sales by defecting to competitors.[17]

"The Ford car will continue to be made the same way," The Boss
kept saying, convinced of his infallibility and hewing to the line of
right as a "single-purpose man," despite all the evidence Edsel
shoved in front of him. Their conference-room disputes escalated to
screaming matches. After a particularly loud argument in full view
of the management team, Ford told Edsel he was "too soft" and to
"shut up." His son left the board room in a silent fury. Ford ordered
Charlie Sorensen to go to Edsel's office, tell him to clean out his
desk, take the next train to California, and stay there until summoned home. "I am not governed by anybody's figures," the father
declared, "but by my own information and observation."

In the end, at high personal cost, the tenacious son won out.
When the Highland Park plant was finally shut down at 3 o'clock
on the rainy afternoon of May 26, 1927, it was the end of an era, a
ritualized show of family solidarity belying deep-seated antago-
nisms that now hovered between the two men. The fifteen-millionth Model T came off the assembly line, and a symbolic serial

number was stamped on the engine-block by eight of the company's oldest employees. Edsel took the wheel. After all, he was at least nominally the president of the company. Henry climbed into the passenger seat of the black coupe. They drove over to the River Rouge Engineering Laboratory and parked the car next to two other historic vehicles. One was the first tiller-steered automobile built by Henry Ford with his own two hands in 1896. The other was the 1908 Model T prototype. Henry took each car for a spin around the plaza, to the respectful applause of several hundred onlookers. There was no announcement from the Ford Motor Com-

"The Fifteen Millionth Ford," May 26, 1927

pany about when and where the next car might be unveiled, what it would look like—or how much it would cost to embark upon an immense, unprecedented (and unplanned) retooling of Ford's manufacturing process across the spectrum from micro-engineering new casting die molds to constructing entirely new machines.[18]

Similarly, to close down the current incarnation of Henry Ford's "Jewish Question" was a mammoth public-relations challenge. As befitting the extreme sensitivity of the subject, it required a dense skein of correspondence, secret meetings, and shadow-diplomacy involving the participation of several likely and unlikely allies.

In the days and weeks following the announcement of the Sapiro mistrial in late April, Ford's emotional state seesawed between poorly veiled anger and impulsive defiance, depending upon whom he was talking to and what he was talking about. He dreaded the thought that with autumn would come yet another court date, almost as much as he dreaded the idea of consigning his beloved "Lizzie" to nostalgia merchants. Yet he understood the necessity for a "clean slate" in both instances. He could not imagine successfully giving birth to a new generation of Ford motorcars with the stigma of Jew-hatred and its economic implications (real or imagined) hanging over his head. There was no way that such a huge undertaking involving the reconstitution of his whole company could be triumphant as a sales stimulus unless Henry Ford were *perceived* as a new industrial leader, shedding his old skin to become reinvigorated in his sixty-fifth year.

The first act in Henry Ford's grand show of rehabilitation came in the person of Arthur Brisbane, who requested a private audience in Dearborn with his friend on May 11, 1927. At the time of their meeting, Brisbane (1864–1936)—the son of leading Fourierist and social reformer Albert Brisbane—was the premier editorial writer for William Randolph Hearst's highly profitable and "decidedly lowbrow" flagship *New York Evening Journal.* Brisbane had known and admired Ford for more than a decade, openly rooted for him during the *Chicago Tribune* libel case ("I am glad to have you as a fellow-citizen"), and was one of the inner circle to encourage Ford to run for president. Brisbane serialized excerpts from Ford's 1926 memoir, *Today and Tomorrow,* and was one of the journalists with whom Ford and his wife associated socially.

"Today," Brisbane's popular column, was faithfully read at its peak by more than one-third of the American population. You could find it without fail six days a week compulsorily slotted for a hefty syndication fee into the upper left-hand corner of the front page of every Hearst morning paper. It was the kind of forum that addressed issues near and dear to Henry Ford, who enjoyed reading worldly wisdom by the "Demosthenes of the Barber Shop" such as "The Automobile Will Make Us More Human," or "Shall We Tame And Chain the Invisible Microbe As We Now Chain Niagara?" or "Your Work Is Your Brain's Gymnasium," or "To Those Who Drink Hard—You Have Slipped the Belt." Ford would have agreed with Brisbane's opinion in one especially outspoken column called, "What Are the Ten Best Books?" that "A man living on a desert island needs no books at all. Reading books is an idle occupation, unless you make your reading profitable to other human beings." Their mutual acquaintance, David Starr Jordan, was inclined to belittle such nuggets as "sciosophy." Be that as it may, Brisbane exalted comrade Ford—along with Washington and Lincoln—as "one of the three most useful men in American history."[19]

There was one issue, however, where the two men had not achieved common ground: Ford's antisemitism. Their differences first surfaced in Brisbane's "Today" column of Sunday, June 20, 1920, in which he harshly criticized the *Dearborn Independent*'s just-beginning series on "the Jewish Question." Among other things, Brisbane wrote that "Every other successful name you see in a great city is a Jewish name.... [They] number less than one per cent of the earth's population [and] possess by conquest, enterprise, industry, and intelligence fifty percent of the world's commercial success." The *Independent* shot back contemptuously in its July 3, 1920, edition, under the provocative headline, "Arthur Brisbane Leaps to the Help of Jewry," accusing Brisbane of having become tainted by living in New York City for so long, surrounded by Jews. The castigating voice sounded suspiciously like Cameron's, a fellow editorial writer, accusing Brisbane of neglecting to do his homework, "not having studied The Question...of knowing nothing about it." The article ended by harping upon Brisbane's natural tendency to heap unmitigated praise upon his subjects. The Hearst writer was cautioned to abandon such indiscriminate sentiments in deference to journalistic objectivity about such an important concern as "the Question."[20]

From that time forward, as unsolicited publicity adviser, Brisbane "implored" Ford on many occasions to discontinue the attacks, saying that he was "committing an injustice against a large body of good, upright American citizens." Brisbane remained convinced that Ford "did not ever realize the full effect of the articles." On May 11, 1927, the two men met and talked for five hours. Brisbane said that Ford told him on that day that "he had made up his mind to discontinue absolutely and permanently in any publication owned by him all articles such as those that had given offense to Jews." Ford said bluntly he was going to "shut the thing down and throw out all the machinery," at which point Brisbane offered $1 million to purchase the *Independent* "for Mr. Hearst." Ford refused.

"No one can charge that I am an enemy of the Jewish people," Ford said to Brisbane, "I employ thousands of them. Among them can be found many of my most talented associates. This building in which we are now located was built by Albert Kahn, a Jewish architect from Detroit, a man who, in my opinion, is without equal."

"I hate those companies which try to control others and make it hard for them to get money," Ford continued, with reference to his antipathy for the banking profession. "It does not matter what religion or race they are—but I am not an enemy of the Jews." The confidential session took place without the knowledge of Cameron, Liebold, or Ford's attorneys. It ended without a hint from Ford about when or how he would go public with his decision.[21]

A month went by. In mid-June 1927, Louis Marshall received word from former U. S. Congressman Nathan D. Perlman, a vice president of the American Jewish Congress, saying that he had been approached recently in Washington by two personal emissaries of Henry Ford: Earl J. Davis, former assistant United States attorney general, a resident of Detroit; and Joseph Palma, of the New York field office of the Secret Service. The men told Perlman that "Henry Ford and his family were anxious to put an end to the controversies and ill feelings" stimulated by the *Dearborn Independent* articles.²²

Perlman advised Davis and Palma to present themselves to Marshall in New York, which they immediately did, telling Marshall that Ford was now ready to do "whatever [he] thought was right." They also said that Ford believed W. J. Cameron had been "deceiving" him and agreed with what Brisbane and others surmised, that Ford did not comprehend the cumulative impact of the articles. Marshall was silent in response to this final assertion, venting incredulousness subsequently to Julius Rosenwald, saying "This God of the Machine (flivver though it be) had the hardihood to say to me through his agents that he knew nothing of the contents of the articles published in his paper."

Marshall did not mince words in condemning Ford for what he had done. He said that "Jews were painfully wounded by these libels, and that mere words would not heal the injury." Marshall stipulated to Davis and Palma that Henry Ford must make "a complete retraction"; he must ask for forgiveness; he must "see to it that such attacks are not made in the future" and make "amends for the wrongs."

The two ambassadors withdrew to Detroit for ten days, and then returned to Marshall with Ford's reply that the "terms were acceptable to him." Ford asked if Marshall would be willing to draft a statement for him. He further offered to make a settlement with Aaron Sapiro as well as with Herman Bernstein, editor of the *Jewish Tribune*, whose libel suit stretching back to the Peace Ship debacle was still pending. Bernstein had joined the original contingent on the *Oskar II* as owner of the Yiddish-language newspaper, *The Day*, and occasional foreign correspondent for the *New York Times*. Toward the beginning installments of the *Dearborn Independent* series, Ford ascribed some of his biases to a conversation he had had with "a Jew on the Peace Ship." This person, Ford said, told him that "Jews controlled the world...and caused wars...through control of gold." When *The History of a Lie*, Bernstein's exposé of the *Protocols of the Learned Elders of Zion*, was published in 1921, Ford made it clear who that Peace Ship informant had been—conveniently forgetting his conference with Rosika Schwimmer six years earlier. With the Sapiro suit coming to the fore, the accused Bernstein saw that his moment for retribution had finally arrived.

During the final days of June, Louis Marshall drafted Ford's apology in consultation with Palma. On June 30, according to Arthur Brisbane, a copy of the apology was transmitted to him by Palma. According to Harry Bennett, Brisbane then came over to the Ford offices in New York City at 1710 Broadway later that same day where, in the presence of Gaston Plantiff, Bennett called Ford on the telephone and tried to read the statement to him, cautioning Ford that it was "pretty bad.... But he stopped me, saying again, 'I don't care how bad it is, you just settle it up.'"

Ford added, "The worse they make of it, the better." Joseph Palma also claimed to have similarly warned Ford about the gravity of Marshall's text. "Go to it," Ford said, in Palma's recollection. "When my real views are explained to the proper people, they will know I am prepared to act honorably and to repair the damage as far as I can." Palma recalled that Ford signed the letter without reading it. Bennett reported that Ford told him on the phone to forge his signature and then send the executed statement over to Louis Marshall.

Marshall "could not believe [his] ears" when he heard that Ford had placed his signature on the apology "without the change of a letter....I do not believe that he will ever hear the last of it."

Henry Ford told all parties involved that the retraction was to be released exclusively by Arthur Brisbane. Proofs were sent from Brisbane's office to newspapers in New York City beyond the Hearst chain, as well as to the International News, Universal Service, the Associated Press, and United Press agencies, with the proviso that the statement be printed in its entirety and that Brisbane's name not be used.

Publication worldwide was on Friday, July 8, 1927. Louis Marshall told Cyrus Adler that he felt washing over him on that day "a great *Nachas Ruach* (spiritual satisfaction)." To the joyous editors of the *Forward*, Henry Ford's words, presented below, attained the same magnitude as the alphabetical *"Al Kheyt"* confession of sins recited by Jews on Yom Kippur:

"For some time past I have given consideration to the series of articles concerning Jews which since 1920 have appeared in *The Dearborn Independent*. Some of them have been reprinted in pamphlet form under the title, 'The International Jew.' Although both publications are my property, it goes without saying that in the multitude of my activities it has been impossible for me to devote personal attention to their management or to keep informed as to their contents. It has therefore inevitably followed that the conduct and policy of these publications had to be delegated to men whom I placed in charge of them and upon whom I relied implicitly.

"To my great regret I have learned that Jews generally, and particularly those of this country, not only resent these publications as promoting anti-Semitism, but regard me as their enemy. Trusted friends with whom I have conferred recently have assured me in all sincerity that in their opinion the character of the charges and insinuations made against the Jews, both individually and collectively, contained in many of the articles which have been circulated periodically in *The Dearborn Independent* and have been reprinted in the pamphlets mentioned, justifies the righteous indignation entertained by Jews everywhere toward me because of the mental anguish occasioned by the unprovoked reflections made upon them.

"This has led me to direct my personal attention to this subject, in order to ascertain the exact nature of these articles. As a result of this survey I confess that I am deeply mortified that this journal, which is intended to be constructive and not destructive, has been made the medium for resurrecting exploded fictions, for giving currency to the so-called *Protocols of the Wise Men of Zion*, which have been demonstrated, as I learn, to be gross forgeries, and for contending that the Jews have been engaged in a conspiracy to control the capital and the industries of the world, besides laying at their door many offenses against decency, public order and good morals.

"Had I appreciated even the general nature, to say nothing of the details, of these utterances, I would have forbidden their circulation without a moment's hesitation, because I am fully aware of the virtues of the Jewish people as a whole, of what they and their ancestors have done for civilization and for mankind and toward the development of commerce and industry, of their sobriety and diligence, their benevolence and their unselfish interest in the public welfare.

"Of course there are black sheep in every flock, as there are among men of all races, creeds, and nationalities who are at times evildoers. It is wrong, however, to judge a people by a few individuals, and I therefore join in condemning unreservedly all wholesale denunciations and attacks.

"Those who know me can bear witness that it is not in my nature to inflict insult upon and to occasion pain to anybody, and that it has been my effort to free myself from prejudice. Because of that I frankly confess that I have been greatly shocked as a result of my study and examination of the files of *The Dearborn Independent* and of the pamphlets entitled 'The International Jew.' I deem it to be my duty as an honorable man to make amends for the wrong done to the Jews as fellow-men and brothers, by asking their forgiveness for the harm that I have unintentionally committed, by retracting so far as lies within my power the offensive charges laid at their door by those publications, and by giving them the unqualified assurance that henceforth they may look to me for friendship and good will.

"It is needless to add that the pamphlets which have been distributed throughout the country and in foreign lands will be withdrawn from circulation, that in every way possible I will make it known that they have my unqualified disapproval, and that henceforth *The Dearborn Independent* will be conducted under such auspices that articles reflecting upon the Jews will never again appear in its columns.

"Finally, let me add that this statement is made on my own initiative and wholly in the interest of right and justice and in accordance with what I regard as my solemn duty as a man and as a citizen."—Henry Ford, June 30, 1927, Dearborn, Michigan.[23]

CHAPTER FIFTEEN

Apostle of Amity

———— ✺ ————

*I don't know as Mr. Ford ever apologized for anything. Of
course, he was supposed to have apologized to the Jews, but I
think everybody knows about that. He never even read that or
never even knew what it contained. He simply told them to go
ahead and fix it up.*

E. G. Liebold[1]

FORD'S settlement with Aaron Sapiro was quickly negotiated,
and, according to William H. Gallagher, "inasmuch as vindication
for himself and his people, and not money" was his client's aim,
Ford paid Sapiro's court costs and attorney's fee in the amount of
$140,000; he also agreed to set up a scholarship fund to educate a
needy orphan. Hailed as "a Jew with guts," a latter-day David who
had the courage to step up against the "tin-lizzie plated Goliath of
Detroit," Sapiro received the Richard Gottheil Medal from B'nai
B'rith for the most distinguished service to the cause of Judaism in
1927. The Herman Bernstein matter was also subsequently
brought quietly to closure. Bernstein was represented by Samuel
Untermyer, law partner of Louis Marshall.[2]

Linked to the conclusion of these suits, Davis and Palma assured
Marshall that it was Ford's further intention to "sever ... relations

with Messrs. Liebold and Cameron." Liebold was relieved of his responsibilities as general manager of the *Independent*, and Cameron was asked to step down as editor of the newspaper. However, both remained on the Ford payroll. Marshall was also told that Ford's apology would be published verbatim in the *Dearborn Independent*. This never happened. Instead, an editorial ran on July 30, 1927, explaining that the many articles about Sapiro's cooperative marketing plan had unfortunately been "accepted at their face value by the Dearborn Publishing Company" and that "Mr. Henry Ford did not participate personally in the publication of the articles."[3]

For the time being, the presses continued to roll at the *Dearborn Independent*, but it was evident that its days as a viable publication were numbered. When his order came down to close the paper, Ford was asked if he would like to sell the presses. He said, "No, don't sell them. I made a deal with those Jews and they haven't lived up to their part of the agreement. I might have to go after those Jews again."[4]

On the warm July day following the retraction announcement, the newspaper office was tense. *Independent* employees said they were not aware of any official change as yet in editorial policy. By this time, Cameron's friend Kurt Ludecke had eloped with an American woman—"dear little Mildred" was librarian for the *Detroit News*—and settled temporarily across the Detroit River in Windsor, Ontario, where he found work part-time as a real-estate salesman and also drafted the occasional article for the *Independent*.

Surprised to read Ford's admission of guilt, Ludecke rushed over to Cameron's office on Saturday morning, July 9, and found him sitting alone gazing out the window in deep thought, "his round, sour face resting in his small, soft hand, his short rather stout body almost crumpled in the chair. He looked forlorn and weak."

Ford's apology had come to Cameron as a devastating shock. He confessed to Ludecke that he was in an emotional state beyond "stunned." Some long moments passed in silence. Ludecke tried to convince Cameron to strike back publicly at Ford, to come out and tell the real truth about the guiding motivations behind the *Independent*. "I don't know yet what I am going to do," Cameron finally said. "But it is certain that I for my part will never make any retraction. What I have written will stand. Not one thing will I take back. You can be sure of that."

"The whole thing is a mystery to me," he continued, "I know Ford too well not to be absolutely sure that the views set forth in [those] article[s] are still his views, and that he thinks today as he always did. I simply cannot understand his alleged statement." After speaking behind closed doors with Ludecke, Cameron left town before mid-day for an inspection trip with a group of engineers on the Ford-owned Detroit, Toledo and Ironton Railroad, saying he "may return tomorrow."[5]

Even if Ludecke's version of Cameron's embittered words is taken with a modicum of restraint, there can be no doubt that after all these years in Ford's employ, the editor comprehended his boss's thought processes as well as anyone; the ink was hardly dry on the retraction before Ford's antilocution leapt forth. A "good friend" took Ford aside at the Dearborn Country Club soon after the apology and asked him why he had gone to the trouble of publishing all the articles in the first place. "I don't hate Jews," Ford insisted. "I want to be their friend. . . . The Jews have gone along during the ages making themselves disliked," Ford nodded as if in agreement with himself "over the good point he thought he was making." "Right? They ignored their own splendid teachers and statesmen. Even they could not get their people to change some of their obnoxious habits." "Well—?" said the friend, trying to determine the conclusion to this line of thought. "I thought," said Ford, "by taking a club to them I might be able to do it." Also at this juncture, "shortly after the repudiation of the Jewish Articles in the *Dearborn Independent*," in the process of a meeting with chemist John Lanse McCloud—a loyal company man since 1914— Ford said "with respect to this lawyer whom he knew, that he was a Jew. He said it," McCloud remembered, "in the most vindictive fashion I've ever heard Mr. Ford express himself. I realized then that when he said that, he characterized the man as being a Jew, and that was the worst possible thing he could say of a man. It kind of scared me."

McCloud was so unnerved by Ford's comment that he repeated it that night at home to his wife: "I was quite sure that Mr. Ford, while he repudiated the articles, hadn't really changed his opinions one iota," McCloud said, as if mimicking Cameron's recently voiced sentiments. Ford's observation was more disturbing because both men knew quite well that the lawyer in question was *not* in fact Jewish; rather, McCloud explained, "[Ford] meant that he had the *characteristics.*"[6]

Let us examine the response to Ford's retraction in concentric circles, first scanning the mainstream press. There E. G. Pipp was one of the most ubiquitous commentators. Pipp brought into the frame of reference the contrasting historic perspective of a former insider—happier times before the *Dearborn Independent* was founded, the era of the five-dollar day, Henry Ford on the ascendancy, building up his great business, providing funds to feed the homeless of Detroit, serving as model citizen. To Pipp, looking with melancholy at a period that now seemed even more unreal, a major turning point arrived in the aftermath of the *Chicago Tribune* suit, when he heard "the same expressions about the Jews [coming] both from Ford and from his secretary, Liebold." As far as Ford's awareness of the nature of every word in the "degenerate" ninety-one article campaign in the *Independent*, in Pipp's opinion that could never be proven. It was a moot point; regardless of the extent of his ongoing knowledge, Ford was the "inspiration, the instigator." In the present moment, at the (supposed) end of the affair, after all the stones had been thrown, Pipp ominously pointed out, "Poison injected into the system by the doctor of medicine or the doctor of public opinion is not wiped out by merely admitting the mistake and saying one is sorry."[7]

A cross-section of editorialists around the heartland echoed in various proportions Pipp's mixture of grudging belief in Ford's apology, coupled with relieved acceptance of his retraction. There was a strong undercurrent of *wanting* to breathe easier. In this mix of observations was added puzzlement and indignant perplexity— but not one rational, feasible explanation for Ford's behavior. "The mass of our citizenry, let us believe, is neither gullible nor bigoted," opined the *Pittsburgh Sun*, trying to take the broader view, referring to Ford by contrast as "this unusual man," noting that the public had been "inexpressibly shocked by such evidences of anti-semitism." The *Chicago Tribune* was more critical, agreeing with Pipp's laying the ultimate responsibility at Ford's feet, because "he has supported [the *Independent*], used it, vouched for it...He was its authority and payroll." To the *Philadelphia Public Ledger*, Henry Ford's retraction was "a queer footnote to the story of our times." The *Cleveland Plain Dealer* was downright scornful, rhetorically asking readers, "What is to be made of a 'dummy publisher,' a man who publishes and broadcasts week after week for years material he knows nothing of?" And an *Indianapolis News* columnist simply threw up his hands, concluding that Ford's antisemitism was "an obsession for which there is no accounting...an inexplicable mystery in the life of a very busy and influential man."[8]

Reaction from conservative Jewish publications was perceptibly more cautious. Close to home, the *Detroit Jewish Chronicle* picked up the sentiments of Julius Rosenwald, that "Mr. Ford's statement is greatly belated. It would have been much greater to his credit had it been written five years ago." However, Rosenwald sounded a theme prevalent among Jews, saying "the spirit of forgiveness is not entirely a Christian virtue."

The *Detroit Jewish Herald* advised its subscribers to wait and see whether the passage of time would prove Ford's sincerity, appropriating Louis Marshall's warning, expressed in the *American Israelite*, "against exaggerated expressions of felicity by Jews...I cannot understand why some of our brethren go from one extreme to the other," Marshall wrote, three weeks following Ford's announcement, invoking the adversary names of the Purim story. "Only last week, Henry Ford was regarded as 'the modern Haman,' and now they are almost willing to declare him a Mordecai."[9]

Cyrus Adler struck a sober and distant pose, condemning the "hysterical outpourings" received in his correspondence, while

dryly complimenting Ford upon finding it within himself to "purge his soul" in the interest of "spiritual satisfaction."[10]

Issuing a measured call for moderation, Marshall and Adler were surely aware of the blazing, all-capital headline in the Sunday, July

The Forward, July 17, 1927

17, English section of the *Forward:* "DRAMATIC COLLAPSE OF THE ANTI-SEMITIC MOVEMENT IN THE UNITED STATES." This was the kind of blind rush to forgiveness of Henry Ford they feared would come, riding the crest of a towering, cathartic wave of hyperbole, even though Marshall's sustained diplomatic role in resolving the matter was highly praised. Correspondent Nathaniel Zalowitz, taking over the entire left-hand half of the page, wasted no time in calling Ford's action "the most significant single event in American Jewish history of the present decade...American anti-semitism has received a death blow." Conceding that he found Ford's anti-semitism to be a riddle that defied solution, leaving Ford to be more of a puzzle than before, Zalowitz dismissed every familiar theory claimed as the root source of Ford's "Jew-mania"—attempts of certain Wall Street firms to gain control of Ford's empire; the machinations of Rosika Schwimmer, "the Hungarian Jewess"; threats of cloak-and-dagger Russian czarists (raising the unnamed spectre of Boris Brasol); Ford as "mere toy," a puppet in the evil hands of E. G. Liebold (sheer nonsense, Liebold was little more than a trusted private secretary); the "nondescript ex-clergyman" W. J. Cameron (absurd, Cameron was little more than a prolific "Yes-man").

FROM a tiny brownstone apartment stuffed with books and papers on West Eighty-Second Street across from Central Park in Manhattan came once again the despondent, plaintive voice of Rosika Schwimmer, mired in an interminable appeal for U.S. citizenship, and near poverty. When news of Ford's public apology reached her,

Two whimsical responses to Henry Ford's apology
in the summer of 1927

she spent the remainder of the summer of 1927 compulsively drafting and redrafting, typing and writing in longhand a lengthy coda to her "Open Letter to Henry Ford" that had been in progress for fits and starts over two years. She, too, craved her day in court—the court of public opinion: "The waste of it, Mr. Ford! To be kept from working when able and passionately desiring to work. To be made a parasite, a burden to oneself and friends, when one is capable to work for one's living! The waste of it, Mr. Ford, I can't clear my name as long as you will not help me to do it!"

"Weeks have passed since your apology to Mr. Sapiro and Mr. Bernstein and the Jews and their Gentile sympathisers," she wrote, "but the Jewish and the Gentile press continue to tell the world—that you had conducted the [antisemitic] campaign to cool your revenge on me."

Aside from a personal interview with Ford—"I must penetrate the walls around you!"—Schwimmer wanted him to issue a similar statement of vindication to her, "refuting the lies broadcast by your intimates." She also wanted Ford to lend her the archives for the Peace Ship expedition so that she could "finish the authentic story" and write a book about the voyage on her own terms. Ford did not respond personally; perfunctory acknowledgment of the "Open Letter" was dispatched through Liebold on September 18. Most likely Ford never saw the letter, as was more often the case with his correspondence by then, especially the more complicated kind.

One year later, during the summer of 1928, an emissary for Schwimmer, Marguerite Dumont, was able to gain an hour's meeting with Liebold, during which he told her that in 1922 there had been a flood in the Highland Park offices before the company moved to the River Rouge plant, and the Peace Ship files, with the exception of some clippings scrapbooks, were damaged and later destroyed. He had no idea of the whereabouts of any other related archives that might have been housed in New York, Stockholm, and Amsterdam. On Schwimmer's behalf, Dumont then asked if her friend could come to Dearborn for a meeting. "This is not possible," Liebold said, "If Mr. Ford and Mme. Schwimmer were to come together, the press would immediately wonder what new venture they are up to... When the expedition was started," Liebold went on, "Mme. Schwimmer and Mr. Ford took the risks attached to it.

Ford got the ridicule and Mme. Schwimmer had the slander...
Were he to vindicate [her] now, it would be out of place, and would
do neither he nor [Mme. Schwimmer] any good."

Well, then, Dumont pressed on, what about some kind of official
statement "that [Schwimmer] was not responsible for Ford's anti-
Jewish campaign?" "There is no point in making it," Liebold replied
flatly, effectively ending the conversation.[11]

ON Yom Kippur in the fall of 1927, temple congregants across the
land gathered solemnly to seek guidance toward paths of introspection on the most holy day of the Jewish year 5688. Rabbis spoke out
en masse about Henry Ford. There was no consistent way for
American Jews to accommodate Ford's apology. The range of pulpit sentiments ran from conciliatory to cynical. Reform Rabbi
Stephen S. Wise of the Free Synagogue in Manhattan was combative. The "picturesque fighter" and champion of free speech was
born in Budapest in 1874, grandson of the chief rabbi of Hungary.
Wise was ordained at the Jewish Theological Seminary in New
York. After a stint as rabbi of Temple Beth Israel in Portland, Oregon, he returned East and was offered a post at the prestigious
Temple Emanu-El. When told by the trustees that his sermons
would have to be approved by the lay heads of the congregation,
Wise immediately turned the Fifth Avenue job down and founded
his own Free Synagogue, so that he could maintain an "unmuzzled
pulpit."

Ever since as a young man he had met Theodore Herzl at the
second World Zionist Council in Basel, Wise was a passionate
believer in the establishment of the Jewish national homeland. In
that spirit, he worked at Justice Louis Brandeis's right hand and
became chairman of the United Eretz-Israel Appeal. Since 1924,
Wise had been president of the American Jewish Congress, to his
way of thinking, an organization more pluralistic and less oli-
garchical than its older sibling, the American Jewish Committee.

Wise was possessed with a vision of rabbi-as-preacher exemplified by the ancient prophets: the truth-speaker, tirelessly encouraging an engagement with the pressing issues of the day, no matter how controversial. Be it woman's suffrage, prohibition, judicial corruption, or, in the current instance, antisemitism—to Rabbi Wise, any course of action was preferable to no action at all, or worse, silence: "Our quarrel is not with Jews who are different," he declared, "but with Jews who are indifferent."[12]

Rabbi Wise ascended to the stage of a packed Carnegie Hall on October 9 (the Free Synagogue building of his dreams had not as yet been constructed). He gripped the sides of the podium tightly and seemed to lean in to the text while his operatic voice rang out

Rabbi Stephen S. Wise

over the assembled crowd. He stressed that the title of his sermon was "Henry Ford's *Retraction*," not "repentance," or even "reparation." In the case of the former, it was presumptuous for a Jew, at Yom Kippur or any time, to think he could look into another man's heart and assess the veracity of his intentions. In the case of the latter, Rabbi Wise believed it was fallacious to try to measure the damage of intangible forces such as libel and defamation compounded over a continuous seven-year stretch, if not longer. The only morally accurate course for the preacher as prophet was to discuss *future* implications of Ford's past actions in the light of his apology.

Here, Wise said, the question may fairly be asked, "Can any man be said to retract, who does not devote as much time and strength and substance to the *cancellation* of the results of his libels as he long devoted to the *publication* of them?" He challenged Henry Ford to demonstrate equal energies now in a constructive direction.

Rabbi Wise believed that Henry Ford's many publications had

taken on an aura of authority based upon the peculiarly American assumption that any "money-king"[13] whose net worth was so astronomical was justified in laying claim to a storehouse of knowledge, regardless of subject matter. The public perception linking omniscience to wealth was pervasive. Rabbi Wise believed its consequences would continue to echo for generations to come—and therein lay an even graver threat to the well-being of American Jews, as well as to the so-called international Jews.[14]

While Rabbi Wise put forth his brand of spiritual pugnacity, "the apostle of amity," Leo Franklin of Detroit, strove to maintain a voice of moderation even though he had always been closer to the center of the storm than any of his rabbinical colleagues—Reform, Orthodox, or otherwise. His Yom Kippur morning remarks to Congregation Beth El addressed the question, "What Is Atonement?" Despite obvious distance with respect to the style of their messages, the two spiritual leaders reached much the same conclusion.

Rabbi Franklin's mission that day was to place into a modern context the three sacred factors that composed atonement: repentance, prayer, and charity. However, he re-cast their meanings as "confession, conversion, and consecration." He did not once in the entire sermon mention the name of Henry Ford, but it is difficult to imagine that Ford was not implied in Franklin's train of thought, considering the rabbi's long summer of agonizing introspection. Unlike the Christian, Rabbi Franklin said, the Jew does not depend upon the public ear for the enactment of his contrition; he does not require the priest in the confessional. God alone sees into the heart of every individual Jew and attends to his still, small voice there. "Personal responsibility," the acceptance of who one is, follows next on the Jewish path toward atonement. And finally, with devotion to service, repentance is consummated. The only way to judge the degree of any man's sensitivity to the rights of others is to evaluate his expressed intention to do good deeds against a record of actions going forward: "Without this desire," said Rabbi Franklin, perhaps to the man who was not present in the sanctuary, "your atonement is a sham and show, a farce, a bit of self-delusion without moral character at all.... When you have come to love the good and hate the evil, you may feel that your atonement has been genuine, has been real."[15]

His Yom Kippur sermon marked the culmination of a vigilant three months for Franklin. From the moment Ford's apology appeared in the morning papers of July 8, the rabbi had been concerned with nothing else. The same day of the announcement, Franklin wrote his former neighbor a long, personal letter, reminding Ford that seven years had gone by since the appearance of the first *Dearborn Independent* article critical of the Jews and that even then he had been among the first to ask Ford to repudiate his attacks. Franklin also reminded Ford that he had never been able to accept that "a man of your native humanitarian instincts would sanction a course that could create nothing but hate and injustice and suffering."[16]

In the days following Ford's apology, Franklin received appeals from Jewish community leaders around the country suggesting or implying that this would be the perfect time to capitalize upon Ford's guilt and vulnerability. Charles F. Joseph, editor of the *Jewish Criterion* in Pitttsburgh, was one of the more blatant. "[K]nowing your former close association with Ford and the fact that you are the leading Jew in his home city," Joseph told Franklin to solicit Henry Ford immediately for a $1 million contribution to the United Jewish Campaign—make his retribution with cash.

Franklin was too diplomatic to follow that obvious route, revealing a touch of the iron hand within the velvet glove. "*No, this isn't the time to ask for money,*" he replied, underlining the words for emphasis. "I want to keep Ford in our debt as long as possible. That's why I was willing at once to accept his apology. The day *may* come when *of his own accord* he may be moved to do the handsome thing. At any rate, give him time." Sounding a strategic tone of caution, Franklin concluded with hope, "Let us be glad he has recanted, but above all let us be the creditors while he remains our debtor."[17]

Within days following Ford's apology, Theodore Fritsch of Hammer Verlag issued a statement questioning its veracity, alleging that it had been "forced [upon Ford] by Jewish bankers...Were it true, Mr. Ford would have withdrawn from me the publication rights for *The International Jew*, thus asserting that he claimed to possess such publication rights." Not until November did Ford—through Liebold—finally tell Fritsch that he would "revoke and terminate" any such rights remaining to publish the book—well aware that the Dearborn Publishing Company had never copyrighted *The International Jew* in the first place. In the interim, behind the scenes, Rabbi Franklin had approached Ford on numerous occasions, pleading with him to take action against the German and other overseas editions of the book. The negative replies always came back through Liebold's office.

Franklin also worked feverishly to try to persuade Doubleday, Page, and Company to delete Ford's venomous section on "Studies in the Jewish Question" from future editions of the first (1922) volume of his memoirs, *My Life and Work*. Isaac Landman, editor of *The American Hebrew*, was one of many who told Rabbi Franklin that he was the only Jewish leader in the aftermath of Ford's retraction who could convince the author to direct the publisher to halt shipment of thousands of copies of the book still in warehouses, and then, most imperatively, to excise in subsequent printings the three most hurtful pages dealing with the "racial problem" of the Jew. The revision was never made.[18]

Scrutiny of Rabbi Franklin's public and private observations during this time and years later reveals the tension between his insightful awareness of Ford's personality and the hope that "the retraction would spell *finis*" to all the troubles. Franklin's well-honed instincts as a student of the human condition are at odds with an equally well-established purpose as his community's minister.

Franklin's well-wrought public statement was an essay in the *Detroit Jewish Chronicle* of August 13, 1927, "Ford the Suppliant vs. Ford the Sinner" (entitled in an earlier, rejected draft, "Saint or Sinner?"). He took aim at colleagues such as Rabbi Wise who "continu-ally ranted against Ford in the pulpit," as distinguished from facing Ford personally, "telling him to his face of his iniquity, repudiating his friendship, returning his gifts." Franklin defended his way of approaching the man, asserting he had always known the futility of attempting to "*drive* Mr. Ford. Those who know his mental make-up must realize the hopelessness of such a course."

Always somewhat of an outsider with respect to the ruling par-ties of the American Jewish Committee, and, given the fissures in his relationship with Louis Marshall, it is not surprising that Franklin never found out that Marshall had drafted Ford's retrac-tion. Twenty years after the fact, Franklin still questioned whether Ford's unnamed "ghost writer" had the right to claim ignorance on his behalf about what was written in the *Dearborn Independent* arti-cles. How could Henry Ford have been "shrewd enough to build up an unparalleled industrial empire, and yet blind to what was hap-pening right before his eyes?" In the reflective solitude of old age, Rabbi Franklin sought solace in the words of the Talmud, "telling us that we must seek, where evil has been done, not to destroy the sinner but to destroy the sin." He was forced to concede sadly, "later events have indicated that my optimism ... was not too well grounded."[19]

CHAPTER SIXTEEN

The Chosen People

———— ✧ ————

*He is an industrial Fascist—the Mussolini of Highland Park,
Fordson and Dearborn.*

WALDEMAR KAEMPFFERT ON HENRY FORD
in *The New York Times Magazine*, January 8, 1928.

ON THE LAST day of 1927, the *Dearborn Independent* shut
down and "sank without a trace, except for the oily slick of bias it
had spread." Dramatizing the closure, Henry Ford traveled to New
York City to meet face-to-face for the first (and only) time with
Louis Marshall at Marshall's law firm on the twenty-third floor of
120 Broadway. With a gentle, genial smile, and a hearty hand-shake
in front of a gaggle of reporters and distracted office workers, Ford
offered his ghost-writer a brand-new Model A Ford, which Marshall politely turned down, saying he was "devoted to pedestrian
locomotion."

The two men spoke privately in Marshall's inner office for over
an hour. Ford told Marshall that "the *Independent* no longer
exists...that he had destroyed every copy of the pamphlet, *The
International Jew*, which he could find, that he never had anything

against the Jews as Jews, and that the ending of the entire affair afforded him the greatest satisfaction." Marshall took the opportunity to tell Ford that Liebold and Cameron must be dismissed, to which Ford "readily acquiesced." Marshall then brought up the continuing sales of the booklet in Germany by Theodor Fritsch as well as editions in a half-dozen other languages. Ford reassured Marshall that a mass-pulping was imminent—neglecting to acknowledge that Fritsch stipulated he would go through with this only if he were reimbursed by Ford for the expense.[1]

For the next five years, the Jewish Question took a sustained hiatus from Henry Ford's explicit public discourse and descended into dormancy. Except for the rare euphemism characterizing the American currency system as "the catspaw of manipulators," Ford managed to keep his rambling mouth shut for awhile. Instead, he rechanneled volatile passions and budgetless financial resources into two other big projects near to his heart. One was a factory. The other was a museum.[2]

To the outside world, Ford needed to demonstrate that the family dynasty was strong. The aging, patrician father appeared to take a back seat to his son. Edsel was assigned to "take care of" the company and see through the transfer of the last assembly lines from the old

Henry Ford, 1928

Highland Park to the new Rouge, the start-up for Model A style redesign, and accelerated production during the fall of 1927. The complicated and costly crash-phase of retooling for the new car in a new era was Edsel Ford's mission. This image of continuity from generation to generation was a marketing necessity: "There is a large field of prospects among the middle-classes," Edsel announced that year, "who are able to pay more for a car—and pride, vanity, a desire for something more impressive, enter very strongly into the sale."[3]

The reality—as was so often the case inside Ford Motor Company—was markedly different. Edsel's nonconfrontational and benign management style was doggedly undermined by his father. Henry directed his old crony, Harry Bennett, head of the personnel department, with Charlie Sorensen at his right hand, to "[get] rid of all the Model-T sons of bitches." Bennett and Sorenson ruled the Rouge plant with the chief's inspiring words ringing in their ears: "A great business," said Henry Ford, "is really too big to be human."[4]

Reflecting Ford's personality, the River Rouge plant was a gigantic contradiction. Architecturally, as a physical plant, it represented the cutting edge in many ways. There were operable ventilation sashes high over the blast furnaces so that heat could escape upward. Broad ranks of sawtooth windows on the roofs faced the four cardinal directions so that natural light came down onto the work areas equally at all times of day. The interior walls were painted eggshell white. The steel structural grids for the dull-yellow-green cement buildings were laid out with an eye to ease of movement about the production floor. Air circulation was aided by giant, quiet fans. The buildings were "sparklingly clean," constantly scrubbed and repainted from end to end. Garbage cans had to be emptied every two hours.[5]

The Rouge *looked* as if it had been built by a humanist "with pretensions of solicitude" rather than a cold-hearted taskmaster. Why, the workers only had to put in a five-day week, for which they were paid $30, unheard of in the rest of the automobile industry toward the end of 1920s. Any man you talked to as he emerged from the place at the five o'clock whistle said that he was grateful to hold a job there. However, he did not have the protection of a labor union, would not be the beneficiary of unemployment payments if he were laid off, and most likely was an immigrant with little other option for other work.

Step inside the Rouge reception lobby, approach the security checkpoints, and sign the log-sheet under the suspicious gaze of "men who look like police-court detectives," then spend some time roaming around, and a different atmosphere came to light. You might think that "Mr. Toil," exemplar of the link between prosperity and industry, one of Henry Ford's favorite childhood heroes from the pages of the McGuffey *Readers*, was running the factory.

"A vast whispering-gallery sown with booby-traps," the Rouge was composed of 126 separate manufacturing and administrative departments. Productivity competition between shifts was encouraged. It was no place for lackadaisicals or weaklings. An army of regimented "machine proletarians" was required, men who could maintain a constant pace, depending upon how fast the conveyor belts were running, eliminating all superfluous motions and often following a printed sheet of instructions dictating the precise sequence of actions to perform their jobs properly—men who worked shoulder-to-shoulder, and when given a break had to scarf down fifteen-cent lunches from the company wagon in exactly fifteen minutes. Talking while working was forbidden. Sitting down while at work or on break was also forbidden. "We are trying to make [the men] do things with a mechanical pace-setter," said A. M. Wibel, a typical remark by a River Rouge line manager at the time.[6]

COMPELLED to secure his niche in the popular imagination as "The Prophet of the New Era," Henry Ford controlled the River Rouge complex—the environment meant to be the preeminent symbol of the American industrial future. The pressure to preserve his reputation was counterbalanced by Ford's equally abiding, ill-concealed fears about the true nature of that modern future. His fears were channeled into a longstanding and omnivorous need to capture, and define, the antique values of the American *past*.

As early as 1912, Ford expressed the intention to direct "his own Smithsonian Institute," a collection of what he liked to call "strictly American" objects, a museum of specimens of all the articles used since the country was settled—"every household item, every kind of vehicle, every sort of tool." It would be a museum-cum-school that exemplified his special view of history, not the abstract, "more or less bunk" kind found in books, but documentary evidence through actual, commonly used old-fashioned, tangible things, the best illustrations of daily life properly conducted by just plain folks since seventeenth-century America.

After a decade, Ford had spent millions of dollars and filled more than five acres of barns and scattered tractor warehouse buildings at Dearborn. The staff called it his "Curio Shop." Here was every example of lamp made in America: hurricane lamp, oil lamp, gas lamp, automobile electric lamp. Here was every kind of doll owned by children in America since the Revolutionary War, hundreds of them. Here was a shelf full of sleigh bells Ford col-

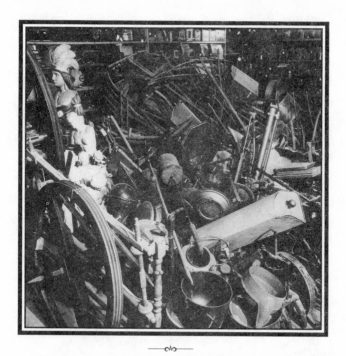

**Temporary storage room of Americana in quonset hut
for Henry Ford Museum**

lected "because I wanted," he told a visitor in 1922, "to find the
exact note that I used to hear from the bells of my father's horses in
winter time." And here was every kind of dinner bell, church bell,
and school bell, too. Here was every known type of reaper. Here
were six different types of threshing machines starting from 1841.
Here was every type of pioneer conveyance from the old Calistoga
wagon to the prairie Schooner. Here was every type of American
pipe, from clay to church warden to water pipe. For that matter,
here was every species of fire-shovel, clock, mattress, spinning
wheel, whiskey jug, chair, candle stick, bird cage, foot warmer (he
had acquired more than fifty), gun, bed, butter churn, china set, fan,
shawl, balancing-wheel, puzzle, and pipe organ.[7]

Ford was not satisfied only to collect the *things* of America. He
would also establish an "Early American Village," dramatizing the
nation's most memorable structures and based upon the Village
Green layout, with restored landmarks, workplaces, and homes of
great men. He began by sending a team of workmen to the site of
his own little white farmhouse birthplace, where they were ordered
to plow the ground six feet down and find "every old knife, spoon,
fork and anything else his Mother and Father used." He built a
complete replica of the Menlo Park laboratory complex in New
Jersey as a tribute to his old friend and mentor, Thomas Edison.
He brought in William Holmes McGuffey's original log schoolhouse, an 1854 general store from Waterford, Michigan, an original stage-coach stop on the Detroit-Chicago Road, the 1840 Logan
Country Court House, site of Abraham Lincoln's law practice, a
brick-by-brick replica of the Detroit workshop at 58 Bagley
Avenue where he built his first motor car in 1896, the 1855 Trip
Saw Mill from Lenawee Country, Michigan, and facsimiles of the
homes of his heroes Edgar Allan Poe, Walt Whitman, and Patrick
Henry. There was even a "spreading chestnut tree" beside a village
blacksmith shop. The collection eventually grew to more than 100
buildings.[8]

Ground-breaking for a central museum within which to house

Ford's cornucopia got under way in April 1929. The centerpiece was a 700-foot-long replica of the façade of Independence Hall in Philadelphia, complete with bell-tower. The structure would cover 350,000 square feet, boasting the largest teak floor in the world, polished to a mirror shine. Henry Ford's Industrial Museum was named the Edison Institute in homage to his dear friend, and the assemblage of old and facsimile buildings was called Greenfield Village in honor of Clara Ford's birthplace. The great foyer of Independence Hall became the scene for old-fashioned dance balls staged weekly by Henry and Clara, reviving the *schottische*, square dances, the polka, the minuet, and the gavotte, partners swooping and swaying to Benjamin Lovett's music played upon vintage instruments in the vast, echoing space, between rows of polished car models and wooden sleighs.[9]

For Henry Ford, all the money spent, all the attention paid to historical veracity, far surpassed indulgence in the simple delights of nostalgia. His fixation upon the material past as manifested by these commonplace talismans was pathological. How else to explain "surrounding himself with bygones" to such an extreme degree? He had the financial wherewithal and used it to become one of the most comprehensive preservationists of all time. It was ironic—and emblematic of his contradictory nature—that the man who did more than anyone else in the twentieth century to modernize America never relinquished his vise-like and possessive grip upon the good old days.[10]

LISTENING to the many hours of William J. Cameron's conversations with Ford Motor Company oral historian Owen Bombard, extensive interviews conducted during the fall of 1951, one hears the mellifluous tones of a reflective, articulate, and introspective seventy-three-year-old man looking back upon twenty-seven years in loyal service to "Mr. Ford"—always "Mr. Ford" except for the rare occasions when Cameron refers to him as "The Boss."

William Cameron always considered himself a religious person, a Christian, although in differing ways. There had been a community church in Brooklyn, Michigan, not far from the town of Jackson, where the Ontario-born Cameron worked as a timekeeper in the rail yards. On occasional Sunday mornings, at the invitation of friends who admired his natural talents as a speaker, Cameron preached informally at the church, even though he was not a member and "*never*," as he put it with great emphasis, "studied theology, I was never a pastor." If anything, Cameron said, that Brooklyn tabernacle was "Unitarian in its trend . . . more like a little group that seceded" from the established institutions in town.

Cameron's Christian orientation extended into the tone of his *Detroit News* editorials, where he wrote an inspirational column called "Reflections," and carried through to his long stint at the *Dearborn Independent.* Cameron viewed the practice of corporate life as religion, too. "Business is one of the great, sacred *originals*, necessary to society," he reminded Bombard. "It provides a gateway into the spiritual world, the world of ideas."

And so in the early days, because he honestly believed that business was not only about making money, when Cameron first came to Ford he basked in the light of the employer's "vision . . . I caught the fire of his vision of business." As the *Independent* rose and fell during the 1920s, it seemed to Cameron (his pauses between replies become lengthy, filled with sadness and caution) that "something just . . . stopped" in the imagination of Henry Ford. The idealistic fire began to die down. Ford never relaxed his manner of authority, but he "stopped *paying attention* to the men. . . . he lost his *touch* with the men on the shop floor," increasing his distance from day-to-day operations, inspiring fear rather than respect.

After the death-rattle of the *Independent,* Cameron confessed poignantly that although "I just went on doing what I had been doing, I never knew what I *was*" for the next two decades. He was called a public-relations man, but there was no public-relations department. Cameron continued to speak for Ford and for the company on a popular radio show, "The Ford Sunday Evening Hour," every week from 1934–1942 over the entire eighty-six station CBS Network and again from 1945–1946 on ABC, even though he never again quite enjoyed the same intimate rapport with "The Boss."[11]

While painting a convincing retrospective self-portrait with a necessary eye to posterity, Cameron understandably never touched upon his most significant and influential ideological affiliation— with the revisionist British- (also known as Anglo-) Israelite Movement.

British-Israelites believed that the *Anglo-Saxon* race "and their ethnic kinfolk—*Isaac's Sons*—throughout the world" were lineally descended from the Ten Lost Tribes of Israel. *They* were the favored, authentic, and legitimately "chosen" people—*not* the tribe of "treacherous" Judah. Inferior, usurper Jews could claim no rightful part in God's original inheritance. The five-score promises originally made by God to Abraham were fulfilled and enacted by the Tribe of Ephraim—Joseph's younger son—on the terrain of England as a company of nations (*Berit-Ish* in Hebrew meaning "man of the covenant"); and, by extension, in the United States, where the "true Children of Israel" knew and recognized the Lord. In America, another of the Lost Tribes, Menasseh—Joseph's elder son—took root with the mandate to establish "a great and *independent* nation" and to "exterminate the aborigines." Jacob crossed his hands—made the Sign of the Cross—over the heads of Ephraim and Menasseh when he blessed them. And as prophesied in Isaiah, 65:15 and 28:11, the true sons of Israel would bear another name, and speak another tongue, that is, English—"a branch of the Aryan stock of languages," *rather than* Hebrew.

British-Israelite doctrine found early articulation in late-eighteenth-century England through the writings of Newfound-land-born Richard Brothers (1757–1824). Possessed by millenarian visions, Brothers imagined himself to be "Nephew of the Almighty, and Prince of the Hebrews" and was author of the two-volume tract, *A Revealed Knowledge of the Prophesies and Times* (1795). He believed Gentiles needed to be made aware that they were "a distinct Nation...the hidden Israel."

Irishman John Wilson's (d. 1871) book, *Lectures on Our Israelitish Origin* (1840, four editions subsequently, and an American edition in 1851), established his reputation as the "True Father of the Rediscovery of Israel." He substantiated the traceable migratory path of the Tribe of Dan, carrying its eagle standard from the Near East by way of the Caucasus Mountains into Western Europe. The only way "erring" Jews could ever be admitted into the Kingdom of Heaven would be to accept Jesus, attending to the "Word of God, gospel for a witness unto all nations." One day, Wilson warned in his many sermons, the land of Israel—Palestine—will have to become repossessed by its rightful Gentile claimants.

A pamphlet by Wilson's disciple, Edward Hine (1825–1891), *Forty-Seven Identifications of the British Nation With the Lost Israel*, published in London in 1871, also connected Biblical Israel with the British Empire. It sold over a quarter of a million copies. Hine was a promoter of his gospel in America and Canada during an ambitious lecture tour in the mid-to-late 1880s, including many speeches in Michigan and Ontario. Hine is considered to be responsible for the "transplantation" of British-Israelism to these shores.

The Reverend W. H. Poole, born in Ontario, took up the banner in Detroit during the decade of the 1880s, through his widely distributed book, *Anglo-Israel, or, The Saxon Race Proved to Be the Lost Tribe of Israel.*

J. H. Allen (1847–1930) was a vice-patron of the British-Israel World Federation, founded in 1920 at Buckingham Gate, directly opposite the palace. Allen promulgated the belief that the Coronation Stone housed in Westminster Abbey was actually the stone upon which Jacob rested his head at Beth El when he dreamed of a ladder reaching from earth to heaven. His *Judah's Sceptre and Joseph's Birthright* (1902)—"Understand us...the great bulk of Israelites are *not* the Jews"—was the major text diffusing British-Israelite doctrines first throughout Canada and then in the northern and midwestern United States, among grassroots Protestant Bible study circles such as the kind Cameron participated in as a young man.[12]

It is difficult to pinpoint the moment of contact between the teachings of British-Israelism and W. J. Cameron. However, Cameron's beliefs were well-known when he signed on with Ford. His colleague John Lanse McCloud recalled "Cameron expound[ing] on his favorite subject of the Lost Tribes of Israel ...a subject [he] loved." In this light, Cameron's complaints to E. G. Pipp that he "hated" writing the Jewish articles require another look. Between 1920–1927, a dozen essays with British-Israelite themes appeared in the *Dearborn Independent*. They demonstrate Cameron's increasingly negative spin, taking the Gentile "chosen" inheritance down a more sinister path to illustrate the basis for the archetypally adversarial relationship between Jews and Christians. According to Cameron, Jewish defensive "propaganda" was beginning to infect the faith of "uninstructed clergy," leading them "astray." He returned repeatedly to the concept of "true Israelitish raciality" while casting aspersions upon the self-defined purity of those who called themselves Jews and were taking the name of Israel in vain, because Israel was not their birthright.[13]

In the September 22, 1923, issue of the *Independent*, the entire second page was given over to the "untenable position" of the Jews. The article is unbylined. Who else but Cameron could make such a production out of the "racial" basis for the Bible? The author triumphantly points to Genesis, Chapter 49, as well as Deuteronomy, Chapter 33, to show that the destiny of the Tribe of Judah, dramatically updated as "the Deserted Prussia of Israel," was far inferior to "the larger branch of the Joseph Tribes," that is, the heroic "tens of thousands of Ephraim" and the "thousands of Menasseh." Modern-day immigrant "Tartars" from Russia and "Slavs" from Poland are therefore anything but "Chosen"—in fact, they are mere remnants, "despised exiles," descendants of minority outcasts.

The essay conjures an image of the End of Days, when the Jews will be unable to withstand the reuniting of the entire Aryan, English-speaking world, the apotheosis of modern British-Israelite doctrine in "the next great war, the real Armageddon." In the *Independent* of May 23, 1925, the words of the Reverend William Pascoe Goard, chief minister of the British-Israel World Federation, are cited at extreme length. "There is not room enough for both Israel and Anglo-Saxondom, if these are two separate conceptions," Goard warns. "It must be one or the other... the International Banking Ring outlined in the *Protocols of the Learned Elders of Zion* ... [against] the Banner of the Lord."[14]

Two years thereafter, Goard lectured in the town of Haverhill, Massachusetts, "very likely" at the invitation of one of its upstand-

The Protocols of the
Learned Elders of Zion in
pamphlet edition sold by
the Anglo-Saxon Federation
of America while W. J.
Cameron was president

PROTOCOLS

of the Learned Elders of

ZION

Translated from the Russian of NILUS

By

VICTOR E. MARSDEN

Late Russian Correspondent of "THE MORNING POST"

PRICE 50 CENTS

ANGLO-SAXON FEDERATION
OF AMERICA
FOX BUILDING DETROIT, MICH.

Issued by

AMERICAN PUBLISHING SOCIETY

P. O. Box 165

Seattle, Washington

ing citizens, a lawyer, inventor, and construction company manager named Howard B. Rand (1889–1991). In 1928, building upon a Bible-study group he led, Rand founded a British-Israelite magazine called *Kingdom Message*, which grew to more than 15,000 subscribers. In the spring of 1930, the Anglo-Saxon Federation of America was jointly founded by Howard Rand and William Cameron, held its first conference in Detroit, and set up headquarters in Suite 601 of the Fox Building downtown. Cameron was elected president of the new organization. Clarence S. Warner, a full-time public relations representative, was appointed at this time. Rand, as secretary and national commissioner, then embarked upon a crusading British-Israelite tour across the country, and over the following years, branches of the new Federation began to spring up everywhere.

And so it was that after having been ousted from his bully pulpit in the *Dearborn Independent*, William J. Cameron arose phoenix-like out of the ashes of Henry Ford's doomed newspaper and found a new venue for his philosophy over the next fifteen years. In 1935, he became the director of *Destiny*, the publishing arm of the Anglo-Saxon Federation of America. Here was a safe haven where this unordained preacher continued to preach unencumbered—preparing the ground for the antisemitic flowering of the Christian Identity movement.[15]

CHAPTER SEVENTEEN

"I Am Not a Jew Hater"

AMONG Henry Ford's private papers formally dedicated at his Fair Lane estate in Dearborn on May 7, 1953, as part of the Ford Motor Company Archives were found hundreds of pocket-sized "reminder books" containing accumulated jottings spanning more than half a century. On the perforated pages were intermingled names and addresses Ford wanted to remember, song titles to be included in the repertory of the next folk-dancing get-together at Greenfield Village, catch-phrases and handy quotes Ford invented or came upon in his reading—as well as "asserted prejudices and fixed ideas, disappointments and frustrations."

This last category was predominantly in evidence in notebooks from the 1930s Depression years, where, according to a *New York Times* reporter permitted an early look at the uncataloged material, "the private jottings reflected [Ford's] dislike of bankers, Jews, the

New Deal and labor unions, and his major competitors, General Motors and Chrysler." Occasionally, Ford merged these components together into an imagined conspiracy against the Ford Motor Company, losing ground in a competitive consumer marketplace. "Our competitors are behind all tax and N. R. A. [National Recovery Administration] plans, with the bankers' international, and they are running all the governments in the world," Ford free-associated. "Unions are created by finance and industry." In another place, he scrawled, as if reminding himself, "The Jew is out to enslave you."

Such tried-and-true Fordisms were reestablished in the public eye after a long silence via his agitated transatlantic telephone interview with the *London Evening Standard* on January 26, 1933. Infuriated by a spontaneous walkout leading to a work stoppage by 9,000 men at the venerable Briggs Manufacturing Company—the supplier of car bodies to Ford occupied leased premises at Highland Park—The Boss lashed out at "certain bankers who caused the shutdown . . . to gain control" of his factories. Ford did not mention that the men at Briggs were fed up with a sweatshop environment where they were paid an average of nine cents an hour. Rather, Ford said, "certain of my competitors are operating against me, supported by these bankers, with the object of preventing another Ford car from leaving the factory . . . but I will fight them and prove that production cannot be stopped."[1]

Four days following Ford's outburst came a different kind of turbulence from overseas. Adolf Hitler was appointed to the chancellorship of Germany, marking the expiration of the Weimar Republic. The new nation, led by "Nazi champions of the conservative Right," embarked upon a cultural path that soon placed Heinrich Ford's name in the foreground.

Within two weeks of taking office, as one of the first official acts defining his "new world order," Hitler delivered the opening address at the International Automobile and Motor-Cycle Exhibition on the Kaiserdamm in Berlin. He described in grandiose detail a nationalistic master plan for a huge system of motorways to be filled with "the people's cars" (*Volksauto*)—"inspired by the American model."

Under the supervision of Edmund C. Heine, a German-born American citizen, the Ford-Cologne plant had opened for business in the spring of 1931 overlooking the Rhine River. It produced the Model A, and then the smaller Model Y, with some components made in Germany. The familiar Ford logo and design were unmistakably American, but "Our work [and] our efforts are German," Heine was fond of saying. Nevertheless, the company was under increasing pressure. Shortly after Hitler's address to the automobile convention, Ford-Germany was handed an explicit ultimatum. The *entire car* had to be "manufactured locally by May 20 [1933] if we are to be considered a national German product, and if our business is not to be jeopardized by arbitrary taxation," Heine reported glumly to his superiors. No further importation of parts from the Dagenham plant in England would be permitted. Hitler's ultimate goal was a wholly German car industry with no foreign dependencies. The Nazi Party "looked coldly on the American firm." Ford-Germany was a deficit operation, reduced to a small fraction of the overall market, claiming only 5.5 percent of new registrations—compared to arch-rival (German-made) Opel-General Motors, which soared to over 50 percent. At one point, the board of directors at Ford-AG secretly considered the embarrassing option of merging with a German automobile firm in a desperate effort to save themselves from ruin.[2]

By the end of February 1933, an ambitious rearmament drive was under way in Germany. Civil liberties were suspended. By the end of March, the Reichstag gave Hitler control. In a long speech to the assembled representatives, he called for "far-reaching moral renewal" in education, the media, and the arts. In early May, as an example of the Nazi "new spirit," thousands of books by authors considered anathema to the regime were burned in public view at the center of the Berlin Opernplatz. By the end of May, the trade union structure of Germany was dissolved. By summer, all opposition parties had been "liquidated." In short, all functions of Hitler's new society were drawn into the compulsory embrace of *Geichschaltung*—"coordination"—falling into place behind his mandates with astonishing speed.[3]

Such rapid "coordination" across all segments of the culture also included, as of April 7, 1933, an "Aryan Paragraph" in the Civil Service Law, barring Jews from any form of government employment. More pernicious was the immediate, widespread relaxation of strictures of violence against Jews—by which was implied more than physical intimidation and economic boycotts. The Hammer-Verlag publisher Theodor Fritsch was an expert in promulgating violence through the written word. In Leipzig, on June 15, he brought out a popular companion volume in tandem with his perennial classic, *The Handbook of the Jewish Question:* the twenty-ninth printing of *Der Internationale Jude* (The International Jew), with Henry Ford's name prominently displayed on the title page. "In America there is to-day no longer a Jewish Question," the first advertisements for the new edition proclaimed, "and Henry Ford is the courageous man who has exposed it.... On this side of the ocean, this problem is moving toward a sure solution, and for the Germans it is of special significance to read the judgements of one of the greatest and most successful Americans."

With renewed fervor, Fritsch reminds his readers of the past history of *The International Jew*, beginning with the trail-blazing first issue of the *Dearborn Independent* thirteen years before—"a blow that took Judah's breath away." It was as if Ford had tossed a stone into the middle of a pool, and ripples were still emanating outward. Fritsch played skillfully upon this argument. In the preface to the German edition, he insists that "the value of Ford's work is constantly growing, and the older it becomes the more its value will grow." As if he were handed Henry Ford's baton directly, "Adolf Hitler under the symbol of the swastika took over the fight against Judah in the spring of 1933." Stepping readily into line to

demonstrate his loyal faith in *Geichschaltung*, Fritsch now enlists
Ford's book as an integral ideological player in the "coalition of all
anti-Jewish movements...this movement will yet eliminate
Judah...After all," the preface concludes, "our final goal is to save
mankind and humanity from destruction."

Fritsch does not stop there. The twenty-ninth German edition
of *The International Jew* is noteworthy for footnotes in which the
translator expresses disagreement with Ford on points where he
feels the automaker does not push far enough. Fritsch disagrees
with Ford's hope that one day "the eyes of the Jews will be opened"
to their mistakes. And he disagrees with the *Dearborn Independent*'s
occasionally drawing the line between "good" and "bad" Jews. Not
possible—all Jews are evil.[4]

As soon as Rabbi Leo Franklin of Detroit got his hands on a
copy of Fritsch's book—sold openly in New York City—he correctly
recognized it as the most extreme co-optation of Henry Ford's
name thus far. Franklin reached out to E. G. Liebold and embarked
upon a fruitless appeal, which extended over the ensuing year and a
half, again attempting to persuade Ford—always through
Liebold—to distance himself once and for all from a publication that
seemed to have taken on a life of its own. It is doubtful that Henry
Ford was made aware of Franklin's efforts.

Rabbi Franklin first sent Liebold copies of the title page, advertisements, and preface of Fritsch's book, and then spoke personally
and by phone with him about the gravity of the problem of the
book's rapid dissemination. He pointed out to Liebold that the Germans were now "*using* Mr. Ford...as the nominal author...most
effectively in their campaign of antisemitism." It was imperative
that Ford reassert what he had said in his famous "Retraction" of
1927: further spread of these sentiments in his name did not enjoy
his sanction.

Under pressure to pursue "backstairs diplomacy" from assistant
secretary Harry Schneiderman and executive secretary Morris D.
Waldman in the American Jewish Committee office, Franklin

gloomingly relayed to them that "Liebold tells me that while Mr. Ford is in deepest sympathy with our people and while he realizes the book is still an instrument of danger to us, he does not at this moment wish to sign the reassertion of his retraction."

"I made it quite clear to him [Liebold] that *NOW* is the time for action, and that even a short delay means unspeakable torture to our co-religionists on the other side."[5]

"I am not a Jew hater." Henry Ford—or someone writing on his behalf, finally spoke out in the pages of the December 1933, issue of *The American Hebrew*, the words syndicated into every Hearst newspaper in the country. "I have never met Hitler. I have never contributed a cent directly, indirectly, or in any other way to any anti-Semitic activity anywhere. Jews have their place in the world social structure, and they fill it nobly. I have Jewish friends—many of them—in my business associations."

The Anti-Defamation League stepped into the fray. In 1934, Executive Director Richard Gutstadt was promoted by ADL Chairman Sigmund Livingston to become the organization's first director of special activities. Gutstadt began his tenure by initiating a letter-writing campaign encouraging members to communicate directly with Rabbi Franklin and alert him to copies of *The International Jew* that they were beginning to find in libraries and bookstores over a wider field, so that Franklin in turn could keep "prevailing upon Ford's secretaries." Franklin continued valiantly to hew to a reasonable tone, writing to Ford that "despite everything that you have tried to do to stop the further publication of the *Dearborn Independent* articles, they seem to bob up here, there, and everywhere."

Tucked away among the rabbi's papers is a harsh letter he received from Richard Gutstadt with the demand that it be passed along to Liebold. Torn between continuing to press his point, and, "knowing the people surrounding Mr. Ford as I do," fearing the consequences of overt anger, Franklin first attempted to edit the letter before filing it unsent. [*Excised portions in brackets*] "[If Mr.

Ford's organization is sincere] It should be evident [to the Ford organization] that a matter of such long standing as this one ought to be for once and for all remedied. Will you be good enough to reopen this matter with Mr. Ford," Gutstadt implored, "and let us know what he is prepared to do in order to remedy the vast evil for which [he] the book bearing his name is responsible?"[6]

Two more years passed before Liebold finally came out publicly to deny authorship of *The International Jew* on behalf of The Boss. Samuel Untermyer, Louis Marshall's law partner, had assumed presidency of an organization in New York City called The Non-

**The International Jew proliferates
in many languages**

Sectarian Anti-Nazi League to Champion Human Rights. Never a man to equivocate, Untermyer had already spoken in the spring of 1933 against the atrocities visited upon Jews in Germany, challenging the Order of B'nai B'rith, "Are you going to sit idly by while your brethren in Germany are humiliated, degraded, deprived of their rights and citizenship and kicked out of their professions and employment and left to starve by this Austrian upstart and his band of ruffians?" As *The International Jew* continued to proliferate, appearing in other languages throughout Europe, the league assailed Ford's dangerous imprimatur. Through Liebold, Ford responded that "the book erroneously refers to [me] as its author... steps will be taken to prevent the continued misuse of [my] name."

In the same accusing telegraph, which he made a fanfare of releasing to the press, Untermyer also called to Ford's attention reports that "several officials of the Ford Motor Company were associated with activities considered anti-Jewish," to which Liebold replied, now speaking for himself, "the writer desires to state that inasmuch as Mr. Ford has always extended to Ford employees the fullest freedom from any coercion with respect to their views on political, religious or social activities, they cannot be reproved by us for exercising such liberties." W. J. Cameron was quick to chime in that "Mr. Untermyer is several years behind the question which he is seeking to discuss. The whole case was settled long ago."[7]

Such oblique references were not new, reconfirming long-held if surreptitiously expressed misgivings about Liebold and Cameron inside the company and without. However, Untermyer was also alluding to another man more recently added to the Ford payroll. Fritz Julius Kuhn, nine months previously had been elected to a four-year term as *Bundesleiter* of the German-American Bund (*Amerika-Deutscher Volksbund*). Born in Munich in 1896, Kuhn served in World War I as a lieutenant in the Bavarian army, seeing action on four different fronts, and was decorated with the Iron Cross. After the war, he studied chemistry at the University in Munich and received a master's degree there. He then joined the paramilitary Epp Freikorps and Oberland Freikorps. A follower of Hitler during the abortive Munich *putsch*, Kuhn emigrated in late 1923 under shady circumstances. He had been convicted of theft, and a friend of his family was able to raise enough funds to spirit him out of the country before Kuhn had to serve substantial prison time.

Fritz Kuhn lived in Mexico City for four years, working as an industrial chemist. In 1927, he entered the United States and made his way to Detroit, where he was given a position in the laboratory of the Henry Ford Hospital. Several years later, he went on to the River Rouge plant. In 1933, he became an American citizen. Shortly thereafter, he joined the Friends of New Germany and became leader of the Detroit chapter, moving up to become head of the *Gau-Mittelwest* (Mid-West District). Kuhn led a Bund delegation to Berlin for the 1936 Olympics, where he was received briefly by Hitler and presented him a $3,000 check for "Winter relief."[8]

The Bund had barely hit its stride as a growing membership organization "preaching the German world viewpoint, the incomparable German miracle," glorying in the post–1933 so-called German Renaissance, when it became the subject of a vigorous congressional investigation led by Representatives John McCormack of Massachusetts and Samuel Dickstein of New York. This inquiry was succeeded in May 1938 by the House Un-American Activities Committee, chaired by Representative Martin Dies, which reiterated that, aided by "nativist allies ... the Bund was an extension into this country of the Nazi purpose and program." By the spring of 1938, it was revealed that 45 percent of all participants in Bund chapter meetings were German citizens. Besides taking thousands of pages of sworn testimony, these two committees performed an adept public-relations job of "unmasking" various forms of Bund propaganda activities in America, especially through the distribution of "tons of literature," such as the virulently antisemitic *Der Sturmer* edited by Julius Streicher, the *Völkischer Beobachter*, as well as the Bund's own official newspaper, *Deutscher Weckruf* (partly German and partly English), and *The International Jew*.

During much of Fritz Kuhn's tenure as head of the Bund, it was alleged that he was on unpaid leave of absence from the Ford

Motor Company. Accusations (never proven) continued during the mid-to-late 1930s that the Bund was subsidized by Henry Ford. These reports were accompanied by those saying that the organization had "financial links to the Fatherland." The flamboyant Kuhn did nothing to dispel such rumors. He went so far as to state that at his Olympic audience with The Fuehrer, Hitler encouraged him to come out in support of Alf Landon, the Republican candidate in the presidential race against Franklin Roosevelt. The German embassy in Washington denied there was any truth to this account.

Fritz Kuhn, February 22, 1939

The German American Bund under Kuhn's inflammatory leadership—eventually disowned by the Nazi government—kindled strong emotional responses from right-wing American fringe groups and was instrumental in keeping home-grown biases alive during the years leading up to World War II.[9]

The pattern of Henry Ford's rhetoric during this period heading into the war circled back to "the approximately one hundred men responsible for wars . . . the small group of men who profit by them," fluctuating over the span of a year to as low as "twenty-five or thirty individuals who are the *real* public enemies . . . the 'underneath government,'" then generalizing about "the financiers and the money lenders." Those same men whom Ford reviled as "the Wall Street crowd, the certain financial interests of New York . . . the basic alien principle behind all New Deal projects" expanded in number to become "sixty families" in April of 1938, and then declined to "twenty-five persons who handle the nation's finances" by June, two months following.[10]

At the apex of this special brand of antisemitism that does not need to make use of the word "Jew," resourceful Sigmund Livingston at the Anti-Defamation League tried to counter Ford's chronic employment of the term "international financiers" in a new, educational way. The league published a statistical study of all foreign loans in the United States between the years 1925 and 1928, during which time non-Jewish bankers floated a total of more than $7.3 billion, and "Jewish bankers" by comparison put forth a little more than $1.1 billion. The amount of outstanding loans currently floated by J. P. Morgan alone, as of the publication of the ADL report in mid-1935, stood at $1.5 billion. As of that same date, only 7 percent of all foreign loans were underwritten by "Jewish" bankers. Finally, Livingston pointed out, nineteen of the largest banks in New York City possessed a combined total of directors on their governing boards amounting to 420 men, of whom thirty were Jews. Given the impermeable management in Henry Ford's outer office, it is doubtful that this corrective survey made its way to him. Even if it did, it is unlikely that he would have read it.[11]

In late 1932, antisemitism in America was still perceived in many quarters as predominantly religious or intellectual in nature, "a subtle, whispered thing, something sensed, felt under the skin, as it were." However, Hitler's early success in his visible campaign to persecute German Jews set off a chain reaction in America. There soon flourished a bumper crop of Americanist-xenophobic, quasi-fascist groups in the United States, eventually more than 120 of them, championed by a colorful assortment of demagogues— William Dudley Pelley's Silver Legion, later the Silver Shirts/Christian Party, founded in California in late January 1933; "Radio Priest" Father Charles Coughlin's National Union for Social Justice/Christian Front, founded in 1935; the American Vigilant Intelligence Federation (established in Chicago to combat "the menace of the Jew" by Honorary General Manager Harry A. Jung in April 1933); Colonel Edwin Marshall Hadley and Mrs. Elizabeth Kirkpatrick Dilling's Paul Reveres, incorporated in November 1932 (she wrote that "Talmudists," otherwise known as Communists, had always hated Christians); and fundamentalist Reverend Gerald Burton Winrod's Defenders of the Christian Faith (established in Wichita in 1925; in February 1933, he condemned "Jewish Bolshevism" as the root cause of the evils of modernism, derived from "the same impulse which killed Jesus Christ"). Facilely characterizing Jews as agents for extreme moral subversion and social upheaval, these and other Fifth Column organizations were infused with a kind of "misty, yeoman ideology." They were energized to frenzied rabble-rousing by hatred of Franklin D. Roosevelt and his "Jew Deal."[12]

By the end of 1933, the climate had substantially darkened for Jews in America. There was discerned an "ever-widening stain of ostracism," in Carey McWilliams's haunting phrase. To be sure, the Depression cut through all ethnic strata, but it had special significance for Jews—representing only 3 percent of the total population—because social discrimination expanded easily into flagrant economic exclusion. As had been the case in the early 1920s, employment quotas were reinstated at the same time that immigration rules were tightened anew, especially against refugees from Poland, Romania, and Germany.[13]

Lingering memories of the "exclusion experience" of the 1920s were fresh in the minds of so many American Jews that a *Fortune Magazine* study in mid-1936 recommended "quieting the Jewish apprehensiveness" as the first priority for improving the morale of society. Anxiety and uncertainty grew, after the passage of the September 1935 Nuremberg Laws "for the protection of German blood and honor."

The *American Jewish Yearbook* looked back with alarm and ahead with desperation at the conclusion of 1936, eerily revising the naïve prediction of Paul Masserman and Max Baker about Jew-hatred—that it would in all probability never amount to more than a tremor beneath the skin of society at large, that this fresh wave of fascism could only be an aberration. Rather, the *Yearbook* editors conceded that in truth "comparatively little provocation was

required" to draw ugly biases up to the surface and make convenient scapegoats out of the Jews.[14]

From Erfurt, Germany, the Nazi World Service (*Weltdienst*),
headed by retired Colonel Ulrich Fleischhauer, disciple of Theodor
Fritsch and friend of Dietrich Eckart, and subsidized by the propaganda ministry, distributed official party literature in eight languages, "the best cure for all public evil," to antisemitic groups in
the United States and across "the Aryan-Christian world...reach-
ing to the furthest corners of the earth." An antisemitic conference
at which twenty-two countries were represented was convened in
Erfurt in 1937.

Henry Ford and the Originators of War was listed fourth on a
lengthy checklist in the *Weltdienst* monthly mail-order bulletin of
most-often-requested pamphlets "to enlighten ill-informed Gentiles [about] the machinations of the Jewish underworld." On the
eve of World War II, according to historian Norman Cohn, *The
Protocols of the Learned Elders of Zion* enjoyed a greater vogue than
they had in 1921.[15]

CHAPTER EIGHTEEN

Hitler's Medal

ON THE evening of April 28, 1938, the Grand Ballroom of the Waldorf-Astoria Hotel in New York City was filled to capacity for the annual banquet of the American Newspaper Publishers Association. Before dinner, the present officers were reelected for another term, led by James G. Stahlman, publisher of the *Nashville Banner*, as president of the association, and John S. McCarrens, publisher of the *Cleveland Plain Dealer*, as vice president. After dinner, the toastmaster, S. E. Thomason, publisher of the *Chicago Times*, introduced the special guest of honor, Mr. Henry Ford.

Resplendent in tuxedo and wing-collar, Ford stood at the dais. The immense room fell silent, for this was to be his first public speech in many years—"and the last," Ford whispered to Thomason. "Mr. Toastmaster, ladies and gentlemen," Ford began, "we are all on the spot. Stick to your guns and I will help you, with the assistance of my son, all I can." Whereupon he sat down, clasping his hands in his lap, smiling thinly.

After dessert, clamoring reporters cornered Ford, while W. J. Cameron hovered at his elbow. Could he venture an elaboration upon such brief remarks? "They're after us," Ford replied instantly. "They're trying to kill competition." But who, pray tell, were "*they*," the members of the Fourth Estate wanted to know. "The powers that be," said Ford, "Not so much the Government as the people behind the Government." Cameron stepped forward and raised a fleshy, protective hand, prohibiting further questions. "Gentlemen, the statement speaks for itself," he said in that trained, ringing voice, pale blue eyes glistening behind round, rimless spectacles. "It requires no amplification. There is nothing more to be said about Mr. Ford's statement."

With that, the two men departed. As they hurried out, Ford brushed past a table where Rosika Schwimmer was seated, as a foreign correspondent assigned to cover the event. But after all the frustrating years of trying to gain a personal audience, she lost her nerve and was too fearful to approach him.

Interpretations of the twenty-nine word speech uttered by the "Oracle of Dearborn" followed thick and fast after Ford had left the room. Why, it was even shorter than the thirty-one word "speech" Ford had delivered a decade earlier, on April 11, 1928, at a testimonial dinner given in his honor by the American Society in London. "He meant the labor people," said Fred Rentz, publisher of the New Castle, Pennsylvania, *News*. "Ford meant he is going to lick hell out of John Lewis and his crowd." "He meant those crackpots in Washington," offered J. M. Stephenson of the South Bend, Indiana, *News-Times*. "If Roosevelt would listen to such men as Ford, instead of the half-witted, brainless Brain Trust, the country would not be in the present condition." William F. Wiley, publisher of the *Cincinnati Enquirer*, opined, "I think he meant that Government was not going to stop squeezing business." "I think he meant that the financiers are trying to control everything, recalling his rather hectic experience with Wall Street a number of years ago," chimed in Fred Schilplin, publisher of the St. Cloud, Minnesota, *Journal*. And so the debate continued over cigars and brandy, onward, deep into the night—the constant and inconclusive debate about the cloudy, elusive language of Henry Ford.[1]

AT the end of the month, the board of directors of Ford AG, chaired by the "dominant" Dr. Heinrich F. Albert—publicly praised in January 1937 by the propaganda office of the Reich Ministry of Economics—voted to enlarge the Cologne plant and also to build an assembly factory in Berlin-Johannisthal for trucks and passenger cars. In June 1938, as a direct signal of approval that Ford cars sold in Germany were finally being made entirely in Germany, the Nazi government placed an order for 3,150 custom-designed, three-ton V-8 trucks. Were these trucks being built for military use? Nonsense, cabled Charlie Sorensen from the home office. There was no danger of war on the horizon; besides, if the German consumer market did not warm overwhelmingly to the four-cylinder Ford "Eifel" sedan, then the company needed to go with the demand for other vehicles. Coming to terms with the necessity of cooperating with the new government was a major breakthrough for Ford AG, one that Albert had been pushing with the powers in the states for several years, beginning when he fired the ineffective Edmund Heine. Albert also encouraged the Dearborn and Dagenham factories to buy tractor parts, transmissions, and axles manufactured in Germany, as a smart diplomatic gesture toward improving German export activity. Stockholders were pleased to see Ford AG foreign sales triple. In 1938, for the first time in its history, Ford AG paid a dividend. A year later, the company changed its official name to Ford-Werke, AG, "as a symbol of its wholly German identity."[2]

In light of these developments, Henry Ford was delighted when, upon the occasion of his seventy-fifth birthday, July 30, 1938, he became the first American recipient of the *Verdienstkreuz Deutscher Adler*—the Grand Service Cross of the Supreme Order of the German Eagle. Contrary to some published accounts, the presentation of this award, created by Hitler in 1937 "as the highest honor given by Germany to distinguished foreigners," was not a surprise. It was announced at Ford's birthday dinner before an invited audience of more than 1,500 prominent Detroiters. William J. Cameron made the keynote speech, in which he praised "the Ford influence upon engineering and production and upon society." The German consul in Cleveland, Karl Kapp, then read the formal, laudatory citation from a parchment scroll signed by Ford's longtime admirer, The Fuehrer, "in recognition of Ford's pioneering auto work in motor-

**Henry Ford Receives the Grand Cross of the German Eagle
on his seventy-fifth birthday, July 30, 1938**

ization and in making autos available to the masses." Flanked by Kapp on his left, and German Consul Fritz Heiler of Detroit on his right, Ford beamed as a red leather box was opened before his eyes. There nestled a golden cross surrounded by four small swastikas, finished in white enamel, strung on a red ribbon with white and black borders. Kapp draped a broad, red satin sash over Henry Ford's right shoulder extending down to his left hip, and then pinned the medal to the breast pocket of his white suit.[3]

On September 10, the Nazi *Official Gazette* in Berlin announced that on October 12, in a dinner at the Harmonie Society Hall in Detroit, Kapp and Heiler would bestow lesser grade *Verdienstkreuz* medals upon three more Americans: Professor Heinrich von Moltke of Wayne State University (Third-Class), John Koos of the Ford Motor Company, a close associate of Harry Bennett (Third-Class), and Ernest G. Liebold (First Class). Thomas J. Watson, the president of IBM, also received the medal, but returned it in 1940.

On October 18, at a predinner reception in the American Embassy in Berlin—this time, it definitely *was* by surprise—Charles "Slim" Lindbergh received the *Verdienstkreuz* from the founder of the Gestapo and minister of the economy, Hermann Wilhelm Goering. Lindbergh did not speak German, and so the American Consul-General in Berlin, Raymond Geist, translated impromptu as Marshall Goering launched into Hitler's citation while he handed the medal to Lindbergh, "By order of *der Fuehrer.*" The decoration was in recognition of "services to the aviation of the world and particularly for his 1927 flight, which postwar Germany had never acknowledged."[4]

Three years later, in a less-hectic moment, sitting serenely on white sand in the shade of a palm tree on the Dry Tortugas islands more than 100 miles southwest of Key West, Florida, watching the sun set and waves break on the beach, Charles Lindbergh's old friend Jim Newton turned to him and said, "Charles, I'd like to hear exactly what happened at that dinner when Goering pinned his medal on you."

Before he knew what was going on, Lindbergh recalled—correcting Newton's wording—Goering thrust the medal into his hand. Ambassador Hugh Wilson was even more flabbergasted than Lindbergh at that instant. "But you didn't hand the medal right back," Newton pressed on. Lindbergh was adamant about providing some background: The dinner had been arranged as the culmination of a long week during which he had visited many German factories to view the latest developments in airplane technology; actually, over a period of years, Goering and his staff had been shepherding Colonel Lindbergh around to aviation plants and research centers, even permitting him to fly the Luftwaffe's newest planes. Lindbergh had earlier made a confidential offer to French Premier Edouard Deladier to sound out Goering about selling airplane engines to the French during this period when there was a (temporary) easing of tensions between the two countries. And finally, Lindbergh told Newton, Ambassador Wilson hoped that he "might have the opportunity to persuade Goering to use his influence with Hitler to alleviate pressure on the Jews." In fact, Lindbergh did not know at the time of the ambassador's diplomatic strategy.

Lindbergh said that handing back the medal would have put an end to any hope of obtaining intelligence information about German air strength and would have looked like an affront to his host, the ambassador. He also told Newton—in an exercise in revisionism—that returning the medal would have quashed even the possibility of progress on "the Jewish Question." Casually disparaging the symbolism of the event, when he returned later that evening to the residence of American military attaché Truman Smith, Lindbergh showed the medal to his wife, Anne Morrow. She had one prophetic word in response: "Albatross."[5]

By the time Henry Ford and Charles Lindbergh received their honors from Hitler, they had been socializing occasionally for more than a decade. Returning to America after his breathtaking solo trans-Atlantic flight, Lindbergh, twenty-five, embarked upon a transcontinental tour covering more than 22,000 miles and touching down in eighty-two cities—"three months of ceaseless adulation." On August 11, 1927, Lindbergh brought *The Spirit of St. Louis* to Detroit, city of his birth, met the sixty-four-year-old Ford for the first time, and took him up, "crouched in the cockpit," for his first spin in an airplane. Edsel Ford followed suit for his own ten-minute flight. While at the Ford Airport, Lindbergh also tried out the one-passenger "Flivver" plane for a spin, and copiloted a Ford Trimotor as well.[6]

Lindbergh went on to become a paid consultant with Henry Ford and the engineers at Dearborn, advising them on airplane as well as bomber design into the early years of World War II. Lindbergh recommended the construction of Ford-built planes equipped with Pratt & Whitney engines for use in the earliest stages of commercial aviation, and he was instrumental in developing a prototypical airline, combined with rail freight, called Transcontinental Air Transport. In conjunction with Ford, this enterprise later became the impetus for TWA.[7]

Since his own first drive in a Model T at the age of eleven, Lindbergh had revered Ford, noting that the Flivver King "combined the characteristics I admire most in men—success

Henry Ford meets Charles Lindbergh, August 1927

with humility, firmness with tolerance, science with religion." He should have added a healthy infusion of tenacity combined with innocent bullheadedness; Lindbergh conceded to Jim Newton on another occasion that "some of Ford's ideas are far out, but they are always stimulating."[8]

By refusing to return or repudiate Hitler's medal, Lindbergh successfully "intellectualized" his opinions about the German people. On the one hand, he admitted that he "shared the repulsion that democratic peoples felt in viewing the demagoguery ... the irrational quality of Hitler." On the other hand—and in this respect, Anne waxed far more enthusiastically than her husband—Lindbergh viewed Nazism glowingly as "the new wave," a social value-system representing the future perfectibility of humankind and a viable "alternative to its decline."

Henry Ford employed a similar rationale in stubbornly holding on to his *Verdienstkreuz* despite an instant wave of indignation from the Jewish press. Ford told E. G. Liebold when Hitler's award was first proposed that he would readily accept "anything the German people have to offer." Having long respected the Germans for their frugal, enterprising, and industrious attributes of character, Ford was certain "they were not as a whole in sympathy with their rulers in their anti-Jewish policies."[9]

Lindbergh's father, Minnesota Congressman C. A. Lindbergh, had been a latter-day agrarian populist and a passionate anti-interventionist in the years leading up to World War I, and he published a book on the subject. He also spoke heatedly on many occasions against the Federal Reserve Board as being "in cahoots with the Money Trust." Young Charles accompanied his firebrand father barnstorming around the state on some of his campaigns, and he developed a sympathetic ear for these and other issues, placing him in harmony with Ford, as the men discovered in their intergenerational, after-dinner chats at Fair Lane during the 1930s and early 1940s.[10]

Henry Ford offhandedly told former Detroit FBI Chief John S. Bugas during an interview in July 1940, "When Charles comes out here, we only talk about the Jews."[11] In addition to commonly held prejudices and stereotypes Ford had grown up with and Lindbergh had inherited from his charismatic father, there were points of convergence in other respects: a shared belief in the existence of "good and bad," the many and farsighted versus the few and avaricious Jews; their conviction that there needed to be a limit to the flow of immigration ("A few Jews add strength and character to a country, but too many create chaos," Lindbergh wrote); their fear of the solidarity of the "internationalists" and alleged hidden Jewish power influencing the media and motion pictures; and their racial, rather than religious, conceptualization of Jews.[12]

While they sought to be consistent on the surface, these two men developed and then gave expression to anti-Jewish biases in starkly divergent fashion. Henry Ford's views were stimulated by proudly held instincts and "hunches." He was not a writer. His inspirations and dicta, as previously shown, emerged into the public and published spheres fashioned and crafted by other men—unless, case in point, at the newspaper publishers' dinner, they were quick enough to catch The Boss, on the run or in a playful mood.

However, as the unsealing of Lindbergh's archives at the Princeton University Library in March 2001 dramatically illustrates, Charles Lindbergh, with frequent editorial assistance and occasional cautionary admonitions by his nuance-sensitive wife, "agonized" over speeches and letters. In one speech draft, for example, according to a new survey of his manuscripts, Lindbergh (as did Ford) blamed unnamed "foreign agents" for the causes of World War II, "only to remove the phrase from later versions."

Henry Ford scribbled fragments in vest-pocket notebooks and never had the time or inclination to be at odds with himself about antisemitic notions. Charles Lindbergh suffered an intense private struggle while wrestling mightily with the strident language he favored. But when the time came to speak out, Lindbergh placed "America First," condemning "Jewish groups in this country" for pushing our nation closer to the brink of war. His youngest child, daughter Reeve, "read a chilling distinction in his mind between Jews and other Americans."[13]

Ambassador Hugh Wilson was recalled from his post in Berlin by President Franklin D. Roosevelt on November 11, 1938, in the aftermath of *Kristallnacht* (The Night of Broken Glass), the newest horror of pogrom antisemitism. Extracting Jews from Germany became the major goal of Jewish organizations in America from that day forward.

Since the *Anschluss* occupation of Austria and the campaign of overt terror against Viennese Jews in March of 1938, the pace of social and legal measures against German Jews had been accelerating. New passports and identity papers stamped with a red J—for *Jude*—were issued. Jews of Polish origin who lived in Germany were expelled. The Polish government refused to accept these refugees, numbering more than 18,000, and at the end of October they were forced to crowd into "transit camps" on the Polish frontier.

On November 7, 1938, a distraught Polish Jew, seventeen-year-old Herschel Grynszpan, angry over the sudden deportation of his family from Hanover, shot the third secretary of the German Embassy in Paris, Ernst vom Rath. As Grynszpan was being led away by police, he cried out, "Being a Jew is not a crime! I am not a dog! I have a right to live, and the Jewish people have a right to exist on earth. Wherever I have been I have been chased like an animal."

Vom Rath died of his wounds two days later. As it happened, November 9 was the fifteenth anniversary of the 1923 Hitler *putsch*, as well as the birthday of Martin Luther, whom Hitler praised in *Mein Kampf* as one of the three greatest figures in German history, along with Frederick the Great and Richard Wagner: "With one blow, [Luther] heralded a new dawn... He saw the Jew as we are only beginning to see him today."[14]

In the words of Joseph Goebbels, emerging from a private audience with Hitler late that night, "He decides... The Jews should for once get to feel the anger of the people." Starting at two o'clock the following morning, a vicious wave of pogroms swept through Germany and Austria. In cities, towns, and rural villages, more than 7,500 shops were vandalized, more than 250 synagogues were burned, archival and art treasures were destroyed. More than one hundred Jews were killed. Hundreds more were dragged out of their beds onto the street and brutally beaten by SA-Reserve and SS men, police, Nazi Party leaders, and local community volunteers. Twenty thousand male Jews were rounded up, arrested, and sent off to concentration camps in Sachsenhausen, Buchenwald, and Dachau. Material damage was estimated well into the hundreds of millions of marks.[15]

Hermann Goering gathered a conference of Nazi officials on November 12 to decide what appropriate further action needed to be taken as a result of the "cowardly" assassination of vom Rath and the "provocation of Aryan wrath." The resulting decree was called the "Atonement Fine," assessed against the Jews of Germany in the amount of one billion marks to be paid to the German Reich.

Out of this same Goering conference came a notice to Jewish store owners that all insurance claims were nullified; shopkeepers were commanded to repair ruined property at their own expense. On that day, Goering also added an amendment to his Four-Year Economic Plan: As of January 1, 1939, Jews would essentially be excluded from the economy, not permitted to own retail stores,

Kristallnacht, destruction of the synagogue at Wiesbaden

mail order stores, or commission houses. They could not hold executive positions in any business. They were not allowed to place advertisements in newspapers.

Four days following, on November 16, it was decreed that German teachers would no longer be expected to give instruction to Jewish pupils. Jewish children would henceforth not be allowed to attend German schools. Local authorities were empowered to prohibit Jews from entering certain neighborhood and shopping areas at specified times of day.

Jewish victims in Germany were blamed for bringing persecution down upon themselves.[16]

CHAPTER NINETEEN

The Radio Priest

THE HARSH, historic lessons of *Kristallnacht* were inevitable, in the opinion of Father Charles E. Coughlin (1891–1979), the "Radio Priest" of Detroit. His weekly broadcast sermon on Sunday afternoon, November 20, was titled, "Persecution—Jewish and Christian." Rich baritone voice rising, Coughlin reminded his audience of more than 3 million listeners that "since the time of Christ, Jewish persecution only followed after Christians were first persecuted.... Students of history," he went on, "recognize that Nazism is only a defense mechanism against Communism." Seen from this logical perspective, the atonement fine levied by Goering paled in significance when measured against the "forty billion dollars' worth of Christian property ... appropriated by the Lenins and the Trotskys, the Zinovieffs and the Kameneffs, the Litvinoffs and the Lapinskys ... by the atheistic Jews and gentiles." Coughlin con-

cluded, his voice permeated with sarcasm, "By all means, let us have
the courage to compound our sympathy, not only from the tears of
Jews, but also from the blood of Christians." To Father Coughlin,
Kristallnacht was not an irrational release of pent-up hate. It was
justified by past events.[1]

Coughlin, born in Hamilton, Ontario, was descended from a
long line of Irish American workingmen. He was educated by the
Basilian Fathers and at the University of Toronto. In his early
years, Coughlin taught English in Sandwich, Ontario. He was
transferred to Kalamazoo and then North Branch, Michigan, before
being assigned in 1926 to the "Shrine of the Little Flower," St.
Therese's Church in Royal Oak, a suburb twelve miles north of
Detroit that had once been a stronghold for the Ku Klux Klan.
Bishop Michael J. Gallagher of Detroit, Coughlin's mentor and a
booster of his career, hoped that the young, energetic priest with
the "mellifluous and appealing" voice would be able to build up the
parish's faltering membership and dwindling funds. Detroit radio
Station WJR gave Coughlin broadcasting time initially for this purpose, and he took to the airwaves of the young medium directly
from his pulpit every Sunday, mixing homiletic afternoon addresses
to children into a potent amalgam of fundraising, politics, and economics. By 1930, encouraged by thousands of letters and donations
from interested listeners, Coughlin branched out to radio stations
in Chicago and Cincinnati, and, within two years, succeeded in
stringing together his own network, growing eventually from
eleven to forty-nine stations, from Maine to Colorado.[2]

Antisemitic nuances tied to the socialistic attributions in his
Kristallnacht speech can be detected in Father Coughlin's radio sermons as early as 1930, even before he had laid down a national network. Proud of his blue-collar lineage, Coughlin liked to think of
himself as a mouthpiece for the working man and small farmer piti-
lessly exploited by the American "billionaires," much like Shylock
in their usurious behavior. "Like grinning devils," he cried, "there

stand at the gates of this Eden of plenty the protectors of privately manufactured money."

"We have lived to see the day," Coughlin said, "that modern Shylocks are grown fat and wealthy." On the cusp of Franklin Roosevelt's inauguration, Coughlin devoted a lengthy February 1933, radio sermon to a stereotype-laden "story of the modern Jew...all related in one sense to our present misery...the commercial gold of the world controlled by private individuals...the Morgans and Kuhn-Loebs and central banks and Rothschilds."[3]

The theme of Jewish money-changers' economic manipulation as the root cause for American entry into World War I as well as the Detroit banking crisis of 1933—the tried and true buzz words, "international bankers"—found a sympathetic listener in Ernest G.

Liebold who, at this time, going into his twenty-third year, still held his post as Henry Ford's general secretary. The "present misery" had been especially hard on Liebold. Immersed in a lengthy and debilitating restructuring of Ford Motor Company finances due to the failure of the Union Guardian Trust Company of Detroit during that unforgiving winter, Liebold suddenly took off on a solo auto trip northward at the bleak middle of February, leaving behind letters of resignation to two Dearborn banks where he served as a board member. Liebold was declared a "missing person" until he was discovered at the Park Place Hotel in Traverse City, Michigan, registered under an assumed name, distressed, disheveled, and exhausted, muttering repeatedly that he "needed rest."

Father Charles Coughlin, 1935

But Liebold would remain, working quietly out of the Ford Engineering Laboratories for another decade and more. He was summarily fired, without comment from either side, by Harry Bennett (according to Bennett, at The Boss's instigation) at the end of May 1944. Liebold's departure from the corporation was accompanied by two divergent waves of emotion in the press. The first was nostalgia: pictures from news clippings files of Henry Ford breaking ground for his new hospital, signing the papers for the acquisition of the Detroit, Toledo and Ironton Railroad, announcing his run for the presidency, with President Calvin Coolidge at the White House, with President Herbert Hoover—and in all of the photos, there was Liebold, "standing at the right hand of Mr. Ford, and helping to guide the destiny of his great industrial empire."

The second wave of responses was more telling: E. G. Liebold would be remembered as "the man who, as general manager of the *Dearborn Independent*, directed a series of anti-semitic articles which involved Mr. Ford in a lawsuit which attracted international attention."[4]

Liebold met Coughlin and they embarked upon a course of regular evenings together, during one of which they "discussed the encyclicals of Pope Leo, and Coughlin tried to compare how closely they lined up with Mr. Ford's ideas." To Liebold, the priest came across as "a man of a very high degree of intelligence" who had command of "facts and figures that could not be refuted"—a quality of character that had always held special importance for Liebold.

Henry Ford and E. G. Liebold

On another memorable occasion, Liebold recalled that Coughlin waxed eloquently about "The Money Question" and talked about "Wall Street money interests controlled by Jews...matters that Mr. Ford was more or less interested in."[5]

By the middle of the decade, Coughlin turned bitterly against President Roosevelt, vilifying him as a "Bolshevik-plutocrat," attacking the movement to join the World Court, and lambasting the New Deal head-on as the economic Depression deepened. Coughlin's public language moved squarely into alignment with the kinds of biases he expressed more candidly with Liebold. Coughlin was "impatient with Roosevelt's moderation," and the president's resounding, spectacular victory at the polls in 1936 was the last straw—rejecting the anti-capitalist, quasi-fascist, neo-populist, isolationist philosophy of the priest's National Union of Social Justice. Detroit's newly appointed archbishop, Edward Mooney, enlisted ecclesiastical censors in an attempt to curtail Coughlin's strident behavior and "self-willed impetuosity." However, Coughlin went on to build up "the largest national following of any demagogue in American history." He received more than 80,000 letters a week, 70 percent of them from Protestants. He employed a staff of over 100 people to open and read them and count the cash and checks enclosed.[6]

By the springtime preceding his *Kristallnacht* speech, Father Coughlin remembered some thirty years on, he was coming to Dearborn for lunch with Henry Ford "at least once a month...He was a sincere man who knew the truth when he saw it." Assisted by material supplied through Liebold's office, Coughlin began to publish—in the "From the Tower" column of his own journal, *Social Justice*—articles by a leading apologist for Nazi Germany, George S. Viereck, and subsequently a series of excerpts from *The Protocols of the Learned Elders of Zion*. The long series was introduced by Henry Ford's terse 1921 testimonial statement to Joseph O'Neill that "The *Protocols* fit with what is going on." The Jewish community of Detroit spoke out against Coughlin as they had against Ford during the early days of the *Dearborn Independent*, arguing that he, too, should "retract" the *Protocols* series just as Ford had done. On the contrary, the priest continued the excerpts, week after week, through Thanksgiving of 1938, insisting that he (just as Henry Ford once said) was "interested in the *factuality*" of the *Protocols*, and that it would be "better for Jews to be less fearful and less sensitive." The shop at the Church of the Little Flower soon became a busy distribution hub for a pamphlet edition of the *Protocols*.

Liebold provided Coughlin with copies of Julius Streicher's popular, cartoon-filled, antisemitic Nazi weekly newspaper, *Der Sturmer* (The Attacker), to which he subscribed faithfully. Hitler's favorite periodical—The Fuehrer read it religiously, from cover to cover—*Der Sturmer* displayed a masthead slogan, *"Die Juden sind unser Ungluck"* (The Jews are our misfortune), had a circulation of over one-half million, and reprinted excerpts from *Social Justice*. Coughlin, reciprocally, published transcripts of Joseph Goebbels' short-wave broadcasts, even going so far as to attribute them under his own byline.[7]

A RADICALLY different response to *Kristallnacht* emerged twenty-four hours following Father Coughlin's radio diatribe. On November 21, 1938, more than 20,000 people jammed into a mass meeting at Madison Square Garden sponsored by the American League for Peace and Democracy in protest against the recent Nazi outrage. An overflow crowd of 2,000 spilled out into the side streets. Dr. Harry F. Ward of Union Theological Seminary, and U.S. Representative Vito Marcantonio, president of the International Labor Defense, roused the crowd to cheers when they declared that "Nazism must be smashed!" Dorothy Thompson, noted columnist for the *New York Herald Tribune*, moved the crowd to applause when she proposed that "Nazi Germany as well as Herschel Grynszpan should be the defendants when the murderer of Vom Rath comes to trial." And President Roosevelt was repeatedly hailed as a "Galahad" and "a man confronted by destiny."

So much for the plaudits. The loudest boos of the night were reserved for the roll call of Adolph Hitler, Joseph Goebbels, Fritz Kuhn—and, last but not least, Henry Ford. It was as if the audience were possessed with prescient awareness that three days hence Field Marshall Goering would announce that his army required another 100,000 trucks. Polls revealed that 80 percent of American men had heard Ford was antisemitic. And more to the point—the consumers' pocketbook—Ford had alienated American Jews to such an extent during the years on the edge of World War II that "they had virtually stopped buying Ford products ... in the most complete boycott of automotive vehicles by any group in American history."[8]

Henry Ford professed to be unimpressed and unmoved by the disconcerting revelation that people had finally peered behind the mask. But a heretofore unpublished account by Rabbi Leo Franklin reveals a different story. Sunday after Sunday, he, too, had been listening to Father Coughlin's campaign of Jew-hatred, "his booming voice punctuated with a bit of Irish accent" traveling over the airwaves—"Had not [the Jews] crucified the Man of Nazareth, and denied His deity, which every Christian child knew He shared with the God of the world? Had not [the Jews] invaded everywhere as aliens and intruders, even in the lands of their birth? Had they not now gained control of every opinion-making agency?" The *New York Times* Berlin correspondent reported that Father Coughlin was the new hero of Nazi Germany. Rabbi Franklin wondered when (or if) all the troubles would ever come to an end.

On Saturday night, November 26, Franklin received a phone call from Albert Kahn's brother, Moritz (1881–1939), who had been at the Ford plant that afternoon discussing a construction project (Albert had vowed, long ago, never to enter Ford's factory door again). Henry Ford himself came into the office, greeted Moritz, left the room briefly, then returned to tell the younger Kahn that he felt a "keen anxiety" to make a statement "in regard to the German situation," and that—as in the past—he would prefer to make it to the rabbi in person.

Franklin was skittish. He had had no contact with Ford for more than ten years and was acutely sensitive to the man's devious behavior. Franklin also knew Ford well enough to suspect the influence of other men in his inner group. And so, before he ventured into the lion's den, Franklin sent off a confidential note to Ford, seeking further information as to why he wanted to see him. Another day went by. No formal meeting date or time had yet been set. However, the rabbi then received an urgent call from Harry Newman, right-hand aide to Harry Bennett, repeating that Mr. Ford wanted to talk "about the German refugees," and would send a car to pick up the rabbi at his convenience wherever and whenever necessary—"How soon can [you] see Mr. Ford?"

After Rabbi Franklin had concluded a meeting with the Detroit Community Fund in the Statler Hotel downtown, he allowed himself to be whisked to Dearborn, arriving just before 3 P.M. on Tuesday, November 29. There he was met—in W. J. Cameron's office—by Henry Ford, Harry Bennett, Harry Newman (essentially a witness to the proceedings), and Cameron. Ford came right out and told Franklin that "he believed the reports of the German atrocities had been exaggerated for propaganda purposes, and that such persecutions as had taken place did not represent the desires of the German people as a whole, but were the work of a few warmongers at the top." This was, Franklin wrote, "his exact expression."

Ford suggested that some kind of formal statement of his position be drawn up for publication. Cameron and Franklin agreed that they would develop two independent drafts and then "compare and perhaps combine them."[9]

Cameron remained in his office to write a draft statement "on his own typewriter," from the point of view as if The Boss's words were narrated *by* Rabbi Franklin: "I found Mr. Ford very understanding and more than sympathetic and characteristically frank in his expression of opinion." Cameron had Franklin attest to the fact that Ford believed America must return to "its traditional role as a refuge for the oppressed"; that Ford would welcome Jewish immigrant laborers with open arms; that he was "indifferent to rumors that his acceptance of a medal from the German people obligated him to Nazism"; and that he "would do everything in his power" to ensure a safe haven for European Jewry.

Meanwhile, Rabbi Franklin's briefer draft statement was dictated in an outer office to a Ford Motor Company secretary and written as if it were being delivered directly *by* Henry Ford, in the first person. It read as if it were a condensed version of what Ford had said to Franklin: "I am sure that all of these Jews [admitted] under our quota system would be beneficial to the country...They will make useful citizens." The disavowal of Hitler's medal was carefully worded, "Those who know me for many years know that anything that breeds hate is repulsive to me."

Upon scanning Cameron's statement, Rabbi Franklin said that he thought it was "considerably stronger" than his, although he had private misgivings about Ford's guarantees that so many Jewish refugees could realistically be employed at the Rouge. Franklin also intimated, in hindsight, that he "took it for granted" that the reason Ford had summoned him to Dearborn was "for the sake of help[ing his] co-religionists."

In the interest of diplomacy, Franklin deferred to Cameron. Before the meeting broke up, Ford suggested that a picture be taken of himself with Rabbi Franklin, to be distributed to the newspapers along with his statement about the Jews. Ever since incredulously reading the first screed in the May 22, 1920, *Dearborn Independent*, Rabbi Franklin wanted desperately to believe there must be a kernel of good intention buried somewhere beneath the defects in Henry Ford's character. This meeting was no exception. He allowed the stilted, posed photograph to be taken.[10]

That evening, Rabbi Franklin received by messenger a copy of the photograph, as well as Cameron's finished text. In the intervening hours, Franklin suffered misgivings about acquiescing so smoothly to Ford and his men: "Upon rereading the statement, I felt that if it were published in the form in which it had been set down, it would be unsatisfactory to all parties concerned." Franklin felt it best not to release the statement that night in the exact form authorized by Ford and Bennett, in order that he might confer further with them.

Early the following morning, the rabbi received a call from Harry Bennett, saying Mr. Ford was "greatly disappointed" that the statement had not appeared in print. Franklin asked to be allowed

**Henry Ford and Rabbi Franklin,
November 29, 1938**

to recast it. He objected to the narrative voice. He said the press release should be put forth in the first person, directly quoting Ford instead of him. At that moment, Henry Ford picked up another telephone extension. Franklin read the two men the new version, revised as to manner of quotation, and Ford said, "That is fine."

Off went the pages to the wire services for publication the next day, Thursday, December 1. Imagine Franklin's shock and surprise when Father Coughlin went on the air the following Sunday, read a signed statement allegedly from Harry Bennett criticizing the rabbi for misrepresenting the sentiments of Henry Ford, and said the words were Franklin's, *not* Ford's. Franklin phoned Bennett immediately at his home and demanded that an apology appear in the paper the next morning. Bennett—who told Franklin he had been taking a nap while the broadcast was airing—expressed mystification as to what Father Coughlin's motives could possibly be. Nevertheless, in Monday afternoon's papers, Bennett reversed his endorsement of Rabbi Franklin's veracity, and in the December 12 issue of *Social Justice*, Bennett was quoted once again, writing "officially for the Ford Motor Company and in the presence of Mr. Ford," saying that the statement given out by Rabbi Franklin "was not totally accurate" and not authorized by Henry Ford. Furthermore, Bennett switched around the dynamic which had set the initial November 29 meeting in motion, insisting that *Franklin had sought out Ford* for the purpose of appealing to the automaker to employ German-Jewish refugees at the River Rouge factory.

The *Detroit Free Press* defended the rabbi, and said that Father Coughlin "had a congenital inability to tell the truth." Coughlin sued the newspaper for $4 million. The newspaper prepared a dossier of dozens of pages of contradictory citations from the priest's radio addresses and from his magazine. Harry Bennett chimed in to say that "Father Coughlin crossed me up." Bennett also swore to Rabbi Franklin that when he saw Father Coughlin in person he was going to "punch that fellow in the nose." Coughlin dropped his suit.[11]

President Roosevelt's curmudgeonly secretary of the interior, Harold L. Ickes, was certain, as was the president, that Henry Ford was financing Father Coughlin during the darkest hours of the Radio Priest's crusade. In late December, following the *contretemps* with Rabbi Franklin, Ickes gave a major speech at a dinner of the Cleveland Zionist Society, practically in Henry Ford's backyard, in which he went further than any public figure to date in condemning Ford. It was Ickes's opinion that any American who accepted a

medal from a dictator "automatically forswears his birthright...
Henry Ford and Colonel Charles Lindbergh...are the only two
free citizens of a free country who obsequiously have accepted
tokens of contemptuous distinction at a time when the bestower of
them counts that day lost when he can commit no new crime
against humanity."

Secretary Ickes connected the motivations of Ford and Lindbergh nine months before Pearl Harbor, in a speech called "Protestantism Answers Hate" delivered at the Hotel Roosevelt in New
York City. Ickes lashed out at those who think "it would be better if
neither England nor Germany won this war. We have heard these
unworthy words from men like Henry Ford and Colonel Lindbergh...Our native fascists are cultivating the soil of hatred."[12]

THE LIVING link between the pre–World War II pro-Nazi movement and the antisemitic movement of the postwar period in America, Gerald Smith (1898–1976), was born in rural Pardeesville,
Wisconsin. He was descended from three generations of fundamentalist preachers and raised by his Disciples of Christ clergyman
father to believe in the Bible as the strict word of God. After graduating from high school in 1915, Gerald worked in the tobacco
fields, then attended Valparaiso University in Indiana, moving
through all his religion courses in under three years. By 1920,
Smith was making use of his natural oratorical skills to find work
as a part-time preacher in scattered Wisconsin towns. He sought a
warmer climate to aid in his wife's recuperation from tuberculosis
and moved to Shreveport, Louisiana, to take over leadership of the
Kings Highway Christian Church. At this point, in his own proud
words, a "rabble-rouser for the Right," he began to broadcast sermons over the radio. Smith fell naturally into the orbit around governor—subsequently senator—Huey P. Long, and joined Long's
populist political organization. Mesmerized by Long's charisma,
Smith left the ministry and went to work full-time for the magnetic
figure he worshipped unhesitatingly as a "superman."

Smith became the national organizer for Long's "Share Our Wealth Society," speaking on his boss's behalf about this utopian idea to level the playing field between rich and poor, which found a willing audience during the Depression. By the end of 1934, appearing in front of frenzied crowds as a "combination of Savonarola and Elmer Gantry," Smith had preached to more than one million people in Louisiana alone, attacking Roosevelt (and his wife as "the female Rasputin") at every turn. Smith envisioned a time in the not too distant future when the society might even be able to "duplicate the feat of Adolph Hitler in Germany." Smith was certain he had hitched his wagon to a star, but when Huey Long was assassinated in September 1935, the star burned out, and Smith quickly found himself removed to the outskirts of Louisiana politics.

He transferred his allegiances to Father Charles Coughlin's National Union for Social Justice. A lively but ultimately destructive competition developed between the two speechifiers during North Dakota Congressman William Lemke's abysmal campaign to unseat President Roosevelt in 1936.

Gerald L. K. Smith speaking at the first session of the "America First" convention, August 29, 1944, Detroit

Undeterred, Smith defected from Coughlin to invent a new brainchild, which he at first called "The Committee of Ten Thousand," soon expanding it to "The Committee of One Million." This grassroots movement was dedicated to demeaning the New Deal, bringing down the CIO, and rooting out Communists spoiling the American ideal and with every passing day bringing the nation closer to Apocalypse. The moment had come for someone to stand tall and make an overt effort to defeat these noxious threats to Christian civilization.

It was only a matter of time before Gerald L. K. Smith and Henry Ford crossed paths. In early 1937, Smith's travels took him through Detroit, where he gave a talk at the Advertising Club. E. G. Liebold was in the audience and became intrigued with Smith's message—"Christian character is the true basis of real Americanism."

Liebold introduced Smith to Ford with the same rationale he had used when speaking of Father Coughlin—a convergence of beliefs on issues that mattered. Within two years, Smith, in serious financial straits, moved to Detroit from New York City, seeking a more comfortable situation for himself in the Midwest. It was, after all, familiar geography—"centrally located, strongly unionized and had good broadcasting facilities." Ford (as well as Horace Dodge and Ransom Olds) provided Smith with financial backing to continue his weekly radio speeches over WJR, the city's largest station. Smith established residence, with Ford's subsidy, at the elegant Detroit Leland Hotel. He was of one mind with Ford in their hatred of the United Automobile Workers and its president, Walter Reuther. Late in 1939, Smith addressed a secret meeting of the Ford Motor Company's anti-union society, The Knights of Dearborn.[13]

Smith felt harmony with Henry Ford on matters pertaining to the Jews. Smith claimed that when the two men first met he "was less anti-Semitic than Ford." He said that Ford told him he had become more wary of the Jews "because of an attempt...by the New York Jews...to take over the Ford Motor Company." Smith also said that Ford once told him early in their association that "No one can understand the issues of this hour unless he understands the Jewish question."

Smith was so enamored of Henry Ford, so inspired by his great example, especially to the young people of America, that he exaggerated the depth of their relationship. After an initial burst of socializing by the Fords and the Smiths, followed by a series of blatant fan letters from Smith to Clara Ford, there was little subsequent contact. Once more, however, the stone had already been cast into the pool, and the ripples were in motion. Liebold presented Smith with a complete run of the *Dearborn Independent* bound in Moroccan leather, and a copy of *The International Jew*, which Smith went on to republish a decade later under the auspices of his Christian Nationalist Crusade, founded in 1947 in Los Angeles.

In the introduction to this 1951 edition, Smith recounted Ford's words at one of their encounters in 1940, thirteen years after his "apology," when Ford, "showing no regret," and in the presence of their wives as well as Liebold, vowed that he "hope[d] to publish *The International Jew* again some time." Smith's edition is one of more than 100 known versions of Ford's book published since 1920 in the English-speaking world alone, predominantly in the United States. As late as 1964, Smith still claimed that Henry Ford had "never changed his original opinion of Jews." Smith brought out bulk quantities of *The International Jew*, and two years later serialized it in his magazine, *The Cross and the Flag*.[14]

With Smith's embittered defeat after a run for the Republican senatorial seat from Michigan in 1942, his ideology began to tilt toward a radical brand of Jew-hatred, drawing upon the essential principles of British-Israelism espoused in W. J. Cameron's *Destiny* magazine. At this time, Smith began regular visits to the West Coast, especially Los Angeles, and over the span of the ensuing decade enjoyed mutual influence there with Wesley A. Swift, preaching at his British-Israelite gatherings—sowing seeds for the nascent white-supremacist "Identity" Movement. Swift, who had been a Ku Klux Klan organizer, went on to found The Church of Jesus Christ Christian after World War II. In this racial phase of his theological development, Smith became a potent cross-pollinator. He took the basic premise of British-Israelism, denying the Jews as "chosen," then tainted it to promote the Manichaean belief that "Jews were God's adversaries on earth ... the Children of Darkness ... a Satanic force" at war with the Children of Light, the Aryans. In the "Genealogy of Israel," the eventual basis for Identity doctrine and a perversion of British-Israelite thought, modern-day Jews stood in a demonic bloodline that linked them to Enoch, patron of Luciferian knowledge; then Cain, history's first murderer, who had made union with the Witch of Nod; and furthest back, to Satan, Cain's direct forebear.[15]

Smith successfully effected the transition from the teachings of his childhood that "the two greatest sins in the world are to deny Jesus Christ is the son of God, and to collect usury," to the fully blown, "extravagant Biblical interpretation" that "we must not confuse the Israel of the Old Testament with the people we now call Jews."[16]

CHAPTER TWENTY

Transitions

— ❧ —

Henry Ford, in an interview at his winter estate in Ways,
Georgia, advised workers to 'shun labor unions.' He said he
believed 'international financiers' were using labor unions to
'reduce competition in industry so as to be able to raise prices
and cut wages... There is no mystery about the connection
between corporation control and labor control. They are two
ends of the same rope. A little group of those who control both
capital and labor will sit down in New York and settle prices,
dividends, and wages.'

HARTFORD COURANT, FEBRUARY 25, 1937,
"Henry Ford Recalls His 'Peace Ship—Says He'd Spend Twice as
Much for What It Taught Him About War and War Makers."

DURING the 1920s, mass production still remained outside the
purview of the American Federation of Labor and its historic tradi-
tion embracing craft workers. With the inspiration of John L.
Lewis' spin-off Congress (originally Committee) of Industrial
Organizations in the mid-1930s, and the implementation of FDR's
Wagner Act—legitimizing the negotiating prerogatives of labor
leaders—the mining, electrical, steel, rubber, cement, aluminum,
and other mass-production sectors fell into line. In May 1935, the
United Automobile Workers held its founding convention in
Detroit. The following summer, at the second constitutional con-
vention in South Bend, Indiana, the UAW formally affiliated with
the CIO, electing Homer L. Martin, a former Baptist preacher from
St. Louis and an accomplished platform speaker, as first interna-

tional president. John Lewis chipped in $100,000 to get the auto industry organizers motivated.

A full-scale revolt among the already-resentful and militant rank and file ensued, leading to an epidemic of "sit-down" strikes in quick, concentrated succession—forty-four days long at General Motors plants in Atlanta, Georgia, Flint, Michigan, and twelve other states; at Firestone, among the tire-builders of Akron, Ohio, spreading to Goodrich and Goodyear; at the Fisher Body plant in Detroit and the Bendix factory in South Bend; at eight Chrysler plants; at North American Aviation; and at J. I. Case—actions eventually resulting in landmark collective bargaining agreements and a dramatic surge in union registration. Within six months in 1937, the UAW quadrupled in size, to over 400,000 strong. "It was like we was soldiers," a General Motors sit-downer joyfully reminisced. "I remember as a kid in school readin' about Davy Crockett and the last stand at the Alamo... Yessir, Chevvy [Plant] No. 4 was *my* Alamo."[1]

Inspired by this momentum, the rallying cry rose up—"Ford Next!" John Lewis was certain that Ford Motor Company, the last of the Big Three, was "in the bag." But it was far easier said than done. Harry Bennett, ex-lightweight pugilist and Navy deep-sea diver, a.k.a. "The Little Fellow," was by now in the management driver's seat at his so-called Bastille, the Rouge factory. As far as Mr. Ford was concerned, Bennett defiantly told the *American Mercury* in April 1937, the union they set out to crush was "irresponsible, un-American, and no god-dam [*sic*] good—We'll *never* recognize the UAW!"

Ford believed he was above the law, telling the *New York Times* on April 14 that in his recalcitrant (and calcifying) opinion, the same subversive "wire pullers" as always were behind the "labor unions, backed by war-seeking financiers, the Wall Street crowd... I haven't given the Wagner Act a thought." In unabashed defiance of the Wagner Act and the National Labor Relations Act, and despite Edsel Ford's unheeded entreaties to the contrary, Ford branch managers and superintendents were ordered "not to talk to anyone [from the outside] about a labor dispute."

Workers entering the factory each day had to open their lunch-pails to show Bennett's security force—a motley assortment of ex-prizefighters, wrestlers, and ordinary parolees "given a second chance"—that they were not smuggling union literature. Personal lockers could be inspected without notice, and clothing searched. Woe to the man whose turned-out pockets revealed a union card; he was in danger of being threatened, or worse, flogged on the spot with blackjacks or lashes fashioned from windshield cord. From 1937 until the summer of 1941, Bennett fired more than 4,000 Ford workers who were actual or suspected members of the UAW. These dismissals, coming to be known as the infamous Ford Purge, were loudly publicized to the rank and file as intimidating examples of what easily could happen to them.[2]

On May 26, 1937, representatives of the UAW, led by Walter Reuther, J. J. Kennedy, Robert Kanter, and Richard Frankensteen, went to the bridge over Miller Road leading to Gate Number 4 at the River Rouge plant with the intent to distribute handbills during the afternoon change of shifts. They were approached by fifty members of Bennett's security squad and warned—"This is Ford property. Get the hell off of here." Reuther and Frankensteen, withdrawing, were nevertheless immediately set upon—"beaten, lifted to their feet, and beaten all over again...kicked and slugged" as they struggled to run away. The Dearborn police stood impassively nearby, watching and waiting as the union men were thrown to the concrete. The police chief was Carl Brooks, an alumnus of Bennett's "Ford Service," and he did not give orders to intervene.

"The Battle of the Overpass" raised the curtain on four more years of stubborn resistance by Henry Ford, despite complaints and censure by the National Labor Relations Board ordering him to "cease and desist" from his repressive manner of discouraging union membership. Dissent and factionalism within the ranks of the UAW at first worked to Ford's advantage, as collective bargain-

ing efforts slowed down in the late 1930s. Further efforts at union-
ization were hampered by the faithful old-timers who had been
working for Ford for twenty or thirty years and still professed allegiance to "The Old Man," even though they never saw him in public anymore.

But by the spring of 1941, Henry Ford's "old shibboleths about
'the outside forces...who are out to get us'"—the nameless, remote,
and shadowy few who would not allow him to run the shop the way
it should be—were tiresome and effete. Sensing a crack in the
armor, the union redoubled its efforts against the company. Organizers began to converge upon Detroit. Ford's harsh practices
resulted in the loss of a multimillion-dollar truck-building government contract as the American defense build-up gathered steam.
Such cash-flow interruptions were writ large, and hard to ignore,
as was the Supreme Court decision finally upholding a suit brought
by the UAW and the NLRB against Ford.

On the first of April 1941, more than 50,000 men at the Lincoln, Highland Park, and Rouge plants stopped work and walked
off the job. Six weeks later, when the union election was held, 70
percent of the men opted to join. Henry Ford told whoever would
listen, as always when he felt constrained by any kind of extreme
change (especially economic), that "the Jews" were persecuting
him. He shouted pathetically at his son to "Close the plant down!...
I don't want any more of this business!" Clara Ford threatened to
sell her shares of stock and divorce Henry if he would not negoti-
ate. This chore he left to Edsel. On June 20, the union contract was
signed.[3]

IN JULY 1939, Ford-Werke, AG entered the first year of its new
identity as a German company, with majority ownership maintained
by the parent Ford Motor Company USA. Edsel Ford and Charles
Sorensen served on the board of directors of Ford-Werke, AG. All
Ford-Werke vehicles—including, by 1941, 1,000 trucks per month,

as well as passenger cars required by the *Wehrmacht*, the SS, and the police—were made in Germany, using materials under German management. More than 60 percent of the popular, three-ton tracked trucks produced for the German army were made by Ford-Werke, AG. Essential strategic raw materials, especially rubber, were bartered for as needed through a special parts-exchange arrangement with American Ford. The German subsidiary also conducted strong export business to Latin America and Japan.

Unlike other American-owned property in Nazi Germany, the Ford plant was never confiscated by the German government. In the aftermath of the German invasion of Holland, Robert H.

**Henry Ford Must Choose, tabloid newspaper
edited by L. M. Birkhead, and published by
The Friends of Democracy, 1941**

Schmidt, who had risen from head of purchasing to become general manager of the Ford-Cologne factory, was selected by the Nazi government to also run Ford-Holland, then Ford-Belgium—and, after Paris was taken, Ford-France as well. Schmidt's appointment was not contested by Ford senior management. Professor Mira Wilkins, in her pathfinding analysis of Ford's business abroad, published nearly forty years ago, established that while the United States was still a neutral nation enjoying full diplomatic relations with Berlin, Ford-Werke was engaged in a secret contract with the German government—unbeknownst, Wilkins writes, to Ford-US—to manufacture the turbine for the V-2 rocket.

At the same period, however, the huge Ford-Dagenham plant in England was also contributing considerable materiel support for the British front in North Africa; the Rouge plant by this point had developed the jeep, various aircraft motors, and medium tanks; and the great "Liberator" bomber would be forthcoming out of Ford's Willow Run facility. The proud "arsenal of democracy" was simultaneously an "arsenal of fascism." Characteristically, one day Henry Ford could say he "hope[d] neither side wins." When asked how he reconciled his professed hatred of war with the fact that his factories were producing war goods, the pragmatic capitalist simply replied, "That's the law of the land, isn't it?"[4]

With American entry into the conflict, the American stake in Ford-Werke had been pared down to 52 percent, still a majority. Schmidt was designated custodian of Ford-Werke, and ran the company in strict agreement with the Nazis, who did not wish to assume a complete takeover. With the United States officially at war with Germany, it was illegal for American car companies to have contact with subsidiaries in Germany. The Treasury Department launched an investigation of American Ford with the suspicion that there was ongoing communication between the home office and Maurice Dollfuss, the collaborationist manager of the Ford-Poissy factory complex in Vichy, France; on at least one occasion, in June 1943, Nazi Party–member Robert Schmidt traveled to Portugal for a meeting with American Ford officials.

American troops entering Cologne during the Liberation came upon "destitute foreign workers confined behind barbed wire [at the Ford plant] according to reports filed by soldiers at the scene." Recent research by German scholar Karola Fings, author of a book on Nazi forced-labor programs, provides graphic descriptions of these foreign captives, predominantly from Eastern Europe and the Soviet Union, and also from France and Italy, making up half of Ford-Werke's workforce and laboring under Gestapo supervision for twelve-hour days on little more than 200 grams of bread and coffee for breakfast.[5]

Sixteen-year-old Elsa Iwanowa was one such unfortunate victim. Abducted from her home in the southern Russian city of Rostov in October 1942, along with hundreds of other women, she was put to work at the Ford Cologne plant. On March 4, 1998, Iwanowa filed a class-action suit against Ford Motor Company seeking financial recompense for unpaid slave labor under inhuman conditions at Ford-Werke. In September 1999, Judge Joseph Greenaway Jr., "threw the case out on the grounds that the statute of limitations had expired."[6]

The haunting image of slave-labor at Ford-Werke hardly seems incongruous, considering what we have learned about Henry Ford's outspoken views over a span of years approaching three decades in the public eye. By the time young Elsa was dragged out of bed, shivering with cold, Henry Ford's outbursts about war and peace, good and evil, right and wrong, Jew and Gentile—and, lest we forget, Adolf Hitler and the essentially "decent" people of Nazi Germany—had already become so confused and muddled that even his designated corporate historians were forced to admit the Flivver King's re-emergent dogma "flared into hallucination... The years of the Mad Hatter were beginning; anything could happen."[7]

On January 7, 1942, one month after Pearl Harbor, Henry Ford dug into his conscience at the insistent prompting of Harry Bennett and dredged up one final apology to the Jews. This time around, it came as the result of a meeting arranged with Richard Gutstadt, national director of the Anti-Defamation League. As Bennett explained, Mr. Ford was "highly indignant" at the charges of anti-Semitism that still dogged him fifteen years after the death of the *Dearborn Independent,* "and with renewed intensity recently."

A succinct letter to Sigmund Livingston, national chairman of the ADL, went out to the press worldwide declaring that "...our present national and international emergency" was the appropriate occasion to state Mr. Ford's judgment that "there is no greater dereliction among the Jews than there is among any other class of citizens...I strongly urge all my fellow-citizens to give no aid to any movement whose purpose it is to arouse hatred against any group."[8]

THE years of unending pressure took their toll on Edsel Ford. Late in 1942, he was diagnosed with gastric ulcers and had two operations. Undulant fever and stomach cancer set in. Heavily sedated with morphine, Edsel fell into a coma and died at home on May 26, 1943, at age forty-nine. At 2:30 P.M. on the day of Edsel's funeral, all Ford factories were silenced for five minutes. "Maybe I pushed the boy too hard," Henry grudgingly remarked two months later. He descended into long spells of depression and silence, appearing in public with Clara always close by his side. Thin and pale, a wan and forced smile on his face, his hair wispy and white, Henry followed "Callie" around docilely. Three weeks following V-J Day, on September 20, 1945, at eighty-two years of age, Henry Ford at last recommended to the board of directors that his twenty-eight-year-old grandson, Henry Ford II, succeed him as president of the company.

It took merely eighteen months for Henry II to declare his first disavowal of antisemitism on behalf of the corporation, stating on March 12, 1947, in a letter to Nathan H. Seidman, president of the

Inter-Racial Press of America, that copies of *The International Jew* published by Gerald L. K. Smith and still in circulation were "without the authorization of his grandfather, the Ford Motor Company, or himself." The *Canadian Jewish Review* predicted tartly that young Henry would probably find himself having to make such pronouncements throughout his life because Old Henry "unloosed an evil which will not be cleaned up in his grandson's time."[9]

On April 7, 1947, Rabbi Leo Franklin sat down in the seclusion of his study to begin what he thought would be the final edits to his work in progress, *Untold Tales of Detroit and Detroiters*—only to wake up the following morning and read on the front page of the newspaper of the death of his old friend Henry Ford. The mighty Rouge River had spilled over its banks after a torrential Easter Sunday rainfall. The Fair Lane power plant blacked out. The Old Man suffered a massive cerebral hemorrhage and passed away at twenty minutes before midnight by flickering gas lamplight in his second-floor bedroom overlooking the river, hands folded upon his chest, watched over by the maid, Rosa Buhler, and faithful Clara.[10]

In a state of emotional agitation, Rabbi Franklin admitted that "No man who has ever lived has been perfect. The greatest personalities in history have had their weaknesses and they have made their mistakes. To this rule, Mr. Ford was no exception." It was indeed a shame, the rabbi thought, that Henry II, so early in his new administration, had to cope with his grandfather's unfortunate legacy.

What better way could there be to conclude his work of many years' labor than with an emblematic tale? Rabbi Franklin chose to invoke the ancient prohibition against *lashon harah* [evil speech, gossip, or slander]. It was written in Leviticus (19:16), "You shall not go about spreading slander among your people; nor shall you stand idly by when your neighbor's life is at stake." The law of Leviticus had subsequently been interpreted in the Mishnah Torah by the scholar Maimonides when he noted that "talebearing, carrying gossip from person to person, motivated to injure someone's reputation, kills three persons: the one who circulates it, the one who listens to it, and the one of whom it is spoken...Whoever glories in the humiliation of others has no share in the future world."

"The story goes," Rabbi Franklin wrote, "that on a certain occasion, a rather pious Jew, smitten by his conscience for having spread a false rumor defaming the character of one of his neighbors, went to his rabbi to ask him what reparation he could make for the great wrong that he had done to a fellow man. To his amazement, the rabbi said to him: 'My friend, you have indeed committed a great sin, but now that you ask me what reparation you can make, I am going to give you a bit of advice that may surprise you. I want you to take a very large sack and to fill it brimful with feathers, and when you have done so, I want you to go about the streets of this town and scatter those feathers over as large an area as you possibly can, and when you have done that, I want you to come back to me and I will tell you what further you must do.'

"The man was indeed surprised at such advice from his rabbi, and he could not at all understand its significance. But he did as commanded. He gathered feathers by the thousands, put them into a bag, and went through the highways and the byways of his city, scattering them abroad. That in itself was not a small task, but having accomplished it, he returned the next morning to his rabbi's home and said, 'Rabbi, I have done as you suggested. I have gathered feathers by the thousands and I have scattered them everywhere in this entire vicinity. Now what further would you have me do?'

"And the rabbi said, 'My friend, now I want you to take your bag again, and go forth and pick up every one of those feathers that you have scattered, and when your bag is full, come back to me.'

"But the man replied, 'Dear Rabbi, you are asking an impossible thing of me. How can I possibly gather these feathers again? The wind has blown them hither and thither, and though I should do my level best to re-gather them, it would be a superhuman—yes, an impossible—task. By this time, some of the feathers must have blown miles and miles away, and I could never regain them.'

"'Exactly so,' said the rabbi, 'I know that you cannot gather the feathers that you have scattered. But I gave you this task with a purpose, and to teach you a lesson. Evil rumors are like feathers. Once they are scattered, no matter what you do to regather them, you can never succeed in doing so. As on the wings of the wind, they take flight, and they lodge far, far away from the place where you laid them down to take lodgement in the hearts and the minds of men.'

"'No, an evil report cannot be completely undone. Do your best to overcome the rumor, but do not, for even a moment, believe that you will wholly succeed in cleansing the thoughts of those who have believed it.'"[11]

AFTERWORD

The epiphany came in 1991, when I was in the throes of research for my biography-in-progress of Thomas Alva Edison. I was sitting patiently, at a polished oak table in the hushed reading room of the Berg Collection on the third floor of The New York Public Library central building ("between the lions") at Forty-Second Street and Fifth Avenue, waiting to examine the pocket diaries of naturalist John Burroughs. I was drafting a chapter about the annual camping trips of the capitalist self-styled "Vagabonds" Edison, Harvey Firestone, and Henry Ford. During and after World War I, through halcyon springs and summers, the men and their wives and comrades launched ten-car caravans into the hills of Appalachia and New England and engaged in their catered, white-tablecloth version of roughing it.

As I leafed through the fragile pages of Burroughs's black notebooks, I sent aloft a silent message of thanks to the white-bearded, gentle spirit for having the presence of mind to listen from his vantage point in the leafy shadows to the captains of industry haggling and swapping stories around the campfire. It was in John Burroughs's sloping, hurried penmanship that I read first-hand evidence of Henry Ford's antisemitism—hurried transcriptions of Ford's vicious after-dinner diatribes against the Jews—and Burroughs's spontaneous, private annotations of shock and dismay.

I tip-toed gingerly into this material, a research minefield that required counterbalancing Ford's prejudicial attitudes against his friend Edison's biases. Where Ford's outbursts over the decades assumed a rapid-fire, repetitive character, Edison's expressions against the Jews were more measured. Ford would shoot clichés from the hip; Edison was discursive in objecting to the Jews' intrusion upon his terrain, the world of commerce.

Henry Ford came across to me as a pro-active antisemite. He did not like the Jews because he believed they were warmongering, manipulative, and alien. Edison did not feel as threatened by the Jews. He simply wished them to stay where they rightfully belonged, within their own circumscribed world of the arts and culture, so they would not compete with his commercial enterprises.

As soon as I finished the Edison book, my publisher took the next logical step, asking if I would like to segue into a full-fledged biography of Henry Ford, since he figured so prominently as Edison's protégé and lifelong admirer. Sixteen years Edison's junior, obsessed with commercial applications for the internal-combustion engine, driven by his unerring feel for market necessities, Henry Ford was the most powerful personification of the next wave of new American technology. But after my encounters with his narrow-minded and parochial sensibility, I could not see myself embarking upon the story of Ford's life. I did not admire Ford's native entrepreneurialism with the same fervor as I marveled at Edison's sheer genius. I recognized Ford's immeasurable contribution to the twentieth-century gospel of progress, and I was impressed with his intuitive, if autocratic, managerial drive and undying faith in one product—but then I would come up with reluctance against his repugnant social traits.

Years passed until one Friday morning, February 21, 1997: I was sipping coffee in my sunny kitchen, scanning the *Business Day* section of the *New York Times*, when I noticed an article about the forthcoming broadcast of Steven Spielberg's *Schindler's List*, to be presented in its entirety for the first time on network television—NBC on Sunday, February 23, from 7:30–11:00 P.M.

"By foregoing commercials during the screening," I read, "the Ford Division of Ford Motor Company will make TV history as the sole sponsor of the program."

Speaking to the *Times* reporter, the Ford Division communications and advertising director, Gerry Donnelley, "denied that the founder's sins had influenced the decision to sponsor the Holocaust film. 'Many of our people were involved in this project, and no one ever mentioned Henry Ford,' Mr. Donnelley said. 'I think quite a few are not even aware of this background,' he added, 'We have great respect and a long association with Mr. Spielberg. For instance, Ford provided the vehicles for the film, *Jurassic Park*. We just felt it was the right thing to do to present this great story of one man's courage.'"

This media event—the mind-bending concept that *Schindler's List* was being packaged as a gift from Ford Motor Company to the American television viewing public—appealed to my sense of irony, but also, more substantially, to my awareness that here resided an inadequately told story in American history. Henry Ford and the Jews, I said to myself, now *there* is something I could delve into and devote my energies to writing about—even though I quickly discovered to my chagrin that another writer had made an attempt when I tracked down an out-of-print book called *Henry Ford and the Jews* by Albert Lee, published in 1980.

I read Lee's book, and I differed with it enough that I was inspired to redouble efforts at recasting the tale. I could not agree with Lee, for example, that William J. Cameron was an unwilling participant in the drama. I could not rest assured with the author's summary overviews of the *Dearborn Independent* articles. I knew that Father Coughlin was showing traces of antisemitism before the late 1930s. I could hardly accept the dismissive premise that "The nation's history is a blank sheet on the subject of Jew-baiting." And after having spent so many years inside the mind of Thomas Edison, I had come to understand that the inventor's stereotypical thinking about Jews was at the other end of the spectrum from Henry Ford's. I closed Lee's book convinced that above all else I needed to discover more—much more—about what was going on within the leadership and among the ranks of the splintered American Jewish community itself in response to Ford's pronouncements.

Albert Lee's discoveries a generation ago were significant impetus for me. I resolved to value them in precisely that way. I replaced his book on my shelf, where it remained for the next four years while I wrote my own *Henry Ford and the Jews.*

As I reflect over the arduous and solitary journey of writing, research, and travel, with a 500-page manuscript sitting in a neat stack on the desk, just touching my right elbow, I try to set Henry Ford's antisemitism in a meaningful context that makes sense at the commencement of a new century.

Constructing this book forced me to revisit the superficial nature of my own Jewishness, which was—and still is—pretty typical of a certain species. Growing up middle-class in New York City, I was a fourth-generation Manhattanite, attending the same Stephen Wise Free Synagogue on the West Side that my great-grandmother, grandmother and mother had. I dressed up and went dutifully to Sunday School from the age of three or four straight through high school, filing into the sanctuary every autumn to observe the two sacred high holy days, but hardly attending temple at all the rest of the year. I learned about the Jewish holidays and celebrated them at home with my family. I studied Jewish history with the learned rabbis of our Reform congregation, and then became Bar-Mitzvah.

The cumulative idea of "being Jewish" was a singularly unde-manding part of my identity, although the saga of the Jews as a people, as I came slowly to understand it, was informed by distant and abstract themes of incessant persecution, enduring strife and struggle, the arduous search for a homeland, and, in modern times—near-annihilation. To me, growing up in the New York City of the 1950s, attending an elite prep school and then an East Coast college in the '60s, being Jewish never felt that "different," and cer-tainly never endangered. Being Jewish didn't feel like an actual reli-gion either, with ritual obligations that possessed deeper meaning; rather, it was a respectable, altogether natural facet of my cosmo-politan and assimilated heritage.

Writing *Henry Ford and the Jews* therefore sent me into intellec-tual shock. I was obligated, for the first time in my mature life as a writer, to become familiar with as much of the documented record of two millennia of Jew-hatred as I could stomach. I was embar-rassed to realize while engaged in my research that I had difficulty believing what I read about the extreme degrees to which Jews had been reviled and marginalized as a matter of course in European society from medieval times. As the pages of early drafts of my manuscript came cascading out of the laser printer, I found myself shaking my head in disbelief, incredulous at what I had just writ-ten, thinking, "This can't be true... This just *can't* be true."

The exercise of writing this book forced me to make the transi-tion from being a biographer heretofore immersed in the realms of poetry, modern art, and high culture, to becoming an historian striking off upon a perilous ideological path through the often shameful course of human action.

The single biggest problem I have encountered in describing "antisemitism" is that it undermines my faith in behavioral logic. Before it is manifested in words or deeds, it is not quantifiable. As an attitude, or feeling, it is latent, unconscious. I remain frustrated by this quality of elusiveness, the first impression I had of young Henry Ford. From what I could determine, he did not know any

Jews until middle age. His impressions and prejudices (*literally, premature judgments*) were drawn from widespread stereotypes common to his tightly circumscribed world of post-bellum midwestern America. However, it is one matter to be exposed to biased images and received impressions of the times, quite another to harbor them, and then quite another to assimilate, believe—and give vent to them.

The historian in me abhors speculation, which is why I tried so hard to avoid it as I wrote this book. I will indulge here, after the fact. Knowing as we do now the unavoidable influence of "the Prussian" E. G. Liebold, the tipping point for Henry Ford, the release of his accumulated prejudices, must have happened after these two men met in 1910, and Liebold was allowed such an influential role in Ford's inner circle for three decades. The same can be said of W. J. Cameron, arriving on the scene a few years after Liebold. Henry Ford was very much at the helm of all of his enterprises; he trusted these two men and a handful of others to help execute his orders and articulate his beliefs. Those men in the Ford Motor Company who outlived their usefulness or crossed him in any way, no matter how faithful or devoted they might have been, were summarily removed.

From the personal level, the people Ford associated with every day, it is then one more step to the economic stage. Prevailing economic forces, *as Henry Ford in his rudimentary way of thinking understood them*, loom as the next important factor in the revelation of his antisemitic bias. Vilifying the "international banker" Jews—the Rothschilds and Warburgs of the world—and their schemes to keep their hands on the cash flow of nations, Ford was, here too, certainly not alone among American business moguls of his generation.

The difference was that Ford willfully set about to acquire an outlet with which to express his philosophy: the *Dearborn Independent* newspaper. Ford had the determination and the money to promulgate his views indefinitely and made a conscious decision to do so, and no one was permitted to impede him.

From its inception, the *Independent* struggled with uneven circulation, was intermittently available on newsstands, and never caught on with the reading public at large. The newspaper seized the panicked attention of American Jews and the fervent allegiance of Christian zealots, racists, and Nazis. Were it not for the sales imperatives imposed by the powers-that-be in Dearborn upon far-flung Ford Motor Company dealers with no choice in the matter, the *Independent* might well have died an earlier death.

The third factor was war. Henry Ford the single-minded, domineering car maker was infuriated to discover that his business could be beholden to the influence of (in his opinion) untrustworthy political forces. Ford announced in 1915 with a clear conscience that he was a "pacifist." By this he meant that he disliked having his grandiose commercial plans challenged by bellicose, far-off kings in alien countries, not to mention a do-nothing president in far-off, East Coast Washington. Someone—the devious race of Oriental peoples—had to take the blame and personify the consolidation of unreachable, immutable powers.

This helps explain why the failed Peace Ship escapade persisted with such preponderant and embarrassing importance. Henry Ford emerging from the public relations debacle of the Peace Ship voyage was a far darker force than Henry Ford going impulsively into it. Between 1910 (when he was already in his late forties and the Model T had been launched) and 1918, Henry Ford metamorphosed from ignorant idealist to embittered antisemite. He found a target to blame for his boredom, disillusionment, and middle-aged unhappiness. He grabbed onto the Jews, and never let go.

Ford's years of propaganda that followed—from the Treaty of Versailles through Pearl Harbor—were not all of a kind. The level of vitriol rose and fell, beyond the screeds in newspaper, booklet, and book form to off-the-cuff remarks to friends and acquaintances over brandy and cigars (theirs, not his); comments under the breath; hard-line negotiations with labor unions; financial and moral support of younger generations of right-wing Christian disciples; false apologies; manufactured photo opportunities; and sanctimonious, third-party press releases.

The barometer of Henry Ford's Jewish antipathies also rose and fell in tandem with the chronically uneven fortunes and missteps of his automobile business. Ford abhorred the inevitable fact that sooner or later the immense corporation he created would have to be run by someone else; his only son, Edsel, was the sacrificial victim. His tenacity led to costly commercial errors traceable to the days of the Model T and even earlier. Henry Ford always believed he was capable of maintaining control over his personal image, too; but his cherished sense of self was gradually ceded to and then appropriated by hired spin-doctors. It was a synthesis of both Henry Ford *and* "Henry Ford" who issued the spectacular 1927 apology to the Jews.

Into the final decade of his life, after several strokes, a nervous breakdown, and the medical diagnosis of senility, Ford's antisemitic statements became repetitive, predictable, and static, like a needle stuck in the dusty groove of one of Thomas Edison's phonograph discs.[1]

Henry Ford's cranky biases were not tolerated blindly. He received his fair share of petitions, high-minded newspaper editorials, critical letters by the bushel, ad hominem sermons and speeches, and, eventually, boycotts. His long-suffering son and strait-laced wife attempted at tremendous emotional strain to put some distance between the patriarch and themselves.

However, imagine by comparison what the social and political fallout would be today, if the C.E.O. of a Fortune–500 corporation in America even so much as intimated at Henry Ford's kind of language. Imagine the instantaneous, indignant response from our multiple media and modern upscale consumer public—and the Flivver King's brand of antisemitism appears downright exotic. It begins to look like a quaint chapter of American history viewed through sepia-toned spectacles—or through the reverse end of a telescope.

The Ford family and the Ford Motor Company embarked upon correctives to his behavior even before the Old Man had passed away. Beginning with Henry Ford II, enlightened and succeeding generations of Fords have sought to put an end to Henry Ford's dark legacy, extending economic credit to the young state of Israel and generously supporting Jewish charities at home and abroad.

During the 1970s, after a gap of twenty-five years—"the quarter-century of grace"[2]—the catastrophe of the Holocaust began to undergo voluminous textual scrutiny in American culture that has continued to build in intensity as the survivors diminish in number and their anecdotal testimony is supplanted by relentless historical examination, as well as refutation of Holocaust "deniers." This widespread attention in literature and the arts, and the establishment of public museums consecrated to unsparing portrayals of the Holocaust, have created a higher profile for Jewish identity.

Surveys commissioned within the past five years by the Anti-Defamation League and the American Jewish Committee have demonstrated that widespread antisemitism in America of the overt kind broadcast by Henry Ford is losing legitimacy. Antisemitism will reside in all cultures, de facto, as long as Jews exist—but in America it is moving toward the distant fringe.[3]

The swastika painted upon the walls of a temple, the vandalism in cemeteries, stand out as the extreme aberrations they have become. The bigoted speech by Louis Farrakhan or Pat Buchanan, the Grenada Hills day-care center attack by Buford Furrow—such inflammatory views and violent actions are reported and condemned. Outposts of white supremacists are scattered in the hinterlands, and members of hard-core Aryan organizations are likewise huddling into niches of leaderless resistance. Contrary to fears that the Web would become overrun with recruitment sites for hate groups, the groups have remained at a constant level.

And so, one might finally be satisfied to imagine the story of *Henry Ford and the Jews: The Mass Production of Hate* beginning to take on an antique patina as an object lesson representing a bygone era in our country's dark underside, almost forgotten in today's sensitized America, where modern-day Jews appear to be vitally engaged, accepted, and enfranchised. Such signs of native progress mean that similar behavior on the scale of Henry Ford's, manifested today by a figure with equal public visibility is well-nigh inconceivable. Twenty-first century American Jews can trust the objective evidence in their favor, feeling a greater measure of respect in our resolutely open society.

ACKNOWLEDGMENTS

This book is dedicated "to the librarians," and could not have been written without them. A perusal of my footnotes will make that abundantly clear. And so, I will start with the selfless and encyclopedically knowledgeable members of this noble profession—to be scrupulously fair, in alphabetical order by institution: Jane F. Westenfeld, Allegheny College; Gary Zola, Kevin Proffitt, Frederic J. Krome, Elise Nienaber, and Camille Servizzi, Jacob Rader Marcus Center of the American Jewish Archives; Cyma Horowitz, American Jewish Committee Library; Harilyn I. Slome, Laura Peimer, and Abigail Schoolman, American Jewish Historical Society; Viola Voss, Leo Baeck Institute; Riva Pollard, Bentley Historical Library, University of Michigan; Diane Spiel-mann, Center for Jewish History; Mark Coir and Amy James, Cranbrook Educational Community Archives; Mark Silverman, Editor and Publisher of the *Detroit News*, Steve Fecht, Photo Department Director, Donna Terek, and Pat Zacharias, *Detroit News* Archives; the staff of the Burton Historical Collections, Detroit Public Library; John A. Sitnik, Glen Ridge Public Library; Linda Skolarus, Nadia N. Blankenbaker, Terry Hoover, Patricia Orr, William

Pretzer, and Andrew Schornick, Henry Ford Museum & Greenfield Village Research Center; Leslie Gowan, former Curator, and Holly Teasdle, present curator, The Rabbi Leo M. Franklin Archives, Temple Beth-El of Detroit; Philip Miller, Hebrew Union College Library, New York; Dana Springer, Hebrew Union College Library, Cincinnati; Elena Danielson, Ronald M. Bulatoff and Dale Reed, Hoover Institution on War, Revolution and Peace, Stanford University; Heidi Christein, Leonard N. Simons Jewish Community Archives, Jewish Federation of Metropolitan Detroit; Mayer E. Rabinowitz, Jerome Schwarzbard, and David Wachtell, Jewish Theological Seminary Library; Julie Miller, former curator, The Ratner Collection, Jewish Theological Seminary; Paul LeClerc, President, Mary Bowling and Melanie Yolles, Manuscripts and Archives Division, Wayne Furman, Office of Special Collections, John Lundquist, Oriental Division, Michael Terry and Roberta Saltzman, Jewish Division, The New York Public Library; Polly Armstrong, Department of Special Collections and University Archives, Green Library, Stanford University; Benjamin Stone, University of Chicago Library, Department of Special Collections; and Aaron Taub, YIVO Institute for Jewish Research.

For many varieties of scholarly assistance, support, and hospitality, I also thank: Edward Ball, Debra Bard, Sidney Bolkosky, Tom Bridwell, Ford Bryan, Ron Chernow, Peter Costiglio, Leonard Gold, Jim Grey, Kim Guise, Renda Hertz, Gene and Ilse Herz, Grant Hildebrand, Eva Justino, Meg Kearney, Laurence Kirshbaum, David Lethbridge, Philip Levine, Celia McGee, Walter Mosley, Rebecca Neuwirth, Keith Newlin, Walter Oliver, Diane Osen, Roger L. Rosentreter, Robert D. Rubic, Robert Rydell, Ellen Ryder, Judith Serrin, Tom Simon, Stephen Steinlight, James Tobin, Lydia Voles, Beth S. Wenger, Gloria Whelan, Mira Wilkins, Victoria Saker Woeste, and Dan Wyman.

For the unique perspective on history that can only be brought to bear by family members of the protagonists in the drama, I thank: Albert Butzel, Leo Butzel, and Steven and Sandra Butzel; William and Ellen Kahn, Ed Pipp, Lydia Robinson, and especially Mary Einstein Shapero, grand-daughter of Rabbi Leo M. Franklin.

I am grateful to Deborah E. Wiley, Chairman, and the Board of Directors of the National Book Foundation, for giving me an unprecedented four-month sabbatical from my responsibilities as Executive Director so that I could become engaged in research for this book, beyond my lifelong restriction of three-day weekends.

My agent, Philippa Brophy, brought this book to Peter Osnos, CEO and Publisher of PublicAffairs. I am grateful to Peter for his unerring instinct in seizing upon the story immediately, and for cheering me on when the going got rough; and to my dedicated editor, Robert Kimzey, for his calm, insightful, and intelligent sensibility.

Rabbi Norman Patz, spiritual leader of Temple Sholom of West Essex, has been a religious mentor and intellectual guide to me during the entire five-year span of this project.

My children, Nicholas and Allegra, were no longer around the house as much as they used to be during the writing of my earlier books. But no matter how immersed I might have been in the work, they were always welcome to take a seat in the spare rocking chair in my study and provide their own special brand of welcome distraction.

My wife, Roberta, was, and always will be, my first and best reader.

N.B., September 13, 2001

BIBLIOGRAPHY

A Note about the Ford Archives

As cited herein, scholars Leo Ribuffo (1980) and Michael Barkun (1994), among others, have noted that "Most of W. J. Cameron's correspondence at Ford has been lost or destroyed," and "Most of the files relating to the Dearborn *Independent* were destroyed," and "The office files of the Dearborn *Independent* were destroyed in 1963, and other records for 1920 have disappeared."

In his autobiography, Lee Iacocca, former president of the Ford Motor Company, alludes to the disinclination of Henry Ford II, his boss during the 1960s and 1970s, to put anything in writing. "Although the two of us ran the company together for nearly eight years, almost nothing in my archives from those days carries his signature," Iacocca wrote. "Henry actually used to boast that he never kept any files. Every now and then he would burn all his papers...His attitude was, 'Destroy everything you can.'" (Lee Iacocca, *Iacocca: An Autobiography* (New York: Bantam Books, 1984), p. 105).

On April 6, 2000, in the course of my research, I wrote to Elizabeth Adkins, manager of archives services for the Ford Motor Company/Ford Industrial Archives, to inquire about the status of several accessions containing materials from the *Dearborn Independent* and housed at the Henry Ford

Museum and Greenfield Village Research Center, formerly known as the Edison Institute. Accession Number 43, described as pertaining to the *Independent*'s "finances, manuscripts, correspondence, payment vouchers," was listed as "Retained by the Ford Motor Company," as was Accession Number 582, "Jewish articles, manuscripts." Accession Number 273, also pertaining to the *Independent*, was listed as "Original accession destroyed."

Adkins, in an email response to my query, wrote back the same day to "confirm that Accessions 43 and 582 were destroyed. Accession 273 still exists, and is on deposit at the Henry Ford Museum [Research Center]... To my knowledge, all of the records that would be of interest to you in your research are now held by the Museum, and I'm sure that the staff there will continue to be of help to you."

Checking back with the Henry Ford Museum, I received word on April 7 from Linda Skolarus, manager of the Museum's Reference Services and Historical Resources, that she had examined Accession 273. It contained "just one folder of information. The rest of the accession has been destroyed. This folder contains, '[a] representative sampling of correspondence reflecting public reaction to Ford's stand on [Aaron] Sapiro ... [and a] ... photostatic copy of subpoena served on W. J. Cameron ... to testify and give evidence in the Sapiro case (2–23–1927)."

On July 3, 2000, I corresponded with Skolarus about my hopes of listening to some of the taped *Reminiscences* by Ford Motor Company old-timers conducted by Owen Bombard and his oral history team in the early 1950s. In response, Skolarus wrote that "The oral history project had been funded by FMC [Ford Motor Company]. Hence, the interviewers did work-for-hire for FMC. The interviewers would reuse the tapes for each interview. Hence, parts of most of the interviews have been taped over and are lost forever."

On August 23, 2000, in response to my query to the Henry Ford Museum Research Center regarding papers relating to the Peace Ship expedition of 1915, I received a "Search Service Report" that "Accessions 62 and 285—Office Papers [and] HF Office papers" contained "nothing" and "one letter," respectively; and that "Accession 79—Peace Ship Papers" contained "nothing." This response confirmed E. G. Liebold's statements to Marguerite Dumont in 1928 when she had been engaged in a similar quest on behalf of Rosika Schwimmer.

.   .   .

Henry Adams. *The Education of Henry Adams.* With an introduction by Leon Wieseltier. Library of America edition, New York, 1990.

Cyrus Adler. *I Have Considered the Days*. The Jewish Publication Society of America, Philadelphia, 1941.

——. *Selected Letters*. Edited by Ira Robinson. The Jewish Publication Society of America, Philadelphia, 1985. [two volumes]

T. W. Adorno, et. al., eds. *The Authoritarian Personality*. Harper & Brothers, New York, 1950.

James A. Aho. *The Politics of Righteousness*. University of Washington Press (A Samuel and Althea Stroum Book), Seattle and London, 1995.

Frederick Lewis Allen. *Only Yesterday: An Informal History of the 1920's*. Harper and Row, New York, 1931.

Gay Wilson Allen. *Waldo Emerson*. Viking Press, New York, 1981.

Gordon W. Allport. *The Nature of Prejudice*. Addison-Wesley, Reading, Massachusetts, 1979.

American Tract Society. *The Illustrated Family Christian Almanac for the United States: 1863*. New York.

Anti-Defamation League, ed. *The Protocols of the Learned Elders of Zion: A Hoax of Hate*. Special Report, June 1990.

Hannah Arendt. *The Origins of Totalitarianism*. New edition with added prefaces. Harcourt Brace and Company, New York, 1979.

Karen Armstrong. *The Battle for God*. Alfred A. Knopf, New York, 2000.

Richard Bak. "Edsel: The Forgotten Ford." *Hour Magazine*, Detroit, Dec. 1997–Jan. 1998, pp. 57–75.

Neil Baldwin. *Edison, Inventing the Century*. Hyperion, New York, 1995.

E. Digby Baltzell. *The Protestant Establishment: Aristocracy and Caste in America*. Random House, New York, 1964.

Michael Barkun. *Religion and the Racist Right: The Origins of the Christian Identity Movement*. University of North Carolina Press, Chapel Hill, 1994.

Harry Barnard. *Independent Man: The Life of Senator James Couzens*. Charles Scribner's Sons, New York, 1958.

Robert N. Bellah and Frederick E. Greenspahn, eds. *Uncivil Religion: Interreligious Hostility in America*. Crossroad Publishing Company, New York, 1987.

Nathan C. Belth. *A Promise to Keep. A Narrative of the American Encounter with Anti-Semitism*. Times Books/Anti-Defamation League of B'nai B'rith, New York, 1979.

Joseph W. Bendersky. *The "Jewish Threat," Anti-Semitic Politics of the U.S. Army*. Basic Books, New York, 2000.

David H. Bennett. *The Party of Fear: The American Far Right from Nativism to the Militia Movement*. Random House, New York, 1995.

Harry Bennett, as told to Paul Marcus. *We Never Called Him Henry.* Fawcett Books, New York, 1951.

Allan L. Benson. *The New Henry Ford.* Funk & Wagnalls, New York, 1923.

A. Scott Berg. *Lindbergh.* Putnam, New York, 1998.

David Berger, ed. *History and Hate: The Dimensions of Anti-Semitism.* Jewish Publication Society, Philadelphia, 1986.

Isaiah Berlin. *The Proper Study of Mankind. An Anthology of Essays.* Farrar, Straus and Giroux, New York, 1998.

Herman Bernstein. *The History of a Lie: "The Protocols of the Wise Men of Zion."* J. S. Ogilvie Publishing Company, New York, [February] 1921. [YIVO Institute for Jewish Research].

Richard J. Bernstein. *Hannah Arendt and the Jewish Question.* MIT Press, Cambridge, Massachusetts, 1996.

Hugo Bettauer. *The City Without Jews: A Novel of Our Time.* Bloch Publishing Company, New York, 1926, 1991.

Bruno Bettelheim and Morris Janowitz. *Social Change and Prejudice.* The Free Press, Glencoe, New York, 1964.

L. M. Birkhead, ed. *Henry Ford Must Choose.* Friends of Democracy, Inc., New York, 1941. [A.J.C. Library]

Sidney Bolkosky. *Harmony and Dissonance: Voices of Jewish Identity in Detroit, 1914–1967.* Wayne State University Press, Detroit, 1991.

Daniel J. Boorstin. *Hidden History.* Vintage Books, New York, 1989.

Norman Brauer. *There to Breathe the Beauty. The Camping Trips of Henry Ford, Thomas Edison, Harvey Firestone, and John Burroughs.* Brauer Publications, Dalton, Pennsylvania, 1995.

Alan Brinkley. *Voices of Protest: Huey Long, Father Coughlin, and the Great Depression.* Vintage Books, New York, 1983.

Arthur Brisbane. "To-Day Ford Attacks Jews, Why?" [AJHS Library, Article excerpted from Hearst Newspapers [review of Joseph Jacobs, Jewish Contributions to Civilization], June 20, 1920.

David Brody. *Workers in Industrial America: Essays on the 20th Century Struggle.* Oxford University Press, New York, 1980.

Stephen Eric Bronner. *A Rumor About the Jews: Reflections on Antisemitism and the Protocols of the Elders of Zion.* St. Martin's Press, New York, 2000.

Thomas R. Brooks. *Toil and Trouble: A History of American Labor.* Delta Books, New York, 1965.

Ford R. Bryan. *Henry's Lieutenants.* Wayne State University Press, Detroit, 1993.

———. *Clara: Mrs. Henry Ford.* Ford Books/Wayne State University Press, Dearborn, Michigan, 2001.

Alan Bullock. *Hitler, A Study in Tyranny.* HarperCollins, New York, 1971.

Luther Burbank with Wilbur Hall. *The Harvest of the Years.* Houghton Mifflin Company, Boston, 1931.

Kenneth Burke. *Attitudes Toward History.* Beacon Press, Boston, 1961.

Roger Burlingame. *Henry Ford, A Great Life in Brief.* Alfred A. Knopf, New York, 1955.

Sarah Burns. *Pastoral Inventions: Rural Life in Nineteenth Century American Art and Culture.* Temple University Press, Philadelphia, 1989.

Sarah T. Bushnell. *The Truth About Henry Ford.* The Reilly & Lee Co., Chicago, 1922.

William J. Cameron. [pamphlet] *Lincoln.* Chicago Historical Society, February 12, 1911.

———. *In Arcady, and other poems.* Macdonald and Company, London, 1913.

Oliver O. Carlson. *Brisbane, A Candid Biography.* Stackpole Sons, New York, 1937.

E. H. Carr. *What Is History?* Alfred A. Knopf, New York, 1967.

Jerome R. Chanes, ed. *Antisemitism in America Today: Outspoken Experts Explode the Myths.* Birch Lane Press, New York, 1995.

Ron Chernow. *The Warburgs.* Random House, New York, 1993.

Christian Science *Watchman*, n.d. [pamphlet ca.1920]. *The Jew and Henry Ford: Has Mr. Ford Unwittingly Become the Jew's Actual Benefactor?* [AJHS Library]

Louise Clancy and Florence Davies. *The Believer: The Life of Mrs. Henry Ford.* Coward-McCann, New York, 1960.

Naomi W. Cohen. *Not Free to Desist: A History of the American Jewish Committee, 1906–1966.* The Jewish Publication Society of America, Philadelphia, 1972.

———. *Encounter With Emancipation: The German Jews in the United States, 1830–1914.* The Jewish Publication Society of America, Philadelphia, 1984.

———. *Jacob H. Schiff: A Study in American Jewish Leadership.* Brandeis University Press, University Press of New England, Hanover, N.H., and London, 1999.

Norman Cohn. *The Pursuit of the Millennium.* Oxford University Press, New York, 1971.

———. *Warrant for Genocide. The Myth of the Jewish World Conspiracy and the Protocols of the Elders of Zion.* Harper & Row, New York, 1967; Serif Press, London, 1996.

Mark Coir. *The Gospel of Work: Henry Ford, Samuel Marquis, and the Five Dollar Day.* Wayne State University Press, Detroit, graduate seminar paper, 1995.

——. *A Brief History of Cranbrook.* Cranbrook Educational Community, Bloomfield Hills, Mich., 1997.

Peter Collier and David Horowitz. *The Fords, An American Epic.* Summit Books, New York, 1987.

Gordon A. Craig. *Germany: 1866–1945.* Oxford University Press, New York, 1978.

Charles Darwin. *The Origin of Species (1859) and the Descent of Man (1871).* Random House/Modern Library, New York [n.d.].

Lucy S. Dawidowicz. *The Holocaust and the Historians.* Harvard University Press, Cambridge, 1981.

——. *On Equal Terms. Jews in America, 1881–1981.* Holt, Rhinehart and Winston, New York, 1982.

Dearborn Independent, eds. *The International Jew, Volume I, The World's Foremost Problem, 1920.* (Vols. I–IV Reprinted 1999 by GSG Associates, San Pedro, California).

—— *The International Jew, Volume II, Jewish Activities in the United States.* Dearborn Publishing Company, Dearborn, Michigan, 1921.

——. *The International Jew, Volume III, Jewish Influences in American Life, 1921.*

——. *The International Jew, Volume IV. Aspects of Jewish Power in the United States, 1922.*

Sigmund Diamond. *The Nation Transformed: The Creation of an Industrial Society.* George Braziller, New York, 1963.

Hasia R. Diner. *The Jewish People in America: A Time for Gathering. The Second Migration, 1820–1880.* Johns Hopkins University Press, Baltimore, 1992.

Leonard Dinnerstein. *Uneasy at Home: Antisemitism and the American Jewish Experience.* Columbia University Press, New York, 1987.

——. *Antisemitism in America.* Oxford University Press, New York, 1994.

Michael Dobbs. "Ford and GM Scrutinized for Alleged Nazi Collaboration." *The Washington Post*, November 30, 1998, p. 1.

Michael N. Dobkowski. *The Tarnished Dream: The Basis of American Anti-Semitism.* Greenwood Press, Westport, Connecticut, 1979.

John Dos Passos. *The U. S. A. Trilogy: The 42nd Parallel (1930); Nineteen Nineteen (1932); The Big Money (1936).* Reprinted 1979, New American Library.

Henry Drummond. *The Greatest Thing in the World.* J. Pott & Company, New York, 1890.

Melvin Dubofsky and Warren Van Tine. *John L. Lewis. A Biography.* The New York Times Book Company, New York, 1977.

Dietrich Eckart. *Bolshevism from Moses to Lenin: A Dialogue Between Adolf*

Hitler and Me. [Translated by William L. Pierce from the German edition published in Munich, March, 1924, from unfinished notes of autumn, 1923]. *National Socialist World,* No.2, Fall 1966. The World Union of National Socialists, Arlington, Virginia.

Daniel J. Elazar. *Community & Polity. The Organizational Dynamics of American Jewry.* The Jewish Publication Society, Philadelphia and Jerusalem, 1995.

Ralph Waldo Emerson. *Gems from Emerson.* Edited by E. Haldeman-Julius. Haldeman-Julius Company, Girard, Kansas (pamphlet, ca. 1904).

——. *Selections from his Works.* Edited by Stephen E. Whicher. Houghton Mifflin, Boston, 1960.

——. *Essays and Lectures.* Edited by Joel Porte. Library of America, New York, 1983.

Richard J. Evans. *In Defense of History.* W. W. Norton & Company, New York, 1999.

Henry L. Feingold. *A Midrash on American Jewish History.* SUNY Press, Albany, New York, 1982.

——. *The Jewish People in America: A Time for Searching. Entering the Mainstream, 1920–1945.* Johns Hopkins University Press, Baltimore and London, 1992.

Egal Feldman. *The Dreyfus Affair and the American Conscience, 1895–1906.* Wayne State University Press, Detroit, 1981.

Otto Fenichel. *The Collected Papers, Second Series.* W. W. Norton and Co., New York, 1954. [*Elements of a Psychoanalytic Theory of Anti-Semitism,* a modified version of a paper first published in *The American Imago,* Vol. I, 1940.]

W. Hawkins Ferry. *The Legacy of Albert Kahn.* Wayne State University Press, Detroit, 1970, 1987.

Henry Ford in collaboration with Samuel Crowther. *My Life and Work.* Doubleday, Page and Company, New York, 1922.

——. *Today and Tomorrow.* William Heinemann, Ltd., London, 1926.

——. *My Philosophy of Industry.* George G. Harrap & Co., Ltd., London, 1929.

——. *Moving Forward.* Doubleday, Doran and Co., New York, 1930.

Leo Franklin. *Some Untold Tales of Detroit and Detroiters.* [*Unpublished restricted MS,* Detroit, 1947. The Leo Franklin Archives, Temple Beth El.]

Sigmund Freud. *The Future of an Illusion.* [1927] W. W. Norton and Co., New York, 1961.

——. *Civilization and Its Discontents.* [1930] W. W. Norton and Co., New York, 1962.

——. *Moses and Monotheism.* [1937] Random House, New York, 1967.

Paul Gagnon, ed. *Historical Literacy.* Houghton Mifflin, Boston, 1989.

Hamlin Garland. *A Son of the Middle Border.* Penguin Books, New York, 1995
edition of 1917 novel.

———. *Afternoon Neighbors: Further Excerpts from a Literary Log.* The Macmillan Company, New York, 1934.

Garet Garrett. *Henry Ford: The Wild Wheel.* Pantheon Books, New York, 1952.

Peter Gay. *Freud, Jews and Other Germans. Masters and Victims in Modernist Culture.* Oxford University Press, New York, 1978.

William Gillespie. *Dietrich Eckart: An introduction for the English-speaking student.* Self-published, Houston, Texas, 1976.

Dan Gillmor, ed. "Proof of Ford's Fascism." *Friday* Magazine, January 24, 1941. [A.J.C. Library]

———, ed. "War in Dearborn." *Unbelievable* Magazine [1941], pp. 27–40. [AJHS Library]

Daniel Jonah Goldhagen. *Hitler's Willing Executioners. Ordinary Germans and the Holocaust.* Alfred A. Knopf, New York, 1996.

Arthur A. Goren. *New York Jews and the Quest for Community. The Kehillah Experiment, 1908–1922.* Columbia University Press, New York and London, 1970.

Thomas F. Gossett. *Race: The History of an Idea in America.* Schocken Books, New York, 1965.

James R. Green. *The World of the Worker: Labor in Twentieth-Century America.* University of Illinois Press, Urbana and Chicago, 1998.

Jeffrey S. Gurock, ed. American Jewish History, Volume 6, Parts I and II: *Anti-Semitism in America.* Routledge, New York, 1998.

Norman Hapgood. "The Inside Story of Henry Ford's Jew-Mania." *Hearst's International,* June–November, 1922. [A.J.C. Library]

W. S. Harwood. *New Creations in Plant Life. An Authoritative Account of the Life and Work of Luther Burbank.* The Macmillan Company, New York, 1906.

Nancy A. Harrowitz, ed. *Tainted Greatness: Antisemitism and Cultural Heroes.* Temple University Press, Philadelphia, 1994.

Jeanine M. Head and William S. Pretzer. *Henry Ford, A Pictorial Biography.* Henry Ford Museum & Greenfield Village, Dearborn, Michigan, 1990.

Konrad Heiden. *Der Fuehrer: Hitler's Rise to Power.* Translated by Ralph Manheim. Houghton Mifflin Company, Boston, 1944.

Maureen Hart Hennessey and Anne Knutson. *Norman Rockwell: Pictures for the American People.* Harry N. Abrams, Inc., New York, 1999.

Will Herberg. *Protestant—Catholic—Jew: An Essay in American Religious Sociology.* The University of Chicago Press, Chicago, 1983.

B. Charles Herring. *The Talmud and Anti-Semitism in Twentieth Century America.* [Unpublished thesis submitted for M.A. in Hebrew Letters and Ordination, Hebrew Union College-Jewish Institute of Religion, Cincinnati, Ohio, 1965.]

Burnet Hershey. *The Odyssey of Henry Ford and the Great Peace Ship.* Taplinger, New York, 1967.

Arthur Hertzberg, ed. *The Zionist Idea: A Historical Analysis and Reader.* The Jewish Publication Society, Philadelphia and Jerusalem, 1997.

Robert E. Herzstein. *Roosevelt & Hitler: Prelude to War.* Paragon House, New York, 1989.

John Higham. *Strangers in the Land. Patterns of American Nativism, 1860–1925.* Rutgers University Press, New Brunswick, New Jersey, 1955.

——. *Send These To Me. Jews and Other Immigrants in Urban America.* Atheneum, New York, 1975.

Grant Hildebrand. *Designing for Industry. The Architecture of Albert Kahn.* The MIT Press, Cambridge and London, 1974.

Adolf Hitler. *Mein Kampf.* Translated by Ralph Manheim. Houghton Mifflin & Co., New York, 1943 translation of 1925 German edition.

——. *Table Talk, 1941-1944.* Introduced and with a new Preface by H. R. Trevor-Roper. Enigma Books, New York, 2000.

Eric Hobsbawm. *The Age of Extremes: A History of the World, 1914–1991.* Pantheon Books, New York, 1994.

——. *On History.* The New Press, New York, 1997.

Richard Hofstadter. *Social Darwinism in American Thought.* Beacon Press, Boston, 1944, 1992.

——. *Anti-intellectualism in American Life.* Random House, New York, 1964.

——. *The Paranoid Style in American Politics, and other essays.* Harvard University Press, Cambridge, 1965.

Barry W. Holtz, ed. *Back to the Sources. Reading the Classic Jewish Texts.* Simon & Schuster, New York, 1984.

Irving Howe. *World Of Our Fathers. The Journey of the East European Jews to America and the Life they Found and Made.* Harcourt Brace Jovanovich, New York, 1976.

Jonathan Hughes. *The Vital Few: American Economic Progress and Its Antagonists.* Oxford University Press, New York, 1973.

Thomas P. Hughes. *American Genesis: A Century of Invention and Technological Enthusiasm, 1870–1970.* Viking Press, New York, 1989.

Lee Iacocca with William Novak. *Iacocca: An Autobiography.* Bantam Books, New York, 1984.

Harold L. Ickes. "Protestantism Answers Hate." [Speech delivered February 25, 1941.] *The Protestant*, New York, 1921. [AJHS Library]

Anne Jardim. *The First Henry Ford: A Study in Personality and Business Leadership*. The MIT Press, Cambridge, 1970.

Glen Jeansonne. *Gerald L. K. Smith, Minister of Hate*. Louisiana State University Press, Baton Rouge, 1997.

David Starr Jordan. *Unseen Empire. A study of the plight of nations that do not pay their debts*. American Unitarian Association, Boston, 1912.

S. T. Joshi. *Documents of American Prejudice. An Anthology of Writings on Race from Thomas Jefferson to David Duke*. Basic Books, New York, 1999.

David S. Katz and Richard H. Popkin. *Messianic Revolution: Radical Religious Politics to the End of the Second Millennium*. Hill and Wang, New York, 1998.

John Keegan. *The First World War*. Random House, New York, 2000.

Ian Kershaw. *Hitler, 1889–1936, Hubris*. W. W. Norton & Company, New York, 1999.

———. *Hitler, 1936–1945, Nemesis*. W. W. Norton & Company, New York, 2000.

John Maynard Keynes. *The Economic Consequences of the Peace. 1971 edition of 1920*. Penguin Books, New York, 1995.

Thomas J. Knock. *To End All Wars: Woodrow Wilson and the Quest for a New World Order*. Princeton University Press, Princeton, New Jersey, 1992.

Barbara S. Kraft. *The Peace Ship*. Macmillan, New York, 1978.

Dominick LaCapra. *Rethinking Intellectual History: Texts, Contexts, Language*. Cornell University Press, Ithaca, New York, and London, 1983.

Barbara Miller Lane and Leila J. Rupp, eds. *Nazi Ideology Before 1933: A Documentation*. University of Texas Press, Austin, 1978.

Lawrence J. Langer. *Preempting the Holocaust*. Yale University Press, New Haven, 1998.

Gavin I. Langmuir. *History, Religion, and Antisemitism*. University of California Press, Berkeley, 1990.

———. *Toward a Definition of Antisemitism*. University of California Press, Berkeley, 1990.

Bernard Lazare. *Antisemitism, Its History and Causes*. University of Nebraska Press, Lincoln, 1995 translation of 1894 edition.

Albert Lee. *Henry Ford and the Jews*. Stein and Day, New York, 1980.

Abram Leon. *The Jewish Question. A Marxist Interpretation*. Pathfinder Press, New York, 1996 edition of 1950 text.

Jonathan Norton Leonard. *The Tragedy of Henry Ford*. G. P. Putnam's Sons, New York, 1932.

William E. Leuchtenberg. *The Perils of Prosperity. 1914–32*. University of Chicago Press, Chicago, 1958.

Mark Levene. *War, Jews, and the New Europe: The Diplomacy of Lucien Wolf, 1914–1919*. The Littman Library, Oxford University Press, Oxford, 1992.

Lee J. Levinger. *Anti-Semitism in the United States: Its History and Causes*. Bloch Publishing Corporation, New York, 1925.

David L. Lewis. *The Public Image of Henry Ford. An American Folk Hero and His Company*. Wayne State University Press, Detroit, 1976.

——. "Henry Ford's Anti-Semitism and Its Repercussions." *Michigan Jewish History Magazine*, XXIV.1, January 1984.

Nelson Lichtenstein and Stephen Meyer, eds. *On the Line: Essays in the History of Auto Work*. University of Illinois Press, Urbana and Chicago, 1989.

Walter Lippman. *Public Opinion*. Pelican Books, New York, 1922.

——. *Drift and Mastery*. Prentice-Hall, Inc., Englewood Cliffs, New Jersey, 1961.

London *Times*. "The Truth About 'The Protocols,' A Literary Forgery." August 16, 17, and 18, 1921. [YIVO]

David Lowenthal. *The Past is a Foreign Country*. Cambridge University Press, Cambridge, 1985.

Kurt G. W. Ludecke. *I Knew Hitler: The Story of a Nazi Who Escaped the Blood Purge*. Charles Scribner's Sons, New York, 1937.

John Lukacs. *The Hitler of History*. Random House, New York, 1997.

William Holmes McGuffey. *First Eclectic Reader, 1879 Edition*. Facsimile Edition by John Wiley & Sons.

——. *Fourth Eclectic Reader*. American Book Company, Cincinnati, 1879.

——. *Fifth Eclectic Reader, 1879 Edition*. With a foreword by Henry Steele Commager. New American Library, New York, 1962.

——. *Sixth Eclectic Reader. 1879 Edition*. With a foreword by Henry Steele Commager. New American Library, New York, 1963.

Carey McWilliams. *A Mask for Privilege. Anti-Semitism in America*. Transaction Publishers, New Brunswick, New Jersey, 1999 reprint of 1947 edition.

Samuel S. Marquis. *Henry Ford: An Interpretation*. Little, Brown and Company, Boston, 1923.

Victor E. Marsden (Translated from the Russian of Sergei Nilus). *Protocols of the Meetings of the Learned Elders of Zion*. Christian Educational Association. [n.d. – ca. 1950]

Karl Marx. *A World Without Jews*. Introduction by Dagobert D. Runes. Philosophical Library, New York, 1959.

Louise A. Mayo. *The Ambivalent Image: Nineteenth-Century America's Percep-

tion of the Jew. Fairleigh Dickinson University Press, Rutherford, New Jersey, 1988.

D. L. Mekler. *Der emes vegen Henri Ford (The Truth About Henry Ford).* Illustrations by Mitchell Loeb. *The Jewish Morning Journal,* New York, 1924

J. Gordon Melton. *Encyclopedic Handbook of Cults in America.* Garland Publishing, Inc., New York and London, 1986.

Paul Mendes-Flohr and Jehuda Reinharz, eds. *The Jew in the Modern World, A Documentary History.* Oxford University Press, New York, 1995.

Charles Merz. *And Then Came Ford.* Decorations by Harry Cimino. Doubleday, Doran & Company, Garden City, New York, 1929.

James Martin Miller. *The Amazing Story of Henry Ford. The Authorized Edition.* Ford Motor Company, Dearborn, Mich., 1922.

Perry Miller, ed. *The American Transcendentalists, Their Prose and Poetry.* Anchor Books, New York, 1957.

Harvey C. Minnich. *William Holmes McGuffey and His Readers.* American Book Company, New York, 1936.

——, ed. *Old Favorites from the McGuffey Readers.* American Book Company, Cincinnati, 1936.

Marsha Miro. *A History of Cranbrook: A Life Without Beauty Is Only Half Lived.* Cranbrook Art Museum, Bloomfield Hills, Michigan, 1999.

Deborah Dash Moore. *B'nai B'rith and the Challenge of Ethnic Leadership.* State University of New York Press, Albany, New York, 1981.

Richard D. Mosier. *Making the American Mind: Social and Moral Ideas in the McGuffey Readers.* King's Crown Press, Columbia University, New York, 1947.

George L. Mosse. *The Crisis of German Ideology: Intellectual Origins of the Third Reich.* Grosset & Dunlap, New York, 1966.

David Nasaw. *The Chief: The Life of William Randolph Hearst.* Houghton Mifflin, Boston and New York, 2000.

Allan Nevins and Frank Ernest Hill. *Ford: The Times, The Man, The Company.* Charles Scribner's Sons, New York, 1954.

——. *Ford: Expansion and Challenge 1915–1933.* Charles Scribner's Sons, New York, 1957.

——. *Ford: Decline and Rebirth 1933–1962.* Charles Scribner's Sons, New York, 1962.

James Newton. *Uncommon Friends. Life with Thomas Edison, Henry Ford, et. al.* Harcourt Brace Jovanovich, New York, 1987.

Peter Novick. *That Noble Dream: The "Objectivity Question" and the American Historical Profession.* Cambridge University Press, New York, 1988.

———. *The Holocaust in American Life*. Houghton Mifflin Company, Boston, 1999.

Sidney Olson. *Young Henry Ford: A Picture History of the First Forty Years*. Wayne State University Press, Detroit, 1963.

James Parkes. *An Enemy of the People: Antisemitism*. Pelican Books, London, 1943.

———. *The Emergence of the Jewish Problem, 1878–1939*. Oxford University Press, London, 1946.

Henry Paynter. "Anti-Jewish Books Still Carry Henry Ford's Name." *PM* Magazine, September 20, 1940. [A.J.C. Library]

Edwin Gustav Pipp. "The Real Henry Ford." *Pipp's Weekly*, Detroit, 1922.

———. "Henry Ford—Both Sides of Him." *Pipp's Magazine*, Detroit, 1926.

———. *Pipp's Weekly*. Detroit, Michigan, February 1921; March 5, 1921; September 30, 1922.

Leon Poliakov. *The Aryan Myth. A History of Racist and Nationalist Ideas in Europe*. Basic Books, New York, 1974.

———. *The History of Anti-Semitism. Volume III. From Voltaire to Wagner*. The Vanguard Press, New York, 1975.

———. *The History of Anti-Semitism, Volume IV, Suicidal Europe, 1870–1933*. The Littman Library, Oxford University Press, Oxford, 1985.

Clive Ponting. *The 20th Century: A World History*. Henry Holt and Company. New York, 1999.

James Pool and Suzanne Pool. *Who Financed Hitler: The Secret Funding of Hitler's Rise to Power, 1919–1933*. The Dial Press, New York, 1978.

Dennis Prager and Joseph Telushkin. *Why The Jews? The Reason for Antisemitism*. Simon & Schuster, New York, 1983.

Hermann Rauschning. *The Voice of Destruction*. G. P. Putnam's Sons, New York, 1940.

William and Marlys Ray. *The Art of Invention: Patent Models and their Makers*. The Pyne Press, Princeton, 1974.

Simon Reich. "The Ford Motor Company and the Third Reich." *Dimensions Magazine: A Journal of Holocaust Studies*. Vol.13, No.2, Winter 1999.

Edward J. Renehan Jr. *John Burroughs, An American Naturalist*. Chelsea Green Publishing Company, Post Mills, Vermont, 1992.

G. J. Renier. *History: Its Purpose and Method*. Harper & Row, New York, 1965.

Charles Reznikoff, ed. *Louis Marshall, Champion of Liberty*. Jewish Publication Society of America, Philadelphia, 1957.

William C. Richards. *The Last Billionaire: Henry Ford*. Charles Scribner's Sons, New York, 1948.

J. M. Roberts. *The Mythology of the Secret Societies.* Charles Scribner's Sons, New York, 1972.

Robert A. Rockaway. *The Jews of Detroit. From the Beginning: 1762–1914.* Wayne State University Press, Detroit, 1986.

Alfred Rosenberg. *Selected Writings.* Edited by Robert Pois. Jonathan Cape, London, 1970.

Leila J. Rupp. *Worlds of Women: The Making of an International Women's Movement.* Princeton University Press, Princeton, 1997.

Robert W. Rydell. *World of Fairs: The Century-of-Progress Exhibitions.* University of Chicago Press, Chicago, 1993.

Howard M. Sachar. *A History of the Jews in America.* Alfred A. Knopf, New York, 1992.

Edward W. Said. *Orientalism.* Random House, New York, 1978.

Maurice Samuel. *The Great Hatred.* Alfred A. Knopf, New York, 1940.

Jonathan D. Sarna, ed. *The American Jewish Experience.* Holmes and Meier, New York, 1986, 1997.

Jean-Paul Sartre. *Anti-Semite and Jew.* Schocken Books, New York, 1948.

Michael Sayers. "Conspiracy of Silence: The Case Against Henry Ford." *Friday* Magazine, November 8, 1920.[AJC Library]

Andrew Schornick. *The Anti-Semitism of Father Coughlin and the End of His Radio Career.* [Unpublished Research Paper] Detroit, 1996.

Joseph A. Schumpeter. *History of Economic Analysis.* George Allen & Unwin, London, 1954.

Binjamin W. Segel. *A Lie and a Libel. A History of the Protocols of the Elders of Zion.* University of Nebraska Press, Lincoln, Nebraska, 1995 translation by Richard S. Levy of 1926 edition.

Andre Siegfried. *America Comes of Age: A French Analysis.* Jonathan Cape, London, 1927.

Ken Silverstein. "Ford and the Fuhrer." *The Nation* Magazine, January 24, 2000, pp. 11–16.

William Adams Simonds. *Henry Ford.* Michael Joseph, Ltd., London, 1946.

Upton Sinclair. *The Flivver King.* Phaedra, Inc., New York, 1969.

Isidore Singer, et al., eds. *The Jewish Encyclopedia.* Funk & Wagnalls Company, New York and London, 1912.

Robert Singerman. "The American Career of the Protocols of the Elders of Zion." *American Jewish History,* No.71, September 1981, pp. 48–78.

——. *Antisemitic Propaganda. An Annotated Bibliography and Research Guide.* Garland Publishing Company, New York and London, 1982.

Harold K. Skramstad Jr. and Jeanine Head. *An Illustrated History of Henry*

Ford Museum and Greenfield Village. Avon Printing Company, Rochester, Michigan, 1990.

Alfred P. Sloan. *Adventures of a White-Collar Man.* Doubleday, Doran & Co., New York, 1941.

Orlando J. Smith. *A Short View of Great Questions.* The Brandur Company, New York, 1899.

———. *The Coming Democracy.* The Brandur Company, New York, 1900.

———. *Eternalism. A Theory of Infinite Justice.* Houghton Mifflin, Boston, 1902.

Thomas Smoot. *Edison in Florida.* [Unpublished MS, 2000]

Charles E. Sorensen. *My Forty Years With Ford.* W. W. Norton, New York, 1956.

Gerald Sorin. *The Jewish People in America. A Time for Building. The Third Migration, 1880–1920.* Johns Hopkins University Press, Baltimore, 1992.

John Spargo. *The Jew and American Ideals.* Harper & Brothers, New York, 1921.

John L. Spivak. *Secret Armies. The New Technique of Nazi Warfare.* Modern Age Books, New York, 1939.

———. *Shrine of the Silver Dollar.* Modern Age Books, New York, 1940.

Raymond L. Stebbins. *Henry Ford and Edwin Pipp: A Suppressed Chapter in the Story of the Auto Magnate.* [Typescript, 8pp. n.d., ca. 1940, Schwimmer/Lloyd Collection, NYPL.]

Theodore Stebbins Jr. and Norman Keyes Jr., eds. *Charles Sheeler: The Photographs.* Little, Brown and Company, Boston, 1987.

George Steiner. *Language and Silence.* Yale University Press, New Haven, 1998.

Charles Herbert Stember, et al. *Jews in the Mind of America.* Basic Books, New York, 1966.

William L. Stidger. *Henry Ford, The Man and His Motives.* George H. Doran Company, New York, 1923.

Donald Strong. *Organized Anti-Semitism in America. The Rise of Group Prejudice During the Decade 1930–1940.* American Council on Public Affairs, Washington, D. C., 1941.

Josiah Strong. *Our Country: Its Possible Future and Its Present Crisis.* Edited by Jurgen Herbst. The Belknap Press of Harvard University Press, Cambridge, Massachusetts, 1963 edition of original 1886 edition.

Keith Sward. *The Legend of Henry Ford.* Rinehart and Company, New York, 1948.

Joseph Telushkin. *Jewish Literacy.* William Morrow and Company, New York, 1991.

Jacob Toury. *"The Jewish Question," A Semantic Approach.* In Publications of the Leo Baeck Institute, Year Book XI, 1966, pp. 85–106. East and West Library, London.

Joshua Trachtenberg. *The Devil and the Jews: The Medieval Conception of the Jew and Its Relation to Modern Anti-Semitism.* Jewish Publication Society, Philadelphia and Jerusalem, 1983.

Barbara W. Tuchman. *The Guns of August.* Macmillan Company, New York, 1962.

Thorstein Veblen. *The Instinct of Workmanship and the State of the Industrial Arts.* B. W. Huebsch, Inc., New York, 1914.

Donald Warren. *Radio Priest: Charles Coughlin, the Father of Hate Radio.* The Free Press, New York and London, 1996.

Beth S. Wenger. "Radical Politics in a Reactionary Age: The Unmaking of Rosika Schwimmer, 1914–1930." *Journal of Women's History,* Vol. II, No.2, Fall 1990, pp. 66–99.

Lee A. White. *The Detroit News, 1873–1917.* The Evening News Association, Detroit, 1918.

Reynold M. Wik. *Henry Ford and Grass-roots America.* University of Michigan Press, Ann Arbor, 1972.

Mira Wilkins. *The Maturing of Multinational Enterprise. American Business Abroad from 1914 to 1970.* Harvard University Press, Cambridge, Massachusetts, 1974.

—— and Frank Ernest Hill. *American Business Abroad: Ford on Six Continents.* Wayne State University Press, Detroit, 1964.

Edmund Wilson. *The American Earthquake. A Documentary of the Twenties and Thirties.* 1996 edition of 1958 first edition.

Richard Guy Wilson, et al. *The American Renaissance, 1876–1917.* The Brooklyn Museum and Pantheon Books, New York, 1979.

——. *The Machine Age in America, 1918–1941.* The Brooklyn Museum, in association with Harry N. Abrams, New York, 1986.

James Waterman Wise (pseud. Analyticus). *Jews Are Like That!* Macmillan, New York, 1928.

Stephen S. Wise. "Henry Ford's Challenge and A Jew's Reply." *Free Synagogue Pulpit.* Vol. VI, No.4, New York, 1920.

——. "Henry Ford's Retraction: Some Further Lessons." *Free Synagogue Pulpit.* Vol. VIII, No.4, 1927–1928.

Ruth R. Wisse. *If I Am Not for Myself... The Liberal Betrayal of the Jews.* The Free Press, New York, 1992.

Robert Wistrich. *Hitler's Apocalypse: Jews and the Nazi Legacy.* St. Martin's Press, New York, 1985.

——. *Antisemitism: The Longest Hatred.* Schocken Books. New York, 1991.

Victoria Saker Woeste. "Lawyers, Public Service, and Anti-Semitism: Aaron

Sapiro's Libel Suit Against Henry Ford, 1922–1927." American Bar Foundation Working Paper #9616. Prepared for the Annual Meeting of the American Society for Legal History, October 18, 1996, Richmond, Virginia.

Lucien Wolf. *The Myth of the Jewish Menace in World Affairs, or, The Truth About the Forged Protocols of the Elders of Zion.* The Macmillan Company, New York, 1921.

C. Vann Woodward. *Tom Watson, Agrarian Rebel.* Oxford University Press, London, Oxford, New York, 1969 edition of 1938.

Ben Yagoda. *Will Rogers: A Biography.* University of Oklahoma Press, Norman, Oklahoma, 2000.

J. Milton Yinger. *Antisemitism: A Case Study in Prejudice and Discrimination.* Freedom Books, New York, 1964.

Leonard Zeskind. *The "Christian Identity" Movement: Analyzing Its Theological Rationalization for Racist and Anti-Semitic Violence.* Center For Democratic Renewal, Atlanta, 1986.

Olivier Zunz. *The Changing Face of Inequality: Urbanization, Industrial Development, and Immigrants in Detroit, 1880–1920.* University of Chicago Press, Chicago, 1982.

NOTES

Chapter One: McGuffeyland

1. Harvey C. Minnich, ed., *Old Favorites from the McGuffey Readers* (Cincinnati: The American Book Company, 1936), pp. 247–252.

2. Richard D. Mosier, *Making the American Mind: Social and Moral Ideas in the McGuffey Readers* (New York: King's Crown Press, Columbia University, 1947), p. 70.

3. Robert N. Bellah and Frederick E. Greenspahn, eds., *Uncivil Religion: Interreligious Hostility in America* (New York: Crossroad Publishing Company, 1987), p. 12.

4. William Holmes McGuffey, *Fourth Reader, Eclectic Series* (Cincinnati: Van Antwerp, Bragg & Company, 1879), p. 44, in Mosier, *Making the American Mind*, p. 70.

5. Harvey C. Minnich, *William Holmes McGuffey and His Readers* (New York: American Book Company, 1936), p. v.

6. Ibid.

7. Henry Steele Commager, Introduction to McGuffey, *Fifth Eclectic*

Reader (1879) (New York: New American Library, 1962 reprint), p. vii.

8.   Gordon W. Allport, *The Nature of Prejudice* (Reading, Mass.: Addison-Wesley, 1979), p. 398; Sidney Olson, *Young Henry Ford: A Picture History of the First Forty Years* (Detroit: Wayne State University Press, 1963), p. 16; Mosier, *Making the American Mind*, p. 15.

9.   Nathan C. Belth, *A Promise to Keep. A Narrative of the American Encounter with Anti-Semitism* (New York: Times Books/Anti-Defamation League of B'nai B'rith, 1979), pp. 43ff.

10.   Ibid., pp. 51–52.

11.   American Jewish Archives, Jacob Rader Marcus Collection, Rabbi Leo Franklin Papers, May 18, 1914.

Chapter Two: The Great Questions

1.   Thomas P. Hughes, *American Genesis: A Century of Invention and Technological Enthusiasm, 1870–1970* (New York: Viking Press, 1989), p. 295.

2.   Harvey Minnich, ed., *Old Favorites from the McGuffey Readers*, pp. 431–440; William Holmes McGuffey, *Fourth Eclectic Reader* (Cincinnati: The American Book Company, 1879), pp. 221–226; Charles Herbert Stember, et al., *Jews in the Mind of America* (New York: Basic Books, 1966), p. 344: "Talcott Parsons' theme of 'instrumental activism' in American values centered around a high regard for energy, work, and accomplishment, illustrated by the habit of saying, 'Well, don't just stand there, *do* something!'"

3.   Neil Baldwin, *Edison, Inventing the Century* (New York: Hyperion, 1995), pp. 301–302.

4.   Baldwin, *Edison*, p. 302; Sidney Olson, *Young Henry Ford*, pp. 29–30.

5.   Allan Nevins with the collaboration of Frank Ernest Hill, *Ford: The Times, The Man, The Company* (New York: Charles Scribner's Sons, 1954), pp. 74–79.

6.   Nevins and Hill, *Ford: The Times, The Man, The Company*, pp. 152–166; Louise Clancy and Florence Davies, *The Believer: The Life of Mrs. Henry Ford* (New York: Coward-McCann, 1960), p. 52.

7.   Baldwin, *Edison*, p. 303.

8.   Allan L. Benson, *The New Henry Ford* (New York: Funk & Wagnalls, 1923), p. 59.

9.   Howard Simpson, Oral History *Reminiscences*, Henry Ford Museum, p. 31.

10. Nevins and Hill, *Ford: The Times, The Man, The Company*, pp. 192, 229.

11. Ford R. Bryan, *Clara: Mrs. Henry Ford* (Dearborn, Mich.: Ford Books/Wayne State University Press, 2001), p. 205.

12. Oliver Barthel, *Reminiscences*, September 26, 1952, Collection of Henry Ford Museum and Greenfield Village, pp. 70–74ff; Bryan, *Clara: Mrs. Henry Ford*, p. 205.

13. HF interview with John Bradford Maine, *Detroit Times*, April 26, 1938.

14. Oliver Barthel, Oral History Interview, Henry Ford Museum and Greenfield Village, pp. 73–75.

15. Orlando J. Smith, *A Short View of Great Questions* (New York: The Brandur Company, 1899), p. 17.

16. The New York Public Library and Henry Ford Museum and Greenfield Village archival copies of Smith, *A Short View*, p. 27.

17. Review and Commentary section of Smith, *A Short View*, pp. 74ff, 40–42.

18. Ibid., pp. 49–50, 64.

19. Ibid., p. 73.

20. Ibid., p. 74.

21. Bernard Lazare, *Antisemitism, Its History and Causes* (Lincoln, Nebraska: University of Nebraska Press, 1995), translation of 1894 edition, p. 117.

22. Smith, *A Short View*, p. 74.

Chapter Three: Tin Lizzie

1. Alfred P. Sloan Jr., *Adventures of a White-Collar Man* (New York: Doubleday, Doran & Co., 1941), p. 41.

2. William L. Stidger, *Henry Ford, The Man and His Motives* (New York: George H. Doran Company, 1923), p. 57; quotation dated from 1900.

3. "Freeing" the farmer: *see*, for example, *Motor World* Magazine, 7, August 16, 1906.

4. Nevins and Hill, *Ford: The Times, The Man, The Company*, pp. 49, 279; *Motor World* Magazine, February 26, 1903; Baldwin, *Edison*, p. 304.

5. Stidger, *Henry Ford, The Man and His Motives*, pp. 77, 120, 153.

6. Baldwin, *Edison*, p. 301. "Consumer vision…": Warren Susman, *Culture Heroes: Ford, Barton, Ruth* (New York: Vintage Books, 1984).

7. Baldwin, *Edison*, pp. 304, 322.

8. Horace Arnold and Fay Faurote, *Ford Methods and Ford Shops*, cited in Nevins and Hill, *Ford: The Times, The Man, The Company*, p. 500.

9. Walter Lippmann, *Drift and Mastery* (Englewood Cliffs, N.J.: Prentice-Hall, 1961), p. 42.

10. *Detroit News*, especially re "alter ego," May 24 and 25, 1944; March 6, 1956, Liebold obituary; also, Bryan, *Clara: Mrs. Henry Ford*, pp. 169–170.

11. Keith Sward, *The Legend of Henry Ford* (New York: Rinehart and Company, 1948), p. 43; Jonathan Norton Leonard, *The Tragedy of Henry Ford* (New York: G. P. Putnam's Sons, 1932), p. 12.

12. Clancy and Davies, *The Believer*, p. 41.

13. Charles Merz, *And then Came Ford* (Garden City, N.Y.: Doubleday, Doran & Company, 1929), pp. 109ff; Bryan, *Clara: Mrs. Henry Ford*, p. 173.; Harry Barnard, *Independent Man: The Life of Senator James Couzens* (New York: Charles Scribner's Sons, 1958), pp. 72, 76.

14. E. G. Liebold, transcripts of *Reminiscences*, Collection of HFMGV, and audio-tape transferred to CD, 1951, pp. 259, 264ff.

Chapter Four: The Christian Century

1. Joseph A. Schumpeter, *History of Economic Analysis* (London: George Allen & Unwin, 1954), pp. 393, 445.

2. Thomas F. Gossett, *Race: The History of an Idea in America* (New York: Schocken Books, 1965), p. 179; Richard Hofstadter, *Social Darwinism in American Thought* (Boston: Beacon Press, 1944, 1992), pp. 93, 187; Hasia R. Diner, *The Jewish People in America: A Time for Gathering. The Second Migration, 1820–1880* (Baltimore: Johns Hopkins University Press, 1992), p. 170; James Martin Miller, *The Amazing Story of Henry Ford. The Authorized Edition* (Dearborn, Mich.: Ford Motor Company, 1922), p. 236.

3. Louise A. Mayo, *The Ambivalent Image: Nineteenth-Century America's Perception of the Jew* (Rutherford, N.J.: Fairleigh Dickinson University Press, 1988), p. 23.

4. Diner, *The Jewish People in America*, p. 115; Kenneth Burke, *Attitudes Toward History* (Boston: Beacon Press, 1961), p. 168; *The Illustrated Family Christian Almanac for the United States* (New York: American Tract Society, 1863), pp. 40, 43.

5. Allan Nevins and Frank Ernest Hill, *Ford: Expansion and Challenge 1915–1933* (New York: Charles Scribner's Sons, 1957), p. 313.

6. Sward, *The Legend of Henry Ford*, p. 146.

7. Nevins and Hill, *Ford: Expansion and Challenge*, p. 574.

8. Mayo, *The Ambivalent Image*, p. 106.

9. C. Vann Woodward, *Tom Watson, Agrarian Rebel* (New York: Oxford University Press, 1969, 1938 edition), pp. 132, 216ff; Leonard Dinnerstein, *Antisemitism in America* (New York: Oxford University Press, 1994), p. 49.

10. Robert A. Rockaway, *The Jews of Detroit. From the Beginning: 1762–1914* (Detroit: Wayne State University Press, 1986), p. 29.

11. Oliver Zunz, *The Changing Face of Inequality: Urbanization, Industrial Development, and Immigrants in Detroit, 1880–1920* (Chicago: University of Chicago Press, 1982), p. 350.

12. Gordon W. Allport, *The Nature of Prejudice*, p. 6.

13. Mayo, *The Ambivalent Image*, pp. 23, 191.

14. Dinnerstein, *Antisemitism in America*, pp. xxvii, 257; Burke, *Attitudes Toward History*, p. 168.

15. John Higham, *Strangers in the Land. Patterns of American Nativism, 1860–1925* (New Brunswick, N.J.: Rutgers University Press, 1955), p. 73; Diner, *The Jewish People in America*, p. 158; Gavin I. Langmuir, *History, Religion, and Antisemitism* (Berkeley: University of California Press, 1990), p. 18.

16. Lucy S. Davidowicz, *Equal Terms. Jews in America, 1881–1981* (New York: Holt, Rhinehart and Winston, 1982), p. 15.

17. Irving Howe, *World of our Fathers* (New York: Harcourt Brace Jovanovich, 1976), pp. 51, 395; Gossett, *Race: The History of an Idea*, p. 219.

18. Howe, *World of our Fathers*, p. 31; Leonard Dinnerstein, *Uneasy at Home: Antisemitism and the American Jewish Experience* (New York: Columbia University Press, 1987), pp. 30, 33.

19. Miller, *The Amazing Story of Henry Ford*, p. 219ff.

20. John Higham, *Send These To Me. Jews and Other Immigrants in Urban America* (New York: Atheneum, 1975), p. 6.

21. Arthur Hertzberg, ed., citing Leo Pinsker, 1882, *The Zionist Idea: A Historical Analysis and Reader* (Philadelphia and Jerusalem: The Jewish Publication Society, 1997), p. 43; Allport, *The Nature of Prejudice*, p. 120; Eric Hobsbawm, *The Age of Extremes: A History of the World, 1914–1991* (New York: Pantheon Books, 1994), p. 119.

22. Howe, *World of our Fathers*, p. 51.

23. Sarah Burns, *Pastoral Inventions: Rural Life in Nineteenth Century American Art and Culture* (Philadelphia: Temple University Press, 1989), p. 239.

24. Josiah Strong, edited by Jurgen Herbst, *Our Country: Its Possible Future and Its Present Crisis*, (Cambridge, Mass.: The Belknap Press of Harvard University Press, 1963 edition of original 1886 edition), p. 247.

25. Ibid., p. 205.

26. Ibid., p. 211.

27. Ibid., p. 42.

28. Ibid., p. 211.

29. Zunz, *The Changing Face of Inequality*, p. 217.

30. Rockaway, *The Jews of Detroit*, pp. 85–91, 132.

31. Karen Armstrong, *The Battle for God* (New York: Alfred A. Knopf, 2000), pp. 64, 135, 140–146.

32. J. Milton Yinger, *Antisemitism: A Case Study in Prejudice and Discrimination* (New York: Freedom Books, 1964), pp. 72–77.

Chapter Five: Working Man's Friend

1. Nevins and Hill, *Ford: The Times, The Man, The Company*, pp. 533–534.

2. Barnard, *Independent Man*, pp.83–94.

3. Henry Ford, *My Life and Work* (New York: Doubleday, Page and Company, 1922), pp. 126–127.

4. *Wall Street Journal*, January 12, 1914.

5. Ford, *My Life and Work*, p. 128.

6. Ida M. Tarbell, *Making Men at Ford's*, twenty-nine page typescript manuscript dated May 12, 1916, Cranbrook Archives.

7. Zunz, *The Changing Face of Inequality*, p. 311, citing J. Schwartz, "Henry Ford's Melting Pot," in *Ethnic Groups in the City*, ed. Otto Feinstein (Lexington, Mass: Heath Education Books, D. C. Heath & Co., 1971), pp. 191–198.

8. Bryan, *Clara: Mrs. Henry Ford*, p. 207, citing the words of Marquis, below.

9. Bryan, *Clara: Mrs. Henry Ford*, p. 206; Ford, *My Life and Work*, p. 130; Mark Coir, *The Gospel of Work: Henry Ford, Samuel Marquis, and the Five Dollar Day* (Detroit: graduate seminar paper, Wayne State University, 1995).

10. William J. Cameron, *Reminiscence*, 1951–52, audio tape transferred to CD, n.p.

11. Samuel S. Marquis Papers, Cranbrook Archives, Folder No.8–2, 1914, "Criticisms of the Sociological Schemes and How Answered."

12. Ford, *My Life and Work*, p. 130.

13. Sidney Bolkosky, *Harmony and Dissonance: Voices of Jewish Identity in Detroit, 1914–1967* (Detroit: Wayne State University Press, 1991), p. 59; Nevins and Hill, *Ford: The Times, The Man, The Company*, p. 553.

14. James Miller, *The Amazing Story of Henry Ford*, p. 41.

15. Zunz, *The Changing Face of Inequality*, p. 312; James Miller, *The Amazing Story of Henry Ford*, p. 40.

16. Zunz, *The Changing Face of Inequality*, p. 312, citing Schwartz, "Henry Ford's Melting Pot," p. 192.

17. Bolkosky, *Harmony and Dissonance*, p. 39; Higham, *Strangers*, p. 243.

18. Walter Lippmann, *Public Opinion*, (New York: Pelican Books, 1992), p. 64.

19. Will Herberg, *Protestant-Catholic-Jew: An Essay in American Religious Sociology* (Chicago: University of Chicago Press, 1983), pp. 21, 75, 264.

20. Benson, *The New Henry Ford*, p. 157.

21. Sarah T. Bushnell, *The Truth About Henry Ford* (Chicago: Reilly & Lee Co., 1922), p. 158; Baldwin, *Edison*, p. 335.

22. Nevins and Hill, *Ford: The Times, The Man, The Company*, p. 586.

23. Edward J. Renehan Jr., *John Burroughs, An American Naturalist* (Post Mills, Vt.: Chelsea Green Publishing Company, 1992), p. 5ff.

24. Baldwin, *Edison*, pp. 327–28.

25. Gay Wilson Allen, *Waldo Emerson* (New York: Viking Press, 1981), p. 624; Baldwin, *Edison*, p. 328.

26. Ralph Waldo Emerson, *Selections from His Works*, edited by Stephen Whicher (Boston: Houghton Mifflin, 1960), p. xiv.

27. Ralph Waldo Emerson, *Essays and Lectures*, edited by Joel Porte (New York: Library of America, 1983), pp. 1131–1137.

28. Renehan, *John Burroughs*, p. 25.

29. Benson, *The New Henry Ford*, pp. 331–332; Bushnell, *The Truth About Henry Ford*, pp. 135, 148; Ralph Waldo Emerson, *Gems from Emerson*, edited by E. Haldeman-Julius (Girard, Kan.: Haldeman-Julius Company, pamphlet ca. 1904).

30. Benson, *The New Henry Ford*, p. 331.

31. Emerson, *Essays and Lectures*, pp. 286–302.

32. Gossett, *Race: The History of an Idea*, pp. 97–98; Emerson, *Essays and Lectures*, pp. 790–792.

Chapter Six: "I Know Who Caused the War"

1. *New York Times*, April 11, 1915.

2. Baldwin, *Edison*, p. 342.

3. Barbara S. Kraft, *The Peace Ship* (New York: Macmillan, 1978), pp. 50, 284.

4. *Detroit News*, June 18, 1915.

5. *New York American*, August 16, 1915.

6. Robert W. Rydell, *World of Fairs: The Century-of-Progress Exhibitions* (Chicago: University of Chicago Press, 1993), p. 38ff; and personal communication, August 21, 2000; Charles Reznikoff, ed., *Louis Marshall, Champion of Liberty* (Philadelphia: Jewish Publication Society of America, 1957), pp. 354–355; LM letter to John Spargo, December 31, 1920.

7. Anne Yoder, Swarthmore College Peace Collection Finding Aid, January 1999, www.swarthmore.edu

8. S. T. Joshi, *Documents of American Prejudice. An Anthology of Writings on Race from Thomas Jefferson to David Duke* (New York: Basic Books, 1999), p. 164ff, citing Jordan, *The Blood of the Nation: A Study of the Decay of Races Through the Survival of the Unfit,* (Boston, Mass: American Unitarian Association, 1902), 1902.

9. Gossett, *Race: The History of an Idea*, p. 145; Higham, *Strangers*, p. 135; Hofstadter, *Social Darwinism*, p. 93ff; Higham, *Send These to Me*, p. 46ff.

10. Bernard Lazare, *Antisemitism, Its History and Causes,* (Lincoln: University of Nebraska Press, 1995), p. 128; Allport, *The Nature of Prejudice,* pp. 119, 124.

11. Michael N. Dobkowski, *The Tarnished Dream: The Basis of American Anti-Semitism* (Westport, Conn.: Greenwood Press, 1979), pp. 89–90, citing Jordan correspondence of 1911 and 1912; David Starr Jordan, *Unseen Empire. A study of the plight of nations that do not pay their debts* (Boston: American Unitarian Association, 1912), p. 4.

12. Jordan, *Unseen Empire*, pp. 19, 62; Margaret Ruddiman, *Reminiscences*, HFMGV, p. 37ff.

13. Jordan, *Unseen Empire*, pp. 75, 81, 177.

14. *New York Times*, September 9, 1915.

15. Barnard, *Independent Man*, pp. 99–100.

16. *San Francisco Examiner*, October 19, 1915, cited in Kraft, *The Peace Ship*, p. 55.

17. Norman Brauer, *There to Breathe the Beauty. The Camping Trips of Henry Ford, Thomas Edison, Harvey Firestone, and John Burroughs* (Dalton, Pa.: Brauer Publications, 1995), pp. 27–28; Rydell, *World of Fairs*, p. 40ff.

18. *Detroit News*, November 15, 1915, cited in Kraft, *The Peace Ship*, p. 55.

19. Beth S. Wenger, "Radical Politics in a Reactionary Age: The Unmaking of Rosika Schwimmer, 1914–1930," *Journal of Women's History*, Vol. II, No. 2 (Fall 1990), p. 66; Burnet Hershey, *The Odyssey of Henry Ford and the Great Peace Ship* (New York: Taplinger, 1967), p. 62.

20. Wenger, "Radical Politics," p. 70.

21. Elinor Lerner, citing Catt-Addams correspondence, September 25, 1914, in Jeffrey S. Gurock, ed., *Anti-Semitism in America*, American Jewish History, Vol. 6, Parts I and II (New York: Routledge, 1998), p. 321ff; Wenger, "Radical Politics," p. 72; Hershey, *The Odyssey of Henry Ford*, p. 63.

22. Leila J. Rupp, *Worlds of Women: The Making of an International Women's Movement* (Princeton: Princeton University Press, 1997), pp. 27ff, 84; Wenger, "Radical Politics," pp. 72–73; Jane Addams papers, Series I, Swarthmore College Peace Collection, Reel 8, no.993, in Thomas Dublin and Kathryn Kish Sklar, eds., *Women and Social Movements, 1830–1930*: www.womhist.binghamton.edu, 1997–2000; Hershey, *The Odyssey of Henry Ford*, pp. 47–48.

23. Rosika Schwimmer, five-page typescript, *The Beginning of Henry Ford's Anti-Semitism*, [n.d. ca.1921–1922], Rosika Schwimmer-Lola Maverick Lloyd Collection, The New York Public Library, Manuscripts & Archives Collection. Photocopy courtesy Beth S. Wenger to the author.

    "Rosika Schwimmer placed her papers on deposit at The New York Public Library in 1940 after her grand project for a World Center for Women's Archives fell through. She formally gave her papers to the Library as a gift in 1942, convincing her friend and collaborator Lola Maverick Lloyd to do the same. The collection contains over 1,000 boxes of material, documenting their activities on behalf of women suffrage, feminism, peace, and world government."—Melanie Yolles, Curator, Rare Books & Manuscripts Division, to the author, August 25, 2000.

24. LML to RS, November 15, 1915, Schwimmer-Lloyd Collection, Box A–64.

25. S-L Coll., typescript MS by RS, *When Henry Ford Was a Pacifist*, Box B–9.

26. Rosika Schwimmer, Box B–9.

27. Benson, *The New Henry Ford*, p. 323.

28. Schwimmer, Box B–9, handwritten ink diagram of seating plan at meeting, dated "1915, Nov.17" in upper right corner.

29. Wenger, "Radical Politics," p. 73.

30. Rosika Schwimmer, article, *The Poisoned Henry Ford, The Jewish Tribune*, December 5, 1924, p. 66.

31. Schwimmer article, ibid.; and earlier version as typescript MS, with handwritten ink revisions, S-L Collection, Box B–8.

32. Rosika Schwimmer, *Ford's Anti-Semitism*, and typescript/holograph MS.

33. S-L Collection, Box B–9, Telegram, Pipp to Addams, dated "11:00 A.M., November 18, 1915."

34. E. G. Liebold, *Reminiscences*, p. 257ff.

35. Liebold, *Reminiscences*, p. 279. On this rhetorical subject, also see Allport, *The Nature of Prejudice*, p. 68: "The familiar expression, 'Jewish international banker' reflects two fused negative attitudes—in defiance of the simple truth that few Jews are international bankers and few such bankers are Jews."

36. Schwimmer MS for *Ford's Anti-Semitism*, pp. 4–5; Schwimmer essay, *Poisoned Henry Ford*, op. cit.

37. Schwimmer MS, ibid.

38. Upton Sinclair, *The Flivver King* (New York: Phaedra, 1969), pp. 56–57; Gavin Langmuir, *History, Religion, and Antisemitism*, p. 297; Wenger, "Radical Politics," pp. 73–74.

39. Hershey, *The Odyssey of Henry Ford*, pp. 14–15; Nevins and Hill, *Ford: Expansion and Challenge*, pp. 26–27.

40. Clancy and Davies, *The Believer*, pp.93–94.

41. Eyewitness account by Lochner, reported in Hershey, *The Odyssey of Henry Ford*, pp. 20–21.

42. Rosenwald Archives, University of Chicago Library, JR to HF, November 29, 1915; Telegrams and Correspondence, HF to DSJ, and DSJ to HF, September 9, 1915–February 15, 1917; David Starr Jordan Collection of the Hoover Institution Archives on War, Revolution and Peace, Box Number 20, folder number 22.

43. *New York Times*, November 24, 1915; and S-L Collection, Box E27, Rosika Schwimmer interview with Keith Sward, March 13, 1939.

44. *New York Times*, November 24, 1915; Baldwin, *Edison*, p. 342ff.

45. Hershey, *The Odyssey of Henry Ford*, p. 119.

46. Rupp, *Worlds of Women*, p. 27ff. Cablegram, RS to Aletta Jacobs, First Vice-Chairman of the International Committee of Women for Permanent Peace, dated in pencil, "November 23 or 24, 1915;" Lola M. Lloyd Telegram, November 23, 1915; and Snowden letter, November 23, 1915. All in S-L Collection, Box E–31.

47. Wenger, "Radical Politics," p. 75.

48. RS manuscript, *An Open Letter to Henry Ford*, pp. 1–5, multiple typescript drafts with holograph pencil emendations, 1925–1927, S-L Collection, Boxes E–29, 30; E. G. Pipp and Henry Ford conversation reported in "History That Really Is Bunk," *Pipp's Weekly*, September 15, 1923, pp. 4–5.

Chapter Seven: The Bolshevik Menace

1. Bolkosky, *Harmony and Dissonance*, p. 81; David L. Lewis, *The Public Image of Henry Ford. An American Folk Hero and His Company* (Detroit: Wayne State University Press, 1976), p. 99ff.

2. Lewis, *The Public Image of Henry Ford*, pp. 97–99.

3. Ibid., p. 101.

4. Woodward, *Tom Watson*, pp. 334, 366, 369.

5. Higham, *Strangers*, pp. 179–181.

6. E. G. Pipp obituary, November 7, 1935, *Detroit News*; *Pipp's Weekly*, Fifth Special Edition, July 1921.

7. *Detroit News*, ibid.; and W. K. Kelsey, "Eight News Editors: Detroit Was Their Life," *Detroit News Sunday Magazine*, August 18, 1963.

8. Nevins and Hill, *Ford: Expansion and Challenge*, p. 124ff; E. G. Pipp, "Henry Ford, Both Sides of Him," *Pipp's Magazine*, Detroit, 1926, pp. 47, 61; Fred Black, *Reminiscences*, March 10, 1951, HFMGV, p. 6.

9. *Pipp's Weekly*, "An Open Letter to Henry Ford," Fifth Special Edition, July 1921; *Pipp's Magazine*, "Ford In Action," September 1927.

10. Clancy and Davies, *The Believer*, p.109.

11. A. J. Lepine (secretary to Edsel Ford) *Reminiscences*; Fred Black, *Reminiscences*, March 10, 1951, HFMGV; Bryan, *Clara*, pp. 37–38.

12. Bryan, *Clara*, pp. 53–54; Pipp, "Open Letter."

13. "Translated": Bryan, *Clara*, p. 53; *Pipp's Weekly*, February 12, 1921, p. 4; Liebold, *Reminiscences*, HFMGV, p. 442, corroborated by Fred Black's *Reminiscences* re. Ford's intention to use his newspaper to "educate" the rank and file, HFMGV, p. 6.

14. Black, *Reminiscences*, p. 9.

15. Nevins and Hill, *Ford: Expansion and Challenge*, p. 271; Black, ibid., pp. 14, 48–51.

16. Nevins and Hill, *Ford: Expansion and Challenge*, pp. 271–274; Black, ibid., pp. 14, 49ff., 51.

17. Roger Burlingame, *Henry Ford, A Great Life in Brief* (New York: Alfred A. Knopf, 1955), p. 97; Lewis, *The Public Image of Henry Ford*, p. 102; Bryan, *Clara*, p.175.

18. Fred Black, *Reminiscences*, p. 14: "It really *was* Mr. Ford's own page... [emph. Black]"; *Dearborn Independent*, first issue, bound volumes in archives of HFMGV; *see also* Ford's similar assertions regarding his initial goals for the *Independent* as expressed to Upton Sinclair, "Henry Ford Tells Just How Happy His Great Fortune Made Him," *Reconstruction* Magazine, Vol. I, No.5, May 1919.

19. *Dearborn Independent,* January 25, 1919.

20. Ibid.

21. *Dearborn Independent,* February 22, 1919.

22. *Dearborn Independent.,* ibid., p. 4.

23. "spectre..." see: Stanley Coben, "A Study of Nativism: The American Red Scare of 1919–1920, *Political Science Quarterly,* No. 79 (March 1964), pp. 52–75; *Pipp's Weekly,* February 12, 1921, p. 4; and March 26, 1921, pp. 1–2.

24. Boris Brasol, *Russian Eagles Fighting Bolshevism,* 1919, in Robert Singerman, *Antisemitic Propaganda* (New York and London: Garland Publishing Company, 1982), pp. 3–4. I am indebted to Prof. Robert Singerman for personal communications on this subject. His exhaustively documented essay, "The American Career of the *Protocols of the Elders of Zion,*" *American Jewish History,* No. 71 (September 1981), pp. 48–78, is the source for much of the biographical information on Boris Brasol cited here.

25. Singerman, ibid., pp. 49–50; Leon Poliakov, *History of Anti-Semitism, Volume IV, Suicidal Europe, 1870–1933* (Oxford: The Littman Library, Oxford University Press, 1985), p. 235.

26. Singerman, ibid., p. 48; Anti-Defamation League, www.adl.org/special_reports/protocols, Introduction; Binjamin W. Segel, *A Lie and a Libel. A History of the Protocols of the Elders of Zion* (Lincoln: University of Nebraska, 1995, translation by Richard S. Levy of 1926 edition), p. 56; Stephen Eric Bronner, *A Rumor About the Jews: Reflections on Antisemitism and the Protocols of the Elders of Zion* (New York: St. Martin's Press, 2000), pp. [1]–12.

27. Bronner, *A Rumor About the Jews,* p. 81ff.; Segel, *A Lie and a Libel,* p. 113.

28. "Chapters in Modern Jewish History," a series presented by the American Jewish Historical Society, No. 115; "The Protocols Come to America," *Jewish Daily Forward,* June 4, 1999; Howe, *World of Our Fathers,* p. 323ff. See also, Joseph W. Bendersky, *The "Jewish Threat," Anti-Semitic Politics of the U. S. Army* (New York: Basic Books, 2000).

29. Poliakov, *Suicidal Europe,* pp. 230–231; Singerman, ibid., p. 51; Herman Bernstein, *The History of a Lie: "The Protocols of the Wise Men of Zion"* (New York: J. S. Ogilvie Publishing Company, 1921), Chapter IV.

30. Segel, *A Lie and a Libel,* from introduction by Richard S. Levy, pp. 3–45; also Segel, p. 56ff; Norman Cohn, *Warrant for Genocide. The Myth of the Jewish World Conspiracy and the Protocols of the Elders of Zion* (New York: Harper & Row, 1967), p. 138ff.

31. "The Russian Lieutenant and Ford's Attack on the Jews," *Pipp's Weekly*, March 26, 1921, pp. 1–3; also See my note about the Ford Archives, in which I describe the removal and destruction of the *Dearborn Independent* records by the Ford Motor Company, and my confirming exchange of letters with the FMC Archivist in Spring 2000.

32. Brasol, *Russian Eagles*, pp. 13–14.

33. *Dearborn Independent*, May 10, 1919.

34. Excerpts from the *Dearborn Independent*, January 11—June 28, 1919.

35. Leonard, *The Tragedy of Henry Ford*, p. 154ff.

36. Baldwin, *Edison*, p. 392; Sward, *The Legend of Henry Ford*, p. 106ff; and especially, re "bunk," see Michael Kammen's essay, "Why Study History? Three Historians Respond," in Paul Gagnon, ed., *Historical Literacy* (Boston: Houghton Mifflin, 1989).

37. Leonard, *The Tragedy of Henry Ford*, pp. 158–170; Brauer, *There to Breathe the Beauty*, pp. 107–109.

38. Baldwin, *Edison*, pp. 333–336; Renehan, *John Burroughs*, pp. 275–276; John Burroughs pocket notebooks, August 4–13, 1919, The Berg Collection of English and American Literature, The New York Public Library; Burroughs notebooks microfilmed and photocopied excerpts, especially August 4–5, 1919, Vassar College, Poughkeepsie, New York; on Edison's correspondence, see Baldwin, *Edison*, p. 492, referencing TAE's original letters in the collections of the Edison National Historic Site, West Orange, New Jersey; and American Jewish Historical Society Manuscript Catalogue for bibliographical information: Markens, Isaac (1846–1928).

39. John Maynard Keynes, *The Economic Consequences of the Peace* (New York: Penguin Books, 1995, 1971 edition of 1920), pp. x–xiii, 37, 225, 236–238, 295; Henry L. Feingold, *The Jewish People in America: A Time for Searching. Entering the Mainstream, 1920–1945* (Baltimore: Johns Hopkins University Press, 1992), p. 179; Donald Strong, *Organized Anti-Semitism in America. The Rise of Group Prejudice During the Decade 1930–1940* (Washington, D.C.: American Council on Public Affairs, 1941), p. 15.

40. Leon Poliakov, *The History of Anti-Semitism, Volume III, From Voltaire to Wagner* (New York: Vanguard Press, 1975), pp. 112, 138, 178.

41. J. J. O'Neill to E. G. Liebold, November 26, 1919, in Lewis, *The Public Image of Henry Ford*, p. 137. Capitalization and punctuation are O'Neill's.

Chapter Eight: Exit Mr. Pipp

1. Higham, *Strangers*, p. 268; Naomi W. Cohen, *Not Free to Desist: A History of the American Jewish Committee, 1906–1966* (Philadelphia: The Jewish Publication Society of America, 1972), p. 123.

2. Higham, *Strangers*, p. 267; Benson, *The New Henry Ford*, pp. 182, 191.

3. Zunz, *The Changing Face of Inequality*, pp. 1, 3, 11, 286, 309–310.

4. Higham, *Strangers*, p. 285; Bolkosky, *Harmony and Dissonance*, p. 79.

5. David H. Bennett, *The Party of Fear: The American Far Right from Nativism to the Militia Movement* (New York: Random House, 1995), p. xiii; Bolkosky, *Harmony and Dissonance*, pp. 82, 173.

6. Bennett, *The Party of Fear*, pp. 190–198, citing Palmer's article, "Where Do The Reds Come From? Chiefly Imported, and So Are Their Red Theories," in the *American Legion Weekly* of January 20, 1920; also, see Palmer's *"The Case Against the 'Reds,"* in *Forum* Magazine (1920), Vol. 63, pp. 173–185.

7. Bennett, *The Party of Fear*; also Zunz, *The Changing Face of Inequality*, p. 324; see also David E. Trask, *World War I At Home: Readings in American Life, 1914–1920* (New York: John Wiley & Sons, 1990), pp. 185–189.

8. "What Started Mr. Ford Against the Jews," *Pipp's Weekly*, March 5, 1921.

9. Liebold, *Reminiscences*, pp. 422, 432, and audiotape transferred to CD, n.p.; J. L. McCloud, *Reminiscences*, p. 337.

10. Nevins and Hill, *Ford: Expansion and Challenge*, p. 274.

11. "Answering the Ford Attacks," *Pipp's Weekly*, March 5,1921, corroborated by Fred Black, Ben Donaldson, and Walter Blanchard, *Reminiscences*, in a joint interview conducted at the Detroit Athletic Club on May 28, 1951, pp. 9, 17, 26.

12. Black, et al., interviewed by Keith Clark, *Reminiscences*, pp. 6, 30–36; Cameron, *Reminiscences*, p. 23; *Pipp's Weekly*, February 12, 1921, p. 5; see also, E. G. Pipp, "Henry Ford, Both Sides of Him," 1926, pp. 68–69.

13. Re British-Israelite doctrine and its effect on Cameron's views of the Jews, *see* Leo Ribuffo's essay in Gurock, ed., *Anti-Semitism in America*, pp. 430–432; and Ben Donaldson, in Black, et al. *Reminiscences*, p. 40; also, *Pipp's Weekly*, March 12, 1921, p. 2ff.; Cameron, *Reminiscences*, pp. 9, 58. See also, Liebold, audio interview, n.p., "Mr. Ford asked me to take over and get the paper going.... Mr. Cameron was in close touch with me at all times."

14. *Dearborn Independent*, excerpts from issues of September 1919 and April 1920.

15. "Letter to the Readers," by Rabbi Samuel S. Mayerberg of Temple B'nai Yeshurun, Dayton, Ohio, in *Pipp's Weekly*, March 15, 1921; E. G. Pipp, "Answering the Ford Attacks," *Pipp's Weekly*, inaugural issue, June 19, 1920.

16. "Ford in Action," *Pipp's Magazine*, September 1927, p. 4.

17. Segel, *A Lie and a Libel*, pp. xii, 23, 60, 122; Bronner, *A Rumor About the Jews*, p. 114; Cohn, *Warrant*, p. 76; Singerman, "The American Career of the Protocols of the Elders of Zion," p. 59; Konrad Heiden, *Der Fuehrer: Hitler's Rise to Power*, translated by Ralph Manheim (Boston: Houghton Mifflin, 1944), p. 93; Barbara Miller Lane and Leila J. Rupp, eds., *Nazi Ideology Before 1933: A Documentation* (Austin, Texas: University of Texas press, 1978), pp. xxiv, 27.

18. Cohn, *Warrant*, p. 78; Singerman, ibid., pp. 59–60; Segel, *A Lie and a Libel*, p. xii.

19. Walter Blanchard, in Fred Black, et al., *Reminiscences*, p.36; Liebold, *Reminiscences*, p. 456ff.

20. Liebold, *Reminiscences*.

21. Mira Wilkins and Frank Ernest Hill, *American Business Abroad: Ford on Six Continents* (Detroit: Wayne State University Press, 1964), pp. 1–163; Mira Wilkins, *The Maturing of Multinational Enterprise. American Business Abroad from 1914 to 1970* (Cambridge, Mass.: Harvard University Press, 1974), pp. 72–73; and Mira Wilkins, personal communication with the author, June 3, 1999.

22. Langmuir, *Definition of Antisemitism*, p. 352ff.

23. Liebold, *Reminiscences*.

24. *Dearborn Independent*, May 22, 1920.

25. "Paper pogrom," E. Digby Baltzell, *The Protestant Establishment: Aristocracy and Caste in America* (New York: Random House, 1964), p. 205; Joshua Trachtenberg, *The Devil and the Jews: The Medieval Conception of the Jew and Its Relation to Modern Anti-Semitism* (Philadelphia and Jerusalem: Jewish Publication Society, 1983), pp. 5, 40, 61, 79, 101, 106, 160, 190, 213; Yinger, *Antisemitism*, pp. 72–77; Cohn, *Warrant*, p. xii; Langmuir, *History, Religion*, pp. 322, 340; Dennis Prager and Joseph Telushkin, *Why the Jews? The Reason for Antisemitism* (New York: Simon & Schuster, 1983), p. 75.

26. James Parkes, *The Emergence of the Jewish Problem, 1878–1939* (London: Oxford University Press, 1946), p. 195; Lazare, *Antisemitism*, p. 158; Leon Poliakov, *From Voltaire to Wagner*, pp. 18, 214, 309; Langmuir, ibid., pp. 23, 340; Cohn, ibid., p. 29, 41; Prager and Telushkin,

Why the Jews?, p. 73; for the derivation of Marr's term, "antisemitism," Yehuda Bauer, in Jerome A. Chanes, ed., *Antisemitism in America Today: Outspoken Experts Explode the Myths* (New York: Birch Lane Press, 1995), p. xv.

Chapter Nine: The Jewish Question

1. Louis Marshall Papers, American Jewish Archives, October 1, 1920.
2. Dawidowicz, *On Equal Terms*, p. 83.
3. For biographical information about Jacob Schiff that follows, with the exception of attributions to material in the American Jewish Archives as well as other critical works, I am indebted to Naomi W. Cohen's *Jacob H. Schiff, A Study in American Jewish Leadership* (Hanover, N.H., and London: Brandeis University Press, University Press of New England, 1999).
4. Poliakov, *Suicidal Europe*, p. 227.
5. Dawidowicz, *On Equal Terms*, pp. 63–64.
6. Jacob Schiff, General Correspondence Files for 1920, American Jewish Archives, Cincinnati.
7. Schiff Correspondence, AJA 1920 General Files, January 23, 1920, ibid.
8. Schiff Correspondence, AJA.
9. Schiff Correspondence, AJA .
10. For biographical details that follow concerning the life of Cyrus Adler, I am grateful for the assiduous scholarship of Ira Robinson in his annotated introductions to many of Adler's *Selected Letters*, Volumes I and II (Philadelphia/New York: Jewish Publication Society of America, 1985).
11. See for example, Adler to Judah L. Magnes, April 5, 1917, in Robinson, p. 329–330; and Adler to Jacob Schiff, January 17, 1918, p. 345–346.
12. Robinson, ibid., Vol. I, pp. 102, 114, citing Adler's 1902 J.T.S. Commencement Address.
13. Robinson, ibid., pp. 123, 208, 212.
14. Marshall to Adler, December 18, 1919, in Charles Reznikoff, ed., *Champion of Liberty*, p. 328; Adler to Marshall, December 29, 1919, in Robinson, ed., *Selected Letters*, pp. 402–403; "Jewish factionalism ... exemplary in their conduct": *see* Adler, unpublished correspondence files, August 15, 1919, and other letters, in Special Collections of the Jewish Theological Seminary Library, Archive I, Box 24, 1916–1922.

15. For biographical background on Louis Marshall (1856–1929), except
     where otherwise noted below, I have drawn upon the two-volume
     standard study, *Louis Marshall, Champion of Liberty,* selected papers
     and addresses assembled under the auspices of the American Jewish
     Committee, edited by Charles Reznikoff with an introduction by Oscar
     Handlin (Philadelphia: Jewish Publication Society of America, 1957).

16. Howe, *World of Our Fathers,* pp. 543–544.

17. Marshall to Stolz, January 12, 1906, cited in Paul Mendes-Flohr and
     Jehuda Reinharz, eds., *The Jew in the Modern World, A Documentary
     History* (New York: Oxford University Press, 1995), pp. 487–488.

18. Marshall to Richard Gottheil, January 8, 1913; S. O. Levinson, January
     8, 1915; and Richard Lindabury, October 24, 1919, in Reznikoff, ed.,
     Champion of Liberty, pp. 245–246; 322–328.

19. "Germany's Reaction Against the *Jew,*" in the *Dearborn Independent,*
     May 29, 1920.

20. Reznikoff, ed., *Champion of Liberty,* p. 329, telegram dated June 3, 1920.

21. Ibid., explanatory note, p. 329; reprinted in *American Jewish Year Book
     5682* (1921–1922), pp. 316, 317; DI letter to Louis Berlin, May 29,
     1920, in Marshall papers, AJA.

22. Marshall papers, AJA; also cited by LM in letters to Julius Rosenwald,
     June 5, 1920, and Henry M. Butzel, September 20, 1920, in Reznikoff,
     ed., *Champion of Liberty,* pp. 330, 335.

23. Adler to Schiff, June 15, 1920, cc'd to LM, in Marshall papers, AJA.

24. Reznikoff, ed., *Champion of Liberty,* LM to David A. Brown, August 13,
     1920, quoting from "an extraordinary letter" LM had received from
     Rabbi Franklin in the first week of June, 1920, pp. 330–333; re corrob-
     oration of Rabbi Franklin's holding LM responsible at the outset for
     Ford's abrupt turn of sentiment, see AJA Archives, David A. Brown to
     Jacob Billikopf, June 10, 1920, and Harris Weinstock to LM, Novem-
     ber 10, 1920. Rabbi Franklin's personal narrative account of his meet-
     ing with Henry Ford is excerpted from a 174-page unpublished
     typescript memoir, completed in 1947, *Some Untold Tales of Detroit &
     Detroiters,* Section II, "Henry Ford, Father Coughlin, and the Jews,"
     Chapter VI, "The Attack Begins," p. 117ff. The memoir was loaned to
     the author with the kind permission of Mrs. Mary Einstein Shapero,
     Rabbi Franklin's granddaughter, and with the cooperation of Leslie
     Gowan, former curator of the Rabbi Leo Franklin Archives, Temple
     Beth El of Detroit.

25. LM to David A. Brown, in Reznikoff, ed., *Champion of Liberty;* and Leo

Franklin, *Some Untold Tales of Detroit and Detroiters* (unpublished MS, Detroit, 1947, the Leo Franklin Archives, Temple Beth El), Chapter VIII, "Ford the Suppliant Versus Ford the Sinner," p. 139ff.

26. Bolkosky, *Harmony and Dissonance*, pp. 69–72; Letter from David Brown to Jacob Billikopf, June 10, 1920, passed along from Billikopf to LM, in Marshall papers, AJA. JB was LM's son-in-law.

27. LM to David A. Brown, August 13, 1920, in Reznikoff, ed., *Champion of Liberty*, p. 332; Bolkosky, *Harmony and Dissonance*, p. 81.

28. Charles F. Mirick, "Architect of Detroit's Soul Reviews 20 Years," *Detroit News*, January 23, 1919. Courtesy *Detroit News* Clippings Library.

29. William C. Richards, "Young Man of High Dreams Becomes Leader of Jewry," *Detroit News*, January 21, 1934. Courtesy *Detroit News* Clippings Library.

30. Excerpts from sermon, thirteen-page holograph manuscript in the Leo Franklin Archives of Temple Beth El, Detroit; for Ahlwardt's sojourn in America, *see* Mayo, *Ambivalent Image*, pp. 134–136.

31. Rockaway, *Jews of Detroit*, p. 122ff; Bolkosky, *Harmony and Dissonance*, p. 23ff.

32. Nevins and Hill, *Ford: The Times, The Man, The Company*, pp. 372–374; Franklin, *Untold Tales*, pp. 96–97.

33. Re Rabbi Franklin's community vigilance campaign, see the Leo Franklin Papers at the American Jewish Archives covering the period May 18, 1914–May 7, 1918; on Detroit Athletic Club, see Rockaway, *The Jews of Detroit*, p. 132.

34. For the historical anecdotes above, I am indebted to Jacob Toury's essay, "The Jewish Question, A Semantic Approach," in *Publications of the Leo Baeck Institute, Year Book XI* (London-Jerusalem-New York, East and West Library, 1966), pp. 85–106; see also: "The Jewish Question," in *Essays on Questions of the Day*, by Goldwin Smith (New York: Macmillan & Co., 1894), posted at *The Journal of Historical Review*, www.ihr.org/jhr; excerpts from Bruno Bauer's essay, *Die Judenfrage* (The Jewish Question) are found, with useful commentary, in Mendes-Flohr and Reinharz, *The Jew in the Modern World*, pp. 321–324.

35. Cyrus Adler, *Selected Letters*, edited by Ira Robinson (Philadelphia: Jewish Publication Society of America), Vol. II, p. 8, June 15, 1920; "Hatred Is Not Without Cost" (unsigned), *Der Veg*, Detroit, June 14, 1920, p. 2. The editor of the newspaper was B. I. Goldstein. Translated from the Yiddish by Aaron Taub, with grateful acknowledgement by the author.

36. Nathan C. Belth, *Promise*, pp. 77–78.
37. Letter from Leo Franklin to Henry Ford, June 14, 1920, Accession 572, Box 2, Ford Archives; Letter from E. G. Liebold to Rabbi Leo Franklin, June 23, 1920, Accession 572, Box 2, Ford Archives: Cited in Anne Jardim, *The First Henry Ford: A Study in Personality and Business Leadership* (Cambridge, Mass.: MIT Press, 1970), pp. 142–144 and Notes, p. 262.
38. Belth, *Promise*, pp. 77–78.
39. Black, *Reminiscences*, pp. 36–40; James Martin Miller, *Amazing Story of Henry Ford*, p. 139ff.; see also Louise Mayo, *Ambivalent Image*, on the popular image of "certain types of Jews" in America, p. 71ff.

Chapter Ten: Retaliation

1. "The Scientific Anti-Fordism," *Der Veg*, June 20, 1920. Translated from the Yiddish by Aaron Taub.
2. For definitive analysis of the concept of community in American Jewish life, see Daniel J. Elazar, *Community & Polity: The Organizational Dynamics of American Jewry* (Philadelphia and Jerusalem: Jewish Publication Society, 1995), especially Elazar's description of the origins and derivation of *kehillah*, pp. 3ff, 190ff. On the origins of the names for the Jewish people, see Lee J. Levinger, *Anti-Semitism in the United States: Its History and Causes* (New York: Bloch Publishing, 1925), Chapter IX, "The Future of the American Mind," pp. 111–118. Also: "Is the Jewish 'Kahal' the Modern 'Soviet?'" *Dearborn Independent*, August 28, 1920, points to the "Council of the Four Lands," proof of "an international relationship" among Jews "in earlier years," leading in a direct historical line to the recently convened World Zionist Congress, updated as a modern-day "Council of the Thirty-Seven Lands."
3. Gerald Sorin, *The Jewish People in America. A Time for Building. The Third Migration, 1880–1920* (Baltimore: Johns Hopkins University Press, 1992), pp. 90–91, 214–218; Mendes-Flohr and Reinharz, *The Jew in the Modern World*, citing Rabbi Magnes's sermon, "A Republic of Nationalities," February 13, 1909, pp. 493–495; Henry L. Feingold, *A Midrash on American Jewish History* (Albany, N.Y.: SUNY Press, 1982), Chapter VII, "Is American Jewry Really Organized?" pp. 110–126; Cohen, *Jacob Schiff*, pp. 112–116. The classic study is Arthur A. Goren, *New York Jews and the Quest for Community: The Kehillah Experiment, 1908–1922* (New York and London: Columbia University Press, 1970).
4. "Rule of the Jewish Kehillah Grips New York," *Dearborn Independent*,

February 26, 1921, and "The Jewish Demand for 'Rights' in America,"
March 5, 1921.

5. "America's Jewish Enigma—Louis Marshall," *Dearborn Independent*,
November 26, 1921.

6. "Finding Another Jewish Goblin in New York," *Pipp's Weekly*, April 26,
1921; Henry L. Feingold, *A Time for Searching*, pp. 155–156; Elazar,
Community & Polity, pp. 203–208.

7. Robinson, ed., *Adler Letters*, Volume II, CA to Harry Schneiderman,
June 25, 1920, pp. 10–11; American Jewish Archives, Minutes of the
Executive Committee Meeting of the American Jewish Committee,
June 23, 1920. Julius Rosenwald requested that Rabbi Leo Franklin be
invited to attend this particular meeting, so that he could report on his
"lengthy interview with Ford." No such invitation was offered. Also
see: Cohen, *Not Free*, p. 245, re the cautious approach of the A.J.C.; and
archives of the Jewish Theological Seminary, Box 24, copies of correspondence by Cyrus Adler to Louis Marshall, June 25 and 28, 1920.

8. Singerman, "The American Career," pp. 59, 63, 64, 73.

9. Liebold, *Reminiscences*, p. 468; Bronner, *A Rumor About the Jews*, pp. 5,
121; Hannah Arendt, *The Origins of Totalitarianism* (New York: Harcourt Brace, 1979), Part I, "Antisemitism," pp. 7, 333.

10. Adler, *Selected Letters*, October 13, 1920, to Racie Adler, p.19; October
17, 1920, to Abraham S. Schomer, p. 20; Cyrus Adler, Jewish Theological Seminary Archive, Letter to Simon Wolf, October 26, 1920;
Reznikoff, ed., *Champion of Liberty*; Louis Marshall letters to G. H.
Putnam, October 13 and 28, 1920, pp. 338–343.

11. G. H. Putnam to Louis Marshall, November 1, 1920, reprinted in Marshall, ibid., p. 343; Singerman, "The American Career of the Protocols
of the Elders of Zion," p. 68.

12. Leo P. Ribuffo, "Henry Ford and the International Jew," in Gurock, ed.,
Anti-Semitism in America, p. 433; Liebold, *Reminiscences*, p. 469; Cohn,
Warrant, pp. 147, 174; on *The International Jew*, see, for example, the
new uniform four-volume paperbound edition published by GSG Associates, San Pedro, California; and also, www.adl.org/special_reports/ij/
international_jew.html.

13. Lewis, *The Public Image of Henry Ford*, p. 142, and p. 510, notes 22 and
23; Marshall papers, American Jewish Archives, Letter to LM from B.
M. Marcus, proprietor of a gas station in Olean, New York, comment-
ing on the Ford quota system, November 13, 1920.

14. Louis Marshall papers, American Jewish Archives: Sachs to LM,
November 16, 1920; Friedenwald to LM, November 24, 1920; English
to LM, November 30 and December 20, 1920.

15. Reznikoff, ed., LM *Letters*, p. 343; *The "Protocols..."* The American Jewish Committee, New York, December 1, 1920, pp. 5–15.

16. "What Some Non-Jewish Leaders Think of Henry Ford's Propaganda," *Cincinnati Gazette*, December 1, 1920.

17. Marshall, Letters, to John Spargo, December 11 and December 31, 1920, pp. 351–355; Poliakov, *Suicidal Europe*, pp. 249–251.

Chapter Eleven: The Talmud-Jew

1. Nevins and Hill, *Ford: Expansion and Challenge*, pp. 167–170; Wilkins, *American Business Abroad*, pp. 107–112; Charles E. Sorensen, *My Forty Years with Ford* (New York: W. W. Norton, 1956), pp. 167–169; Bryan, *Clara*, pp. 153–159, 267–273; Harry Bennett, as told to Paul Marcus, *We Never Called Him Henry* (New York: Fawcett Books, 1951), pp. 23–31; Sloan J., *Adventures of a White-Collar Man*, pp. 137–138.

2. "Ford's Penchant for Discharge Disrupts Wonder Organization Built from Nothing, Auto King Lets Out Heads of All Departments," *Louisville Courier-Journal*, February 1, 1921, via wire from the *Wall Street Journal*. Collection Cranbrook Educational Community Archives. See also, reflective of the general reaction to Ford's erratic executive behavior, "Ford, Sober Up!," *Forbes* Magazine, January 22, 1921:"Henry Ford imagines that he has become a tin god."

3. Mark Coir, *A Brief History of Cranbrook* (Cranbrook Archives, 1997).

4. Samuel S. Marquis, *Henry Ford, An Interpretation* (Boston: Little, Brown and Company, 1923), pp. 118–119, 176–177; Correspondence, Bruno Lasker, *The Survey* Magazine; Loring Pickering, North American Newspaper Alliance; and H. F. Jenkins, Little, Brown & Company, to Samuel S. Marquis, November 11–December 19, 1922, Cranbrook Archives; and Mark Coir, Archivist, Cranbrook Educational Community, personal communication with the author, December 15, 2000.

5. Marquis, *Henry Ford: An Interpretation*, pp. 29–30.

6. Sorensen, *My Forty Years*, pp. 144–146, 150; Ford R. Bryan, *Henry's Lieutenants* (Detroit: Wayne State University Press, 1993), pp. 204–210; Nevins and Hill, *Ford: Expansion and Challenge*, pp. 349–354; Sinclair, *The Flivver King*, p. 110; Marquis, *Henry Ford: An Interpretation*, pp. 42, 46, 78–79, 160.

7. Bennett, *We Never Called Him Henry*, pp. 32–38; Bryan, *Henry's Lieutenants*, pp. 29–34 (re Bennett) and 89–95 (re Dahlinger).

8. Ford Bryan, personal communication to the author, June 25, 2001, with reference to unpublished archival correspondence between Clara Ford and Sidney Houghton, January 31–February 11, 1921; and also

Henry Ford Museum Oral History testimony by Thomas Sato, Ford
family driver and cook at Fair Lane during this period of time.

9. Bryan, *Clara*, p. 171 re Clara and Edsel Ford; Karl A. Bickel, "Ford
Planning for a New Era, Sees Changes Coming in Industrial World
and Prepares to Meet Them, Borrows on Own Terms," *Detroit News*,
February 1, 1921.

10. Kraft, *The Peace Ship*, pp. 115, 178; Lewis, *The Public Image of Henry
Ford*, pp. 504–505, footnote 44.

11. The O'Neill interview is in Joshi, ed., *Documents of American Prejudice*,
pp. 387–390; on "defensive action..." see *Dearborn Independent*, January
29, 1921, p. 8; Liebold, *Reminiscences*, p. 468; on the issue of quoting
Henry Ford, see also Higham, *Strangers in the Land*, p. 404: "Although
Ford hired professional journalists to speak for him in the pages of the
Independent, supplementary evidence consistently indicates that the
views expressed there corresponded roughly to his own"; *Pipp's
Weekly*, expanded edition on *Ford and the Jews*, February 1921, p. 1,
with apology for doubling the price from the customary five cents,
"leaving out all advertising made it necessary to charge ten cents for
this special edition."

12. O'Neill, *New York World*, February 11, 1916; Kraft, *The Peace Ship*, pp.
141, 159.

13. Kraft, *The Peace Ship*, p. 275.

14. Wenger, "Radical Politics," pp. 82–84.

15. *Jewish Activities in the United States*, Volume II of *The International Jew,
The World's Foremost Problem*, April 1921, Preface, pp. 3–4; and *Jewish
Influences in American Life*, Volume III of *The International Jew*, Novem-
ber 1921, pp. iii–iv.

16. *Dearborn Independent*, issues of January–March, 1921, and Volume III,
The International Jew, p. 75.

17. "What's Your Answer to Young Jews, Mr. Ford?" *Pipp's Weekly*, March
12, 1921, pp. 1–2.

18. *The International Jew, Volumes III and IV*, selected excerpts spanning
March–December, 1921; "Let it go on...," p. 254. Also: HFMGV Card
catalogue file, category drawer: *Jews*, typed checklist annotating *Dearborn Independent* articles on the subject, 1920–1927 inclusive.

19. LM Letters, Reznikoff, ed., *Champion of Liberty*, pp. 353–366; "lingering death...," LM to Felix Vorenberg, April 26, 1921, p. 357. London
Times, August 12, 1921.

20. Nevins and Hill, *Ford: Expansion and Challenge*, pp.305–308; William C.
Richards, *The Last Billionaire: Henry Ford* (New York: Charles Scrib-

ner's Sons, 1948), pp. 95–98; "the power of the Jewish race ...," *New York Times*, December 5, 1921, p. 33.

21. Nevins and Hill, *Ford: Expansion and Challenge*, p. 316; Benson, *The New Henry Ford*, p. 358.

22. Bryan, *Clara*, pp.182–183.

23. Raymond L. Stebbins, *Henry Ford and Edwin Pipp, A Suppressed Chapter in the Story of the Auto Magnate*, nine-page unpublished typescript monograph, Collection of the American Jewish Archives.

24. "An Address to 'Gentiles' on the Jewish Problem," *Dearborn Independent*, January 14, 1922; G. K. Chesterton, *What I Saw in America*, 1922, cited in Poliakov, *Suicidal Europe*, pp. 245–246; *Pipp's Weekly*, September 30, 1922, p. 3, under the subhead, *Personal With Ford*.

25. Pipp, *Henry Ford, Both Sides of Him*, p. 71; *Pipp's Weekly*, September 30, 1922; CA, Letter to Judge Horace Stern, November 8, 1921, Jewish Theological Seminary Archives.

26. Barry W. Holtz, ed., *Back to the Sources. Reading the Classic Jewish Texts* (New York: Simon & Schuster, 1984), Chapter Two, "Talmud," by Robert Goldenberg, pp. 129–175; Rabbi Joseph Telushkin, *Jewish Literacy*, Sections 82–84: Oral Law; Written Law; Babylonian and Palestinian Talmud; and Marquis, *Henry Ford*, pp. 148–158.

27. William E. Leuchtenberg, *The Perils of Prosperity, 1914–32* (Chicago: University of Chicago Press, 1958), p. 138.

28. Joshua Trachtenberg, *The Devil and the Jews*, pp. 178–180.

29. Fritz B. Voll, *A Short Review of a Troubled History*, www.jcrelations.net/res/incidents.htm; Telushkin, Section 99, Burning of the Talmud, p. 186; B. Charles Herring, *The Talmud and Anti-Semitism in Twentieth-Century America*, unpublished thesis, Hebrew Union College-Jewish Institute of Religion, Cincinnati, Ohio, 1965, Introduction.

30. Herring, ibid., pp. 4, 40; Singerman, *Antisemitic Propaganda, A Bibliography*, pp. 3, 10–11, 44, 363; Michael Terry, Dorot Chief Librarian, The Jewish Division, NYPL, personal communication re "Talmud Paranoia," April 7, 2000, to the author.

31. Herring, *The Talmud and Anti-Semitism*, pp. 4, 31–32, and p. 12: "There are no 'secret' Jewish writings. Within the whole of Judaism there is neither a written nor an oral tradition which is inaccessible to learned Christians"; Telushkin, *Jewish Literacy*, Section 294, Yom Kippur, pp. 569–569.

32. Lazare, *Antisemitism*, p. 18ff; Dobkowski, *The Tarnished Dream*, pp. 31–40.

33. Higham, *Strangers*, pp. 308–316; Adler, *Letters*, Volume II, p. 52, August 22, 1922, to Lucien Wolf.

34. Gossett, *Race*, esp. Chapter XV, "Racism in the 1920's," pp. 370–408; and Burton J. Hendrick, *The Jews in America*, 1922, excerpted in Joshi, ed., *Documents of American Prejudice*, pp. 391–395.

35. I am grateful to John M. Lundquist, The Susan and Douglas Dillon Chief Librarian of the Oriental Division, The New York Public Library, for his personal communication and scholarly advice, December 1999.

36. Ford, *My Life and Work*, pp. 17, 250–252; Ford quoted in *Pipp's Weekly*, February 12, 1921, p. 5. Samuel Crowther (1880–1947), a popular economist, business writer, and magazine journalist, also co-authored books with Alfred P. Sloan Jr. and Harvey Firestone.

Chapter Twelve: Heinrich Ford

1. Kurt G. W. Ludecke, *I Knew Hitler: The Story of a Nazi Who Escaped the Blood Purge* (New York: Carles Scribner's Sons, 1937), p. 119; James Pool and Suzanne Pool, *Who Financed Hitler: The Secret Funding of Hitler's Rise to Power, 1919–1933* (New York: Dial Press, 1978), pp. 90–91; *PM* Magazine, New York, April 9, 1947.

2. Segel, *A Lie and a Libel*, pp. xiii, 21, 63, 70–71, 122; Mendes-Flohr and Reinharz, *The Jew in the Modern World*, pp. 350–351; Poliakov, *Suicidal Europe*, pp. 253–254, 386.

3. For the concept of *"idees fixes,"* I am grateful to Ian Kershaw's magisterial biography, *Hitler, 1889–1936* (New York: W. W. Norton and Company, 1999), p. 241.

4. "Berlin Hears Ford Is Backing Hitler. Bavarian Anti-Semitic Chief Has American's Portrait and Book in His Office," *New York Times*, December 20, 1922, p. 2, column 3; Mendes-Flohr and Reinharz, *The Jew in the Modern World*, p. 636.

5. George L. Mosse, *The Crisis of German Ideology: Intellectual Origins of the Third Reich* (New York: Grosset & Dunlap, 1966), pp. 4–5, 172, 285; Hermann Rauschning, *The Voice of Destruction* (New York: G. P. Putnam's Sons, 1940), p. 255ff, on Hitler's affinities for the great outdoors; Kershaw, *Hitler, 1889–1936*, pp. 125–153; for another overview of *Völk* ideals, see Daniel Jonah Goldhagen, *Hitler's Willing Executioners. Ordinary Germans and the Holocaust* (New York: Alfred A. Knopf, 1996), pp. 66–86; Levinger, *Anti-Semitism in the United States*, p. 16.

6. John Lukacs, *The Hitler of History* (New York: Random House, 1997), pp. 104–108; Mosse, *The Crisis of German Ideology*, pp. 115, 121, 151, 176.

7. Robert Pois, ed., *Alfred Rosenberg, Selected Writings*, (London: Jonathan Cape, 1970), pp. 11–13; Lane and Rupp, *Nazi Ideology*, pp. xiii-xv, 44–74; Kershaw, *Hitler*, pp. 189, 153, and *see* pp. 650–651 notes 107–110; Heiden, *Der Fuehrer*, pp. 96, 138, 305, 327.

8. For introductory biographical information on Dietrich Eckart, www.motlc.wiesenthal.com, The Simon Wiesenthal Center Web Site; and Wolf Schwarzwaller, *The Unknown Hitler*, n.d.

9. Adolf Hitler, *Hitler's Table Talk, 1941–1944*, introduced and with a new preface by H. R. Trevor-Roper (New York: Enigma Books, 2000), pp. 217, 347; Ludecke, *I Knew Hitler*, p. 83; Kershaw, *Hitler*, p. 155.

10. Lane and Rupp, *Nazi Ideology*, citing excerpts from texts by Eckart, pp. 3–9, 16–26, and 30–32; Adolf Hitler, *Mein Kampf* (New York: Houghton Mifflin, 1943), translated by Ralph Manheim, p. 687, note 2.

11. See Albrecht Tyrrell, studies from 1975–1979, refuting initial claims by Ernst Nolte in 1961, as cited in Kershaw, *Hitler*, pp. 651, 795.

12. Dietrich Eckart, *Bolshevism from Moses to Lenin: A Dialogue Between Adolf Hitler and Me*, English translation, by William L. Pierce, published in *National Socialist World*, Number 2, Fall 1966, Arlington, Virginia, pp. 13–14, 17–18, 22, 24.

13. Ibid., pp. 16, 21, 29–30, 33.

14. Ibid., pp. 19–20.

15. Kershaw, *Hitler*, pp. 235, 240; Hitler, *Mein Kampf*, trans. Manheim, introduction by Konrad Heiden, p. xvii.

16. Heiden, *Der Fuehrer*, p. 360; Hitler, *Mein Kampf*, p. 639.

17. Hitler, *Mein Kampf*, p. 14.

18. Ibid., pp. 51, 307–308.

19. Kershaw, *Hitler*, pp. 261–262; Heiden, *Der Fuehrer*, pp. 131, 252, 438; Ludecke, *I Knew Hitler*, pp. 94, 95, 119; Hughes, *American Genesis*, p. 288, and note p. 496; "Hitler's Papers and Books in 5th Av. Display," *New York Herald Tribune*, May 22, 1946.

20. Ludecke, *I Knew Hitler*, pp. 9–12; 192–193.

21. Ibid., pp. 15–16.

22. Kershaw, *Hitler*, p. 190; Leonard, *Tragedy of Henry Ford*, p. 208, quoting from an article published in the *New York Times* on February 8, 1923.

23. Pool and Pool, *Who Financed Hitler?*, pp. 117ff; Wilkins, *American Business Abroad*, pp. 96, 138.

24. Charles W. Wood, "If I Were President: Henry Ford Tells Where He Stands on All of the Great Issues of the Day," *Collier's Magazine*, August 4, 1923, pp. 5–7.

25. Benson, *The New Henry Ford*, p. 350; Cyrus Adler letter to Louis Marshall, JTS Archives, March 13, 1923; Rabbi Samuel Schulman letter to Lee Kohns, AJA Collections, June 26, 1923; Adolf Hitler interview, *Chicago Tribune*, March 8, 1923.

26. Reynold M. Wik, *Henry Ford and Grass-roots America* (Ann Arbor, Mich.: University of Michigan Press, 1972), pp. 178–179; Ludecke, *I Knew Hitler*, pp. 189–194.

27. Kershaw, *Hitler*, p. 186ff., and p. 658 n.90, cites extensively from the London edition of Ludecke's *I Knew Hitler* published in 1938, one year following Scribner's first American edition. Kershaw endorses Ludecke's "general reliability." However, he chooses not to discuss at any point Ludecke's several sojourns in the United States.

28. Winifred Wagner, interview with James Pool, October 1977, in Pool and Pool, *Who Financed Hitler?*, pp. 124–127.

29. Ludecke, *I Knew Hitler*, p.194

30. Ibid., Chapter XII, "Anti-Semitism: Model T," pp. 191–218.

31. Wilkins, *American Business Abroad*, p. 235; and p. 491, notes 7 and 8.

32. Ibid., pp. 138–140.

33. "leaders..." *New York Times*, October 3, 1930, as cited in Wilkins, *American Business Abroad*, p. 206; Lukacs, *The Hitler of History*, pp. 154–155; Trevor-Roper, *Table Talk*, xxii, p. 279, spoken on the evening of February 2, 1942, regarding "the superiority of American technique."

34. Hughes, *American Genesis*, especially the illuminating section, "Weimar and the American Model," pp. 284–294, and notes, pp. 496–497.

Chapter Thirteen: Sapiro v. Ford

1. Grant Hildebrand, *Designing for Industry. The Architecture of Albert Kahn* (Cambridge, Mass., and London: MIT Press, 1974), pp. 44–54.

2. Hildebrand, *Albert Kahn*, pp. 91–92, 111; Theodore Stebbins Jr. and Norman Keyes Jr., *Charles Sheeler: The Photographs* (Boston: Little, Brown and Company, 1987), p. 25.

3. Nevins and Hill, *Ford: Expansion and Challenge*, pp. 279–289.

4. For biographical material on Albert Kahn, I am indebted to two landmark studies: *The Legacy of Albert Kahn*, by W. Hawkins Ferry, with an

essay by Walter B. Sanders (Detroit: Wayne State University Press, 1970, 1987), especially pp. 8–27; and the previously cited *Designing for Industry: The Architecture of Albert Kahn,* by Grant Hildebrand (Cambridge, Mass., and London, MIT Press, 1974). I am grateful to Professor Hildebrand for personal communications of December 25–26, 2000. Five essays also contributed to the preceding section of Chapter XIII: "Albert Kahn," www.si.umich.edu/Project/march/architects/kahn.html; "History of Albert Kahn Associates," www.albertkahn.com/cmpny_history.cfm; "Albert Kahn, the architect of the auto industrialists," by Vivian M. Baulch, *Detroit News,* n.d., www.detroitnews.com/history/kahn/kahn/htm; "Ford and Kahn," by David L. Lewis, *Michigan History Magazine,* September/October, 1980; and "Albert Kahn, His Son Remembers," by Edgar Kahn, M. D., *Michigan History Magazine,* July/August 1981, provided through the courtesy of William and Ellen Kahn.

5. "Ford and Ideas," *The New Republic,* October 31, 1923.

6. Grant Hildebrand, personal communications, December 26, 2000, citing comments to him made by Albert Kahn's daughter, Rosalie Kahn (Mrs. Martin) Butzel, deceased October 4, 2000; Albert Butzel, son of Rosalie Kahn Butzel, personal communications, January 8, 2001; Sandra (Mrs. John) Butzel, daughter-in-law of Rosalie Kahn Butzel, personal communications, January 13, 2001; William Kahn, son of Louis Kahn, personal communications, and telephone conversation with NB, January 9–12, 2001; also, Bolkosky, *Harmony and Dissonance,* pp. 72–74.

7. Bolkosky, *Harmony and Dissonance;* Hildebrand, *Albert Kahn,* pp. 59, 100, 214; Lewis, *The Public Image of Henry Ford,* pp. 26–28; Edgar Kahn essay, pp. 29–31; Sandra Butzel personal communications, January 13, 2001; William and Ellen Kahn, personal communications, March 7, 2001.

8. Leo P. Ribuffo, 1980, in Gurock, ed., American Jewish History, Part I, pp. 462–463.

9. Julius Rosenwald Collection, The University of Chicago Library, File labeled: "1923, Ford attack, Dearborn Independent, Feb. 10, 1923."

10. "Henry Ford Adds to Horrors of War," *Chicago Tribune,* August 2, 1923; Henry Ford, "If I Were President,"*Collier's Magazine,* August 4, 1923, p. 6ff.; Helen Baker, "How Did the Women's International League for Peace and Freedom Respond to Right-Wing Attacks, 1923–1931?" SUNY at Binghamton, www.binghamton.edu/womhist/wilpf/intro.html

11. Leonard, *The Tragedy of Henry Ford*, pp. 217–18, 223; "Why They Love Henry," *The New Republic*, June 27, 1923, pp. 111–112.

12. Marshall, *Champion of Liberty*, p. 366; Howe, *World of Our Fathers*, "The Culture of Yiddish/The Yiddish Press," fn., p. 532, and pp. 543–545.

13. Wik, *Henry Ford and Grass-Roots America*, especially Chapter VII, "Ford and the Farm Cooperative Movement," pp. 126–141; *Vancouver Farm & Home Magazine*, Report on Aaron Sapiro's visit to British Columbia, January 4, 1923; Victoria Saker Woeste, *Lawyers, Public Service, and Anti-Semitism: Aaron Sapiro's Libel Suit Against Henry Ford, 1922–1927*, American Bar Foundation, Chicago, 1996, p. 1; "The Farmer's Salvation," editorial (no byline), *Chicago Tribune*, August 2, 1923.

14. www.progressivefarmer.com/century/sapiro/copy.asp; Randall Torgerson, Bruce J. Reynolds, and Thomas W. Gray, *Evolution of Cooperative Thought, Theory and Purpose* (Madison, Wis.: University of Wisconsin Center for Cooperatives, 1997), pp. 1–3; Woeste, *Lawyers, Public Service, and Anti-Semitism*, pp. 4, 6.

15. Charles M. Morgan, "Co-Worker Tells Impressions He Gained About Aaron Sapiro," *Phoenix (Arizona) Republican*, n.d. [ca. April, 1925]; Wik, *Henry Ford and Grass-roots America*, p. 131; Woeste, *Lawyers, Public Service, and Anti-Semitism*, pp. 6, 7, 11, 12; Wik, *Henry Ford and Grass-roots America*, p. 132, citing HF interview with Andrew S. Wing, editor of *Farm and Fireside* Magazine, 1924.

16. Issue of September 4, 1920, anthologized in *The International Jew*, Vol. I, pp. 181–193.

17. Wik, *Henry Ford and Grass-roots America*, pp. 133–135, and notes 16–18, pp. 251–252; Ribuffo, *Henry Ford and The International Jew*, pp. 463–464.

18. Ribuffo, *Henry Ford and The International Jew*, p. 465; Wik, *Henry Ford and Grass-roots America*, p. 136; *Jewish Daily Bulletin*, Vol. IV, No. 716, New York City, March 14, 1927, p. 1. Foregoing citations from the *Dearborn Independent* series by Robert Morgan, issues dated April 12; April 19; April 26; July 19; July 26; August 2; August 9; August 16; August 23; August 30; September 6; September 13; September 20; December 13; and December 20, 1924; and April 12, 1925: Courtesy of The Collections of the Henry Ford Museum and Greenfield Village Research Center.

19. Bryan, *Henry's Lieutenants*, chapter on "Roy Donaldson McClure," pp. 197–203; Liebold, *Reminiscences*, p. 484.

20. The definitive account of Paul M. Warburg's role in the genesis of the

Federal Reserve Bank is Ron Chernow, *The Warburgs* (New York: Random House, 1993), pp. 131–140; also, RC, personal communication with NB, May 11, 2000; Michael A. Whitehouse, *Paul Warburg's Crusade to Establish a Central Bank in the United States*, Publications of the Federal Reserve Bank of Minneapolis, May 1989; Feingold, *A Midrash*, especially Chapter II, p. 42ff., "The Success Story of German Jews in America"; and re "nativist vilification," of Warburg, see B. C. Forbes in *Frank Leslie's Illustrated Weekly*, January 16, 1916; and *The Creature from Jekyll Island*, http://a-albionic.com.

21. *The International Jew*, Volume III, *Jewish Influences in American Life*, pp. 191–229.

22. Chernow, *The Warburgs*, pp. 267–270.

23. *Jewish Daily Bulletin*, New York City, March 14, 1927, pp. 1–2.

24. Biographical chapter on Nathan Straus, in James Waterman Wise, (pseud. Analyticus), *Jews Are Like That!* (New York: Macmillan Company, 1928), pp. 207–232.

25. The *Dearborn Independent*, editorial (no byline), December 25, 1926, p. 2. The Straus essay was released two weeks prior to being published in the Christmas Day edition of Ford's newspaper.

26. In the House of Representatives, 69th Congress, 2nd Session, Resolution, December 18, 1926; "Ford Indiscreetly Definite," editorial, *New York World*, December 16, 1926.

27. *New York Times*, December 20, 1926, "[Bloom] Wants Ford Called to Give His Facts," "Dr. Nathan Krass [Rabbi of Temple Emanu-El in New York City] Says Ford Slanders All Jews," and December 26, 1926, "Bloom Urges Ford to Submit Facts, Asks for His Evidence That Federal Reserve System is Under Jewish Control."

28. Adler, *Selected Letters, Volume II*, January 3, 1927, to Sol Bloom, pp. 137–138.

Chapter Fourteen: Apology

1. *Jewish Daily Bulletin*, p. 2; Ribuffo, *Henry Ford and The International Jew*, p. 442, and *Note*, as of June 1980, "The files relating to the Sapiro suit have been removed from the Ford Archives [HFMGV Collections] by the Ford Motor Company"; Wik, *Henry Ford and Grass-roots America*, p. 139; Richards, *The Last Billionaire*, pp. 96–98. Also, Bennett, *We Never Called Him Henry*, pp. 49–52. Bennett told his co-author, Paul Marcus, in 1951 (p. 49) that Ford told him he had expected Sapiro to be represented by "a Jew lawyer from New York";

Ford therefore considered William H. Gallagher, a Catholic, to be "a Christian front" for Sapiro.

2. "Cameron Kept on Libel Stand—Gallagher Continues Attempts to Prove Ford Responsible for Sapiro Articles—Checked by Objections," *Detroit News*, March 25, 1927; Garet Garrett, *Henry Ford: The Wild Wheel* (New York: Pantheon Books, 1952), p. 147; WJC, Oral History *Reminiscences* (June 1952) HFMGV Collections, pp. 3–23; Nevins and Hill, *Ford: Expansion and Challenge*, pp. 319–321; Bennett, *We Never Called Him Henry*, p. 52.

3. Bryan, *Clara*, p. 201.

4. Correspondence, LM to G. Lowenstein, March 29, 1927, in Reznikoff, ed., *Champion of Liberty*, pp. 371–372; *New York Graphic*, April 1, 1927; and *Detroit Times*, April 1, 1927; Bennett, *We Never Called Him Henry*, pp. 52–53.

5. Wise, *Jews Are Like That!* pp. 156–164; Woeste, *Lawyers, Public Service, and Anti-Semitism*, p. 15; Ribuffo, *Henry Ford and the International Jew*, p. 443–444; Detroit *News*, April 10, 1927, "Liebold Gets Libel Subpena [sic]—Sapiro's Counsel Serves Summons to Stand on Officer of Independent—Reed Continues His Quiz," *New York Times*, April 12, 1927; Bennett, *We Never Called Him Henry*, p. 54.

6. "Ford Closing Stirs A Crop of Rumors—Talk of a New Car Heard—This Is Also Denied, Although it is Generally Admitted That Competition is Keen," *New York Times*, December 3, 1926.

7. Black, *Reminiscences*, p. 50; Stebbins and Keyes, eds., *Charles Sheeler, Photographs*, pp. 24–25.

8. Leonard, *The Tragedy of Henry Ford*, pp. 221–227.

9. Ibid., p. 228; Wilkins and Hill, *American Business Abroad*, pp. 154–158.

10. Sloan, *Adventures of a White-Collar Man*, pp. 133–166, 183; Nelson Lichtenstein and Stephen Meyer, eds., *On the Line: Essays in the History of Auto Work* (Ubana, Ill., and Chicago: University of Illinois Press, 1989), pp. 81, 82; Sorensen, *My Forty Years with Ford*, p. 224; Sward, *The Legend of Henry Ford*, Chapter Fifteen, "Death of the Model-T," pp. 194–205.

11. Hamlin Garland, *Afternoon Neighbors: Further Excerpts from a Literary Log* (New York: Macmillan Company, 1934), pp. 161–164, 218. The cited passage was written in 1924. Grateful acknowledgment to Keith Newlin, Hamlin Garland bibliographer, for personal communication directing me to the archival repositories for HG's "literary logbooks," December 30, 1999.

12. Garland, *Afternoon Neighbors*, pp. 338ff, 398.

13. Hamlin Garland, *A Son of the Middle Border* (New York: Penguin Books, 1995 edition of 1917 novel), pp. 91–92; Garland, *Afternoon Neighbors*, p. 365.

14. Garland, *Afternoon Neighbors*, pp. 398–400.

15. Ibid., p. 403; Marquis, *Henry Ford, An Interpretation*, pp. 77–78; *New York World*, March 21, 1927, in Compendium of "statements by Henry Ford relating directly to Jews, 1927–1942," twenty-three-page typescript, dated January 31, 1942. Collection of the American Jewish Committee Library, New York City, p. 3.

16. Allport, *The Nature of Prejudice*, p. 14.

17. William Adams Simonds, *Henry Ford* (London: Michael Joseph, Ltd., 1946), pp. 174–175; Wilkins, *American Business Abroad*, pp. 154–158. Sward, *The Legend of Henry Ford*, p. 203.

18. Simonds, *Henry Ford*, Chapter 18, "In Memory of a Friend," p. 178ff.; Sorensen, *My Forty Years*, p. 222; "Ford to Fight It Out With His Old Car," *New York Times*, December 26, 1926; Nevins and Hill, *Ford: Expansion and Challenge*, p. 437.

19. See David Nasaw's definitive biography, *The Chief: The Life of William Randolph Hearst* (Boston and New York: Houghton Mifflin, 2000), pp. 110–111, 323, 386, 430; also, Oliver O. Carlson, *Brisbane: A Candid Biography* (New York: Stackpole Sons, 1937), re "Demosthenes..."; Lewis, *The Public Image of Henry Ford*, p. 131, and fn. 65, p. 509; Henry Ford, May 1, 1926: "Brisbane is a great writer. Everybody ought to read his column"; Wik, *Henry Ford and Grass-roots America*, pp. 46, 54.

20. *The International Jew*, Volume I, pp. 79–86.

21. "Ford asks forgiveness from Jews," *The Forward*, July 8, 1927; and "Ford Conferred With Louis Marshall," July 9, 1927, translated from the Yiddish by Aaron Taub, for the author; "Jews Divide on Sincerity of Apology from Ford," *New York Herald Tribune*, July 9, 1927.

22. Despite the fact that the unease of Henry Ford's wife and son have been referred to here and elsewhere by people who knew them, it has been impossible to find more detailed, documented examples of Edsel's and Clara's antipathies regarding Henry Ford's antisemitism. Richard Bak wrote in his study, "The Edsel Enigma," *Hour* Magazine, Detroit, January 1988—one of the few biographical profiles of the troubled son—"Getting to know Edsel Ford has never been easy [and] continues to be difficult.... At the Ford Archives in Dearborn ... his personal files are distressingly threadbare. One day in the early 1960's [1963], Henry II had the files purged. 'Hank the Deuce'—who before his own death would destroy his personal papers in order to thwart biogra-

phers—was determined that nobody would ever examine his life, or the life of his unsung father, in great detail."

23. The sequence of events leading up to Henry Ford's retraction was reconstructed from the following sources: *Louis Marshall Champion of Liberty*, ed. Reznikoff, To G. Lowenstein, March 29, 1927; To Fred M. Butzel, June 30, 1927; To Samuel Untermyer, July 1 and July 4, 1927; To Henry Ford, July 5, 1927; To Cyrus Adler, July 10, 1927; and To Julius Rosenwald, July 22, 1927, pp. 371–382; Richards, *Henry Ford, The Last Billionaire*, pp. 99–102; Bennett, *We Never Called Him Henry*, pp. 55–56; "Ford Conferred with Louis Marshall...," *The Forward*, July 9, 1927; "Jews Divide On Sincerity of Apology from Ford," *New York Herald Tribune*, July 9, 1927.

Chapter Fifteen: Apostle of Amity

1. Liebold, *Reminiscences*, October–December 1951, p. 1384.
2. "Ford Overtures to End Suit in Sapiro's Hands," *New York Herald Tribune*, July 9, 1927, p. 2; Woeste, *Lawyers, Public Service, and Anti-Semitism*, p. 16; Wise, *Jews Are Like That!*, pp. 153, 154, 175.
3. Cameron, *Reminiscences*, p. 34, Question: "Part of the Bernstein, Sapiro, Ford and the whole Jewish question and settlement was predicated upon the idea that you and Liebold would no longer work with the Ford Motor Company. Was there any truth to that?" Cameron: "I never heard of that"; also see: Louis Marshall, Letter to Earl J. Davis, in Reznikoff, ed., *Champion of Liberty*, pp. 384–385, August 25, 1927.
4. Liebold, R*eminiscences*, p. 504.
5. Ludecke, *I Knew Hitler*, Chapter XVII, "Selling Hitler in America," pp. 308–315; "Ford Overtures...," *New York Herald Tribune*, p. 2.
6. Emphasis mine. Richards, *The Last Billionaire*, p. 102; John Lanse McCloud, *Reminiscences*, p. 348.
7. "Pipp Explains Ford Attitude," *New York Times*, July 15, 1927; "Ford and the Jews," *Pipp's Magazine*, July 1927; "Ford in Action," *Pipp's Magazine*, September 1927.
8. Newspapers cited above, all editions of Saturday, July 9, 1927.
9. The first antisemite on record is Haman, who appears in the Book of Esther, 3:8. Haman told King Ahasuerus that he should exterminate the Jews because they were "scattered abroad... and their laws are different from all other people's..." Even more than Pharoah, Haman has become for Jews the symbol of the Jew-hater. *See* Martin S.

Bergmann, in Chanes, ed., *Antisemitism in American Today*, p.101; and also Telushkin, ed., *Jewish Literacy*, p.108.

10. *Jewish Chronicle*, July 15, 1927; Julius Rosenwald, *Chicago Tribune*, July 9, 1927; *Jewish Herald*, July 27, 1927; *American Israelite*, July 21, 1927. These citations are drawn from the "Ford Retraction" Clippings Scrapbook, Rabbi Leo M. Franklin Archive, Temple Beth El, Detroit.

11. Wenger, "Radical Politics," pp. 82–85; Rosika Schwimmer, typescript and holograph pencil drafts for "Open Letter to Henry Ford," Schwimmer-Lloyd Collection, The New York Public Library, Box E26; also, Marguerite Dumont, three-page letter to Rosika Schwimmer, June 26, 1928; E. G. Liebold, *Reminiscences*, p. 267: "It's too bad all those [Peace Ship] records were destroyed, because it throws me off the exact dates and the real chronology of these happenings."

12. Stephen S. Wise biographical information, World Zionist Organization and Progressive Jewish Alliance sites, www.wzo.org.il; www.pjalliance.org; and Wise, *Jews Are Like That!*, pp. 80–103.

13. Clancy and Davies, *The Believer*, p. 186: "The man who had dispensed with his stockholders, the man who carried a billion-dollar company in his breast pocket..."

14. Stephen S. Wise, "Henry Ford's Retraction: Some Further Lessons," *Free Synagogue Pulpit*, New York City, Volume VIII, No. 4, 1927–1928, pp. 1–15. Grateful acknowledgment to Roberta Saltzman, Jewish Division, The New York Public Library, for bringing this landmark sermon to my attention.

15. Characterization of Rabbi Franklin as "the apostle of amity": "Long Ministry Ends," by Henry George Hoge, Church Editor, *Detroit News*, November 1, 1941; excerpts from Rabbi Franklin's Yom Kippur 1927 sermon are drawn from nine-page typescript original manuscript with Franklin's holograph editing, in the Collections of the Franklin Archive, Temple Beth El, Detroit.

16. Correspondence, Leo Franklin to Henry Ford, July 8, 1927, Franklin Archives, Temple Beth El.

17. Correspondence, Charles F. Joseph to Leo Franklin, and LF to CFJ, July 13 and July 17, 1927, Franklin Archives, Temple Beth El.

18. Unpublished manuscript by Rabbi Leo M. Franklin, *Some Untold Tales...*, 1947, pp. 161–165, Franklin Archives, Temple Beth El; also see, Louis Marshall, Letter to Henry Ford, December 21, 1927, ed. Reznikoff, *Champion of Liberty*, pp. 386–387.

19. Leo Franklin, *Untold Tales*, MS, pp. 114–116, 137–143.

Chapter Sixteen: The Chosen People

1. Richards, *The Last Billionaire*, p. 265; LM *Letters*, to Robert Marshall, January 11, 1928, in Reznikoff, ed., *Champion of Liberty*, pp. 387–389; LM account of meeting with Ford conveyed to Julius Rosenwald by Jacob Billikopf, January 16, 1928, in Julius Rosenwald Archive, The University of Chicago Library; Z. H. Rubinstein, "Henry Ford Deplores Roumanian Outrages," *The Day*, January 15, 1928; *New York Times*, January 16–17, 1928.

2. Henry Ford, *My Philosophy of Industry* (London: George G. Harrap & Co., 1929), p. 85.

3. mediaford.com: Edsel Ford, Executive Bio., i.d. no. 3407.

4. Jardim, *The First Henry Ford*, pp. 224–225, quoting Sorensen; Nevins and Hill, *Ford: Expansion and Challenge*, pp. 453, 524–525.

5. Hildebrand, *Designing for Industry*, pp. 110–123; Nevins and Hill, *Ford: Expansion and Challenge*, p. 511.

6. Richards, *The Last Billionaire*, p. 217; James R. Green, *The World of the Worker: Labor in Twentieth-Century America* (Rubana, Ill., and Chicago: University of Illinois Press, 1998), p. 110, quoting eyewitness visitor Charles Reitell to the River Rouge plant in 1924; Edmund Wilson, "Detroit Motors" (originally published in *The New Republic*, 1930–1931), in *American Earthquake, A Documentary of the Twenties and Thirties* (New York: Farrar, Straus, & Giroux, 1958), pp. 219–220, 238, 245; Wayne Lewchuk, "Fordism and the Moving Assembly Line," in Lichtenstein and Meyer, eds., *On the Line*, p. 24.

7. Leonard, *The Tragedy of Henry Ford*, p. 243; Henry Ford, in collaboration with Samuel L. Crowther, *Moving Forward* (New York: Doubleday, Doran and Co., 1930), pp. 125, 251, 266–272; William L. Stidger, Chapter XXV, "Ford's Americanism," in *Henry Ford, The Man and His Motives*, pp. 176–181.

8. Stidger, *Henry Ford, The Man and His Motives*, p. 180; Baldwin, *Edison*, pp. 392–395; Merz, *And Then Came Ford*, p. 265.

9. The definitive contemporary account of the vast Dearborn site is Harold K. Skramstad Jr. and Jeanine Head, *An Illustrated History of Henry Ford Museum and Greenfield Village* (Dearborn, Michigan: Henry Ford Museum and Greenfield Village, 1990.) I am indebted to John Bowditch, at that time curator of industry at the HFMGV, for a fascinating behind-the-scenes tour of the museum and environs on April 27, 1993.

10. David Lowenthal, *The Past Is a Foreign Country* (Cambridge: Cambridge University Press, 1985), pp. 11, 43, 244.

11. Owen Bombard, taped interview with William J. Cameron, from which WJC's *Reminiscences* were subsequently transcribed, fall 1951. Collections of HFMGV. Grateful acknowledgment to Terry Hoover, Archivist. Also, Bryan, *Henry's Lieutenants*, pp. 54–55.

12. On the informing origins and texts of British-Israelism: Isidore Singer, Cyrus Adler, Richard Gottheil, et al., eds., *The Jewish Encyclopedia,* (New York: Funk & Wagnalls Company, 1912), pp. 600–601; *Encyclopaedia Judaica Jerusalem* (New York: Macmillan, 1971), p. 1381; Langmuir, *Toward a Definition of Antisemitism*, p. 58, re "doctrinal anti-Judaism"; Edward Wheelock Tullidge, *The Ten Lost Tribes of Israel in England and America* (New York: 1881), re "treacherous Judah" including exhaustive Biblical exegesis; J. Gordon Melton, ed., *Encyclopedic Handbook of Cults in America* (New York: Garland Publishing Company, 1986), pp. 53–54; David S. Katz and Richard H. Popkin, *Messianic Revolution: Radical Religious Politics to the End of the Second Millennium* (New York: Hill and Wang, 1998), Chapter 7, "From British Israel to Christian Identity and Aryan Nation," especially pp. 171–186; and Michael Barkun, *Religion and the Racist Right: The Origins of the Christian Identity Movement* (Chapel Hill, N.C.: University of North Carolina Press, 1994), especially Chapters 1 and 2, "The Origins of British-Israelism" and "British-Israelism in America," pp. 3–31.

13. John Lanse McCloud, *Reminiscences*, March–May, 1952, p. 336; *Dearborn Independent*, "Angles of Jewish Influence in American Life," May 21, 1921; "Jewish 'Kol Nidre' and 'Eli, Eli' Explained," November 5, 1921.

14. *Dearborn Independent*, September 22, 1923, "Are the Jews 'God's Chosen People'?"; May 23, 1925, "Where Are Israel's Lost Tribes?"; December 18, 1926, Editorial, "The Pritchett Report," delegitimizes Zionism, in this context, as "a diversion of public attention," because Palestine cannot be said to "belong" to the Jews; February 19, 1927, "Why the Anglo-Saxons Are the Descendents of the Lost Ten Tribes of Israel," by Mark John Levy, "a British Jew who had converted to Christianity," cf. Barkun, *Religion and the Racist Right*, p. 39.

15. James A. Aho, *The Politics of Righteousness* (Seattle: University of Washington Press, 1995), p. 52ff.; Barkun, *Religion and the Racist Right*, p. 30; David Lethbridge, Director, The Bethune Institute, Salmon

Arm, B.C., Canada, personal communications with the author regarding the origins of the Anglo-Saxon Federation of America, February 27 and March 6, 2001; Melton, *Encyclopedic Handbook of Cults*, p. 54; Leonard Zeskind, *The "Christian Identity" Movement: Analyzing Its Theological Rationalization for Racist and Anti-Semitic Violence* (Atlanta: Center for Democratic Renewal, 1986), on the lineage of Christian Identity in the United States, pp. 12–13; and Donna Kossy, "The Anglo-Israelites," www.teleport.com/dkossy/anglo.html, pp. 1–7.

Chapter Seventeen: "I Am Not a Jew Hater"

1. "Ford Papers, to be Dedicated at Home Today, Yield Mountain of Treasure and Trash Linked With His Life," *New York Times*, May 7, 1953; "Bankers Caused Ford Shutdown, Says Interview. They Seek Control of His Plants, London Paper Quotes Him," *Chicago Daily News*, January 27, 1933; and Lichtenstein and Meyer, ed., *On the Line*, pp. 63 and 134.

2. Wilkins, *American Business Abroad*, pp. 246–248, 270–274.

3. Kershaw, *Hitler*, Volume I, pp. 431–490 provides an overview of Hitler's first five months as chancellor. See also, Dawidowicz, *On Equal Terms*, p. 101.

4. For translations from the German language of the June 1933, advertisements, the preface to *The International Jew*, and selected footnotes, I have relied upon Rabbi Leo M. Franklin's unpublished manuscript, pp. 159–162; and Poliakov, *Suicidal Europe*, pp. 253–254, and notes, p. 387.

5. Cohen, *Not Free to Desist*, pp. 20–22; Rabbi Leo M. Franklin, unpublished manuscript, pp. 161–162; Correspondence, LMF to and from E. G. Liebold, Harry Schneiderman and Morris Waldman, Temple Beth El Archives, October 2, October 4, October 13, October 16, 1933.

6. Correspondence, LMF and Richard Gutstadt, Temple Beth El Archives, May 17 and December 25, 1934; January 15, 17, and 18, 1935; also, Deborah Dash Moore, *B'nai B'rith and the Challenge of Ethnic Leadership* (Albany, N.Y.: State University of New York Press, 1981), p. 119.

7. Moore, *B'nai B'rith*, p. 172; *New York Times*, December 18, 1936, "Anti-Nazis Ask Ford to Repudiate a Book—German Volume Slurring Jews Is Being Linked to Him," and January 7, 1937, "Ford Disclaims Book—Not Author of Anti-Jewish Book, He Assures Untermyer."

8. Belth, *A Promise to Keep*, pp. 120–126; Strong, *Organized Anti-Semitism in America*, Chapter III, "The German-American Bund," pp. 21–39.

9. Belth and Strong, ibid., *Report of the McCormack Committee*, Report No.153, 74th Congress, First Session, February 15, 1935; and Peter H. Peel, "The Great Brown Scare: The Amerika Deutscher Bund in the Thirties and the Hounding of Fritz Julius Kuhn," *The Journal for Historical Review*, Winter 1986, VII, 4, p. 419ff. Peel discusses Samuel Untermyer's accusations of Kuhn's antisemitism as related to his employment at Ford Motor Company.

10. Citations from *New York Times*, March 8, 1934; July 22, 1934; March 25, 1936; November 1, 1936; November 2, 1936; April 14, 1937; April 28, 1938; and June 8, 1938.

11. Sigmund Livingston, *A Problem of American Jewry*, pamphlet by The Anti-Defamation League of B'nai B'rith, Chicago, 1935, pp. 19–20: "We frequently hear the phrase, 'the Jewish international bankers...'"

12. Strong, *Organized Anti-Semitism in America*, pp. 40–123; Singerman, *Antisemitic Propaganda*, pp. 92–202; Bennett, *The Party of Fear*, p. 244ff.; John L. Spivak, *Secret Armies. The New Technique of Nazi Warfare* (New York: Modern Age Books, 1939), especially Chapter VIII, "Henry Ford and Secret Nazi Activities," pp. 102–117.

13. Carey McWilliams, *A Mask for Privilege. Anti-Semitism in America* (New Brunswick, N.J.: Transaction Publishers, 1999 reprint of 1947 edition), pp. 40–46; Dawidowicz, *On Equal Terms*, pp. 101–104; Howard M. Sachar, *A History of Jews in America* (New York: Alfred A. Knopf, 1992), especially Chapter XIV, "Nazism and the Quest for Sanctuary," p. 475ff.

14. Feingold, *A Time for Searching*, pp. 251–256.

15. Cohen, *Not Free to Desist*, pp. 180–181; Henry Paynter, "Anti-Jewish Books Still Carry Ford's Name—Nazi Propagandists Circulate Pamphlets in Eight Languages," *PM Magazine*, September 30, 1940, pp. 13–16; Norman Cohn, *Warrant for Genocide. The Myth of the Jewish World Conspiracy and the Protocols of the Elders of Zion* (New York: Harper & Row, 1967; London: Serif Press, 1996), pp. 239–240; 256–268.

Chapter Eighteen: Hitler's Medal

1. Malcolm Logan, "Publishers Split on Translation of Ford Speech," *New York Post*, April 29, 1938; Rosika Schwimmer, Letter to Henry Ford, July 25, 1938, Schwimmer-Lloyd Collection, NYPL.

2.   Wilkins, *American Business Abroad,* pp. 270–285, and notes 21–24, p. 498.

3.   David L. Lewis, "Henry Ford's Anti-Semitism and Its Repercussions," *Michigan Jewish History,* XXIV.1, January 1984, pp. 5–6; *New York Times,* July 31, 1938; *Detroit News,* July 31, 1938. For description of the medal, A. Scott Berg, *Lindbergh* (New York: Putnam, 1998), p. 375.

4.   *Detroit News,* September 10, 1938, "Nazi Organ Confirms Awards to Detroiters," and October 13, 1938, "Liebold Is Presented With Hitler Award"; *The American Freeman,* (Girard, Kansas, n.d., ca. March, 1942); Berg, *Lindbergh,* pp. 375–376.

5.   James Newton, *Uncommon Friends, Life with Thomas Edison, Henry Ford, et. al.* (New York: Harcourt Brace Jovanovich, 1987), pp. 221–222; 237–248; Berg, *Lindberg,* pp. 375–377.

6.   Berg, *Lindbergh,* p.168ff; Bryan, *Clara,* p. 202.

7.   Newton, *Uncommon Friends,* p.109; Nevins and Hill, *Ford: Expansion and Challenge,* p.245.

8.   Newton, *Uncommon Friends,* pp. 218, 267; Allan Nevins and Frank Ernest Hill, *Ford: Decline and Rebirth 1933–1962* (New York: Charles Scribner's Sons, 1962), pp. 169–171.

9.   I am grateful to A. Scott Berg's biography for the concept of Lindbergh's propensity to "intellectualize his feelings," pp. 378–379, and p. 467; Nevins and Hill, *Ford: Decline and Rebirth,* pp. 168–171; "Ford Denies Sympathy With Nazism," *New York Times,* November 30, 1938.

10. Nevins and Hill, *Ford: Decline and Rebirth,* p. 169ff.; Berg, *Lindbergh,* p. 49ff; also see: Arthur Schlesinger Jr., responding to a series of questions about Charles Lindbergh for *The American Experience,* www.pbs.org/wgbh.

11. Peter Collier and David Horowitz, *The Fords, An American Epic* (New York: Summit Books, 1987), p. 205, and note, p. 457. The citation is from the FBI file of Harry Bennett.

12. Arthur Schlesinger Jr., in his PBS *American Experience* interview, takes up the issue of Lindbergh's "conditioning" by his father; see also Berg, *Lindbergh,* p. 379–380, 384–385, 391, 424.

13. Newton, *Uncommon Friends,* p. 234: "Anne had urged him to change the remark…"; Mark Mueller, "Lindbergh's Inner War; Unsealed Papers Chronicle Unpopular Position," *Newark Star-Ledger,* March 30, 2001, pp. 1, 12 ; Reeve Lindbergh, "The Flyer, Charles Lindbergh," *Time 100 Heroes and Icons,* www.time.com; Berg, *Lindbergh,* pp. 424–425.

14. Cohen, *Not Free to Desist,* p. 187; Mendes-Flohr and Reinharz, *Jew in the Modern World,* p. 651; Prager and Telushkin, *Why the Jews?,* p. 107.

15. Goldhagen, *Hitler's Willing Executioners*, pp. 98–104; Kershaw, *Hitler, Volume II*, pp. 136–144.

16. Mendes-Flohr and Reinharz, *The Jew in the Modern World*, pp. 651–656; Kershaw, *Hitler*, p. 143.

Chapter Nineteen: The Radio Priest

1. Donald Warren, *Radio Priest: Charles Coughlin, the Father of Hate Radio* (New York and London: The Free Press, 1996), pp. 154–157; Andrew Schornick, *The Anti-Semitism of Father Coughlin and the End of His Radio Career* (unpublished research paper, Detroit, 1996), pp. 26–32.

2. Strong, *Organized Anti-Semitism*, pp. 57–59; Dinnerstein, *Anti-Semitism in America*, p. 115; Alan Brinkley, *Voices of Protest: Huey Long, Father Coughlin, and the Great Depression* (New York: Vintage Books, 1983), pp. 90–91.

3. Warren, *Radio Priest*, pp. 132–133; Brinkley, *Voices of Protest*, pp. 149, 270–271.

4. *New York Times*, March 1, 1933, "Ford Secretary, Missing, Is Found. Telephones From Traverse City, Mich., He Has 'Just Woke Up, Totally Exhausted'"; May 24, 1944, "Liebold Dismissed as Ford's Secretary; Was Power in Auto Company For 30 Years"; *Detroit News*, May 24, 1944, "Ford and Liebold Separate."

5. Warren, *Radio Priest*, pp. 145–146.

6. Belth, *A Promise to Keep*, pp. 131–134; Cohn, *Warrant for Genocide*, p. 258; Dinnerstein, *Anti-Semitism in America*, pp. 115–118.

7. Warren, *Radio Priest*, pp. 146–153; Brinkley, *Voices of Protest*, p. 267; Cohn, *Warrant for Genocide*, pp. 258–259; Liebold, Oral History interview, p. 471: "As shown in this publication of *Der Sturmer*, [the Germans] used *The International Jew* to enhance the value of their work..."; Rauschning, *The Voice of Destruction*, p. 236.

8. Lewis, "20,000 Jam Garden in Reich Protest. Fund of $4,655 Is Raised. Resolutions Ask Roosevelt to Call World Parley and to Ban Trade With Germany," *New York Times*, November 22, 1938; Lewis, "Henry Ford's Antisemitism and Its Repercussions," p. 6; Lewis, *The Public Image of Henry Ford*, p. 153; Wilkins, *American Business Abroad*, p. 283.

9. Leo Franklin manuscript, *Some Untold Stories*, Chapter IX, "Coughlin Enters the Picture," pp. 144–148.

10. On Rabbi Franklin's conception of the classic role of the community-oriented rabbi, see for example, his essay, "Pulpit Seen as Mediator,"

Detroit News, June 4, 1921: "...in order to stand as a sponsor for social justice," Franklin writes, "one must align oneself with no group and with no party, but must take a large view of the whole situation..."

11. Leo Franklin manuscript, *Some Untold Stories,* Chapter X, "Who Told the Truth?" pp. 149–157; Lewis, *The Public Image of Henry Ford,* p. 151; *Detroit Free Press,* December 5, 1938.

12. "'Brutal Dictator' Lashed By Ickes In Recent Talk," *New York Times,* December 23, 1938; Harold L. Ickes, *Protestantism Answers Hate,* pamphlet published by The Protestant Magazine, March 1941.

13. For biographical overview, see Glen Jeansonne, *Gerald L. K. Smith: Minister of Hate* (Baton Rouge, La.: Louisiana State University Press, 1997), pp. 1–74; also, Bennett, *The Party of Fear,* pp. 252–253, 261–263, 265–266; and the investigative article, "War in Dearborn," *PM* Magazine, n.d. (ca. 1940), pp. 28–41.

14. *The International Jew,* "Abridged from the original as published by the world renowned industrial leader Henry Ford, Sr. Copy prepared for the printer by Gerald L. K. Smith," pp. 5–11; Richard S. Levy, "Introduction" to *A Lie and a Libel,* pp. 26–27, and note 7, pp. 45–46; Lewis, *Henry Ford's Antisemitism,* pp. 6–7.

15. Zeskind, *The "Christian Identity" Movement,* p. 13; Bennett, *The Party of Fear,* p. 438; Aho, *The Politics of Righteousness,* pp. 102–103, Table 4.1; see also, Richard Hofstadter, *Anti-Intellectualism in American Life* (New York: Random House, 1964), p. 135, "The fundamentalist mind is essentially Manichaean. It looks upon the world as an arena for conflict between absolute good and absolute evil."

16. Katz and Popkin, *Messianic Revolution,* pp. 180–187; Jeansonne, *Gerald L. K. Smith,* pp. 102–103; Bolkosky, *Harmony and Dissonance,* p. 174; Melton, *Encyclopedic Handbook of Cults,* pp. 53–61.

Chapter Twenty: Transitions

1. Green, *The World of the Worker,* Chapter 5, "The Depression, the New Deal, and the New Industrial Unions," p. 133ff; David Brody, *Workers in Industrial America: Essays on the 20th Century Struggle* (New York: Oxford University Press, 1980), Chapter 3, "The Emergence of Mass-Production Unionism, p. 82ff; Thomas R. Brooks, *Toil and Trouble: A History of American Labor* (New York: Delta Books, 1965), pp. 180–181;

also, www.uaw.org for an overview of United Auto Workers history from a union perspective.

2. "War in Dearborn," *PM* Magazine, pp. 32–35; Sward, *The Legend of Henry Ford*, Chapter 27, "Call-to-Arms," p. 370ff.

3. Nevins and Hill, *Ford: Decline and Rebirth*, Chapter VI, "A New Deal for Labor," p. 133ff.; re "the Jews..." p. 165; on the perceived threat to the "natural economy" as a classic trigger for incipient antisemitism to rise to the surface, see Abram Leon, *The Jewish Question, A Marxist Interpretation* (New York: Pathfinder Press, 1996 edition of 1950 text), pp. 72, 133: "The 'real Jew' is the Jew in his economic and social role."

4. Wilkins, *American Business Abroad*, pp.320,329, and fn.11, p. 502; "Ford and GM Scrutinized for Alleged Nazi Collaboration," by Michael Dobbs, *Washington Post*, November 30, 1998, p. A1.; for the view that Ford-Werke "did not enjoy unjust enrichment" during the war years, see Simon Reich, "The Ford Motor Company and the Third Reich," in *Dimensions, A Journal of Holocaust Studies*, The Anti-Defamation League, 13:2 (Winter 1999). Nevertheless, Professor Reich conceded to *Post* reporter Dobbs, "GM and Ford did absolutely everything they could to ingratiate themselves to the Nazi state." On Henry Ford's unstoppable contradictions, see *New York Daily Mirror*, November 17, 1940, HF interview by James L. Kilgallen, and *New York Journal*, December 31, 1941.

5. Dobbs, ibid.; Ken Silverstein, "Ford and the Fuehrer," *The Nation*, January 24, 2000, pp. 11–16.

6. Silverstein, ibid., p. 11

7. Nevins and Hill, *Ford: Decline and Rebirth*, pp. 176, 242; on the syndrome of "re-emergent anti-semitic expression," see Goldhagen, *Hitler's Willing Executioners*, p. 44.

8. "Ford Repudiates Bias Against the Jews—Anti-Semitism Is 'Weakening National Unity,' He Writes B'nai B'rith Leader," *New York Times*, January 12, 1942.

9. Rabbi Leo Franklin manuscript, p. 167; Lewis, "Ford's Antisemitism," p. 6; Lewis, *The Public Image of Henry Ford*, p. 154.

10. Bryan, *Clara*, p. 297.

11. Rabbi Leo Franklin typescript, pp. 167–169. For *lashon harah*, Philip Birnbaum, *Encyclopedia of Jewish Concepts*, as cited by Diane Osen to the author, April 27, 2001.

Afterword

1. Medical diagnoses by Dr. Frank Sladen of Henry Ford Hospital, cited
    in Bryan, *Clara*, pp. 179, 235, 243, 283, 286. Dr. Roy D. McClure was
    chief of surgery and Sladen was chief of medicine at the hospital.

2. Ruth R. Wisse, *If I am Not for Myself... The Liberal Betrayal of the Jews*
    (New York: Free Press, 1992), p.117.

3. See for example, Summary of ADL Audit of Anti-Semitic Incidents ©
    1996 Anti-Defamation League; *Anti-Semitism and Prejudice in America*,
    Highlights from ADL Survey, November 1998 © 2001 Anti-
    Defamation League; and also, Harold Meyerson, "America the Armed,"
    L. A. Weekly, August 11, 1999; and "Lieberman," by the editors, *The
    New Republic*, August 21, 2000.

PERMISSIONS

TEXT

Correspondence, Henry Ford and David Starr Jordan, Box 20, Folder 22, Hoover Institution Archives, Copyright © Stanford University.

Correspondence, editorial department Little, Brown & Co., and Samuel S. Marquis; unpublished manuscripts of Samuel S. Marquis. Published by permission of the Cranbrook Archives.

Excerpts from unpublished correspondence and manuscripts of Henry Ford; excerpts from Oral History *Reminiscences*. From the Collections of the Henry Ford Museum and Greenfield Village.

The Cyrus Adler Unpublished Correspondence Files; excerpts from Cyrus Adler to miscellaneous addressees. Published by permission of the Library of the Jewish Theological Seminary.

The Louis Marshall Papers, published by permission of the Jacob Rader Marcus Center of the American Jewish Archives, Cincinnati, Ohio.

Selections from the Schwimmer-Lloyd Collection, Manuscripts and Archives Division, published by permission of The New York Public Library, Astor, Lenox, and Tilden Foundations.

Correspondence from the Julius Rosenwald Papers, published by permission of The University of Chicago Library.

Compendium of "Statements by Henry Ford relating directly to Jews, 1927–1942," published by permission of the American Jewish Committee Library.

PHOTOGRAPHS

3 *Shylock in 1860.* Illustration by G.H. Thomas for *The Merchant of Venice* (London: Sampson & Low), General Research Division, The New York Public Library, Astor, Lenox and Tilden Foundations.

5 *Henry Ford perusing...* Collections of the Henry Ford Museum & Greenfield Village.

9 *William Ford, circa 1895* and *Mary Litogot Ford, circa 1860.* Collections of the Henry Ford Museum & Greenfield Village.

10 *Henry Ford at age eighteen...* Collections of the Henry Ford Museum & Greenfield Village.

11 *Henry Ford at age twenty-three.* Collections of the Henry Ford Museum & Greenfield Village.

12 *Henry Ford with son, Edsel, 1899.* Collections of the Henry Ford Museum & Greenfield Village.

13 *"Crazy Henry"...* Collections of the Henry Ford Museum & Greenfield Village.

15 *Oliver Barthel...* Collections of the Henry Ford Museum & Greenfield Village.

16 *"At Full Speed,"...* Illustration from *Munsey's Magazine...* Collections of the Henry Ford Museum & Greenfield Village.

22 *The First Ford.* Illustration by Harry Cimino, in Charles Merz, *Along Came Ford* (Garden City, New York: Doubleday, Doran & Company, 1929).

23 *The classic Ford logo...* Collections of the Henry Ford Museum & Greenfield Village.

24 *E. G. Liebold, April 26, 1925.* Collections of the Henry Ford Museum & Greenfield Village.

32 *Immigrants arriving in "the golden land."* Illustration from *Frank Leslie's Weekly,* n.d. Collections of the American Jewish Historical Society, Waltham, Massachusetts and New York, NY.

40 *The Ford Americanization School at Highland Park.* Collections of the Cranbrook Archives, Bloomfield Hills, Michigan.

41 *The Melting Pot ceremony, July 4, 1917.* Illustration from an article in *National Magazine,* July, 1920, p.156. Collections of the Henry Ford Museum & Greenfield Village.

44 *Henry Ford and John Burroughs...* Collections of the Henry Ford Museum & Greenfield Village.

57 *E. G. Pipp. Detroit News* Archives.

62 *Rosika Schwimmer...* Collections of the Henry Ford Museum & Greenfield Village.

66 *Rosika Schwimmer on board the Peace Ship.* Collections of the Henry Ford Museum & Greenfield Village.

68 *Highland Park assembly line, two views.* Collections of the Henry Ford Museum & Greenfield Village.

73 *Dearborn Publishing Company...* Collections of the Henry Ford Museum & Greenfield Village.

74 *Fred Black.* Collections of the Henry Ford Museum & Greenfield Village.

77 *Henry Ford and W. J. Cameron...* Collections of the Henry Ford Museum & Greenfield Village.

78 *The inaugural "Mr. Ford's Own Page,"...* Collections of the Henry Ford Museum & Greenfield Village.

81 *Boris Brasol.* "Proof of Ford's Fascism," an "exposé" by Dan Gilmor, *Friday Magazine,* January 24, 1941.

83 *Antichrist and his emblems...* From Norman Cohn, *Warrant for Genocide: The Myth of the Jewish World Conspiracy and the* Protocols of the Elders of Zion (London: Eyre and Spottiswoode, 1967), p. 101.

88 *"Roughing it" around the lazy Susan...* Collections of the Henry Ford Museum & Greenfield Village.

102 *"The International Jew," May 22, 1920.* Collections of the Henry Ford Museum & Greenfield Village.

103 Pipp's Weekly *strikes back.* The Burton Historical Collections, Detroit Public Library.

109 *Jacob Schiff.* Collections of the American Jewish Historical Society, Waltham, Massachusetts and New York, NY.

113 *Cyrus Adler.* Collections of the American Jewish Historical Society, Waltham, Massachusetts and New York, NY.

117 *Louis Marshall.* Collections of the American Jewish Historical Society, Waltham, Massachusetts and New York, NY.

122 *Rabbi Leo Franklin in his study.* The Rabbi Leo M. Franklin Archive, Temple Beth El, Bloomfield Hills, Michigan.

128 *"The Jew in the United States"...* Collections of the Henry Ford Museum & Greenfield Village.

129 *"The Jewish Question"...* Collections of the Henry Ford Museum & Greenfield Village.

136 *Judah L. Magnes.* Collections of the Jacob Rader Marcus Center of the American Jewish Archives, Cincinnati, Ohio.

144   The International Jew, *Volume I, November, 1920*. Collections of the Henry Ford Museum & Greenfield Village.

147   *Editorial in* The Day/The Warheit (Der Tog)...Schwimmer-Lloyd Collection, Manuscripts Division, The New York Public Library, Astor, Lenox and Tilden Foundations.

153   *Henry Ford, P. E. Martin, and Charles "Cast-Iron Charlie" Sorensen...* Collections of the Henry Ford Museum & Greenfield Village.

155   *Rev. Samuel S. Marquis and his wife, Gertrude.* Collections of the Cranbrook Archives, Bloomfield Hills, Michigan.

158   *Ray Dahlinger (left) and Harry Bennett.* Collections of the Henry Ford Museum & Greenfield Village.

164   *Henry Ford and Herman Bernstein...* Collections of the Henry Ford Museum & Greenfield Village.

167   *Papal bull of Julius III...* Rare Books Division, The New York Public Library, Astor, Lenox and Tilden Foundations.

173   *Reprint of "Heinrich Ford" article...* "Proof of Ford's Fascism," an "exposé" by Dan Gilmor, *Friday Magazine*, January 24, 1941.

183   *Kurt Ludecke, October 1938. Detroit News* Archives.

187   *The dwarf against giants...Der emes vegen Henri Ford* (The truth about Henry Ford), David Mekler, New York, 1923. Captions translated by Roberta Saltzman, The Jewish Division, The New York Public Library.

187   *Ford on Uncle Sam's scale* and *The Klan's Toy. Der emes vegen Henri Ford* (The truth about Henry Ford), David Mekler, New York, 1923. Captions translated by Roberta Saltzman, The Jewish Division, The New York Public Library.

190   *The Ford Plant in Cologne.* Collections of the Henry Ford Museum & Greenfield Village.

193   *The criss-crossed conveyors...* Collections of the Henry Ford Museum & Greenfield Village.

195   *Albert Kahn in his office. Detroit News* Archives.

201   *Julius Rosenwald.* Jacob Rader Marcus Center of the American Jewish Archives.

204   *Aaron Sapiro.* Jacob Rader Marcus Center of the American Jewish Archives.

208   The Dearborn Independent, *August 30, 1924*. Collections of the Henry Ford Museum & Greenfield Village.

212   *Paul Warburg.* Jacob Rader Marcus Center of the American Jewish Archives.

216   *Nathan Straus.* American Jewish Historical Society, Waltham, Massachusetts and New York, NY.

226 *Hamlin Garland...* Collections of the Henry Ford Museum & Greenfield Village.

228 *Fair Lane, on the banks of the Rouge River.* Collections of the Henry Ford Museum & Greenfield Village.

232 *"The Fifteen Millionth Ford," May 26ᵗʰ, 1927.* Collections of the Henry Ford Museum & Greenfield Village.

246 The Forward, *July 17, 1927.* Collection of the author.

247 *Two whimsical responses to Henry Ford's apology in the summer of 1927.* The Rabbi Leo M. Franklin Archives, Temple Beth El, Bloomfield Hills, Michigan.

250 *Rabbi Stephen S. Wise.* Jacob Rader Marcus Collection of the American Jewish Archives.

256 *Henry Ford, 1928.* Collections of the Henry Ford Museum & Greenfield Village.

259 *Temporary storage room...* Collections of the Henry Ford Museum & Greenfield Village.

266 The Protocols of the Learned Elders of Zion *in pamphlet edition...* Collections of the Henry Ford Museum & Greenfield Village.

274 The International Jew *proliferates in many languages.* "Proof of Ford's Fascism," an "exposé" by Dan Gilmor, *Friday Magazine,* January 24, 1941.

277 *Fritz Kuhn, February 22, 1939. Detroit News* Archives.

284 *Henry Ford receives the Grand Cross...* Collections of the Henry Ford Museum & Greenfield Village.

287 *Henry Ford meets Charles Lindbergh, August, 1927.* Collections of the Henry Ford Museum & Greenfield Village.

291 *Kristallnacht...* Courtesy of the Leo Baeck Institute, New York.

295 *Father Charles Coughlin, 1935. Detroit News* Archives.

296 *Henry Ford and E. G. Liebold.* "Proof of Ford's Fascism," an "exposé" by Dan Gilmor, *Friday Magazine,* January 24, 1941.

302 *Henry Ford and Rabbi Franklin, November 29, 1938.* Collections of the Henry Ford Museum & Greenfield Village.

305 *Gerald L. K. Smith... Detroit News* Archives.

313 *Henry Ford Must Choose ...* Collection of the author.

INDEX

Abraham (patriarch), 263

Addams, Jane, 55, 56

Adler, Cyrus, 170; vs. American Jewish Congress, 115; birth and early career, 112–13; vs. *Dearborn Independent*, 121, 132; vs. Ford, 184, 217; Ford's apology to the Jews and, 246; Jewish factionalism and, 115; vs. *The Protocols of the Learned Elders of Zion*, 116, 143; Zionism and, 113–14

Adolf Hitler, His Life and Speeches, 177

Advertising, 203–04

Agassiz, Louis, 50

Agriculture, 52, 210–11. *See also* Farming

Ahlwardt, Hermann, 126

Aked, Charles, 161

Alabama, 164

Albert, Heinrich F., 283

Aldrich, Nelson W., 212

All Vows (*Kol Nidre*), 166, 169

Allen, J. H., 264

Allport, Gordon, 8, 230

America, 92, 330; antisemitism in, 329; Brasol on, 82; British-Israelism and, 263; Fascist movement and Ford, 185; the Great Migration, 31; identity and, 33, 42; Jewish congregations in, 33; migration of southern Negroes, 86, 201; as the new Israel, 28; quasi-fascist groups in, 278–79. *See also* Public, the

American Broadcasting Company (CBS), 263

American Constitutional League, 82

American Farm Bureau Federation, 206

American Federation of Labor, 309

American Hebrew, The, 139, 253, 273

American Institute of Architects, 200

American Israelite, 245

American Jewish Committee (AJC), 114, 137, 254, 272, 329; vs. *Dearborn Independent*, 139–40, 166; vs. Ford, 147–48, 184; *The International Jew* and, 145, 146; Marshall and, 118, 163; vs. Schiff, 112

American Jewish Congress, 112, 115, 215, 235, 249

American Jewish Historical Society, 113

American Jewish Yearbook, 279

American League for Peace and Democracy, 298

American Mercury, 310

American Newspaper Publishers Association, 281

American Peace Society, 63

American Tract Society's Illustrated Family Christian Almanac, 28

American Zionist Federation, 136

Americanism, 93, 118, 306

Amerika (Goethe), 31

Anderson, Warren C., 152, 184

Anglo-Israel, or, The Saxon Race (Poole), 264

Anglo-Saxon Federation of America, 267

Anglo-Saxons, 27, 42, 98, 171, 263, 266

Antichrist, 83

Anti-Defamation League (ADL), 6–7, 128, 132, 145, 273, 316, 329

Antisemitism, 322, 329; vs. behavioral logic, 325; blame and, 327; Chesterton, 165–66; Christian identity and, 35, 267; Coughlin, 293–95, 296–98; *Dearborn Independent* vs. *Der Veg*, 132; economics and, 326; Ford compared to Lindbergh, 289; vs. Ford II, 316–17; Ford on, 273; Ford vs. Kahn, 199, 200; Ford vs. Wilson, 150, 151; Ford's pacifism and, 61; Franklin on, 126–27; German-American Bund and, 275–77; in Germany, 172, 177, 183, 273; Hitler on, 174; image and, 30, 134; the Jewish aim and, 179; Jewish emancipation and, 107; Ku Klux Klan, 93–94; Kuhn, 275–77; Populism and, 29; repetition and, 328; Schiff and, 110; Smith, 19, 304–08; vs.

Spargo, 150; vs. the Talmud, 166–69; Zionism and, 181. *See also International Jew, The*; *Protocols of the Learned Elders of Zion, The*; Racism

Architecture, 195; factories by Kahn, 197, 199, 200; homes by Kahn, 198–99; Nettleton, Kahn, and Trowbridge established, 196; River Rouge Plant, 257

Arendt, Hannah, 142

Armageddon, 34, 42, 52, 266

Arnold, Matthew, 44

Aryans, 33, 34, 191, 263, 266, 329

Association of Licensed Automobile Manufacturers, 22

Atonement, 251–52

Auer, Erhard, 183

Auf Gut Deutsch, 177

Auf Vorposten, 100

Automobile industry, 39, 93, 257, 270

Automobile manufacturing: Ford and war, 49; Ford Motor Co. in Germany, 283; Model A, two-cylinder, 21; Model T, 23, 171, 192; River Rouge Plant, 258; Tin Lizzie, 22

Automobiles: early Ford prototypes, 12; Ford racing cars, 15–16; Hitler and, 190; Model A, 224, 256, 270; Model A (two-cylinder), 21, 103; Model N, 153(photo); Model Y, 270. *See also* Model T

Aviation: Lindbergh and, 287; Lindbergh and Goering, 286

Baker, Max, 279

Balch, Emily Greene, 56

Balfour Declaration, 119

Banking, 9, 220–21, 266; as a cause of war, 48; establishment of Highland Park State Bank, 24–25; Federal Reserve Bank and Jews, 211–14; vs. Ford, 269; the press and, 71; the Rothschilds, 29, 51; vs. Texas farmers, 210–11. *See also* Financiers; Jewish bankers; Moneylenders

Barthel, Oliver, 15,16, 17, 23

Bauer, Bruno, 130–31
Bavarian Diet, 183
Beek, Gottfried zur, 100
Ben-Hur (film), 162
Bennett, Harry Herbert, 157–58, 222, 237, 257, 316; fires Liebold, 296; Ford's statement on German persecution of Jews and, 300, 302, 303; *Sapiro v. Ford* and, 219–20, 224; vs. United Automobile Workers, 310, 311
Benson, Allan, 46, 184
Berlin, Louis L., 120
Bernstein, Herman, 84–85, 115, 164, 236–37, 241
Bible, the, 3, 4, 46, 265
Billikopf, Jacob, 124
Black, Fred Lee, 72, 133, 223, 224, 227
Bloom, Sol, 216–17
B'nai B'rith, 145, 241, 274. *See also* Anti-Defamation League
Bogory, Natalie de, 82
Bolschewismus, Der (Eckart), 179
Bolshevism, 80, 83, 84, 85, 94
Bombard, Owen, 261
Bonbright, Howard, 230
Book of the Kahal (Brafman), 168
Boyer Machine Co., 197
Brafman, Jacob, 168
Brandeis, Justice Louis, 94, 134, 249
Brasol, Boris, 81–82, 83–84, 85, 140
Briggs Manufacturing Co., 269
Brisbane, Arthur, 233–35, 237
British Peace Conference, 90
British-Israel World Federation, 264, 266
British-Israelites, 98, 263–67, 307–08
Brooks, Carl, 311
Brothers, Richard, 263
Brown, David, 123–24
Brownell, Charles A., 58
Bryan, William Jennings, 55, 125, 150
Buckeye Harvester Co., 11
Bullitt, William C., 65
Burbank, Luther, 53
Burroughs, John, 43, 44–45, 88–89, 227, 321–22
Bushnell, Sarah, 43

Business, 327; farm cooperatives and, 205; Ford on, 257; vs. Jewish bankers, 326; Jewish moneylenders, 106; the spiritual and, 262. *See also* Financiers; Wall Street
Butzel, Judge Henry, 67, 124

Cain (son of Adam), 308
California, 205
California State Market Bureau, 204
Cameron, William John, 78, 100, 123, 137, 227, 236, 247, 261, 282, 284, 307, 326; as a British-Israelite, 98, 265; as a Christian, 261; Ford's apology to the Jews and, 242; Ford's statement on German persecution of Jews and, 300–301; hired to the *Dearborn Independent*, 73–74; vs. Jews, 163; Lee and, 324; Ludecke and, 187, 188; "Mr. Ford's Own Page" and, 75, 77; vs. Pipp, 86; *Sapiro v. Ford* and, 219–21; steps down as editor of the *Dearborn Independent*, 242, 262, 267; vs. Untermyer, 275
Canada, 103, 208
Canadian Jewish Review, The, 317
Capitalists, 29, 77, 314. *See also* Business; Wall Street
Catt, Carrie Chapman, 55, 65
Cause of World Unrest, The, 143–44
Central Conference of American Rabbis, 145
Central Greenback Club, 29
Cerny, Josef, 180
Chalmers Motor Co., 197
Chesterton, G. K., 165–66
Chevrolet, 154, 225
Chicago, 201–02
Chicago Times, 281
Chicago Tribune, 86–87, 245
Chosen people, the, 33, 98, 141, 263
Christ Church, 156
Christian National Crusade, 307
Christiana, 64, 65
Christianity, Christians, 3, 4, 28, 30, 33, 35, 106, 167–68, 262, 293–94, 306

Chrysler, 189, 310
Church of the Jesus Christian, 308
Cincinnati *Enquirer*, 282
Civil liberty, 118, 270
Civilization: Anglo-Saxon, 33; nativism and 34; roads and 190
Cleveland Plain Dealer, 245, 281
Cleveland Zionist Society, 303
Cohn, Norman, 145, 280
Collier's Magazine, 184
Cologne, 189, 270, 283, 314, 315
Columbia Broadcasting System (CBS), 263
Commerce. *See* Business
Committee of Fifteen, 201–02
Committee of One Million, The, 306
Communism, Communist party, 95, 293
Compensation (Emerson), 47
Congress, 54, 68, 94, 212, 216–17, 276
Congress of Industrial Organizations, 309
Coolidge, Calvin, 185
Coughlin, Charles E, 293–95, 296–98, 302–03, 305, 324
Council of Four, 90
Couzens, James, 23, 24–25, 36, 53, 128
Cross and the Flag, The, 307
Crowther, Samuel, 171
Culture: academia and racial discrimination, 170; advertising and, 203; German, 174; German social theory and, 191; the Holocaust and, 329; Jewish within American, 136. *See also* Society

Daily Forward, The, 203
Daughter of the Middle Border, A (Garland), 227
Davis, Earl J., 235, 241
Davison, Henry, 213
Days of Man (Jordan), 50
Dearborn, 30, 194, 259
Dearborn Independent, 69, 159, 227, 301, 316; anthology of, 144; vs. Bernstein, 236; Black hired, 72–73; Brasol and, 81, 85, 140; British-Israelism and,

265, 266; vs. *Der Veg*, 132, 135; Ford vs. Kahn, 199; Ford's retraction to the Jews and, 238, 239, 240; vs. Franklin, 121, 132–33; Fritsch and, 271–72; vs. Jewish unity, 134–35; vs. the Kehillah, 138; Liebold vs. Pipp, 96; Liebold's first article, 85–86; Ludecke and, 182; vs. Marshall, 119–21; "Mr. Ford's Own Page," 78(photo); objects of, 77; Pipp as editor, 75, 79–80; vs. *Pipp's Weekly*, 99–100, 138; policy of, 75, 218; *The Protocols of the Learned Elders of Zion* and, 141; resignation of Pipp, 98–99; vs. Rosenwald, 201–02; vs. Sapiro, 207–10, 218, 219, 220–21; vs. Schiff, 108, 112; sensationalism and, 91; similarities to the *Völkischer Beobachter*, 176; Smith and, 307; vs. Spargo, 149–50; the Talmud and, 166–69; "The International Jew," 100, 102–03, 104; "The Jew in Character and Business," 104–05; "The Jew in the United States," 128(photo); "The Jewish Question," 129(photo), 130, 131, 133; vs. Warburg, 213–14. *See also* Ford, Henry
Dearborn Publishing Company, 160, 242, 253; established, 72; *The International Jew* and, 145–46; vs. Marshall, 120; produces *The International Jew*, 144; *The Protocols of the Learned Elders of Zion* and, 142, 144; resignations of Clara and Edsel, 158; Sapiro libel suit, 211, 219
Delavigne, Theodore, 52, 66
Destiny, 267, 307
Detroit, 30, 34, 93
Detroit Americanization Committee, 41–42
Detroit Athletic Club, 34, 128
Detroit Automobile Co., 14
Detroit Free Press, 52, 89, 166, 303
Detroit Industrial Removal Office, 39
Detroit Interdenominational Thanksgiving, 128

Detroit Journal, 57
Detroit News, 57, 60, 69, 132, 156, 262
Detroit, Toledo and Ironton Railroad, 296
Deuteronomy, 265
Deutscher Weckruf, 276
DeWitt, Clinton C., 42
Dickstein, Samuel, 276
Dies, Martin, 276
Discrimination (bias), 118, 128–29, 170, 279
Dodge, John and Horace, 67
Dollfuss, Maurice, 314
Donaldson, Benjamin R., 227
Donin, Nicholas, 167
Donnelley, Gerry, 323
Doubleday, Page & Co., 170, 253
Dow, Alexander, 13, 14
Dumont, Marguerite, 248

Eckart, Dietrich, 177–78, 180, 183
Economics, 92, 279; antisemitism and, 326; Christian identity and, 35; depressions and, 29, 30, 35, 92, 279; farm cooperatives and, 205; Jews and, 30, 131, 295; Kahn and, 199; Populism and, 29
Edison Illuminating Co. (Detroit Edison), 11–12, 14
Edison, Thomas Alva, 43, 53, 54, 88, 164, 321; on Jews, 89–90; vs. Jews, 322, 324; and laboratory of, 260; meets Ford, 13–14
Emergency Peace Federation, 55
Emerson, Ralph Waldo, 45–47
Encyclopedia Judaica, 168
England, 130, 231, 263, 304, 314
English, Ivan G., 147
English language, 40, 263
English Traits (Emerson), 47
Espionage and Alien Acts, 94
Essays: First Series (Emerson), 45
Eternalism (Smith), 17
Eugenics, 49, 53
Europe, 32; dip in Ford sales and, 231; Ford on, 202; International Congress

of Women for Peace, 56; vs. Jewish secret knowledge, 105; Jews vs. the spiritual, 179; Keynes and, 90; moneylenders and war, 48, 52; the Rothschilds and, 51
Eynon, W.G., 140
Eyre and Spottiswood, 101

Fairchild, Henry Pratt, 170
Farming: cooperative, 204–06; Ford on, 202; Fordson tractors and, 204; vs. Jews, 207; John Ford and, 8; technology and, 21. *See also* Agriculture
Fascism, 185, 279
Federal Census Schedule, 30
Federal Reserve Act, 213
Federal Reserve Bank, 211–14
Federal Reserve System, 215–16, 221
Federation of Jewish Charities, 124
Ferdinand, Archduke Franz, 55
Financiers, 90, 108–12, 209, 277, 278, 282, 310. *See also* Banking; Moneylenders
Fings, Karola, 315
Firestone, Harvey S., 14, 53, 54, 87, 321
First Zionist Congress, 113
Fitzmorris, Charles C., 201
Ford, Clara Jane (Bryant – HF's wife), 11, 46, 72, 157, 312
Ford, Edsel: birth, 12; death, 316; fifteen-millionth model T and, 232; vs. Ford, 231, 257, 310; Ford's pacifism and, 71–72; Ford-Werke AG and, 312; marriage, 71; Model A and, 224, 256; named secretary-treasurer of Dearborn Publishing Co., 72; redesigns the Lincoln, 165; temporary president of Ford Motor Co., 76
Ford, Eleanor Lowthian (Clay – HF's daughter-in-law), 71
Ford, Henry
Character, health, personality, 15, 39; as a boss, 14, 21; death, 317; on good will, 37; libel suit against the *Chicago Tribune,* 86–87; management style, 23–24, 25; nervous

Ford, Henry (*cont.*)
     breakdown, 158; reminder books,
     268; Sapiro files for libel, 211
     Dearborn Independent, 72, 104; vs.
     American Jewish Committee,
     139–40; Black on, 75–76; vs. Bris-
     bane, 234–35; Cameron on, 262;
     car dealers and, 146, 327; Chester-
     ton and, 165–66; establishes Dear-
     born Publishing Co., 72; vs.
     Franklin, 252, 254; hires Pipp,
     70–71; the Jewish Program and,
     162; Jews and, 96, 97, 243;
     LaGuardia on, 167; vs. Liv-
     ingston, 145; "Own Page," 74–75,
     77, 80, 86, 99; vs. Rosenwald, 202;
     vs. Sapiro, 204, 207, 211, 214,
     219–22, 223, 241, 242; shutting
     down the press, 224, 235, 242,
     255; stagnant circulation and, 91;
     vs. Straus, 215–16. *See also Dear-
     born Independent*
Ford Motor Company, 326; advertis-
     ing and, 203; buys out stockhold-
     ers, 76; Christ and, 38; dividend
     disbursement and, 67–68; vs.
     Edsel, 231, 257, 310; fifteen-mil-
     lionth Model T and, 232; vs. Gen-
     eral Motors, 225; Highland Park
     design limitations, 194; imagined
     conspiracies against, 269; incorpo-
     ration of, 21; Liebold hired as per-
     sonal secretary, 24; presents
     Franklin with a Model T, 127; the
     press and, 158, 159; vs. progress,
     226; seventy-fifth birthday,
     283–84; vs. United Automobile
     Workers, 306, 310–12; vs. Wall
     Street, 93; workers and, 157–58.
     See also Ford Motor Company
Hitler, Adolph, 185, 273, 301; Eckart
     and, 180; *The International Jew*
     and, 172–73, 271–72; Kuhn and,
     277; Ludecke and, 186–89; simi-
     larities, 175, 181, 190
Homes, 43, 45
Jews, 88–89, 235, 269, 316; agricul-

ture and, 207; vs. American Jewish
     Committee, 147–48; vs. the Amer-
     ican public, 299; blame and, 327;
     vs. Bloom, 216–17; business and,
     328; Chesterton and, 165–66;
     closing the *Dearborn Independent*
     and, 242; Coughlin and, 297; Edi-
     son compared to Ford, 322; vs.
     Franklin, 122–23, 132–33;
     Franklin and, 127; vs. Fritsch,
     272; *Henry Ford and the Originators
     of War*, 280; industrialization of,
     40; Kahn and, 198, 200; Lee and,
     323–24; Liebold and, 95; Lind-
     bergh and, 288–89; vs. Marshall,
     119–21, 123, 124, 148, 255–56;
     moneylenders and, 52, 106; *My
     Life and Work* and, 170–71;
     O'Neill on, 159–60; vs. public
     relations, 232–33; slave labor at
     Ford-Werke AG and, 315; Smith
     and, 306–07; vs. Spargo, 149–50;
     and statement on German perse-
     cution of, 299–303; "The Interna-
     tional Jew" and, 103; unions and,
     312; Wood on, 185; Zalowitz and,
     246–47. *See also* Jews
Jews, apology: Adler on, 246; ambas-
     sadors to Marshall, 235–36; apol-
     ogy drafted by Marshall, 237;
     apology fails to appear in the
     Dearborn Independent, 242; apol-
     ogy published, 238–40; atonement
     and, 251–52; Cameron and,
     242–43; Franklin on, 253–54;
     Fritsch on, 253; image and, 328;
     Liebold on, 241; McCloud on, 244;
     Pipp on, 244; response of the Jews,
     249; response of the press, 244;
     Wise and, 250–51
Memoirs: *My Life and Work*, 181–82,
     253; *Today and Tomorrow*, 191,
     233
Pacifism, 99, 202; the Aryan species
     and, 50; on the causes of war, 48,
     49; Edsel and, 71–72; vs. Jewish
     bankers, 59, 61; peace educational

campaign, 52; the Peace Ship and, 63–66, 164, 236–37, 248, 327; vs. the press, 63–64; Schwimmer and, 56–66, 160–61, 247–48, 282; vs. Wilson, 63; vs. World War II, 314

Photographs, 256; age eighteen, 10; age twenty-three, 11; with Cameron, 77; with Franklin, 302; Grand Cross of the German Eagle, 284; Green Island holiday, 88; "Heinrich Ford," 173; with Liebold, 296; with Lindbergh, 287; with Lochner and Schwimmer, 62; McGuffy Homestead, 5; with Model N, 153; Old 999 racing car, 16

Politics, 68, 184, 296

Public statements: American Newspaper Publishers Assoc., 281–82; competitors and, 269; government and, 184; Jews and, 159–60, 232–33, 299; Liebold on, 26; unions and, 309; war and, 48, 52

Religion, 38, 46

Travel, 43, 53–54, 87–88, 321; Alabama, 164; the Peace Ship, 64–65

Youth, 20; *American Tract Society's Illustrated Family Christian Almanac*, 28; birth and parents, 8–9; early jobs, 10–11; early prototypes of the horseless carriage, 12; first business venture, 14; Jewish population in Detroit and, 30; *McGuffey's Eclectic Reader* and, 3; meets Edison, 13–14; Miller School, 1; Populism and, 29; racing cars and, 15–16; Smith and, 17

Ford II, Henry, 316–17, 329

Ford, John (HF's grandfather), 8, 27–28

Ford, Mary (Litigot – HF's mother), 10–11

Ford Motor Company, 295, 326; advertising in Jewish newspapers and, 203–04; anti-Jewish activities and, 275; Archives and, 268; Archives and *Sapiro v. Ford*, 221; buys Lincoln

Motor Co., 165; in Canada, 103; car dealers and competitors, 231; car dealers and the *Dearborn Independent*, 146; departures of various managers, 152–56; vs. the Dodge Brothers, 67–68; early hierarchy, 23; Edsel and, 71–72; establishment of Highland Park State Bank, 24–25; foreign plants, 104; in Germany, 183–84, 189, 270, 283, 312–15; Highland Park Plant, 22, 191–94, 312; Highland Park Plant shut down, 231; incorporation of, 21; Kuhn and, 276–77; Lincoln Plant, 312; logo, 23(fig.); Ludecke and, 182; McCloud and, 28–29; Melting Pot ceremony, 42; resignation of Couzens, 53; River Rouge Plant, 194–95, 257–58, 312; *Schindler's List* and, 323; Sociological Department, 38–39, 41, 42, 154; stock and, 21, 76; V–2 rockets and, 314; wage increase of 1914, 36–39; wages and, 257. *See also* Automobiles; Ford, Henry; Photographs; Workers

Ford Motor Company AG, 189, 283

"Ford Sunday Evening Hour, The," 263

Ford, William (HF's father), 8

Fordson tractor, 88, 204

Ford-Werke AG, 283, 312–15

Fortune Magazine, 279

Forty-Seven Identifications of the British Nation With the Lost Israel (Hine), 264

Forward, The, 238, 246

France, 103, 107, 130, 231, 314

Frank, Leo, 118

Frank Leslie's Illustrated Weekly, 126

Franklin, Rabbi Leo: on atonement, 251–52; birth and early career, 125; death of Ford and, 317; vs. Ford, 121–23, 132–33; Ford and, 127; Ford's statement on German persecution of Jews and, 299–303; vs. *The International Jew*, 273; vs. Liebold, 272–73; Marshall and, 124; vs. *The Merchant of Venice*, 6–7, 128

Freund, Herman, 34

Friedenwald, Herbert, 146

Friends of New Germany, 276
Fritsch, Theodor, 173, 214, 253, 256, 271–72
Frost, Robert, 227
Funk and Wagnalls, 113

G. H. Putnam & Son, 143
Galicia, 32
Gallagher, William Henry, 218, 220–21, 223, 241
Garland, Hamlin, 226–30
Gems (Emerson), 46
General Committee on National Defense, 81
General Motors, 154, 189, 270, 310
Genesis, 265
Gentiles, 207, 264
George, David Lloyd, 54–55
Georgia, 213
German Liberty Movement, 185
German-American Bund, 275–77
Germany, 89, 304; army, 299, 313; *Dearborn Independent* and, 119–20; Ford Motor Co. and, 183–84, 231, 270, 283, 312–15; Four-Year Economic Plan, 291–92; *Geichschaltung*, 271; Hitler appointed chancellor, 269; *The International Jew* and, 145, 172–73, 271—72, 274–75; Keynes and, 90; *Kristallnacht* pogroms, 289–91; *My Life and Work* and, 190; *The Protocols of the Learned Elders of Zion* and, 100–101; the *Völkisch* movement, 174–75
God, 4, 33, 251, 263, 308
Goebbels, Joseph, 290, 298, 299
Goering, Hermann Wilhelm, 285–86, 291, 293, 299
Goethe, Johann Wolfgang von, 31
Goldman, Sachs & Co., 210–11
Goldsmith Bryant and Stratton Business College, 11
Gossip, killing and, 317
Gottl-Ottlilienfeld, Friedrich von, 191
Gould, Jay, 89, 106
Government, 312; Ford on, 269, 277, 282; National Reserve Association and, 213; Nazi, 269, 283, 313–14; Palmer and, 94–95; Rules Committee of the House vs. Ford, 216–17; Treasury Dept. investigates Ford Motor Co., 314. *See also* Congress
Graves, William C., 201
Great Britain, 98
Great Migration, the, 31
Greeneway, Judge Joseph, Jr., 315
Gregory IX, Pope, 167
Grynszpan, Herschel, 290, 298
Gutstadt, Richard, 273–74, 316

Hammer Verlag, 173, 214, 271
Hanfstaengel, Ernst, 181, 182
Harding, Warren G., 185
Harper & Brothers, 149
Hartford Courant, 309
Hausen, Ludwig Muller von, 100
Hawthorne, Nathaniel, 9
Hearst, William Randolph, 233
Heine, Edmund C., 270
Henry Ford & Son, 71
Henry Ford and the Originators of War, 280
Henry Ford, An Interpretation (Marquis), 157
Henry Ford Company, 15
Henry Ford Hospital, 211, 222, 276
Henry Ford Museum, 258–61
Herzl, Theodore, 34, 84, 111, 141, 249
Hess, Rudolf, 180
Higham, John, 94
Hill, Frank Ernest, 164
Hine, Edward, 264
History: Ford and, 160; Ford on, 87, 142; Henry Ford Museum and, 261; Hitler and, 290; Hitler on, 181; Strong and, 33–34
History of a Lie, The (Bernstein), 164, 236
Hitler, Adolf, 271, 273, 299; appointed chancellor, 269; car industry and, 270; *Der Sturmer* and, 298; Eckart and, 177, 178, 179; *The International*

Jew and, 172; on Jewry as a race vs. a religion, 174; Kuhn and, 276, 277; Ludecke and, 182–83, 185–86, 187–88; quasi-fascist groups in America and, 278; on racial comrades, 101; *Völkischer Beobachter* and, 176
Hoheneichen Verlag, 178
Holocaust, the, 329
Holy Land, the, 98
Hoover, J. Edgar, 95
Houghton, Harris Ayres, 82, 84, 140, 149
House of the Masses, 95
House Un-American Activities, 276
Howe, Frederick C., 58
Howe, Irving, 118

Ickes, Harold L., 303–04
Ideology, 307. *See also* Philosophy
Illustrations: Antichrist and emblems of, 83; "Crazy Henry," 13; Ford and anti-semitism, 187; Ford and the Ku Klux Klan, 187; Ford logo, 23; immigrants, 32; Papal bull, 167; responses to Ford's apology to the Jews, 247; Shy-lock, 3; Tin Lizzie, 22. *See also* Photographs
Immigrant Press and Its Control, The (Park), 169
Immigrants, 32, 40–42, 99, 265
Immigration, 30, 92, 169, 288, 300–301; antisemitism and, 110; the Depression and, 279; the Great Migration, 31; quota (1922), 170
Indianapolis News, 245
Industrial Workers of the World, 94
Industry: agriculture as, 205; booze and, 202; in the *Dearborn Independent* and, 80; Ford on, 239, 269, 309; German, 89; Ku Klux Klan and, 93; labor strikes, 91, 310, 312; the spiritual and, 37. *See also* Automobile industry; Unions
International Automobile and Motor-Cycle Exhibition, 269
International Committee of Women for Permanent Peace, 56, 65

International Congress of Women for Peace, 56
International Jew, The, 144–46, 276; vs. the Anti-Defamation League, 145, 273; vs. Ford II, 317; Ford's apology to the Jews and, 253, 255–56; in Germany, 172–73, 256, 271–72, 274–75; Ludecke and, 182; Smith and, 307; vs. Spargo, 149; vs. Untermyer, 274–75; vs. Warburg, 214
International Labor Defense, 298
Inter-Racial Press of America, 317
Isaiah, 263
Israel, 28, 98, 263, 264, 265, 329
It Is Near at Our Doors! (Nilus), 83
Iwanowa, Elsa, 315

J. P. Morgan & Co., 52, 213, 278
Jacob (son of Isaac), 263, 264. *See also* Israel
Jacobs, Aletta, 65
Jacobs, Joseph, 139
James Flower & Brothers Machine Shop, 10
James, Henry, 44
James I, King, 167
Jekyll Island, 212, 213
Jenkins, H. F., 156, 231
Jerusalem, University of, 137
Jesus Christ, 3, 28, 38, 98, 308
Jew According to the Talmud, The (Rohling), 168
Jew and American Ideals, The (Spargo), 149
Jewish bankers, 59, 61, 209, 253, 278, 326
Jewish Chronicle, 245, 253
Jewish Communal Register (New York City), 136
Jewish community, the, 108; factionalism in, 115; hostility toward in Detroit, 34; the Kehillah as, 135–138; Franklin and, 127–28, organizations co-signing manifesto against Ford, 147
Jewish Criterion, The, 252

Jewish Encyclopedia, 113
Jewish Herald, 245
Jewish Peril, The, 101
Jewish Publication Society, 113
Jewish Question, the, 286; Bauer and,
    130–31; Brisbane and, 234–35; Ford
    vs. Strauss, 215; *Handbuch der Juden-*
    frage, 173, 271; *The International Jew*
    and, 145; the Jewish Program and,
    162; Jewry as a race vs. a religion,
    174; Marquis and, 157; Miller on,
    133; Schwimmer on, 60
Jewish State, The (Herzl), 34
Jewish Theological Seminary, 114, 117
Jews: vs. American quasi-fascist groups,
    278; Baldwin as, 324–25; Bernstein,
    84–85, 115, 164, 236–37, 241; boy-
    cott of Ford vehicles, 299; vs. British-
    Israelism, 98, 263, 264, 265, 307–08;
    Brown, 123–24; Butzel, 67, 124; vs.
    Cameron, 163; vs. Christ, 28; Christ-
    ian identity and, 35; vs. Coughlin,
    293–95, 296–98; vs. the *Dearborn*
    Independent, 96, 97, 104–05, 106; eco-
    nomics and, 30, 35; Edison on, 89–90;
    and emancipation of, 106–07; Emer-
    son on, 47; Federal Reserve Bank
    and, 211–14; Federal Reserve System
    and, 215–16; vs. Ford, 88–89;
    Franklin, 6–7, 121–28, 132–33,
    299–303, 317; vs. Garland, 227; Gut-
    stadt, 273–74; Herzl, 34, 84, 111, 141,
    249; Hitler on, 101, 181; Kahn,
    22–23, 127, 195–200, 235; Klingen-
    smith, 154; the Law and, 166; vs.
    Ludecke, 187–88; Magnes, 136, 137;
    McGuffey's Eclectic Reader and, 2–3,
    6–7; Mendes, 108; nationality and,
    131; "Oriental," 170–71; population,
    America, 129; population, Detroit, 30;
    vs. *The Protocols of the Learned Elders*
    of Zion, 82–85, 116; Rosenwald,
    Julius, 148, 201–02; the Rothschilds,
    29; Sapiro, 204–11, 214, 217; *Sapiro v.*
    Ford and, 219, 221, 223; Sartre on,
    134; Schiff, 89, 108–12, 121, 212;
    Schwimmer, 54–63, 65–66, 246,

247–49, 282; vs. Smith, 18–19;
    Spargo and, 149–51; Straus, 99,
    215–16; *tzedakah* and, 110;
    Untermyer, 117, 241, 274–75; vs. the
    Völkischer Beobachter, 176; Warburg,
    212–14; Wise, 249–51; Yom Kipper,
    169, 249; Zalowitz, 246. *See also*
    Adler, Cyrus; Ford, Henry; Marshall,
    Louis; Zionism
Jews, Eastern European, 31, 32, 39, 119,
    170
Jews, German, 31, 59, 180, 271, 274–75,
    291–92
Johnson, Hiram, 201
Joint Distribution Committee, 111, 115,
    123–24
Jordan, David Starr, 49, 52, 53, 62–63,
    151, 234; books written, 50, 51
Joseph, Charles F., 252
Judah (son of Jacob), 263, 265, 271–72
Judah's Sceptre and Joseph's Birthright
    (Allen), 264
Judaism, 18, 113, 114, 126, 241

Kaempffert, Waldemar, 255
Kahn, Albert, 22–23, 127, 195–200, 235
Kahn, Moritz, 299
Kehillah, the, 135–38
Keynes, John Maynard, 90
Kingdom Message, 267
Kings Highway Christian Church, 304
Kingsford, Edward G., 87
Klingensmith, Frank L., 154
Knights of Dearborn, 306
Knudsen, William S., 153–54
Kol Nidre (All Vows), 166, 169
Kristallnacht pogroms, 289–91, 293–94,
    298
Ku Klux Klan, 93, 94, 187(fig.), 308
Kuhn, Fritz, 275–77, 299
Kuhn, Loeb & Co., 89, 108, 109, 111, 212

Labor strikes, 91, 310, 312
LaFollette, Robert, 201
LaGuardia, Fiorello, 167

Landman, Isaac, 253
Landon, Alf, 277
Landsberg prison (Germany), 180, 181
Latin America, 104
Lawsuits: Dodge Brothers vs. Ford
    Motor Co., 67–68; Ford vs. *Chicago
    Tribune*, 86; Iwanowa vs. Ford Motor
    Co., 315; United Automobile Workers
    vs. Ford Motor Co., 312; Warburg vs.
    Fritsch, 214. *See also Sapiro v. Ford*
Lectures on Our Israelitish Origin (Wil-
    son), 264
Lee, Albert, 323–24
Lee, John R., 38, 39, 41
Lehmann, Paul, 173
Lemke, William, 305
*Leo Frank v. the Sheriff of Fulton County,
    Georgia*, 118
Lessing, Gotthold, 19
Leviticus, 317
Lewis, John L., 309
Leybold, Otto, 180
Liberty Motor Car Co., 129
Libre Parole, La, 101
Liebold, Ernest Gustav, 60–61, 75, 95,
    123, 137, 152, 154, 186, 247, 248,
    326; birth and early career, 24; Brasol
    and, 85; Coughlin and, 296–98; dis-
    tress and, 295; fired from Ford Motor
    Co., 295; on Ford's apology to the
    Jews, 241; vs. Franklin, 133, 272–73;
    given power of attorney, 25; hires
    Black, 72; "The International Jew"
    and, 102–03; McClure and, 211–12;
    vs. Pipp, 80–81, 96; *The Protocols of
    the Learned Elders of Zion* and, 140,
    141–42; receives a *Verdienkreuz*, 285;
    relieved of position as general man-
    ager of the *Dearborn Independent*, 242;
    Sapiro v. Ford and, 223; vs. Schwim-
    mer, 66; Smith and, 307; vs.
    Untermyer, 275
Lincoln Motor Company, 165
Lindbergh, Anne (Morrow), 286, 288
Lindbergh, Charles, 285–89
Lippmann, Walter, 24
Little, Brown and Company, 156

Livingston, Sigmund, 145, 278, 316
Lloyd, Lola Maverick, 57
Lochner, Louis Paul, 62–63
Loeb, Solomon, 109
London Evening Standard, 269
London Spectator, The, 101
London Times, 163
Long, Huey P., 304–05
Lowell, A. Lawrence, 200
Lucking, Alfred, 58
Ludecke, Kurt, 182–83, 185–89, 242
Lusitania (ship), 49

M. M. Warburg & Co., 212, 214
MacDougall, William, 170
Madison Square Garden, 298
Madison Square Garden Automobile
    Show, 20
Magill, Robert, 10
Magnes, Judah Rabbi, 136, 137
Maimonides, 317
*Manual of the Vertebrates of the Northern
    United States* (Jordan), 50
Manufacturing, 21, 93, 194. *See also*
    Automobile manufacturing
Marcantonio, Vito, 298
Markens, Isaac, 89
Marquis, Samuel Simpson, 38, 57, 58, 59,
    64, 65, 154–157
Marr, Wilhelm, 107
Marshall, Louis, 92, 145; American Jew-
    ish Committee and, 118; vs. American
    Jewish Congress, 115; early career,
    116–17; vs. Ford, 119–21, 123, 124,
    148; vs. Ford advertising in Jewish
    newspapers, 203; Ford's apology to
    the Jews and, 235–36, 237–38, 242,
    245–46, 255–56; Franklin and, 254;
    the Kehillah and, 138; vs. *The Proto-
    cols of the Learned Elders of Zion*, 116,
    143–44, 163; *Sapiro v. Ford* and, 222
Martin, Homer L., 309
Marx, Robert S., 218
Mason and Rice, 196
Mason, George D., 196
Masserman, Paul, 279

Maurice, Emil, 180
Maybury, William C., 17
McCarrens, John S., 281
McCloud, John Lanse, 28–29, 243–44, 265
McClure, Roy Donaldson, 211–12
McCormack, John, 276
McGuffey's Eclectic Reader (McGuffy), 2–5, 229
McGuffy, William Holmes, 4, 5–6, 7, 228, 260
McKinley, William, 17
McWilliams, Carey, 172, 279
Media, the, 162, 203, 323, 328. *See also* Press, the
Mein Kampf (Hitler), 176, 180, 290
Mendes, Rabbi Henry Pereira, 108
Merchant of Venice, The (Shakespeare), 6–7, 116, 128
Metempsychosis, 17, 18
Mexico, 87, 103
Michigan, 94
Michigan Car Company Works, 10
Michigan, University of, 127
Migration, 86, 201
Militarism, 52
Miller, James Martin, 40, 133
Miller School, 1
Mishnah Torah (Maimonides), 317
Model T, 22, 67, 171, 257; advertising and, 203; fifteen-millionth, 231–32; first factory, 23, 192; in Germany, 189; sales (1919), 104; sales (1921), 165; sales decline and, 224, 230; Sorensen and, 153
Moneylenders, 48, 52, 106. *See also* Banking; Financiers
Mooney, Edward, 297
Morgan, J. P., 106
Morgan, Robert (Harry Dunn), 209, 211
Morning Journal, 204
"Mr. Toil," 9, 258
Munich, 172, 175, 178, 182
My Battle With the House of Warburg (Fritsch), 214
My Life and Work (Ford), 181–82, 190, 253

N. W. Ayer & Son Agency, 224
Nashville Banner, 281
National Americanization Day, 42
National Association of Edison Illuminating Companies, 13
National Broadcasting Company (NBC), 323
National City Bank, 213
National Council of Farmer's Cooperative Marketing Associations, 206
National Council of Jewish Women, 145
National Labor Relations Act, 310
National Labor Relations Board (NLRB), 311, 312
National Monetary Commission, 212
National Socialist German Workers' Party, 101, 172, 175
National Union of Social Justice, 297, 305
Nationalism, 33, 110, 114
Nativism, 35, 115
Nature, 44, 45, 47, 174–75
Nature of Prejudice, The (Allport), 8, 230
Nazis, 269, 290, 298; book burning and, 270; *Der Sturmer* and, 276, 298; forced labor and Ford-Werke AG, 315; Ford Motor Co. and, 283, 313–14; Fritsch and, 173; Hitler appointed German chancellor, 269; Kuhn, 275–77; Ludecke and, 185; purchase of *Völkischer Beobachter*, 175
Nazism, 176, 293, 298, 301
Nevins, Allan, 164
New Deal, the, 277
New York City, 33, 136–37, 165, 255, 278, 324, 325
New York Evening Journal, 233
New York *Herald*, 84–85
New York Herald-Tribune, 298
New York Times, 65, 115, 212, 222, 236, 268, 310, 323
New York *World*, 40, 91, 159, 161, 230
Newberry, Truman H., 68
Newman, Harry, 300
Newton, Jim, 285–86
Nichols, Dudley, 230
Nilus, Sergei, 82, 83

Non-Sectarian Anti-Nazi League to Champion Human Rights, 274
Norway, 64, 65

Official Gazette (Berlin), 285
Ohio, University of, 4
Old Favorites from McGuffey Readers, 6
Old Testament, the, 3
O'Neill, Joseph Jefferson, 91, 159, 161
Oskar II, 64, 236. *See also* Peace Ship, the
Our Country (Strong), 33

Pacifism, 50, 111. *See also* Ford, Henry
Palestine, 99, 119, 215, 264
Palma, Joseph, 235, 241
Palmer, A. Mitchell, 94–95
Pan-German League, 100
Park, Robert E., 169
Peace activism, 52, 55, 62–63. *See also* Schwimmer, Rosika
Peace Ship, the (*Oskar II*), 58, 63–66, 161, 248
Perils of Racial Prejudice, The (Spargo), 150–51
Perlman, Nathan D., 235
Perry, Percival, 104
Persecution, 28, 30, 167–68, 289–91, 293–94
Peter Beckwith Company, The, 144
Philadelphia Public Ledger, 245
Philanthropy, 52, 64, 110, 124, 201–02, 215, 329
Philosophy, 18–19, 191. *See also* Ideology
Photographs: Adler, 113; Barthel, 15; Bennett, 158; Brasol, 81; Cameron, 77; Cologne assembly line, 190; Coughlin, 295; Dahlinger, 158; Dearborn Publishing Co., 73; Fair Lane, 228; Ford Americanization School, 40; Ford, Edsel, 12, 153; Ford, Mary and William, 9; Ford Melting Pot ceremony, 41; the *Forward,* 246; Franklin, 302; Garland, 226; Green Island holiday, 88; Henry Ford Museum artifacts, 259; "Henry Ford

Must Choose," 313; Highland Park assembly lines, 68; "The International Jew," 102; *The International Jew,* 144, 274; "The Jew in the United States," 128; "The Jewish Question," 129; Kahn, 195; *Kristallnacht,* 291; Kuhn, 227; Liebold, 24, 296; Lindbergh, 287; Lochner, 62; Ludecke, 183; Magnes, 136; Marquis, Gertrude and Samuel, 155; Marshall, 117; Model N, 153; Model T, fifteen-millionth, 232; "Mr. Ford's Own Page," 78; Pipp, 57; *Pipp's Weekly,* 103; *The Protocols of the Learned Elders of Zion,* 266; River Rouge Plant, 193; Sapiro, 204; "Sapiro's Dream," 208; Schiff, 109; Schwimmer, 62, 66; Smith, 305; Sorensen, 153; Straus, 216; Warburg, 212; Wise, 250. *See also* Ford, Henry; Illustrations
Pipp, Edwin G., 60, 66, 72, 85; birth and early career, 69–70; vs. Cameron, 86; vs. Ford, 160, 162; on good will, 71; hires Cameron as writer for the *Dearborn Independent,* 73–74; vs. Liebold, 80–81, 96; resigns from the *Dearborn Independent,* 98–99; response to Ford's apology to the Jews, 244
Pipp, Gaylord, 72–73
Pipp's Weekly, 99–100, 138
Pittsburgh Sun, 245
Plantiff, Gaston, 165, 237
Player, Cyril Arthur, 79
Poison Pen, The (Livingston), 145
Poland, 265, 290
Poliakov, Leon, 90–91, 151
Politics, 34, 68, 118, 131, 135, 184, 296, 327
Poole, W. H., 264
Populism, 29
Posekel, E. F., 184
Pranaitis, Justin Bonaventura, 168
Prejudice, 30, 150, 230, 326
Prentiss, John W., 230
Press, the: *Dearborn Independent* vs. German, 120; Ford and O'Neill, 91, 159; vs. Ford's pacifism, 63; Jewish,

Press, the (*cont.*)
117–18, 132, 135, 139, 141,
147(photo), 210; Jewish, Ford adver-
tising and, 203–04; Jewish, response
to Ford's apology to the Jews, 238,
245; Liebold's departure from Ford
Motor Co. and, 296; as owned by
bankers vs. Ford, 71
Princeton University Library, 289
Progress, 21, 22, 33, 46, 226, 322, 330
Protocols and Jewish World Policy, The
(Rosenberg), 176
"Protocols" Bolshevism and the Jews, The
(AJC), 148
Protocols of the Learned Elders of Zion,
The, 280; vs. Adler, 116, 143; vs.
Bernstein, 164, 237; Brasol and, 82,
140; British-Israelism and, 266;
Coughlin and, 297–98; farming and,
207; Ford vs. Kahn, 199; Ford's
retraction to the Jews and, 238; in
Germany, 100–101, 173; *The Interna-*
tional Jew and, 145; the Kahal and,
135; Liebold and, 140, 141–42, 160;
vs. Marshall, 116, 143–44, 163; vs.
Spargo, 149
Prussia, 130
Public, the, 26, 31, 328, 330
Putnam, Major George Haven, 143–44

R. H. Macy's Department Store, 215
Rabinovitsh, Yisrael, 135
Rachkovsky, Pyotr Ivanovich, 83
Race, Racism, 35, 49, 50–51, 101, 104,
107, 170, 219
Rackham, Horace, 36
Radio, 263, 293–94, 306
Rand, Howard B., 267
Rath, Ernst vom, 290, 291
Raymond, Judge Fred S., 219, 223
Red Scare, 80, 202
Reed, James M., 219, 223
Religion, 17–19, 131. *See also* Christian-
ity; Judaism; Theology
Rentz, Fred, 282
Republican National Convention (1916),
68

Reuther, Walter, 306, 311
Revealed Knowledge of the Prophesies and
Times, A (Brothers), 263
Ribuffo, Leo P., 200
Rockwell, Norman, 13(fig.)
Rohling, August, 168
Rohm, Ernst, 182
Roosevelt, Franklin, 282, 305
Roosevelt, Theodore, 145, 213, 279, 289,
297, 298
Rosenberg, Alfred, 101, 175–77, 180, 182
Rosenwald, Julius, 148, 201–02, 245
Rothschilds, the, 29, 51
Rules Committee of the House, 216–17
Rumania, 32
Rumor, evil of, 318–19
Russia, 32, 81, 265; *The Book of the Kahal*,
168; Ford Motor Co. and, 104;
Palmer on, 94; *The Protocols of the*
Learned Elders of Zion and, 83, 84;
Schiff and, 109
Russian Officers' Union, 81

Sachs, Henry, 146
San Francisco Panama-Pacific Interna-
tional Exposition, 49, 53
Sapiro, Aaron, 204–11
Sapiro v. Ford, 214, 217; Cameron's testi-
mony, 219–21; Ford's automobile
accident during, 222; jurors and,
223–24; mistrial granted, 224; plain-
tiff's opening statement, 218; Sapiro
files for libel, 211; Sapiro's testimony,
222–23; settlement, 236, 241
Sartre, Jean-Paul, 134
Satan, 99, 308
Schechter, Solomon, 114
Schiff, Jacob H., 89, 109–12, 121, 212
Schilplin, Fred, 283
Schindler's List (film), 323
Schirach, Baldur von, 172
Schmidt, Robert H., 313–14, 315
Schneiderman, Harry, 272
Schopenhauer, Arthur, 18, 179
Schulman, Samuel, 184
Schwimmer, Rosika, 54–66, 160–61,
246–49, 282

Scribe, The, 210
Scribner Book Store, 182
Sears, Roebuck, 201
Second National Conference on Race
   Betterment, 49
Secret Societies and Subversive Movements
   (Webster), 169
Senate Finance Committee, 212
Senate, the, 68
Seventh Congress of the International
   Woman Suffrage Alliance, 54
Shakespeare, William, 6
Shanks, George, 101
Shelly, Rebecca, 57
Short View of Great Questions, A (Smith),
   17, 46, 179
Shylock (Shakespeare character), 2–3,
   116, Allport
Sladen, Frank, 158, 211
Slander, evil of, 317
Sloan, Alfred P., Jr., 20
Small, Maynard & Co., 140
Smith, Gerald, 304–08
Smith, Orlando J., 17, 179
Social Darwinism, 17–18, 51
Social Justice, 297, 303
Social theory, progressive, 191
Society, 279, 330; Christ and, 38; com-
   pensation and, 47; *Geichschaltung*,
   271; vs. Jewish collective identity,
   131; Jewish emancipation and, 107;
   vs. Jewish secret knowledge, 105; vs.
   the Kehillah, 135; Pipp on the *Dear-
   born Independent* and, 71, 79; *The Pro-
   tocols of the Learned Elders of Zion*
   and, 141; xenophobia and, 32–33. *See
   also* Culture
Sombart, Werner, 191
Son of the Middle Border, A (Garland),
   227
Soncino Press, 167
Sorensen, Charles Emil, 153–55, 199,
   231, 257, 283, 312
Southern Race Conference, 86
Spargo, John Webster, 148–51
Spiritual, the, 37, 179, 262. *See also* Religion
Stahlman, James G., 281

Stanford University, 50
Stephen Wise Free Synagogue, 249, 324
Stephenson, J. M., 282
Stevenson, Elliott G., 87
Straus, Nathan, 99, 215–16
Straus, Oscar, 99
Streicher, Julius, 276, 298
Strong, Josiah, 33
Sturmer, Der, 276
Swift, Wesley A., 307–08

Talmud, the, 166–69, 179
Talmud Unmasked, The (Pranaitis), 168
Talmud-Jew, The (Rohling), 168
Technology, 21, 322
Temple Beth El (Reform), 6, 121, 126,
   197, 198, 251
Temple Emanu-El (Reform), 109, 117,
   124, 136, 249
Tennessee Valley Authority, 164, 185
Texas, 210–11
Theology, 45, 98, 263–67. *See also* Reli-
   gion
Thesing, Curt and Marguerite, 181
Thomason, S. E., 281
Thompson, Dorothy, 298
Thoreau, Henry David, 45
Thrasher, Samuel P., 201
Times of London, 101
Tin Lizzie, 22, 225
Titus Publishing Co., 168
Today and Tomorrow (Ford), 191, 233
Tog, Der (*The Day*), 147(photo), 203, 236
Tom Watson: Agrarian Rebel (Woodward),
   29
Tom Watson's Magazine, 69
Transcontinental Air Transport, 287
Treaty of Versailles, 90

Under the Maples (Burroughs), 89
Union Guardian Trust Co., 295
Union Theological Seminary, 298
Unions, 91, 202, 269, 271, 309. *See also*
   Labor strikes
United Automobile Workers (UAW),
   306, 309–12

United Eretz-Israel Appeal, 249
United Jewish Charities, 127
United States, 49, 56, 98, 263, 278
U.S. Bureau of the Census, 93
U.S. Department of Agriculture, 206
U.S. Treasury Department, 314
United Synagogue of America, 114
United Zionists of Detroit, 34
Unseen Empire (Jordan), 51
Untermyer, Samuel, 116, 241, 274–75
Upbringing of Mankind, The (Lessing),
    19

Vanderlip, Frank, 213
Veg, Der (*The Way*), 132, 135
Viereck, George S., 297
Virginia, University of, 4
Vladeck, Baruch Charney, 203
Völkischer Beobachter, 101, 175–77, 183,
    214, 276

Wagner Act, 309, 310
Wagner, Winifred, 186
Waldman, Morris D., 272
Wall Street (financial center), 25, 48, 93,
    98, 295
Wall Street Journal, 37, 156
War, 48, 49, 54, 277, 327
War Memoirs (George), 55
Warburg, Max, 214
Warburg, Paul, 212–14, 221
Ward, Harry F., 298
Weber, Max, 191
Webster, Nesta Helen, 169
Wednesday Night Club, 120–21
Weimar Republic, 269
Weinstock, Harris, 204
Weltdienst, 280
Westinghouse Engine Co., 11
Westminster Abbey, 264
White supremacism, 307, 329
Whitman, Walt, 45, 260
Who Financed Hitler? (Pool and Pool),
    184
Wibel, A. M., 258

Wiley, William F., 282
Wilhelm IV, King Friedrich, 130
Wilkins, Mira, 314
Wilson, Hugh, 285, 286, 289
Wilson, John, 264
Wilson, Woodrow, 55, 56, 58, 63, 150,
    151, 213
Wise, Rabbi Stephen S., 249–51
Wister, Owen, 31
Woman's Peace Party, 55, 64
Women's International League for Peace
    and Freedom, 202
Wood, Charles W., 184–85
Woodward, C. Vann, 29
Workers, 93, 94
Workers (Ford Motor Co.), 192; Ameri-
    canization of, 40–42; European lay-
    offs and, 231; Ford and, 157–58;
    Ford-Werke AG, 315; River Rouge
    Plant, 194, 257–58; vs. Sociological
    Department investigators, 39; wage
    increase of 1914, 36–39. *See also*
    Labor strikes
World as Will and Idea, The (Schopen-
    hauer), 18
World War I, 99; vs. agriculture, 52;
    causes of, 88, 295; Ford vs. Wilson,
    63; Jewish bankers and, 59; Keynes
    and, 90; U.S. neutrality and, 56; vs.
    Woman's Peace Party, 55
World War II, 289, 314

Xenophobia, 32

Yidishe Velt, 118
Yom Kipper, 169, 249, 250–51
Yonker, Ralph, 57, 58, 60
Young Men's Hebrew Association,
    162

Zalowitz, Nathaniel, 246–47
Zangwill, Israel, 99
Zionism, Zionists, 84, 94, 99, 110–11,
    119, 163, 179, 181, 215